VIET NAM

History, Documents, and Opinions on a Major World Crisis

Edited, with an Introduction by
MARVIN E. GETTLEMAN

A FAWCETT CREST BOOK

Fawcett Publications, Inc., Greenwich, Conn.
Member, American Book Publishers Council

For

Daniel

and Todd

CONTENTS

	page
INTRODUCTION	6

PART ONE: BACKGROUND TO REVOLUTION

EDITOR'S INTRODUCTION	9
Vietnam: The Historical Background by Roy Jumper and Marjorie Weiner Normand	10
Edict of the Emperor Minh-Mang:	28
The Path to Leninism by Ho Chi Minh	30
Ho Chi Minh on the Condition of the Peasants	32
Founding of Communist Party of Indochina	33

PART TWO: WAR AND INDEPENDENCE

EDITOR'S INTRODUCTION	36
Independence for Vietnam? by Harold Isaacs	37
Founding of the Doc-Lap Dong Minh Hoi	55
Vietnam Declaration of Independence	57
Abdication of Bao Dai	60
Agreement on the Independence of Vietnam	61

PART THREE: THE FIRST INDOCHINESE WAR

EDITOR'S INTRODUCTION	62
Genesis of the First Indochinese War by Ellen J. Hammer	63
Onset of the War for Independence	86
Vietminh Directives	87
The Origin of U. S. Military Involvement	89
Dulles: Opposition to the Spread of Communism	89
Fear of Impending French Defeat: Nixon	91
SEATO	92
The Day We Didn't Go to War by Chalmers M. Roberts	96
Dienbienphu: A Battle to Remember by Bernard B. Fall	105

                                                              page
PART FOUR: THE CONFERENCE AT GENEVA

EDITOR'S INTRODUCTION 115
Power Politics at the Geneva Conference
   by Donald Lancaster 118
Agreement on the Cessation of Hostilities.............137
Final Declaration of the Conference...................151
Close of the Conference.............................154

PART FIVE: THE FATE OF THE GENEVA AGREE-
MENTS: TESTIMONY OF THE INTERNATIONAL COMMISSION
FOR SUPERVISION AND CONTROL IN VIETNAM

EDITORS' INTRODUCTION 160
The First Six Months of the International Commission
   for Supervision and Control......................166
Vietminh Compliance with the Agreements............167
Differences in Compliance (1955)...................169
Differences in Compliance (1956)...................170
The Agreements after the Deadline for Elections......172
Airfields and U. S. Arms 174
Violations of the Agreements by South Vietnam.......177
Achievements and Setbacks of the Commission.......179
"Democratic Freedoms" in 1961....................181
Military Operations in Vietnam.....................182
Aggression, Subversion: A Divided Commission......185
The Commission in Escalating War..................189

PART SIX: THE REIGN OF NGO DINH DIEM

EDITOR'S INTRODUCTION 191
Diem on Elections in Vietnam.......................193
South Vietnamese Policy on Reunification............194
Vietnam's Democratic One-Man Rule
   by Wesley R. Fishel............................195
Eisenhower–Diem Correspondence 204
Joint Declaration: Johnson and Diem................205
Diem–Kennedy Correspondence 206

                                                        page
*Ngo Dinh Diem and the Struggle for Reunification
  in Vietnam* by Philippe Devillers.....................210
*The Genesis of United States Support for
  Ngo Dinh Diem* by Robert Scheer...................235
Program of the National Liberation Front..............253
Repression in the South: Law 10/59...................256
South Vietnam's Policy on Former Resistance Members..260
The Buddhist Crisis in Vietnam by David Halberstam....262
The Coup in South Vietnam by David Halberstam......271

PART SEVEN: PROBLEMS OF ESCALATION: AN AMERICAN CRISIS

EDITOR'S INTRODUCTION 282
U. S. "White Paper"................................284
A Reply to the White Paper by I. F. Stone.............317
A Pattern for Peace in Southeast Asia:
Johnson's Johns Hopkins Speech......................323
American Foreign Policy and International Law
  by Dean Rusk....................................330
Military Requirements for U. S. Victory in Vietnam
  by Frank N. Trager...............................337
Revolutionary Warfare by Eqbal Ahmad.............351
Fight on in Vietnam by Hanson W. Baldwin...........362
Vietnam and the National Interest
  by Hans J. Morgenthau 365
Dissent in the Senate...............................376
National Teach-in, Washington, D. C.................389
A Local Teach-in, Brooklyn, New York...............407
Militancy of the National Liberation Front............409
"Johnson's Swindle Will Certainly Fail"
  by Hoang Quoc Viet...............................419
Mainland China's Warning...........................425
The Situation in Vietnam by Max Clos................429

Maps 439

Index 443

INTRODUCTION

In the early 1960s the international Cold War showed some signs of easing. The Nuclear Test Ban Agreement of 1963 and the amicability that followed in the wake of the Cuban missile crisis seemed to augur at long last a *détente* between the Soviet Union and the United States. But this hopeful progression has been reversed by a series of conflicts in Asia, Africa, and Latin America, of which the war in Vietnam is the most dramatic and dangerous.

In midsummer 1965, President Lyndon B. Johnson declared: "this is real war," [1] adding an official gloss to what had long been privately admitted. What is the nature of this war? What are its historical roots? How did it begin? How can it end? These are the questions that are probed in the pages that follow. The emphasis of the book is historical. It provides a selection of reportage, scholarly analysis, and documentary material drawn from the entire range of Indochinese history.[2] It is the editor's conviction that the contemporary crisis can be understood only in the perspective of the past. This is especially true when applied to Vietnam. The Vietnamese boast a long history of continual struggle, defeat, and triumph, which is meaningful and relevant to the present. An attempt is made here to document this relevance.

[1] The New York Times *(July 29, 1965)*.

[2] *"Indochina" is the name the French applied to Vietnam, Laos, and Cambodia. As an accidental by-product of European imperialism the term has neither ethnic nor geographical precision. Nevertheless there is no generally agreed-upon substitute. The term appeared in the name of the Indochinese Communist Party, and is still used (see for example Radio Hanoi [June 28,1957]). On these terminological problems, see Joseph Buttinger,* The Smaller Dragon: A Political History of Vietnam *(New York, 1958), pp. 17-26.*

In order to achieve this editorial purpose, permission has been obtained to reprint portions of major scholarly works. The selections from Donald Lancaster's *Emancipation of French Indo-China* (1961) and George McT. Kahin's *Government and Politics of Southeast Asia* (1964) fall into this category.

Interpretative analyses of controversial problems in the evolution of Vietnam comprise a second type of material to be found in this book. Can the United States mount successful counter-guerrilla action? Why did the French lose their war against the Vietminh? What political role did the Buddhists play? What groups and individuals in America influence policy toward Vietnam? How did the insurrection in South Vietnam begin? How significant is infiltration from North Vietnam? What is the impact of the teach-ins? Many similar issues are explored. The opinions of a wide range of observers have been included, including Hans Morgenthau, I. F. Stone, Frank Trager, Wesley Fishel, and many others.

Last, and most important, this book contains a rich selection of what historians call primary documents—writings and speeches of key political leaders, policy statements of interested governments, monitored radio broadcasts,[3] and texts of such major documents as the Geneva Agreements of 1954, and the Treaty of Manila of the same year, which established the Southeast Asia Treaty Organization. A major section of the book is given over to the extremely important, but little-known Reports of the International Commission for Supervision and Control in Vietnam. It is this primary material which best serves the educational aims of the book

---

[3] *Special mention must be made of this extremely valuable material, lest anyone conclude that this editor has sat since 1954 beside a shortwave radio tuned to Vietnam. Monitored radio reports in English translation from 1942 to the present are available in major university and research libraries. I have used the New York Public Library. The U. S. government agency which does the monitoring and provides the transcripts requests that it not be mentioned as a source. (The bibliographical note to Roy Jumper and Marjorie Weiner Normand, "Vietnam," in George McT. Kahin [ed.], Government and Politics of Southeast Asia [2d ed., Ithaca, N.Y., 1964], p. 516, provides a relatively explicit description). This material shall be simply cited here as: "Radio Hanoi," "Liberation Radio/South Vietnam," "Cao Dai Radio," etc.*

by providing its readers with the basic data on which policymakers themselves rely, or choose not to.

In bringing this data together, the major editorial criteria were scope, balance, and diversity. But the very edit-
ing of a book, the intent of which is to stimulate informed
public concern, reveals a position. It is a political act, which
indicates my conviction that foreign policy is not some
erudite mystery to be delved into only by statesmen and
diplomats in the world's capitals. Democratic societies, to
the extent that they are true to their ideals, must move toward more extensive and meaningful popular participation
in decision-making. This book is offered in the hope that
it will aid this evolution and help fulfill the promise of
democracy.

I have been fortunate in having the advice and criti-
cism of many of my friends and colleagues, Laurence R.
Birns, Joseph H. Crown, Helmut Gruber, Irving Markovitz,
John McDermott, Stanley Millet, Martin Nicolaus, Robert
Scheer and Sol Stern. Special mention must be made of the
help given by Mr. Otto Bauer of the Library for Political
Studies, and Professor David Mermelstein of the Polytechnic
Institute of Brooklyn. The staff of the New York Public Library, Economics Division, has been extraordinarily helpful
as have been the librarians at the Polytechnic Institute of
Brooklyn. Edward Dong fulfilled the tasks of research assistant with efficiency and intelligence. Marge Gettleman, the
mother of the two boys to whom this book is dedicated,
not only joined in the work at many stages, but far more
important, shared the concern which prompted it.

New York City
September 1965

Part One

BACKGROUND TO REVOLUTION

When William Graham Sumner published his classic *Folkways* in 1906, he coined the term "ethnocentrism." He defined it as the tendency of every group or nation to nourish its own vanity, boast its own superiority, exalt its own divinities, and to look with contempt on outsiders.[1] A modern form of ethnocentrism is to deny the relevance, or even the existence, of the historical experience of peoples with which we become involved. This tendency is particularly acute in the United States, the unique breeding ground of what C. Vann Woodward has called "the American legend of success and victory, a legend that is not shared by any other people of the civilized world." Woodward goes on to say:

> This unique good fortune has isolated America, I think rather dangerously, from the common experience of the rest of mankind, all the great peoples of which have without exception known the bitter taste of defeat and humiliation. It has fostered the tacit conviction that American ideals, values, and principles inevitably prevail in the end. . . . [this] assumption exposes us to the temptation of believing that we are somehow immune from the forces of history.[2]

The history of Vietnam is full of bitterness and humiliation but also encompasses many achievements and triumphs over foreign enemies. It has been the particular fate of this region to define itself in reaction to influences beyond its borders. In this section devoted to the background of modern Vietnamese history we shall see the Vietnamese re-

[1] *William Graham Sumner,* Folkways: A Study of the Sociological Importance of Usages, Manners, Customs, Mores and Morals *(1906, reprinted New York, 1959), p. 13.*

[2] *C. Vann Woodward, "The Irony of Southern History," in* The Burden of Southern History *(1960, reprinted New York, 1961), pp. 168-169.*

sponse to both Chinese and French expansionism.[3] From
this record it is easy to trace the emergence of Communism
in Vietnam from its roots in resistance to French conquest
and control. Ho Chi Minh himself entered the international
communist movement through nationalism and patriotism.[4]

It is in the context of this particular historical evolution
that the people of Vietnam understand the American appearance there in the 1950s and '60s. The United States, no
matter how pure its announced motives, cannot escape being
seen as the latest in a succession of foreign interlopers.
Earlier invaders as every Vietnamese is proud to claim,
were driven out. For America to ignore this history is to
indulge in exceedingly costly ethnocentrism.

Vietnam: The Historical Background

BY ROY JUMPER AND
MARJORIE WEINER NORMAND*

Vietnam stands unique as the only country in Southeast
Asia subjected to pervasive and continuous Chinese influence
and domination for over a thousand years. The Vietnamese,
their origins and early history obscure, began to figure in
ancient Chinese annals during the third century B.C. The
first verified date of importance in Vietnamese history is the
founding of the kingdom of Nam-Viet, in 208 B.C. Composed
of parts of present-day southern China together with three
provinces in northern Vietnam, Nam-Viet during the Han
dynasty was an autonomous kingdom under a vague Chinese

* Roy Jumper is Associate Professor of Political Science, Wake
Forest College. He was with the Michigan State University Ad-
visory Group in Vietnam (1962-1963).
The selection is from "Vietnam," in George McTurnan Kahin,
(ed.), *Government and Politics of Southeast Asia* (2d ed.;
Ithaca, N. Y., 1964), pp. 375-390. By permission of the Cornell
University Press.

3 *See pp. 10–28.* 4 *See pp. 30–32.*

suzerainty.[1] In 111 B.C. it was annexed by China, and for the next millennium, until A.D. 939, it was governed as a Chinese province, Giao Chi.[2]

Vietnamese history is that of a people more than of a geographic area, for present-day Vietnam is far more extensive than it was under Chinese rule, when the Vietnamese were centered on the Red River delta and the northeastern coastal plain. They pushed south slowly, their progress shaped by the geographical configuration of the country. What is known today as Vietnam occupies the eastern seaboard of a peninsula curving into the South China Sea at the southeastern tip of Asia. Vietnam is shaped like the letter S. In the north is the intensively cultivated and highly productive Red River delta; these flatlands give way to a long undulating coast with small fertile plains interspersed by rocky prominences jutting out to the sea; and farther south the thin coastal strip widens and eventually slopes into the rich alluvial soil of the Mekong delta, the farthest limit of Vietnamese expansion. Inland, the mountains of the north merge into the Annamite chain which runs parallel to the coast and descends into a series of plateaus in the west inhabited by primitive mountain tribes.

TRADITIONAL VIETNAM

The era before 939 was marked by the gradual imposition of Chinese economic, social, and political institutions. Chinese governors brought in their political and economic organization, instituted a mandarin-type bureaucracy, and introduced Confucian ethics and the Chinese writing system. It is unclear, however, to what extent Chinese culture and in-

[1] *D. G. E. Hall,* A History of Southeast Asia *(London: Macmillan, 1960), p. 170.*

[2] *Vietnam was also known by the Chinese as An Nam, or "pacified South." The name Viet Nam, preferred by the Vietnamese, was officially adopted in 1802 by Emperor Gia Long. ["Vietnam," or "distant south" are Vietnamese characters for the Chinese term Yueh-nan, which literally means "South of Yueh" (ancient name for the South Chinese province of Kwangtung). See Edgar Snow,* The Other Side of the River: Red China Today *(New York, 1962), p. 682.—ed.]*

stitutions, channeled to the upper levels of society, actually modified the political condition of the peasantry.[3]

Frequent attempts to overthrow Chinese rule culminated in a victory in 939, when the Vietnamese were able to capitalize on the anarchy prevalent in China following the fall of the T'ang dynasty to throw off direct Chinese domination. For the next 500 years, although nominally united under a centralized kingship, the country was in fact almost constantly rent by dynastic struggles and the wars of rival princely families. Successful dynasties had a threefold task: to maintain their authority against internal competitors, to protect the Red River delta against Chinese invasion, and to provide land for an expanding population by pushing southward.

The issue with China was finally settled in 1427 when the great warrior Le Loi recaptured Hanoi from Chinese forces which had held it for some twenty years, proclaimed himself emperor, and established the Le dynasty. From this time until the Tay Son rebellion in the 1770s, the Le emperors held nominal sway over Vietnam. Strife continued among the great mandarin houses, however, and rivalries eventually coalesced into two dominant factions: the Trinh in the north and the Nguyen in the south. Despite their predominant power, the Trinh never succeeded in conquering the Nguyen, nor did they dare usurp the throne, for fear of Chinese intervention. The victory in 939 did not bring a decisive break with the past; until the time of the French conquest, Vietnam remained a tributary state of China, sending triennial payments of ivory, precious stuff, and gold as symbolic tokens of submission, in return for the seal of investiture through which Peking confirmed the legitimate succession.[4] Even Le Loi hastily sent the requisite tribute to procure the Chinese emperor's acquiescence to his accession, forestall any direct intervention, and ensure the concomitant guarantee of support from China in times of military crisis.

If the tributary tie with China was not found incompatible

---

[3] On the Chinese imprint see Léonard Aurousseau, "La première conquête chinoise des pays annamites: Origine du peuple annamite," Bulletin de l'Ecole Française d' Extrême-Orient, XXIII (1932), 137–264.

[4] Tran Trong Kim, Viet Nam Su Luoc ("Brief History of Vietnam"; Hanoi: Tan Viet, 1951), p. 410.

with real independence, neither was the widespread acceptance of Chinese cultural and political borrowings. Perhaps the most important aspects of Chinese civilization adopted by the Vietnamese were the political and social organizations represented by the mandarinate; the examination system; and the moral precepts embodied in Confucianism. Absolute authority in principle emanated from the emperor, who held the "mandate of heaven" as the representative of divine power on earth, similar to the celestial sovereigns of China. Below the emperor, an elaborate central administration functioned, modeled on that of China but substantially modified by local Vietnamese conditions. The real basis for power during these war-torn times was military might rather than legalized imperial authority. The court in fact was isolated from its people and largely confined to ritual; it did not constitute an effective channel of communication or control.[5]

Officials staffing the administrative service—the mandarinate—were divided into two branches, military and civil, each subdivided into nine grades. They were recruited by a complicated system of competitive examinations based on Confucian scholarship. To become a mandarin, the candidate spent many years in preparation for the examinations which would determine his degree of knowledge and resultant official rank. Study centered on rhetoric, ancient Vietnamese and Chinese history, poetry, and ethics, and the ability to write poetry and draft government regulations. Candidates worked themselves up through a series of examinations beginning at provincial and regional levels, success in which procured entry into the teaching field and the lower levels of rural administration. Those who succeeded at the national or the court examinations normally entered directly into the corps of mandarins.

In its pure form the mandarinate system meant that the country's ruling class was identical with its educated minority. The ideal of advancement according to ability was not always realized, however. Although in theory even the poor-

[5] *The court was composed of all high officials, including high dignitaries and mandarins above the rank of bureau chief (Roy Jumper and Nguyen Thi Hue, Notes on the Political and Administrative History of Vietnam, 1802–1962 [Saigon: Michigan State University, Vietnam Advisory Group, 1962], p. 29).* [On the activities of Michigan State University in Vietnam, see pp. 248-252.—ed.]

est peasant competed equally with the highest noble, in practice only the sons of great and wealthy families could devote their time exclusively to study in order to attain the necessary scholarly background.[6]

The Chinese Confucian ideal on which the mandarinate was based represented a single hierarchy of values that the mandarins had a vested interest in maintaining. What Hsiaot'ung Fei says of traditional China is also applicable to traditional Vietnam: the mandarins "monopolized authority based on wisdom of the past. . . . Their main task was the perpetuation of established norms in order to set up a guide for conventional behavior." [7] The values inherent in Confucianism and manifest in the mandarin system gave rise to few impulses for social change. This static world view failed to cope with the kinds of dynamic problems generated by later outside events; however, it served to provide an internal order which helped compensate for the harsh social and economic conditions produced by almost constant warfare. Confucian principles emphasized the personal virtues of loyalty, morality, and obedience and the social importance of hierarchy, status, and order.

Life in Vietnam was very much rural-oriented. Even in the eighteenth century there were few urban centers. The basic administrative and social unit was the village, which in the north formed a nearly autonomous unit, fulfilling political, economic, social, and religious needs. As the Vietnamese moved southward, the villages they established played a less important role because of their rootless, even frontier, qualities. In both cases, since the great majority of the population was involved in rice cultivation, the village was the primary unit for facilitating rice production. On a national scale, the improvement and expansion of agriculture and the maintenance of an elaborate system of dikes constituted the major responsibilities of the central government.[8]

During this time, Vietnamese efforts were also directed to-

---

[6] *The historians Tran Van Giap, De Lanessan, and Dumarest emphasized the hereditary character of administration (cited in Jumper and Hue, op. cit., p. 68).*

[7] *Hsiao-t'ung Fei, China's Gentry (Chicago: University of Chicago Press, 1953), p. 74.*

[8] *In return, the central government required the village to pay its taxes, provide military recruits, and maintain internal order*

ward removing the two obstacles to their territorial expansion southward: the kingdom of Champa along the coastal plains of central Vietnam and, to the southwest beyond Champa, the powerful Khmer empire. Champa was eliminated as a major rival after a series of wars culminating in a decisive battle in 1471 which the Vietnamese won. They subsequently annexed the Cham kingdom, destroying forever its unity and military strength. Today, little remains of Champa except for a few Indic ruins and a small, fast-disappearing minority of Cham in villages along the southern coast, centered around Phan Rang.

Under the Nguyen lords, who established a rival principality south of the Gianh River near the present site of Hué, the march south was continued, this time at the expense of the Khmers. The Vietnamese met with little formal resistance and followed up their successful forays with settlements. They easily moved into Khmer territory in the rich Mekong delta, which presented vast reaches of relatively unpopulated land ideally suited for rice cultivation. By the mid-eighteenth century, the Vietnamese had reached the Gulf of Siam, the farthest limits of their conquest.

The last phase of Vietnamese territorial expansion coincided with the beginning of regular European contact. From the seventeenth to the nineteenth century four European nations—England, France, the Netherlands, and Portugal—competed for commercial and religious privileges in Vietnam. Although by the beginning of the eighteenth century European trade with Vietnam had declined, Western missionary activity, particularly by the French, continued despite the opposition of the mandarinate, which viewed Christianity as a threat to the ordered social structure that maintained the ruling class in its dominant position. During both the seventeenth and eighteenth centuries, periods of intense persecution alternated with edicts of toleration in the domains of the Trinh in the north and those of the Nguyen in the south.[9]

---

[9] *On the eve of the French intervention the Christian community was estimated to have numbered 300,000, despite recurrent persecution. Two basic studies on this subject are Tran Minh Tiet, Histoire des persécutions au Vietnam (Paris: Imp. Notre Dame de la Trinité, 1955), and John R. Shortland, The Persecutions of Annam: A History of Christianity in Cochin China and Tonkin (London: Burns and Oates, 1875).*

The relative equilibrium established by the rival houses was disrupted by an uprising known as the Tay Son revolt, led by three brothers.[10] They succeeded in putting the Nguyen ruling house to flight, then defeated the Trinh armies and a Chinese invading force, and brought substantial unity to Vietnam. Their victory proved ephemeral, however. A Nguyen prince, Nguyen Anh, began the slow and arduous task of reconquering his territory. He first regained Saigon and the southern regions, moved up toward the center, reconquering Hué, invaded the north, and captured Hanoi. His military victories were abetted by Monsignor Pigneau de Behaine, bishop of Adran, who had tried to enlist official support from the French government [11] and, this failing, procured the aid of French volunteers from Pondicherry. They trained Nguyen Anh's army, equipped his navy, and directed the construction of fortifications. On June 1, 1802, more than twenty-five years after the Tay Sons raised the standard of revolt, Nguyen Anh proclaimed himself emperor of Vietnam at Hué and took the name Gia Long.[12]

Gia Long ruled from 1802 to 1820, and many of the early years were devoted to military activity, to the difficult task of pacifying and rebuilding the empire after decades of a shattering civil war. His personal qualities of leadership, courage, and intelligence were offset by less fortunate aspects of his rule; his government was in effect an oppressive, military despotism. Gia Long was no innovator. He conserved the traditional administrative framework and reinstituted the competitive examinations. While continuing the always heavy burden of taxes and the use of forced labor without recom-

---

10 *The brothers were Nguyen Van Hue, who established himself at Hanoi and was proclaimed Emperor Quang Trung; Nguyen Van Nhac, who ruled at Hue; and Nguyen Van Lu, who was located in the extreme south.*

11 *Pigneau de Behaine journeyed to France in 1787, accompanied by the four-year-old heir apparent of Nguyen Anh, Prince Canh. He concluded a treaty of alliance with France in the name of Nguyen Anh but discovered in Pondicherry that French promises of aid were not forthcoming. [Pondicherry was formally transferred from France to India in August, 1962—ed.]*

12 *He sought and was granted formal investiture by the Chinese in 1803 in return for tribute sent every two years and homage performed every four years (Hall, History of Southeast Asia, p. 371).*

pense (*corvée*) for constructing the government's numerous public works, he is also credited with attempting to alleviate his people's distress by redistributing ricelands, revising and unifying the code of law, standardizing weights and measures, and reforming land registration (*cadastre*).[13]

His successor, the Emperor Minh Mang, ruled from 1820 to 1841. Nurtured, like his father, on a military heritage, Minh Mang undertook to extend a uniform administrative system throughout his empire and to create a strongly centralized regime. He was well educated and particularly devoted to Chinese literature and law and Confucian traditions. This attachment to Confucian ethics spurred him to oppose the spread of Christianity, a religion which preached against the Confucian concept of an absolute and divine monarchy. An imperial edict issued in 1833 declared the profession of Christianity a crime punishable by death, and in the following years French missionaries were hounded out of the country, imprisoned, or executed.[14] Persecution was intensified after a revolt in Lower Cochin China was reputedly supported by Vietnamese Christians, and a French missionary, Father Marchand, was found among the rebel captives.[15] Before his death, Minh Mang appears to have reconsidered this policy of persecution in the fear of antagonizing France. The next

[13] *Pierre Huard and Maurice Durand,* Connaissance du Viet-Nam *(Paris: Imprimerie Nationale, 1954), pp. 34–35. Several accounts in English by foreign visitors emphasize the oppressive and brutal nature of government in traditional Vietnam. Officials constantly thrashed people with bamboo rods for the slightest offense. Nobody other than an official enjoyed any rights or personal freedom. See John White,* History of a Voyage to the China Sea *(Boston: Wells and Lilly, 1823); John Crawford,* Journal of an Embassy from the Governor General of India to the Courts of Siam and Cochin China *(2d ed.; London: Colburn and Bentley, 1830); George Finlayson,* The Mission to Siam and Hué, the Capital of Cochin China in the Years 1821–2 *(London: John Murray, 1826). In an earlier work Samuel Baron describes "the most material passages of trade, government, and customs of the country, and vice and virtue of the people, at least so far as will content and satisfy a moderate mind" (A Description of the Kingdom of Tonqueen [n.p., 1685]).*

[14] *On Minh Mang's anti-Christian policy, and the edict of 1833, see pp. 28–30.—ed.*

[15] *Jules Silvestre, "L'insurrection de Gia Dinh,"* Revue Indochinoise, *XXIV (1915), 1–37.*

emperor, Thieu Tri (1841–1847), pursued an anti-Christian policy with even more vigor, however, leaving the Emperor Tu Duc (1848–1883) to cope with the consequent breakdown of relations with France and its unhappy results.

The reign of the first two Nguyen emperors, and especially that of Minh Mang, is sometimes referred to nostalgically as a "golden age" of Vietnamese history,[16] and it is imperative to look behind the facade of regulated hierarchical authority for a realistic appraisal of the power structure. There was, in fact, a weak kingship system, bolstered not only by the authority of the civil mandarinate but also by the might of the army. Under Gia Long, generally insecure conditions prevailed in many rural areas, and he exercised only nominal control over a large part of the countryside. Even his successors failed to impose law and order in all parts of their realm. Furthermore, the emperor shared real power with the governors-general of the several regions, although in principle his authority extended directly into the province and district down to the canton and village. Nor was the relationship between the emperor and high mandarins always clearly defined. The emperor's councilors were chosen from among the top mandarins, who in practice often held several high positions at once, making it difficult for them competently to fulfill all their functions. Rivalries among mandarins were notorious and especially vicious during the reign of Minh Mang.[17] The situation was exacerbated by the personal remoteness of the emperor, sheltered behind the high walls of the imperial capital at Hué and largely deprived of contact with and knowledge of the state of the peasantry in rural areas. Imperial isolation was encouraged by the mandarins, who sought to enhance their personal power by confining the court largely to ritualistic functions and ceremonies.

The policy of the Nguyen emperors toward the West, especially on the accession of Tu Duc, represented an attempt to maintain the old order by closing off the country to

---

[16] See Marcel Gaultier, Gia Long (Saigon: Ardin, 1933) and Minh Mang (Paris: Larousse, 1935), and also Charles B. Maybon, "Nguyen Anh, Empereur et fondateur de dynastie: Gia Long (1802–1820)," Revue Historique Coloniale (Paris), 1919, pp. 47–126.

[17] Tran Trong Kim, Viet Nam Su Luoc, p. 50.

foreign influences, both religious and commercial. Maltreatment of the missionaries, however, provided the French with a pretext for intervening in local affairs, and during the 1840s French naval vessels stormed into Vietnamese ports to demand—and obtain—the release of imprisoned missionaries. Matters came to a head when Tu Duc decided to isolate Vietnam completely and stamp out all Christian communities.[18] Following the death of French and Spanish missionaries, a joint Franco-Spanish task force invaded Tourane [Danang] and in February 1859 they turned south and took Saigon. The French moved inland to capture the three provinces adjacent to Saigon and by a treaty signed with Tu Duc in 1862 confirmed this conquest. French occupation of Cochin China was completed in 1867 when Admiral de la Grandière occupied the three western provinces on the grounds that anti-French rebels were using the provinces still under Vietnamese control as a base of operations and refuge.

The French next turned their attention to the north, where the Emperor Tu Duc exercised very little control. The conquest of Hanoi by a small French force in 1873 was soon thereafter disavowed by the French government. Tu Duc's prestige was so impaired by his defeat, however, that he was unable to extend government authority in Tonkin and appealed to the Chinese emperor, under the terms of vassalage, to re-establish order.[19] In response to the movement of Chinese troops into the north, the French sent a squadron to Haiphong, and, in 1883, a force of some 600 men again attacked and took the citadel of Hanoi. By the terms of the treaty signed on August 25, 1883, the court at Hué formally recognized the French protectorate over Tonkin and Annam —Tu Duc having previously granted France sovereignty over Cochin China—but guerrilla warfare raged on in several parts of the country. Vietnamese independence had come to an end, but Vietnamese resistance to French rule, in both

---

[18] *Hall*, History of Southeast Asia, *pp. 558–559.*

[19] *Hall maintains that Tu Duc was playing the Chinese against the French by emphasizing his vassalage to the former despite French admonitions, in the hope that they would get embroiled in a dispute which would sap the strength of both* (History of Southeast Asia, *pp. 570–571.) A Franco-Chinese treaty signed May 11, 1884, formally recognized the validity of treaties between France and Vietnam.*

the north and the south, continued into the twentieth century.[20]

THE FRENCH IMPACT

The pattern of French colonial rule had a major impact on the course of Vietnamese history: it introduced economic, political, and social changes which dislocated the traditional mode of life and produced a poorly integrated society in which a small, urban-oriented Westernized elite was largely alienated from the bulk of the village-based population. It also inspired a violent nationalist response to the displacement of the traditional system of government by French colonial power, a response characterized by innumerable attempts to overthrow French rule, led first by the traditional elite and then by new leaders born during the period of foreign subjugation.

By terms of the treaty of 1884 defining the limits of French authority in Vietnam, Tonkin was to be administered indirectly by French *résidents* operating alongside the existing hierarchy of mandarins, while Annam was also to retain the emperor and court. Technically, only Cochin China ranked as a colony and was placed under direct French control. Annam and Tonkin, together with Laos and Cambodia, were classed as protectorates and joined with Cochin China in the Indochinese Union in 1887. The distinction between direct and indirect rule, however, constitutes one of the great myths of colonial administration; its effect was legal rather than practical, since in fact French authority throughout Indochina was absolute.[21]

The pattern of French colonial administration in Indochina was hierarchical, "government from the top down rather than from the bottom up." [22] The Indochinese Union was administered by a Governor-General directly responsible to the Ministry of Colonies in Paris. French rule was characterized by a succession of vacillating policies emanating from Paris, accompanied by a rapid turnover of high officials and frequent administrative reorganization. Much of

[20] *On the other hand, much of Vietnam was immediately pacified, and thus French rule brought peace and security for the first time to an important part of the population.*

[21] *Hall*, History of Southeast Asia, *p. 644.*

[22] *Rupert Emerson*, Representative Government in Southeast Asia *(New York: Institute of Pacific Relations, 1955), p. 171.*

the difficulty was attributable to Paris, which lacked firsthand knowledge of Vietnamese affairs yet was unable to refrain from constant meddling through administrative directives or by appointing new governors-general who were often selected for political reasons and not on the basis of experience in colonial administration. Between 1892 and 1930, Indochina had twenty-three governors-general in addition to an even greater number of colonial ministers. Theoretically the Governor-General disposed of great power, but since he was rarely a professional colonial administrator, his authority was often effectively blocked by career colonial officials.

The Governor-General's scope of authority was further circumscribed by the concentration of power in the hands of French regional and provincial officials. Cochin China, Tonkin, and Annam were each administered separately and only tenuously linked in the Indochinese Union. Cochin China was ruled directly by a governor assisted by two assemblies.[23] At the provincial level it was administered by French chiefs of province assisted by a provincial council which voted the provincial budget. In Tonkin, French power was increased gradually, all of it concentrated eventually in the hands of the French *Résident*.[24] In Annam, the emperor was retained as a symbolic monarchy at Hué, and the French even intervened at this level, exiling recalcitrant emperors.[25] In short, while a façade of Vietnamese control was permitted in Annam and Tonkin, French authority permeated all levels of the central administrative hierarchy in all three regions, though the form differed. In Cochin China especially, it even penetrated to the district and village level. There, the civil system of separation of judicial and administrative powers

[23] *They were the Private Council, of an advisory character, and the Colonial Council, which voted the budget.*

[24] *The French had first established the office of viceroy (kinh luoc), held by a Vietnamese mandarin who, as official representative of the emperor, would serve as a liaison with the French Résident Supérieur in Tonkin. The multiple powers of this official were transferred to the French Résident in 1897, thus ending even the pretext of a traditional system of regional super vision.*

[25] *Imperial authority was further diminished by depriving the Co Mat, the traditional Secret Council of the emperor, of executive powers and transforming it into the principal Vietnamese advisory body to the French administration.*

served to strip the canton chiefs and village elders of their police and judicial powers, which were given to French policemen and judges.

Another policy which facilitated the penetration of French control was the widespread use of French personnel at local administrative levels, in positions which, in other colonies in Southeast Asia, were usually filled by indigenous officials. Virginia Thompson wrote of the plethora of French *fonctionnaires*, whose salaries devoured the colonial budget: they were too numerous for what they accomplished and far too few to do what was necessary.[26] Vietnamese mandarins, especially in Cochin China and Tonkin, lost all initiative and responsibility and filled only secondary positions. The debasement of their authority, plus the substitution of Western education for Confucian culture based on traditional morality, contributed to the increased venality and corruption of those mandarins who cooperated with the French, thus compromising them hopelessly in the eyes of the local population.

French colonial policy as it evolved under Governor-General Paul Doumer (1897–1902) and subsequent administrations was largely shaped by the concept of Indochina as a profitable economic enterprise to be exploited for the benefit of the mother country. The economy was dominated by a combination of private French investors and the Bank of Indochina, which developed into the real political and financial nerve center of all Indochina. Established to provide the colony with monetary exchange and to encourage economic development by extending credit, the Bank of Indochina became the instrument for channeling metropolitan capital into the colony and directing its investment at highly profitable rates. French interests permeated all sectors of the economy but exercised almost exclusive control over mineral extraction, the rubber industry, and manufacturing. The Chinese community controlled the rice trade and was active in retailing, while Vietnamese economic ambitions were generally confined to landowning, where profits were derived from high rents and usurious rates of interest on money advanced to tenant farmers.

The economic impact of French rule did not change the

[26] *Virginia Thompson*, French Indochina (*London: George Allen & Unwin, 1937), p. 86.*

preponderantly agrarian nature of the Vietnamese economy, and by 1940 the peasantry still constituted 85 to 90 per cent of the total population. The structure of landownership, however, was considerably altered. In Tonkin and Annam the pattern had been fairly well fixed in advance of the French so that, despite the economic changes that took place, a large proportion of proprietors still cultivated their own lands. But because of population pressures, holdings were fragmented and provided little more than subsistence for the majority of the population.[27] In contrast to Tonkin and Annam, land was abundant in Cochin China, and vast projects of reclamation added considerably to the available acreage. This land was concentrated in large estates devoted to rice production and owned by both Vietnamese and French landlords or in French-owned rubber plantations. The growth of the rubber industry further modified the economic organization of Cochin China by creating a labor shortage met by transplanting thousands of Tonkinese workers to the south, where they lived and worked under conditions approximating peonage.

Although a higher proportion of peasants rented land from absentee landlords in Cochin China than in Tonkin and Annam, the lot of the peasant was miserable in all three regions. High taxation was a contributing factor in forcing owners to sell or mortgage their property, and usurious interest rates produced a vicious system of rural indebtedness.[28] Another abuse causing great misery in the countryside resulted from the establishment of governmental monopolies on the purchase and distribution of alcohol, opium, and salt, thus depriving many villages of their secondary means of livelihood. In general, then, French economic achievements were not shared by the rural population, which was little affected by the extensive program of public works and road building.

[27] *In Tonkin 62 percent of the peasantry eventually owned less than .9 acre and 30 percent less than .4 acre. Conditions in Annam were only slightly better (Ellen J. Hammer,* The Struggle for Indochina *[Stanford: Stanford University Press, 1954], p. 65).*

[28] *Also contributing to rural poverty were the occasional crop failures and very large expenditures upon marriages, funerals, dead ancestors, and the celebration of festivals such as the New Year.*

The French colonial system also acted to destroy the village as a social and economic unit producing social security for the poor. French-trained Vietnamese officials were given authority formerly exercised by the village notables, who thereby lost prestige and with it much of their tradition-based authority over the villagers. With the breakdown in local authority, much village communal land was lost to speculation by notables and mandarins, and following upon the disruption of this traditional form of social insurance came an increase in pauperism and vagrancy. The growth of urban centers and a cash economy also contributed to the destruction of communal life, as did the French emphasis on individual as against communal responsibility. The village persisted as the primary locus of rural life, but it lost much of its cohesiveness and autonomy.[29]

Colonial rule did not completely restructure Vietnamese society, which remained essentially peasant-oriented, though it did upset the social setting at many points. The most injurious social measure in Cochin China was the introduction of a French legal code administered by French judges. Most judges were ignorant of Vietnamese customs and language and relied on Vietnamese interpreters, who were often open to bribery and corruption. The traditional mode of life was further modified by the process of urbanization; this gave rise to a rootless indigenous proletariat and absorbed the attention of many of the wealthy landowners who had hitherto played an important role in village society.

Finally, the introduction of French education did much to reshape the class structure. Guided in the early days of French rule by the ideals of assimiliation [30]—with the goal of turning Indochina into a cultural carbon copy of the mother country—the colonial regime reformed the Vietnamese schools and substituted French-type education for traditional moral teachings and the French language and *quoc ngu* (the romanized transcription of Vietnamese) for Chinese characters. Both the reformed Vietnamese schools and the new French schools emphasized quality rather than quantity, and

[29] See Ho Chi Minh's bitter attack on France's mission civili-satrice in Indochina, pp. 32-33.—ed.

[30] Initially, there was a great debate between those who advocated "assimilation" and those who favored a policy of "association" based upon respect for indigenous institutions.

he system, wholly inadequate to fulfill the Vietnamese demand for learning, produced a talented though small Vietnamese leadership group.[31]

Lucian Pye comments that the Vietnamese proved the most gifted of all Southeast Asians in assimilating Western culture and adapting to Western standards and they alone, of the peoples of the region, have successfully followed careers in Europe.[32] This elite education served to create a disgruntled educated class aspiring to the high political and administrative posts closed to them by the colonial regime. Unemployed or underpaid in secondary governmental positions, the disillusioned elite formed the nucleus around which patriotic and anti-French activity would coalesce at the earliest opportunity. Within the elite it is important to distinguish the members who attended French schools from those trained in the re-formed Vietnamese schools. Those educated in the French schools tended to become non-Communist Nationalists, while those who made up the Communist leadership [33] attended either the re-formed Vietnamese schools or none at all.

THE GROWTH OF NATIONALISM

The roots of Vietnamese national unity extended back to

[31] *On the eve of the French intervention, the traditional system of education, patterned on that of ancient China, included at the village level an estimated 20,000 one-teacher private schools supplemented by state-supported provincial and district classes. At the summit of the system was the National College (Quoc Tu Giam) for royal princes and mandarins. During French rule there were only 14 secondary schools in all Vietnam, including several excellent French lycées which they still operate. A single university of Hanoi was founded in 1917 but was subsequently closed on several occasions because of student political agitation.*

[32] *"This is a reflection," Pye says, "not only of French policy but also of the fact that the Vietnamese are the products of a sophisticated traditional civilization that placed high value on intellectual attainment and the disciplining of the mind"* (Lucian W. Pye, "The Politics of Southeast Asia," in G. A. Almond and J. S. Coleman, eds., Politics of the Developing Areas [*Princeton: Princeton University Press, 1960*], p. 95).

[33] *Hardly any leaders or members of the Workers' Party were educated in French schools. Two things most leaders of the Communist North Vietnam have in common are periods of training in China during the 1920s under the auspices of the Revolutionary Youth League and of imprisonment by the French in the early 1930s.*

the period of Chinese domination, and the Vietnamese struggle for independence has an equally long historical tradition. Armed opposition to French rule, led by high-ranking mandarins and members of the imperial family, continued until 1916; the objectives were to oust the hated foreigner and restore the former dynastic order. During the decade before the First World War, both the leadership and the purpose of the Vietnamese resistance began to change. French economic and cultural penetration, and especially the French educational system, gave rise to a small group of Western-oriented intellectuals convinced of the need to modernize and industrialize their country and to broaden the primarily political anti-French struggle to include goals of social and economic change.

During the 1920s, several attempts were made by Vietnamese scholars and nationalists to achieve moderate reforms through co-operation with the colonial regime. When their programs were flatly rejected, they turned once again to violent methods and to clandestine organizations. Many underground nationalist societies were Marxist-oriented, although the dominant Nationalist organization in the twenties, the Viet Nam Quoc Dan Dang (VNQDD—Vietnamese Nationalist Party), was not. Its aim was the revolutionary overthrow of French rule and the establishment of a republican government along the lines of the Chinese Kuomintang, which served as its organizational model. The VNQDD led an uprising which began on the night of February 9, 1930, when the Vietnamese garrison at Yen Bay on the Chinese border rose in revolt. This was expected to foment a general revolution, but French authorities had been alerted and they easily quelled the disturbances. The VNQDD was destroyed as an effective organization for nearly fifteen years, reappearing under Chinese auspices during the Second World War.

The disappearance of the VNQDD from the political scene greatly facilitated the rise of Vietnamese Communism to a position of dominance. The fusion of three competing Communist groups into a united Indochinese Communist Party (ICP) [34] was arranged in 1930 by the Comintern representa-

[34] I. Milton Sacks, "Marxism in Vietnam," in Frank N. Trager, ed., Marxism in Southeast Asia (Stanford: Stanford University Press, 1959), pp. 115–124.

tive in Southeast Asia, Nguyen Ai Quoc,[35] who gave the fledgling organization clearly defined relations with the international Communist apparatus.[36] Soon after its inception, the ICP sought to rival the VNQDD uprising by organizing mass peasant demonstrations to dramatize the widespread agrarian misery then prevalent as a result of successive crop failures. These were followed by a series of strikes in plantations and factories and culminated in peasant revolts and the creation of "soviets" in the two provinces of Ha Tinh and Nghe An.[37] French retribution was swift and

[35] *Nguyen Ai Quoc (Nguyen the Patriot) was the pseudonym used by Nguyen Tat Thanh, better known to the world today as Ho Chi Minh. Born in 1890, he left Vietnam in 1911 as a cabin boy on a merchant vessel and was known to be in Paris at the time of the Versailles conference. He became active in the French Socialist Party and attended its congress in 1920, voting with the majority which split off and formed the French Communist Party. In 1923 he was sent to Moscow as the French Communist Party delegate to the Peasant International (Krestintern). He remained there for more than a year to study Communism and attend the Fifth Congress of the Communist International (Comintern) in 1924. He then accompanied Mikhail Borodin, the senior Soviet adviser to the Kuomintang, to Canton, where he ostensibly worked as a translator, a cover for his task of organizing an Indochinese Communist movement. In 1925 he created the Association of Revolutionary Youth, a precursor of the ICP* (Sacks, "Marxism in Vietnam," in *Trager* (ed.), Marxism in Southeast Asia, pp. 108–111; Donald Lancaster, The Emancipation of French Indochina [*London: Oxford University Press, 1961*], pp. 79–83; Bernard B. Fall, The Two Vietnams [*New York: Praeger, 1963*], pp. 81–103. [*see below, pp. 48–50.—ed.*]

[36] *At the time of its formation, the ICP had a membership of 211 Vietnamese Communists in all, according to an official source* (Thirty Years of Struggle of the Party [*Hanoi: Foreign Languages Publishing House, 1960*], p. 24). *One year later, ICP membership had reputedly grown to about 1,500, augmented by some 100,000 peasants affiliated in peasant organizations* (Hammer, Struggle for Indochina, p. 82).

[37] *These "soviets" apparently distributed communal land to peasants and took over local administration* (Le Thanh Khoi, Le Viet-Nam [*Paris: Editions de Minuit, 1955*], p. 445). *For an official Communist evaluation of the strength and weakness of ICP policy during this period, including criticisms of the party "line,"* see Thirty Years of Struggle, pp. 31–37.

brutal. By 1932 an estimated 10,000 political prisoners languished in jail, and many Communist leaders were executed.[38] The organization of the ICP was further disrupted, and its ties to the Comintern severed, by the arrest of Nguyen Ai Quoc in 1931 in Hong Kong.

Unlike the VNQDD, the ICP was weakened but not decimated by French repression. By 1933 the party was again operative. It soon regained pre-eminence in the revolutionary movement, although it shared this leadership in Cochin China with several Trotskyist groups. During the late 1930s ICP adherence to the Popular Front, its rationale deriving from European politics, cost the party a sizable portion of its support. By 1938, with the fall of the Popular Front in France, the ICP was driven underground and many of its militants were arrested. The eve of the Second World War found the leadership of the ICP forced to reorganize in exile in southern China. However, by its activities and organizational skill, the ICP had come to dominate the revolutionary scene in Vietnam and had laid the foundation for its subsequent claims to historic leadership of the Vietnamese Nationalist movement.

Edict of the Emperor Minh-Mang: Hostility to Christianity (1833)*

I, Minh-Mang, the king, speak thus. For many years men from the Occident have been preaching the religion of Dato [1] and deceiving the public, teaching them that there is a mansion of supreme bliss and a dungeon of dreadful misery. They have no respect for the God Phat [2] and no reverence for ancestors. That is great blasphemy indeed. Moreover,

---

[38] *Edgar Snow points out that "[b]y the time the Japanese arrived [in Vietnam in 1941], the French were operating eighty-one prisons, not counting labor-reform camps."* (The Other Side of the River, p. 683). —ed.

* Translated by Marge Gettleman from the text in Georges Taboulet, *La Geste Française en Indochine* (2 vols., Paris, 1955–1956), I, pp. 328-329. By permission of the publisher, Adrien-Maisonneuve.

[1] *Christianity.*

[2] *Buddha.*

hey build houses of worship where they receive a large number of people, without discriminating between the sexes, in order to seduce the women and young girls; they also extract the pupils from the eyes of sick people. Can anything more contrary to reason and custom be imagined?

Last year we punished two villages steeped in this depraved doctrine. In so doing we intended to make our will known, so that people would shun this crime and come to their senses.

Now then, this is our decision: although many people have already taken the wrong path through ignorance, it doesn't take much intelligence to perceive what is proper and what is not; they can still be taught and corrected easily. Initially they must be given instruction and warnings, and then, if they remain intractable, punishment and pain.

Thus we order all followers of this religion, from the mandarin to the least of the people, to abandon it sincerely, if they acknowledge and fear our power. We wish the mandarins to check carefully to see if the Christians in their territory are prepared to obey our orders, and to force them, in their presence, to trample the cross underfoot. After this they are to pardon them for the time being. As for the houses of worship and the houses of the priests, they must see that these are completely razed and, henceforth, if any of our subjects is known to be guilty of these abominable customs, he will be punished with the last degree of severity, so that this depraved religion may be extirpated.

This is our will. Execute it. 12th day of the eleventh moon, 13th year of our reign.　　　　[the royal seal]

SECRET ANNEX TO THE EDICT

The religion of Jesus deserves all our hatred, but our foolish and stupid people throughout the kingdom embrace it *en masse* and without examination. We must not allow this abuse to spread. Therefore we have deigned to post a paternal edict, to teach them how they must correct themselves.

The people who follow this doctrine blindly are nonetheless our people; they cannot be turned away from error in a moment. If the law were followed strictly, it would require countless executions. This measure would cost our people dear, and many who would be willing to mend their ways would be caught up in the proscription of the guilty. Moreover, this matter should be handled with discretion, following the [Confucian] maxim, which states: "If you want to destroy a bad habit, do so with order and patience," and continues: "If you wish to root out an evil breed, take the hatchet and cut the root."

We order all the *tong doc* [3] and all others who govern:

1. Carefully to attend to the instruction of their inferiors, mandarins, soldiers, or populace, so that they may mend their ways and abandon this religion;

2. To obtain accurate information about the churches and homes of missionaries, and to destroy them without delay.

3. To arrest the missionaries, taking care, in doing so, to use guile rather than violence; if the missionaries are French, they should be sent promptly to the capital, under the pretext of being employed by us to translate letters. If they are indigenous, you are to detain them in the headquarters of the province, so that they may not be in communication with the people and thus maintain them in error. Take care lest your inferiors profit from this opportunity by arresting Christians indiscriminately and imprudently, which would cause trouble everywhere. For this you would be held guilty. . . .

You, provincial prefects, act with caution and prudence, do not stir up trouble; thus you will make yourselves worthy of our favor. We forbid this edict to be published, for fear that its publication might cause trouble. As soon as it reaches you, you alone are to acknowledge it. Obey.

Ho Chi Minh: "The Path Which Led Me To Leninism" *

After World War I, I made my living in Paris, now as a retoucher at a photographer's, now as painter of "Chinese antiquities" (made in France!). I would distribute leaflets denouncing the crimes committed by the French colonialists in Vietnam.

* Written in April 1960 for inclusion in the Soviet Review *Problems of the East* on the occasion of the 90th anniversary of Lenin's birthday, in Ho Chi Minh, *Selected Works* (4 vols.; Hanoi, 1960-1962), IV, pp. 448-450.

[3] *Provincial governors.*

At that time, I supported the October Revolution only instinctively, not yet grasping all its historic importance. I loved and admired Lenin because he was a great patriot who liberated his compatriots; until then, I had read none of his books.

The reason for my joining the French Socialist Party was that these "ladies and gentlemen"—as I called my comrades at that moment—had shown their sympathy toward me, toward the struggle of the oppressed peoples. But I understood neither what was a party, a trade-union, nor what was Socialism nor Communism.

Heated discussions were then taking place in the branches of the Socialist Party, about the question whether the Socialist Party should remain in the Second International, should a Second-and-a-half International be founded or should the Socialist Party join Lenin's Third International? I attended the meetings regularly, twice or three times a week and attentively listened to the discussion. First, I could not understand thoroughly. Why were the discussions so heated? Either with the Second, Second-and-a-half or Third International, the revolution could be waged. What was the use of arguing then? As for the First International, what had become of it?

What I wanted most to know—and this precisely was not debated in the meetings—was: which International sides with the peoples of colonial countries?

I raised this question—the most important in my opinion —in a meeting. Some comrades answered: It is the Third, not the Second International. And a comrade gave me Lenin's "Thesis on the national and colonial questions" published by *l'Humanité* to read.[1]

There were political terms difficult to understand in this thesis. But by dint of reading it again and again, finally I could grasp the main part of it. What emotion, enthusiasm, clear-sightedness, and confidence it instilled in me! I was overjoyed to tears. Though sitting alone in my room, I shouted aloud as if addressing large crowds: "Dear martyrs, compatriots! This is what we need, this is the path to our liberation!"

[1] V. I. Lenin, *Selected Works* (2 vols., Moscow 1952), II, pp. 462-470.—ed.

After that, I had entire confidence in Lenin, in the Third International.

Formerly, during the meetings of the Party branch, I had only listened to the discussion; I had a vague belief that all were logical, and could not differentiate as to who were right and who were wrong. But from then on, I also plunged into the debates and discussed with fervor. Though I was still lacking French words to express all my thoughts, I smashed the allegations attacking Lenin and the Third International with no less vigor. My only argument was: "If you do not condemn colonialism, if you do not side with the colonial people, what kind of revolution are you waging?"

Not only did I take part in the meetings of my own Party branch, but I also went to other Party branches to lay down "my position." Now I must tell again that Comrades Marcel Cachin, Vaillant Couturier, Monmousséau, and many others helped me to broaden my knowledge. Finally, at the Tours Congress, I voted with them for our joining the Third International.

At first, patriotism, not yet Communism, led me to have confidence in Lenin, in the Third International. Step by step, along the struggle, by studying Marxism-Leninism parallel with participation in practical activities, I gradually came upon the fact that only Socialism and Communism can liberate the oppressed nations and the working people throughout the world from slavery.

There is a legend, in our country as well as in China, on the miraculous "Book of the Wise." When facing great difficulties, one opens it and finds a way out. Leninism is not only a miraculous "Book of the Wise," a compass for us Vietnamese revolutionaries and people; it is also the radiant sun illuminating our path to final victory, to Socialism and Communism.

Ho Chi Minh on the Condition of the Peasants in Vietnam (1924)*

The Annamese in general are crushed by the blessings of French protection. The Annamese peasants especially are still

* *La Vie Ouvrière* (January 4, 1924), in Ho Chi Minh, *Selected Works* (4 vols.; Hanoi, 1960-1962), I, pp. 62-65.

more odiously crushed by his protection; as Annamese they are oppressed, as peasants they are robbed, plundered, expropriated, and ruined. It is they who do all the hard labor, all the corvées. It is they who produce for the whole horde of parasites, loungers, civilizers, and others. And it is they who live in poverty while their executioners live in plenty, and die of starvation when their crops fail. This is due to the fact that they are robbed on all sides and in all ways by the Administration, by modern feudalism, and by the Church. In former times, under the Annamese regime, lands were classified into several categories according to their capacity for production. Taxes were based on this classification. Under the present colonial regime, all this has changed. When money is wanted, the French Administration simply has the categories modified. With a stroke of their magic pen, they have transformed poor land into fertile land, and the Annamese peasant is obliged to pay more in taxes on his fields than they can yield him. . . .

One can see that behind a mask of democracy, French imperialism has transplanted in Annam the whole cursed medieval regime, including the salt tax; and that the Annamese peasant is crucified on the bayonet of capitalist civilization and on the cross of prostituted Christianity.

Founding of the Communist Party of Indochina (February 1930) *

Workers, peasants, soldiers, youth, and pupils!
Oppressed and exploited compatriots!
Sisters and brothers! Comrades!
Imperialist contradictions were the cause of the 1914-1918 World War. After this horrible slaughter, the world was divided into two camps: one is the revolutionary camp including the oppressed colonies and the exploited working class throughout the world. The vanguard force of this camp is the Soviet Union. The other is the counter-revolutionary

* This program (dated February 18, 1930) was drafted by Comintern representative Nguyen Ai Quoc (Ho Chi Minh), and adopted at a conference of Communists from Tonkin, Annam, and Cochin China held in Hong Kong. It appears in Ho Chi Minh, *Selected Works* (4 vols., Hanoi, 1960–1962), II, pp. 145-148.

camp of international capitalism and imperialism whose general staff is the League of Nations.

During this World War, various nations suffered untold losses in property and human lives. The French imperialists were the hardest hit. Therefore, in order to restore the capitalist forces in France, the French imperialists have resorted to every underhand scheme to intensify their capitalist exploitation in Indochina. They set up new factories to exploit the workers with low wages. They plundered the peasants' land to establish plantations and drive them to utter poverty. They levied many heavy taxes. They imposed public loans upon our people. In short, they reduced us to wretchedness. They increased their military forces, firstly to strangle the Vietnamese revolution, secondly to prepare for a new imperialist war in the Pacific aimed at capturing new colonies; thirdly to suppress the Chinese revolution; fourthly to attack the Soviet Union because the latter helps the revolution of the oppressed nations and the exploited working class. World War Two will break out. When it breaks the French imperialists will certainly drive our people to a more horrible slaughter. If we give them a free hand to prepare for this war, suppress the Chinese revolution, and attack the Soviet Union, if we give them a free hand to stifle the Vietnamese revolution, it is tantamount to giving them a free hand to wipe our race off the earth and drown our nation in the Pacific.

However, the French imperialists' barbarous oppression and ruthless exploitation have awakened our compatriots, who have all realized that revolution is the only road to life; without it they will die out piecemeal. This is the reason why the Vietnamese revolutionary movement has grown ever stronger with each passing day: the workers refuse to work, the peasants demand land, the pupils strike, the traders boycott. Everywhere the masses have risen to oppose the French imperialists.

The Vietnamese revolution has made the French imperialists tremble with fear. On the one hand, they utilize the feudalists and comprador bourgeois in our country to oppress and exploit our people. On the other, they terrorize, arrest, jail, deport, and kill a great number of Vietnamese revolutionaries. If the French imperialists think that they can suppress the Vietnamese revolution by means of terrorist acts, they are utterly mistaken. Firstly, it is because the Vietnamese revolution is not isolated but enjoys the assistance of the world proletarian class in general and of the French working class in particular. Secondly, while the French imperialists are frenziedly carrying out terrorist acts, the Vietnamese Communists, formerly working separately, have now united into a single party, the Communist Party of Indochina, to lead our entire people in their revolution.

Workers, peasants, soldiers, youth, pupils!

Oppressed and exploited compatriots!

The Communist Party of Indochina is founded. It is the party of the working class. It will help the proletarian class lead the revolution in order to struggle for all the oppressed and exploited people. From now on we must join the Party, help it and follow it in order to implement the following slogans:

1—To overthrow French imperialism, feudalism, and the reactionary Vietnamese capitalist class.

2—To make Indochina completely independent.

3—To establish a worker-peasant and soldier government.

4—To confiscate the banks and other enterprises belonging to the imperialists and put them under the control of the worker-peasant and soldier government.

5—To confiscate all of the plantations and property belonging to the imperialists and the Vietnamese reactionary capitalist class and distribute them to poor peasants.

6—To implement the eight hour working day.

7—To abolish public loans and poll tax. To waive unjust taxes hitting the poor people.

8—To bring back all freedoms to the masses.

9—To carry out universal education.

10—To implement equality between man and woman.

NGUYEN AI QUOC

Part Two

WAR AND INDEPENDENCE

On July 4, 1964, Dean Rusk delivered an address at Independence Hall, Philadelphia, on "The Universal Appeal of the Declaration of Independence." [1] There was only one mention of Vietnam in Rusk's talk, a brief reference to the "gangster war . . . of terror and aggression" the Communists are "waging against the people of . . . South Vietnam." [2] He missed an opportunity to comment on the irony of the fact that the very communists he was referring to chose to begin their national history with the words: "All men are created equal . . ." [3]

The August 1945 revolution, which created the Democratic Republic of Vietnam, came about in the wake of the Japanese defeat in World War II. Far from fanatically seeking to defend their Asian empire by military force, the Japanese were attempting to curry favor with indigenous nationalists in the hope of retaining maximum Japanese influence in Indochina. The Chinese, too, invited into Vietnam at Potsdam, did not interfere with the political arrangements of the new Democratic Republic.

As Harold Isaacs shows, [4] it was not the Oriental but the Western nations, Britain and France, who interfered with the self-determination of the Vietnamese. The motive seems to have been mainly the imperatives of empire. Later, when the United States would take up what appeared to be the imperial burden in Indochina, simple anti-Communism would be motive enough.

[1] Department of State Bulletin, *LI* (July 20, 1964), pp. 74-78.
[2] Ibid., *p. 75.*
[3] *Vietminh Declaration of Independence, see pp. 57–59.*
[4] *See p. 37.*

Independence for Vietnam?

BY HAROLD ISAACS*

Nguyen Va Ba was a grizzled man of perhaps forty-five. He had gone as a youth to France to study, was briefly a teacher, then wandered around the world as a sailor on French merchant ships. He spoke familiarly, with long-cherished memories, of glimpses he had of New York and London and New Orleans and Hamburg, and of his years in France. "In France I liked the French," he said. "They were *chic* and generous, and we had many friends among them. I have happy memories of Frenchmen in France. But Frenchmen here?" He leaned across the table. "I hate them," he said slowly. "We all hate them with a hatred that must be inconceivable to you, for you have not known what it is to live as a slave under a foreign master."

This hatred of the Annamites for the French was a living, leaping thing in the land. You read it in the faces of the ordinary people, in the faces I saw in the yard of the Saigon Sûreté.[1] You heard it in the voices of the educated Annamites, speaking impeccable French. I even found it in the bearing of a rich and timid Annamite businessman who mortally feared the "anarchy" of a nationalism that had become too popular. He wanted protection against it, anybody's protection but that of the French. It was like a social disease of the subjected, this passionate loathing. Whole generations had been infected with it, by the vermin in French prisons or by the slower poison of an enforced inferiority haunting every step of their lives from cradle to grave.

This was a hatred compounded of many things. The dull and weary sense of unrepaid toil was part of it; and so was chronic injustice never articulately understood. There was also the nettle of racialism in it, for the masters were white and the least of them was greater than the greatest of the

* An eye-witness of many of the events he describes here, Mr. Isaacs is a member of the Center for International Studies of MIT. He is the author of *The Tragedy of the Chinese Revolution* (2nd ed., Stanford, Calif., 1961), *The New World of Negro Americans*, (New York, 1963), *India's Ex-Untouchables* (New York, 1965), and other books. The selection is from *No Peace for Asia* (New York, 1947), pp. 145-154, 158-159, 162-170, 172-175. By permission of Harold R. Isaacs.

[1] The French political police.—ed.

land's own sons. Racialism, where it does not impose dumb submission, outrages manhood and breeds violence. The French in their own country are not a people who practice the American kind of Jim Crowism. But freedom is not among the exports of any imperial nation. The great French libertarian tradition was never carried by Frenchmen east of Suez, because it is not a commodity from which profits can be made. Only the small number of Annamites who were sent to France for higher schooling encountered it when they reached the homeland of their masters. The France of the great classic revolutionary tradition, of free thinkers and free livers, was a new France to them. They had seen no trace of it in the physiogonomy of France overseas. In Paris they discovered at least the roots of the freedom they were denied in their own land. The result, in most ~ases was that their French schooling did not train them, as was intended, to become pliant adornments of the colonial regime but to become rebels against it and leaders of rebels when they came back home. "This is a movement led against France," an Annamite told me, "by intellectuals who were all educated in France. Almost all who went to France returned as revolutionists. That is why so many Frenchmen here regret having provided any education at all for any Annamites. There was a governor general of Cochin China named Cognac about twenty years ago who said: 'We want no intellectuals in Indochina. They are a misfortune for the country.'" And it was indeed a fact that almost every Annamite graduate of a French lycée or university took his post-graduate degree in French colonial culture at any of a score of prisons, at Sonla or Ban Me Thuot, or on the island penal colony of Poulo Condore.

Annamite nationalism has a history as long as the history of French rule. The line of French priests and conquerors and colonial governors is matched by a line, no less long, of Indochinese fighters and martyrs and leaders of the people. But Annamite nationalism had long been a scattered, dispersed, underground movement, cleft in many segments. It had burst into violence sometimes out of sheer circumstance and without benefit of any prepared organization. It was for many a mood rather than a movement, a condition rather than a program. So isolated uprisings, like those in Vinh province in 1930 and 1931, could be drenched in the blood of the rebels and the rest of the world was little the wiser. By the time of the next big flareup, in Cochin China in 1941, all the currents of Annamite nationalism had begun to flow into a single, widening stream under the banner of the Vietminh.

"Vietminh" is the popular contraction of Viet Nam Doc Lap Dong Minh, the League for the Independence of Vietnam. Vietnam, meaning Land of the South, is the ancient name of this ancient country. The Vietminh was first formed in 1939 as a coalition of various groups, democrats, Socialists, Communists, and other less well defined sections of the independence movement. They agreed primarily on a program of common struggle for independence and a social program based on the idea of a democratic republic. Clashes and incidents in Mytho province of Cochin China grew into an open revolt under the Vietminh banner in December 1940. The French at that time were already under the pressure of Japanese penetration and were being attacked by the Siamese in the west. They were unable or unwilling to oppose effectively either the Japanese or the Siamese, but they turned with ruthless cruelty on the revolting Annamites. During the repressions, some 6,000 were killed or wounded and thousands more arrested. French courts-martial for months afterward were grinding out condemnations to long years of penal servitude or to death.[2]

During the long years of the Japanese occupation, the Vietminh carried on increasingly strong underground activity under the slogan: "Neither the French nor the Japanese as masters! For the Independence of Vietnam!" The French and Japanese joined in an equally persistent but unsuccessful attempt to stamp out the movement. Early in 1943 when Vietminh partisans contacted certain French officials and offered collaboration in an anti-Japanese underground, they received the reply: "You want arms now to use against the Japanese. But later you will use them against us. Nothing doing!" After the Japanese coup against the French on March 9, 1945, the Vietminh gathered forces

[2] *It should be remembered that the French government at the time was the pro-Nazi Vichy regime. See Adrienne Doris Hytier,* Two Years of French Foreign Policy: Vichy, 1940-42 [Études d'histoire . . . xxv] (Paris/Généve, 1958); Donald Lancaster, The Emancipation of French Indochina (London/New York/Toronto, 1961), chap. VI.—ed.

with increasing strength and boldness. The Japanese never had the time to develop a police apparatus in the colony as efficient as the French had, and their Annamite puppets were few, weak, incompetent, and somewhat affected themselves by the Nationalist upsurge. Many an Annamite patriot joined the puppet militia only to get his hands on a rifle and then to melt away into the hinterland to join the Vietminh partisans. After March 9, Vietminh guerrilla activity took on major proportions in the north. They secured arms from abandoned French stores, from attacks on isolated Japanese detachments and supply depots, and at long last arms began to filter across the Chinese frontier from American army sources. A small quantity of tommy guns, automatics, radios, and other supplies was parachuted to the partisan bands and was soon followed by teams of American officers who entered Indochinese territory and joined the partisan bands in operations against the Japanese. Between March and August the Vietminh guerrillas cleared large sections of five of the northernmost provinces of Tonkin and engaged the full attention of the bulk of the Japanese 21st Division. In the city of Hanoi, principal center in the north, the Japanese imprisoned 2,000 Vietminh followers but they never, by their own means or through their monarchist puppets, brought the movement under control. In the south there was partisan activity on a smaller scale, raids on Japanese communications and supply dumps. Then the war suddenly ended. "Too suddenly," ruefully smiled Pham Ngoh Thach, one of the Vietminh leaders. "We were doing so well!" But the Japanese collapse was the Vietminh opportunity. The puppet regimes in Saigon and Hanoi all but collapsed at the same time. The Vietminh moved in to take over.

A Vietminh congress was held at Caobang, near the Chinese border, the week the Japanese surrendered. A provisional government was formed. On August 19, after a few scattered clashes with Japanese troops and puppet militia, this government took power in Hanoi. Bao Dai, for twenty years the puppet king of Annam under the French and briefly under the Japanese, wearily and gladly laid down his scepter. In a remarkable document, the puppet ruler abdicated, saying: "We cannot but regret the thought of our twenty years' reign during which it was impossible for us to render any appreciable service to our country. . . . We have known much bitterness. Hereafter we shall be happy to be a free citizen in an independent country. Long live the independence of Vietnam! Long live the democratic republic!" The new government gave him his wish and even appointed him, as plain M. Nguyen Vinh Thuym, a counsellor of state in the new regime. Even Bao Dai, from his early boyhood educated in France for his puppet role, proved to be a "misfortune" for the French.[3]

The new government quickly restored quiet in Hanoi. The new banner of the republic, a yellow star on a red field, fluttered throughout the city, in Annamite hands now for the first time since Francis Gardenière conquered it for the French in 1873. In the South, at Saigon, the Vietminh on August 25 called for a popular demonstration. A throng estimated at more than 100,000 turned out and marched, amid perfect order, past the Cochin China government buildings under banners proclaiming the new power of the Vietnam Republic. The monarchist puppets had already largely melted away. The Vietminh People's Committee, announcing itself as a subordinate arm of the provisional government in Hanoi, took power the next day. There were a few clashes, with Japanese at nearby Tay Ninh and Thu Dau Mot and with a puppet group in the Saigon suburbs. But fighting quickly ended. The Vietminh was solidly in power in the north and south. In Hanoi on September 2 the new leaders issued a declaration of independence in which they said:

> They have deprived us of all liberties. They have imposed upon us inhuman laws. . . .
>
> They have built more prisons than schools. . . . They have despoiled our ricelands, our mines, our forests. . . .
>
> They have drowned our revolutions in blood. . . .
>
> For these reasons we, members of the Provisional Government, representing the entire population of Vietnam, declare that we shall henceforth have no connection with imperialist France; that we cancel all treaties which France has signed on the subject of Vietnam; that we abolish all the privileges which the French have arrogated to themselves on our territory. . . .
>
> We solemnly proclaim to the entire world: Vietnam has the right to be free and independent, and in fact has become free and independent.[4]

See pp. 59–61.—ed.
For the full declaration, in a different translation, reminiscent of the American document of 1776, see pp. 57–59.—ed.

Thus the Republic of Vietnam came into being, while the occupying Japanese army stood by, awaiting its fate, and thousands of unmolested but unarmed Frenchmen looked helplessly on. The new regime took swift hold. In the cities and the countryside there was order. Markets thrived, utilities and public services continued to function. In government bureaus Annamites set about the exciting business of creating a government of their own. There were scarcely any incidents. In all the month of August, by subsequent official French acknowledgment, only one Frenchman was killed in a street clash. The Vietnam government opened wide the prison gates. Thousands of political prisoners came blinking into the light from the sordid dungeons of Saigon and Hué and Hanoi and other cities. A fleet of seagoing junks was hastily mobilized and sent off the island penal colony of Poulo Condore to rescue the victims of French and Japanese justice held there.

It seemed indeed, for a breathless interval, that the new dispensation had come. The Annamites believed that what they had won for themselves, the victorious Allies would never take away. "We are convinced," they said in their declaration of independence, "that the Allies who recognized the principles of equality at the conferences of Tehran and San Francisco cannot fail to recognize the independence of Vietnam." That they believed. But the Vietminh ruled in Saigon for only one month. By the time the prisoners of Poulo Condore approached the coast in their fleet of junks with their brown-patched sails, they landed, not to join a freely functioning republic but to enter a harshly renewed struggle to be free.

By agreements made at the Big Three Potsdam Conference just as the war ended, all of southeastern Asia was acknowledged to be within the sphere of British influence and control. Here, in the form of responsibility for enforcing the surrender terms and "restoring law and order," the British were given a free hand to pick up the broken pieces of empire. In Indochina, however, owing to special circumstances, they had to divide this opportunity with the Chinese. For occupation purposes, the French colony was cut in half at the 16th Parallel. North of that line was the Chinese zone, south of it the British. The French, sidetracked by events and quite powerless at the moment, were given no choice. The Chinese and British received identical mandates: to concentrate, disarm, and repatriate the defeated Japanese armies. But events in the two zones soon showed how the special interests of the occupying powers could produce different interpretations of this mandate. In the north the Chinese, for their own reasons, interpreted "law and order" to mean recognition of the insurgent Annamite regime as the *de facto* government. In the south the British, for their own reasons, interpreted "law and order" to mean the overthrow of the Annamite regime and the restoration of the French to power.

The first British representatives arrived in Saigon during the last days of August to set up the headquarters of the Allied commission. The Annamites covered the city with Allied flags in welcome. The Vietminh People's Committee called a demonstration for September 2, both as a welcoming gesture and as a show of Vietminh strength. Several hundred thousand people turned out that afternoon, paraded through the city for three hours, listened to speeches by their leaders, and began to disperse, quite peacefully, just before five o'clock. Suddenly, on the fringes of the crowd, shooting started. The Vietminh later charged that French provocateurs had used drunken liberated prisoners of war to provoke disorders. The French version was that Annamites, inflamed by the day's speeches, had begun attacking Europeans. The Annamites scornfully rejected this charge, pointing out in correspondence with the British headquarters that there had been Europeans in the watching crowd all afternoon without incident. The Annamites, moreover, had every interest in maintaining order. The French had every interest in fomenting disorder. In any case, the shooting occurred. Initial French and British claims that 100 Europeans had been killed boiled down eventually to the officially acknowledged fact that the afternoon's dead totaled three. The angry Annamites that evening rounded up and arrested nearly 200 Frenchmen, but most of these were released at the request of the small American team that had arrived to take care of American war prisoners.

This was the beginning, and it set the tone for all that followed. The British refused to treat directly with the Vietminh Government. They insisted it was a creature of the

Japanese, the product of Japanese plotting and intrigue against the Allies. So they communicated with the local Vietminh authorities only through the Japanese army headquarters. Pham Ngoh Thach, the young foreign affairs secretary of the committee, patiently wrote the British commander day after day, requesting direct contact and offering fullest Vietminh assistance in the task of concentrating and disarming the 70,000 Japanese in the southern zone. His letters were ignored. The British ordered the Japanese to keep their troops in full war kit, to sit tight where they were, retaining all arms and holding all garrisoned points until Allied forces could take them over.

The British had come to "restore" order, and they began by promptly disrupting the order they found prevailing throughout their zone. They declared martial law. They suppressed Annamite newspapers. They rearmed the bulk of 5,000 French troops who had been under Japanese internment. They ordered the disarmament of Vietminh militia and police. As their own troops—almost all Indian—began arriving on September 12, they moved even more directly against the local regime. They evicted it from the Cochin China government building and sent troops to take over from Vietminh police most of the important police stations in the city. Vietminh representatives were evicted from the Bank of Indochina and the Treasury. Annamites in general were excluded from arrangements made for bank withdrawals and rationing scarce commodities. Each one of these acts was formally protested by the Vietminh Committee, with warnings that they would lead to conflict for which only the occupying authority could be held responsible. These protests were ignored. The British were proceeding upon a deliberate course and with a deliberate object in view. The ranking French officer in the city, a Colonel Cedile, regrouped the French soldiers who had been rearmed and joined them to the small force of about 150 commandos whom he had brought in with him. With these forces, he prepared to seize power.

This was accomplished by a coup d'état, carried out with armed stealth in the early morning hours of September 23. With Cedile personally commanding, the French troops moved against the Hotel de Ville, the new seat of the Vietminh government. They attacked the post office and the

Sûreté. Annamite sentries were shot down. Occupants of the building were either killed or taken prisoner. Records were seized and scattered. Scores of Annamites were trussed up and marched off. Foreign eyewitnesses that morning saw blood flow, saw bound men beaten. They saw French colonial culture being restored to Saigon. There was a house-to-house roundup in which many more prisoners were taken, but the principal Annamite leaders, warned in time, made good their escape into the nearby countryside. By 9 o'clock that morning the tricolor again flew over Saigon. In the city and in neighboring Cholon, the large Chinese quarter, Annamite resistance immediately began. There was street fighting. Grenades were thrown. And as these first battles began, Major General Douglas Gracey, the British commander, issued an invitation to Vietminh leaders to come in for negotiations with the French around his table.

"But why," Gracey's chief political spokesman was asked, "why would you not talk with the Vietminh before the shooting started?"

"Because you cannot negotiate when a pistol is held at your head," the British official replied.

"You mean you can negotiate only when you hold a pistol at the other party's head?"

He shrugged.

Saigon was swiftly paralyzed by a general strike of all Annamites. Shops and markets closed. Trams stopped running. Rickshas disappeared from the streets. The city was dead except when it rippled with gunfire at night or with the thudding explosions of grenades. An uneasy truce began on October 3 when the Vietminh leaders, at Gracey's repeated invitation, finally came in to parley. The French offered negotiations on the basis of an extremely limited autonomy in which French control was assured. The Annamites demanded recognition of their independence, restoration of their position in Saigon, and disarmament of the French. There was, of course, no agreement. The truce, already broken by minor clashes and largely ineffective in the countryside where Japanese and British Indian troops were skirmishing with Vietminh partisans, came to an end. The only thing gained was six days' steaming time for the French cruiser *Gloire* coming up the coast with the first contingent of French reinforcements. On October 12 the British and

French, with Japanese troops assisting, opened a formal campaign to widen the perimeter around Saigon. Five days later the Annamites counter-attacked in the city itself, and the fighting came to within a few blocks of the French and British headquarters. That was the last major Annamite challenge in Saigon itself. After that the fighting spread across the swampy flatlands of the Saigon River delta. By grace of the British, and with the aid of the Japanese, the French had regained a toehold in Indochina. . . .

There was no secret about the use of Japanese troops against the Annamites. The British command did make it quite difficult for correspondents to get firsthand information on this subject, and they forbade Japanese officers to talk to newsmen. However, due recognition to Japanese assistance was given in official communiqués issued by British mission headquarters. A sample on October 22: "Japanese troops supported by armored cars manned by troops of the 16th (Indian) Cavalry extended the perimeter west of Cholon against slight opposition." Again, the same week, the Japanese "repelled an attack" on the RAF petrol dumps at the Saigon airfield. These dumps, incidentally, went up in flames two weeks later when the Annamites tried again and succeeded. At Cap St. Jacques, downriver, Japanese naval contingents repelled an Annamite attack on gun positions there. The British spokesman announced on October 18 that the headquarters had thanked General Terauchi, the Japanese commander, "with highest praise" for his cooperation. The British were delighted with the discipline shown by the late enemy and were often warmly admiring, in the best playing-field tradition, of their fine military qualities. It was all very comradely.[5]

The French slowly gathered enough strength to be firm. Before Christmas there were about 50,000 French troops in the southern zone, and the British prepared to withdraw. "We have done our best for the French," General Gracey told me. "They are our allies, and we have discharged our

[5] *General Douglas MacArthur, commenting in Tokyo on the use of Japanese troops passionately exclaimed: If there is anything that makes my blood boil it is to see our allies in Indochina and Java deploying Japanese troops to reconquer the little people we promised to liberate. It is the most ignoble kind of betrayal." Edgar Snow, The Other Side of the River: Red China Today (New York, 1962), p. 686.—ed.*

obligation to them. Now it's up to them to carry on." The French were soon left alone to complete, by force and by guile, the jobs of "pacification." They had been restored in the south by the British and had brought overwhelmingly superior forces to the spot. They could pacify Cochin China now, if it meant leveling every village in it. . . .

The seat of the provisional government of the Vietnam Republic was in Hanoi. It is a pleasant city lying quietly in the sun on the Red River plain in northern Tonkin, not far from the Chinese frontier. Like most cities in the colonial east, it has its spacious foreign quarter, built here in the familiar French provincial style with its broad avenues and comfortable, ugly homes. Back of these avenues are the seamy, crowded alleys where the Annamites and the Chinese live. But when I drove into Hanoi from the airfield in the sleepy warmth of that mid-November afternoon, many evidences of great change flickered past on the walls and on the shop fronts. The Vietnam flag flew everywhere. Across every open surface there were slogans chalked or painted or printed: *"Doc lap hay chet!"* ("Independence or death!"); *"Nuoc Viet Nam sua nguh Viet Nam!"* ("Vietnam to the Vietnamese!"); *"Tha chet cou hon trelaine le!"* ("Death rather than return to slavery!").

All the French street signs were gone, and in their places were Annamite names. On inquiry I found that Boulevard Henri Rivière, Rue Amiral Courbet, Rue Miribel, all named for French conquerors, had become Dailo Phan Boi, after a famous Annamite revolutionist, Duong Lethaite, after a fifteenth century king of Annam, and Duong Nhan Ton, after the first king of Vietnam ever to call a popular assembly, sometime in the fourteenth century. The street names, the old and the new across the entire city, were like chapter headings in two histories, one of conquest, the other of resistance. There was no question about who was writing the current chapter. It showed in the boarded-up fronts of the slick French shops on the main avenues, on the banners waving over the crowded, busy, streaming Pipe Street, Cotton Street, Wood Street, and Copper Street, in the flags and signs draped over the tramcars traveling their appointed routes, or bobbing from rickshas, or flying proudly from flagstaffs in what used to be the government quarters of the ruling French.

When I saw his picture painted on a huge banner on one of the main streets, I was fairly certain. When he walked into the sitting room on the second floor of the Résidence Supérieure and held out his hand smiling, I knew he was indeed my Shanghai friend of long ago.

"You have changed," he said, looking me over with cocked head. "So have you," I replied. "You used to have black hair and you were thinner," he said. "And I? How have I changed?"

Ho Chi Minh had become an old man in these twelve years. His hair had turned gray. He wore now a scraggly little moustache and a beard of thin long strands. His cheeks were deep hollows, his skin like old paper. His brown eyes shone with a quizzical brightness. He wore a faded khaki jacket and trousers, a white shirt and old slippers.

"And now," he said, "I'm president of the provisional government of the Republic of Vietnam. They call me 'Excellency.' Funny, eh?"

He spoke much better English than I remembered him speaking. As he told me of what had passed with him in these years, I understood his painful thinness and the two teeth missing, fallen from the front of his mouth. He had gotten to Europe, then returned to Hong Kong. He made his way to the Indochinese frontier region, where for years he lived the life of a wanderer in the mountains, meeting friends, tortuously keeping contact with his fellows farther south, slipping into Indochina again and again and making good his escape. There was a long siege in Chinese prisons. "All the way up to Liuchow and Kweilin," he grinned. "It was at Kweilin that my teeth began to fall out. I looked at myself once and then tried never to look again. I was skin on bones, and covered with rotten sores. I guess I was pretty sick." The Chinese held him as, of all things, a French spy!

Clear finally of his Chinese jailers, he returned to the border region, began organizing guerrillas in the mountains that rim southern Kwangsi and the Tonkin frontier. In March he crossed over and was the leader of the bands which made contact with the Americans, received arms and training and liberated large areas in the northern provinces. When the Vietminh congress met at Coabang just as the Japanese surrendered, they named him president of the provisional government. He entered Hanoi and was riotously greeted in streets jammed with demonstrators.

Ho Chi Minh put on a battered old cork helmet and picked up a bamboo cane. "Come on," he said, "you will have dinner with the president of·the republic!" Out in the corridor smart young Vietminh guards snapped to attention and saluted. Two of them, very businesslike-looking youngsters with Sam Browne belts and holstered revolvers, got into the car with us. He chuckled, "How funny life is!" he said. "When I was in prison in China, I was let out for fifteen minutes in the morning and fifteen minutes in the evening for exercise. And while I took my exercise in the yard, there were always two armed guards standing right over me with their guns. Now I'm president of the Vietnam Republic, and whenever I leave this place there are two armed guards right over me, with their guns." . . .

The French identified Ho Chi Minh as Nguyen Ai Quoc, the most persistent, canny, and dangerous of all the revolutionary nationalists in Indochina. He never once fell into their hands, although he had often been within reach. If they had ever caught him, he would have been given short shrift. Nguyen Ai Quoc shipped to France as a laborer during the last war. There, like so many other Asiatic laborers— Chinese, Korean, Indian—he caught a glimpse of what it was not to be a slave. He became a Communist. He wrote eloquent articles and pamphlets. He became an international figure, the representative of his country's struggle for liberation from the French. In the years that followed, his name became universally known throughout Tonkin, Annam, and Cochin China. It became synonymous with the most dogged and persevering attempts to create and keep alive kernels of resistance to French rule. Nguyen Ai Quoc was like a shadow across French mastery in Indochina. His presence was reported everywhere. His name was spoken in whispers. His influence stirred young people in the villages and towns.

Ho Chi Minh was born in the province of Vinh, in northern Annam. "The home of revolutionists," the Annamites call that place with its sparse hills and valleys, its thickly crowded population. From out of that mass grubbing in the soil to live has come a peculiarly large proportion of Indochina's greatest national leaders. As a boy of twelve, Ho began his revolutionary career as a courier, carrying messages from village to village for his conspiring elders. Today, at fifty-five, he likes to think of himself as a man who has cast aside parties and programs. He speaks not in class political terms but in nationalist terms. "My party is my country," he liked to say; "my program is independence." In long discussions we had of the problems of the Nationalist movement in general and in Indochina in particular, he would impatiently wave aside all misgivings. "Independence is the thing," he said. "What follows will follow. But independence must come first if there is to be anything to follow at all later on."

Ho Chi Minh, however, was under no illusions about the difficulties faced in the newborn republic. It stood alone and no one in the world seemed interested in its fate.[6] It had the powerful support of its own people, but it faced far more powerful and hostile forces with almost empty hands. The French return to power in the south had been a blow. The Annamites would organize partisan war. They would fight and keep on fighting, "and our children will keep on fighting if need be," Ho said. In the north they were at the mercy of the Chinese, and while the Chinese were being momentarily friendly—at least not unfriendly—no one in the Vietminh government, least of all Ho Chi Minh, could mistake the rapacious Kuomintang militarists for apostles of freedom.

The Chinese were in northern Indochina by a fluke of interpower politics. There is an ancient and well established Chinese institution known in pidgin English as *cumshaw*, which roughly translated means a tip, an extra cut, a slight premium, an additional reward, or in current American parlance: gravy. Temporary occupation of northern Indochina was *cumshaw* handed out to the Chinese by the Big Three at Potsdam. It was an easy piece of Anglo-American-Russian generosity, at French expense. The French, having been pushed well down to the lower rungs of international authority, were in no position to protest. Their status as a great power, like that of China, was purely complimentary, subject to change without notice. The Chinese had been heavily bilked at the Yalta Conference. They were due to suffer heavily from the grants made to Russia in Manchuria. It seemed only fair, by Big Three standards, to give them some slight compensation in the south. Accordingly the authority to occupy Indochina down to the 16th Parallel and there to enforce the surrender terms was

[6] *Even the U.S.S.R. waited a full five years after the appearance of the independent Democratic Republic of Vietnam, and granted diplomatic recognition only in 1950.—ed.* .

given to Chiang Kai-shek as commander of the China theater
of operations.

The Kuomintang government had certain outstanding issues
to settle with the French. There was French extraterrito-
riality in China and the concessions which had been yielded
by the other powers in 1943. There were French holdings in
the Yunnan railway. China wanted to recover these and,
reversing the historic process, wanted certain privileges for
herself in northern Indochina. Many Chinese militarists and
politicians in adjacent southern Chinese provinces had long
looked covetously across the border at the wealth of Tonkin.
There were half a million Chinese in the French colony, most
of them merchants and traders, who suffered under legal
disabilities and discriminations. There was, in the language
of the powers, a Chinese "interest" in Indochina. The occupation, it was understood, would be temporary, but it would
last long enough to be profitable. So when Chinese troops
poured in great numbers across the frontier, there was no
Chinese desire at all for any early return of French power.

The Chinese military authorities promptly recognized the
de facto authority of the Vietminh government at Hanoi. The
3,500 French troops they found in Hanoi without arms were
kept without arms and were held in semi-internment at the
Hanoi citadel. Some 1,000 French soldiers who had escaped
across the Chinese border in March were not permitted to
return. As a result, in sharp contrast to conditions in the
south, perfect order reigned in the north and the disarmament
of the Japanese was carried out quietly and with relative
speed. In Hanoi, correct though wary relations were established with Ho Chi Minh and the insurgent Annamite regime.
There was no great mutual trust—the Annamites suspected
Chinese designs, and the Chinese suspected Annamite radi-
calism—but protocol was observed by both sides. Vietnam
and Chinese flags were entwined on many a ceremonial arch,
and leaders of both sides wined and dined each other amid
much formal cordiality. The Chinese military guaranteed
"law and order," but most of the policing and all administration was left in the hands of the Vietminh government. Toward the French, the Chinese adopted a highly satisfying
attitude of authority. The French mission was kept cooped
up in a small residence over which they dared not fly the
tricolor. French officers arriving from the south were frisked

for arms, at aggravating length, before they were allowed to leave the airfield.

For there was much anomalous irony in this Chinese penetration of foreign territory, especially territory that had once owed distant allegiance to the Chinese emperor and had been wrested from Chinese control by a treaty exacted at the cannon's mouth. Here the Chinese could taste the unfamiliar fruits of conquest. Here the European had lost face immeasurably and the Chinese was master. He could keep French troops under humiliating restrictions. Here all his orders had to be obeyed by deliciously reluctant Frenchmen. Here, for a change, the Chinese kept "order" to which the European had to submit. He could demand, requisition, seize, pre-empt, in the time-honored style of Europeans in China, and he could not be denied. And here, most importantly of all, there was rich territory to exploit, fabulous profits to be swiftly gained. This was a heady draught indeed for the Chinese militarists and politicians in on the deal, and on a lesser scale, for the Chinese soldiery for whom, in turn, there was the *cumshaw* of selective looting.[7]

For however long it lasted—and as things turned out it lasted more than four months—the Chinese occupation of northern Indochina was a profitable foray long to be remembered by all, French, Chinese, and Annamite alike. For the French it was painful and costly, and for the Chinese merchants long established in the area it was an unhappy interlude. But for the Annamites it was a grievous additional burden laid on the already heavy load of the threatening famine. The previous year nearly two million people had died in Tonkin, it was said, because the French had taken the bulk of the rice crop to satisfy Japanese demands. In addition Tonkin ricelands—never sufficient to feed the area, which had to import additional supplies from the south—were taken out of rice production and cultivation of castor beans was ordered, because the Japanese wanted the oil. The Japanese coup in March and the sub-

[7] *The Indochina deal was in every way a felicitous one for Chiang Kai-shek, even serving his domestic political purposes. As the occupying force, he sent in the best units of the Yunnan provincial armies controlled by Governor Lung Yun, Lu Han's brother-in-law. Then Chiang Kai-shek knocked over Governor Lung in a swift coup at Kunming and acquired full control, for the first time, of Yunnan Province.*

sequent war conditions in Tonkin had resulted in neglect of the irrigation system controlling the turbulent waters of the great Red River that comes down from the Chinese mountains across the Tonkinese plain to the sea. The river overflowed the crumbling dikes. When the Vietminh took power in Hanoi, the ricelands of eight provinces were under water, all the crops ruined. When the Chinese came in, they did nothing about it and even took for their own use the meager rice supplies still available. The Hanoi government was desperately trying to apply emergency measures and to stem the spread of the flood, but its resources were few and the outlook was grim. The Chinese, the French, and all the greater powers of the outside world, and even the more malignant forces of nature itself were all conspiring, it seemed, to throttle the new born republic of the Vietnamese. . . .

Upon whom could [the Vietnamese now] . . . count? Certainly not now upon the Chinese. China was so immensely larger than the little Republic of Vietnam—and perhaps there would come a day when China would have realized her capacities and assumed her place as the leader of Asia. On that day Vietnam would profit, perhaps, from being China's neighbor. But China now was weak and assailed, rent by internal struggles and external pressures. It was ruled by the kind of men who were in northern Indochina now, sucking at the land like leeches. Because they held the French at arm's length, they were temporarily helpful. But that could not last. The Chinese were already negotiating their settlement with the French and would be interested only in gaining their own immediate ends. From those ends, Annamite nationalism had little enough to gain.

What of the Russians? Would they bring any strong political support to the Annamite cause? I met no Annamite who thought so; and I spoke to many Annamite Communists. The Annamite Communists, like all their fellow nationalists, suffered from a terrifying sense of their isolation. They were unusually frank and cynical about the Russians. Even the most orthodox among them, like shaggy-haired Dran Van Giau, the partisan organizer, granted that the Russians went in for "an excess of ideological compromise," and said he expected no help from that quarter, no matter how distant or verbal it might be. "The Russians are nationalists for Russia first and above all," another Annamite Communist said with some bitterness. "They would be interested in us only if we served some purpose of theirs.

Right now, unfortunately, we do not seem to serve any such purpose."

"How about the French Communists?" I asked. He snorted with disgust. "The French Communists," he said, "are Frenchmen and colonialists first and Communists after. In principle they are for us, but in practice? Oho, that is quite another thing!" One of the top-ranking Annamite Communists spoke contemptuously of Thorez, who in a Paris speech had said he was in favor of the Annamites "finally arriving at their independence." He laughed sourly. "A fine rubber phrase, is it not? You can stretch it into any shape or any meaning. No, I am afraid we cannot depend on these fine gentlemen. They are the dominant party in France now. And look what Frenchmen are doing now in Indochina."

From the small handful of French Communists in Indochina, the Annamite comrades learned a remarkable lesson in their kind of politics. There were only twenty in the French Communist group in Saigon. "Of these only one," said my Annamite Communists companion, *only one* solidarized with us. The rest stood aside." The French group prepared a document for the Indochinese Communist Party which bore the date of September 25—two days after the French had seized power in the city. I was able to read the document, but not to copy it, so the notes I made immediately afterward are not verbatim. But the substance was as follows: It advised the Annamite Communists to be sure, before they acted too rashly, that their struggle "meets the requirements of Soviet policy." It warned that any "premature adventures" in Annamite independence might "not be in line with Soviet perspectives." These perspectives might well include France as a firm ally of the USSR in Europe, in which case the Annamite independence movement would be an embarrassment. Therefore it urged upon the Annamite comrades a policy of "patience." It advised them in particular to wait upon the results of the French elections, coming up the following month, in October, when additional Communist strength might assure the Annamites a better settlement. In the meantime it baldly proposed that an emissary be sent not only to contact the French Communist Party but also the Russians "in order to acquaint yourselves with the perspectives of coming events."

This document displayed with remarkable and unusual bluntness the Communist Party's notion of the relation between a revolutionary movement and Soviet foreign policy. It apparently came as a shock to the Annamite Communists, who were thrown into considerable confusion by it. There was a sharp internal argument within the party which ended in a decision to dissolve the party entirely, to cease functioning within the Vietminh as a distinct unit but to work in it purely as individuals. In this way the party apparently figured on avoiding any responsibility at a time when its responsibility was the heaviest. I do not know what the internal development was in any detail, but I do know that the Annamite Communists I met were men bitten deeply with the bitterness of having been abandoned by their ideological comrades overseas. They had consequently taken refuge in a pure and simple nationalism. Ho Chi Minh was making no idle phrase when he said: "My party is my country." They were oppressed, in common with all the non-Communist Annamite nationalist leaders, by a fearful sense of loneliness. There seemed to be support for them against the French nowhere, none from the Chinese they could count on, none that could be anticipated from the Russians, none from the French Communists, who did gain enormous strength in those October elections without effecting any noticeable change in Indochinese affairs. What then of the United States?

Annamite nationalists spoke of the United States as men speak of a hope they know is forlorn but to which they desperately cling all the same. Could all the fine phrases of the Atlantic Charter, of the United Nations pact, of President Roosevelt and his successor, really have meant nothing at all? Nothing? All right, let us make allowances for expediency, for big-power politics, for all the shabby realities. Would not the United States still find it wiser for the sake of its position in the Far East to win support among the people rather than to cling to the rotten imperial system of the past? It seemed not. For the only indication the Annamites had of America's role in their struggle came in the form of lend-lease weapons and equipment being used against them by the French and British, and the stunning announcement of an American deal with France for the purchase of $160,000,000 worth of vehicles and miscellaneous industrial equipment for the French in Indochina. To the Annamites this looked like American underwriting of the French reconquest. The Americans were democrats in words but no help in fact, just as the Russians were communists in words but no help in fact. "We apparently stand quite alone," said Ho Chi-minh simply. "We shall have to depend on ourselves."

Founding of the Vietnam Doc-Lap Dong Minh Hoi (June 1941)*

Elders! Prominent personalities! Intellectuals, peasants, workers, traders, and soldiers! Dear compatriots!

* Revolutionary League for the Independence of Vietnam (Vietminh). The selection is from a letter dated June 6, 1941, of Nguyen Ai Quoc (Ho Chi Minh), in Ho Chi Minh, *Selected Works* (4 vols., Hanoi, 1960–1962), II, 151–154.

Since the French were defeated by the Germans, their forces have been completely disintegrated. However, with regard to our people, they continue to plunder us pitilessly, suck all our blood, and carry out a barbarous policy of all-out terrorism and massacre. Concerning their foreign policy, they bow their heads and kneel down, shamelessly cutting our land for Siam [1]; without a single word of protest, they heartlessly offer our interests to Japan. As a result, our people suffer under a double yoke: they serve not only as buffaloes and horses to the French invaders but also as slaves to the Japanese plunderers. Alas! What sin have our people committed to be doomed to such a wretched plight!

Now, the opportunity has come for our liberation. France itself is unable to dominate our country. As to the Japanese, on the one hand they are bogged in China, on the other, they are hamstrung by the British and American forces, and certainly cannot use all their forces to contend with us. If our entire people are united and single-minded, we are certainly able to smash the picked French and Japanese armies.

Some hundreds of years ago, when our country was endangered by the Mongolian invasion, our elders under the Tran dynasty rose up indignantly and called on their sons and daughters throughout the country to rise as one in order to kill the enemy. Finally they saved their people from danger, and their good name will be carried into posterity for all time. The elders and prominent personalities of our country should follow the example set by our forefathers in the glorious task of national salvation.

Rich people, soldiers, workers, peasants, intellectuals, employees, traders, youth, and women who warmly love your country! At the present time national liberation is the most important problem. Let us unite together! As one in mind and strength we shall overthrow the Japanese and French and their jackals in order to save people from the situation between boiling water and burning heat.

Dear compatriots! National salvation is the common cause to the whole of our people. Every Vietnamese must take part in it. He who has money will contribute his money, he who has strength will contribute his strength, he who has talent will contribute his talent. I pledge to use all my modest abilities to follow you, and am ready for the last sacrifice.

Revolutionary fighters! The hour has struck! Raise aloft the

Taking advantage of the French defeat in Europe, Siam (Thailand) raised ancient claims to French territory in Indochina. She backed up these claims with military moves that the French could halt only with the aid of a Japanese fleet. By negotiations carried out through 1941 France was obliged to cede considerable territory to Siam. See Donald Lancaster, The Emancipation of French Indochina (London/New York/Toronto, 1961), pp. 94–95.—ed.

insurrectionary banner and guide the people throughout the country to overthrow the Japanese and French! The sacred call of the fatherland is resounding in your ears; the blood of our heroic predecessors who sacrificed their lives is stirring in your hearts! The fighting spirit of the people is displayed everywhere before you! Let us rise up quickly! Compatriots throughout the country, rise up quickly! Unite with each other, unify your action to overthrow the Japanese and the French. Victory to Vietnam's Revolution! Victory to the World's Revolution!

Declaration of Independence of the Democratic Republic of Vietnam*
(SEPTEMBER 2, 1945)

"All men are created equal. They are endowed by their Creator with certain inalienable rights, among these are Life, Liberty, and the pursuit of Happiness."

This immortal statement was made in the Declaration of Independence of the United States of America in 1776. In a broader sense, this means: All the peoples on the earth are equal from birth, all the peoples have a right to live, to be happy and free.

The Declaration of the French Revolution made in 1791 on the Rights of Man and the Citizen also states: "All men are born free and with equal rights, and must always remain free and have equal rights." Those are undeniable truths.

Nevertheless, for more than eight years, the French imperialists, abusing the standard of Liberty, Equality, and Fraternity, have violated our Fatherland and oppressed our fellow-citizens. They have acted contrary to the ideals of humanity and justice. In the field of politics, they have deprived our people of every democratic liberty.

They have enforced inhuman laws; they have set up three distinct political regimes in the North, the Center and the South of Vietnam in order to wreck our national unity and prevent our people from being united.

They have built more prisons than schools. They have mercilessly slain our patriots; they have drowned our uprisings in rivers of blood. They have fettered public opinion; they have practiced obscurantism against our people. To weaken our race they have forced us to use opium and alcohol.

In the fields of economics, they have fleeced us to the

* From Ho Chi Minh, *Selected Works* (4 vols.; Hanoi, 1960-1962), II, pp. 17–21.

backbone, impoverished our people, and devastated our land.

They have robbed us of our rice fields, our mines, our forests, and our raw materials. They have monopolized the issuing of bank-notes and the export trade.

They have invented numerous unjustifiable taxes and reduced our people, especially our peasantry, to a state of extreme poverty.

They have hampered the prospering of our national bourgeoisie; they have mercilessly exploited our workers.

In the autumn of 1940, when the Japanese Fascists violated Indochina's territory to establish new bases in their fight against the Allies, the French imperialists went down on their bended knees and handed over our country to them.

Thus, from that date, our people were subjected to the double yoke of the French and the Japanese. Their sufferings and miseries increased. The result was that from the end of last year to the beginning of this year, from Quang Tri province to the North of Vietnam, more than two million of our fellow-citizens died from starvation. On March 9, the French troops were disarmed by the Japanese. The French colonialists either fled or surrendered, showing that not only were they incapable of "protecting" us, but that, in the span of five years, they had twice sold our country to the Japanese.

On several occasions before March 9, the Vietminh League urged the French to ally themselves with it against the Japanese. Instead of agreeing to this proposal, the French colonialists so intensified their terrorist activities against the Vietminh members that before fleeing they massacred a great number of our political prisoners detained at Yen Bay and Caobang.

Notwithstanding all this, our fellow-citizens have always manifested toward the French a tolerant and humane attitude. Even after the Japanese putsch of March 1945, the Vietminh League helped many Frenchmen to cross the frontier, rescued some of them from Japanese jails, and protected French lives and property.

From the autumn of 1940, our country had in fact ceased to be a French colony and had become a Japanese possession.

After the Japanese had surrendered to the Allies, our whole people rose to regain our national sovereignty and to found the Democratic Republic of Vietnam.

The truth is that we have wrested our independence from the Japanese and not from the French.

The French have fled, the Japanese have capitulated, Emperor Bao Dai has abdicated. Our people have broken the chains which for nearly a century have fettered them and have won independence for the Fatherland. Our people at the same time have overthrown the monarchic regime that has reigned supreme for dozens of centuries. In its place has been established the present Democratic Republic.

For these reasons, we, members of the Provisional Government, representing the whole Vietnamese people, declare that from now on we break off all relations of a colonial character with France; we repeal all the international obligation that France has so far subscribed to on behalf of Vietnam and we abolish all the special rights the French have unlawfully acquired in our Fatherland.

The whole Vietnamese people, animated by a common purpose, are determined to fight to the bitter end against any attempt by the French colonialists to reconquer their country.

We are convinced that the Allied nations which at Tehran and San Francisco have acknowledged the principles of self-determination and equality of nations, will not refuse to acknowledge the independence of Vietnam.

A people who have courageously opposed French domination for more than eighty years, a people who have fought side by side with the Allies against the Fascists during these last years, such a people must be free and independent.

For these reasons, we, members of the Provisional Government of the Democratic Republic of Vietnam, solemnly declare to the world that Vietnam has the right to be a free and independent country—and in fact it is so already. The entire Vietnamese people are determined to mobilize all their physical and mental strength, to sacrifice their lives and property in order to safeguard their independence and liberty.

Abdication of Bao Dai, Emperor of Annam (August, 1945)*

The happiness of the people of Vietnam!

* *La République* [Hanoi], Issue no. 1 (October 1, 1945), translated in Harold R. Isaacs (ed.), *New Cycle in Asia: Selected Documents on Major International Developments in the Far East, 1943–1947* (New York, 1947), pp. 161–162. By permission of the American Institute for Pacific Affairs.

The Independence of Vietnam!

To achieve these ends, we have declared ourself ready for any sacrifice and we desire that our sacrifice be useful to the people.

Considering that the unity of all our compatriots is at this time our country's need, we recalled to our people on August 22: "In this decisive hour of our national history, union means life and division means death."

In view of the powerful democratic spirit growing in the north of our kingdom, we feared that conflict between north and south would be inevitable if we were to wait for a National Congress to decide us, and we know that this conflict, if it occurred, would plunge our people into suffering and would play the game of the invaders.

We cannot but have a certain feeling of melancholy upon thinking of our glorious ancestors who fought without respite for 400 years to aggrandize our country from Thuan Hoa to Hatien.

Despite this, and strong in our convictions, we have decided to abdicate and we transfer power to the democratic Republican Government.

Upon leaving our throne, we have only three wishes to express:

1. We request that the new Government take care of the dynastic temples and royal tombs.

2. We request the new Government to deal fraternally with all the parties and groups which have fought for the independence of our country even though they have not closely followed the popular movement; to do this in order to give them the opportunity to participate in the reconstruction of the country and to demonstrate that the new regime is built upon the absolute union of the entire population.

3. We invite all parties and groups, all classes of society, as well as the royal family, to solidarize in unreserved support of the democratic Government with a view to consolidating the national independence.

As for us, during twenty years' reign, we have known much bitterness. Henceforth, we shall be happy to be a free citizen in an independent country. We shall allow no one to abuse our name or the name of the royal family in order to sow dissent among our compatriots.

Long live the independence of Vietnam!

Long live our Democratic Republic!

Agreement on the Independence of Vietnam (March 1946)*

1. The French Government recognizes the Republic of Vietnam as a free state, having its Government, its Parliament, its army, and its finances, and forming part of the Indochinese Federation and the French Union.

With regard to the unification of the three Ky (Nam Ky, or Cochin China, Trung Ky, or Annam, Bac Ky, or Tonkin), the French Government undertakes to follow the decisions of the people consulted by referendum.

2. The Government of Vietnam declares itself ready to receive the French army in friendly fashion when, in accord with international agreements, it relieves the Chinese troops. An annex attached to the present Preliminary Convention will fix the terms under which the operation of relief will take place.

3. The stipulations formulated above shall enter into effect immediately upon exchange of signatures. Each of the contracting parties shall take necessary steps to end hostilities, to maintain troops in their respective positions, and to create an atmosphere favorable for the immediate opening of friendly and frank negotiations. These negotiations shall deal particularly with the diplomatic relations between Vietnam and foreign states, the future status of Indochina, and economic and cultural interests. Hanoi, Saigon, and Paris may be indicated as the locales of the negotiations.

Signed: [Jean] Sainteny, Ho Chi Minh, Vu Huong Khanh.

* *Bulletin Hebdomadaire,* Ministère de la France d'Outremer, no. 67 (March 18, 1946), translated in Harold R. Isaacs, *New Cycle in Asia, Selected Documents on Major International Developments in the Far East, 1943–1947* (New York, 1947), p. 169. By permission of the American Institute for Pacific Affairs.

Part Three

THE FIRST INDOCHINESE WAR

Although they were ultimately defeated in one of the most humiliating military setbacks of any modern nation at Dienbienphu in 1954,[1] the French began their post-World War II military adventure in Vietnam by holding their enemy in contempt. French officers referred to the Vietminh as *les jaunes*,[2] as if their yellow color were a sign of cowardice. The systematic underestimation of the Vietminh enemy had much to do with the final shape of the French defeat, as Jules Roy suggests in his brilliant *The Battle of Dienbienphu*.

In the 1960's the First Indochinese War was replaced, in Bernard Fall's useful terminology, by the Second Indochinese War[3]—with the Americans playing the role that the French had earlier discharged with so little credit to themselves. One should be alert to parallels, and one finds them in the occasional expressions of American contempt for the Vietnamese enemy. Under-Secretary of State George W. Ball explained in 1962:

> The guerrillas whom the Vietnamese Army is fighting are under distinct handicaps. In many cases they are poorly trained and equipped and not motivated by deep conviction. Rather, they are merely unsophisticated villagers or peasants who have been conscripted by terror or treachery. In such a case they are likely to have had only rudimentary training in weapons-handling and tactics. Their equipment may be makeshift, often just what they can capture or fabricate themselves.
>
> Only the leaders and the hard core have a strong ideological commitment. The rank and file are their puppets—those whom they have bought, coerced, or intimidated.[4]

[1] See pp. 105–114.

[2] *Denis Warner*, The Last Confucian (*New York, 1963*), p. 73.

[3] The Two Vietnams: A Political and Military Analysis (*revised ed., New York/London, 1964*), chap. 15.

[4] *Ball*, Vietnam: Free-World Challenge in Southeast Asia [*Department of State Publication 7388: Far Eastern Series 113*] (*Washington, D.C., 1962*), p. 15.

Niel Sheehan, a former UPI correspondent in Vietnam, reported that U. S. military men were wont to dismiss the Vietcong as "raggedy little bastards in black pajamas." [5]

In comparing the First and Second Indochinese wars, one is struck with the relevance of George Santayana's aphorism: those who refuse to learn from history are doomed to repeat it.

Genesis of the First Indochinese War: 1946-1950

BY ELLEN J. HAMMER[*]

By the summer of 1946 the French had . . . reached agreements with the three regimes ruling Indochina—the Democratic Republic of Vietnam, the Kingdom of Cambodia, and the Kingdom of Laos—but the area was not quiet. Free Cambodians and Free Laotians (known as Issaraks or free men), dissatisfied with the accords signed with France, took to the bush against the French, and a number of them fled to Thailand. In Vietnam, clashes were unavoidable with French and Vietnamese troops so close together. Had an atmosphere of understanding and co-operation existed between the two peoples, these might have been smoothed over, but the Accord of March 6, 1946 [1] was little more than an armistice that provided a transient illusion of agreement where no agreement actually existed. Even though the March 6 treaty had allowed French troops to move peaceably into Tonkin and north Annam, the situation was potentially grave. Cochin China was still nominally under French control, the French were trying in vain to pacify the area, and no referendum was in sight.

"Unity and independence" was the demand that the Vietnamese put forward at conferences with the French, first at

---

[5] *Introduction to Jules Roy*, The Battle of Dienbienphu (*New York*, 1965), p. xix.

[*] Author of *The Struggle for Indochina* (Stanford, Calif., 1954). The selection is from "Indochina," in *The State of Asia: A Contemporary Survey*, by Lawrence K. Rosinger and Associates (New York, 1951), pp. 240-267. By permission of Alfred A. Knopf, Inc.

[1] *See p. 61.*—ed.

Dalat in Annam during the spring of 1946 and later in France at Fontainebleau during July and August 1946. By unity, they meant the unconditional inclusion of Cochin China within Vietnam, not merely the promise of a referendum at some indefinite date (it would be held as soon as peace was restored, the French said). They claimed Cochin China by ethnic, cultural, and historical right as well as by economic necessity. The French, however, had good reason for wanting to separate Cochin China from Vietnam: the separation would safeguard their considerable economic interests in the province and emasculate the Republic from the start. Cochin China, with its large rice fields and rubber plantations, was the most economically developed and therefore the richest part of Vietnam, and three-fifths of all French holdings in Indochina were in Cochin China.

By the March 6 Agreement, the Vietnamese had accepted limitations on their independence—they were to have a "free" (not an "independent") state, and it was to belong to the Indochinese Federation and the French Union. But only at Dalat and Fontainebleau did either side get around to telling the other what it had in mind by these words. Use of "free" was a semantic compromise; how free Vietnam would be depended upon how many of the attributes of sovereignty it would have to share with the Indochinese Federation and the French Union. The latter, the new postwar name for metropolitan France and its empire, had not yet come into legal existence, for the French did not adopt a constitution for the Fourth Republic until October 1946. But if the place of Vietnam within the French Union could only be guessed at during the French-Vietnamese negotiations, each side had its own definite idea of the Indochinese Federation. The Vietnamese saw it as little more than a formal link between the several independent parts of Indochina; the French wanted it to be a real entity with considerable power through which France would continue to exercise a decisive control over Vietnam (with or without Cochin China), Laos, and Cambodia. They used federation as an excuse for attempts to break up Vietnam, proposing the establishment of a separate Moi state in 1946. Two years later they encouraged a minority group in Tonkin to proclaim itself a separate Thai state. Within the framework of federation the French hoped to counterbalance the power of the Republic by keeping

Cochin China separate, by maintaining French influence in Laos and Cambodia, and by insisting on a direct French voice in the working of the federal machinery. Thus, on independence, as on unity, the French and the Vietnamese were diametrically opposed during the spring and summer of 1946.

French policy in these crucial days was made in Paris and in Saigon, and it was not always the same in both places. In France, liberal ideas of empire had evolved among the Free French during the war. These ideas had a following not only among leftists but also among those who wanted to strengthen the empire against threats to French control, both from nationalists in the colonies and from critics abroad (notably in the United States, which the French suspected of desiring to see Indochina under an international trusteeship). The French Provisional Government had promised on March 24, 1945 to transform the Indochinese Union into an Indochinese Federation after the war, to develop it economically, culturally, and socially, and to give it broader economic and administrative autonomy. Politically the structure of French control was not to be substantially altered, and the country was to remain divided into five parts. But the proclamation of the Vietnam Republic six months later and the March 6 Accord, which recognized the Republic, turned much of the March 1945 declaration into a dead letter. The old colonialism was out of date. That, at least, was the viewpoint of a number of officials in Paris and of some of the emissaries sent out to Indochina. It was not the view of Admiral d'Argenlieu [2] or of most of the men around him.

The majority of the Frenchmen in Indochina, colonists and administrators alike, refused to recognize that their position in the country had changed since the war. They were opposed to making any concessions to Vietnamese demands. D'Argenlieu himself seemed never to have wholly accepted the March 6 Accord as superseding the 1945 French statement of Indochina policy. He pursued an independent course, supporting groups and individuals who opposed the Republic. He made abortive efforts to persuade the Annamese royal family to return to the throne. Among the small Cochin Chinese bourgeoisie, he found an unrepresentative group of

---

[2] *French High Commissioner for Indochina.—ed.*

Cochin Chinese separatists, almost all of them French citizens, who feared the encroachment of the Hanoi government upon their privileges. He drew upon them to set up a puppet regime in Cochin China, and on June 1, 1946 recognized this government as a "free republic." He permitted French troops to move into the Moi Plateaus in southern Annam, despite an agreement with the Republic to maintain the military status quo, which would have left these minorities under Vietnamese rule. And finally, in August 1946, he convened a second conference at Dalat, a so-called "federal" conference of Laotians and Cambodians as well as people from Cochin China and southern Annam, areas claimed by the Republic but still governed by France.

D'Argenlieu seemed to be trying to settle the status of Cochin China and the organization of the Indochinese Federation, the very subjects the Vietnamese had come to discuss with the French at Fontainebleau. To the Vietnamese delegates in France the second Dalat conference seemed designed to confront them with a *fait accompli*. Encouraged by the French left-wing parties and press, they broke off negotiations with France. All that was salvaged from the months of negotiations since the March 6 Agreement was a *modus vivendi* signed in Paris on September 14, 1946 by Ho and Marius Moutet, the minister for Overseas France, which provided safeguards for the economic and cultural position of Frenchmen in Vietnam—equality of treatment and status with the Vietnamese for French nationals and property, priority for French advisers and technicians, no change in the status of French property or enterprises without the approval of the French government, and the free functioning of French schools in Vietnam. It also provided for an Indochinese customs union and a single Indochinese currency. And it called for an end to all acts of hostility and violence in Cochin China. But even this agreement, which skirted the major issues between the two governments, was never fully carried out.

Inside Vietnam, during this period of negotiations with France in the spring and summer of 1946, the alignment of political forces changed. The Vietminh took military and political steps to consolidate itself in power. As members of the Ho government, some leaders of the Vietnam Nationalist party and the Vietnam Revolutionary League had shared responsibility for the March 6 Agreement, but they soon made clear their opposition both to it and to the Vietminh. By this time, however, their Chinese friends had left the country, and the French troops who replaced them did not share the Chinese army's feelings for its Vietnamese protégés. Convinced by the militant xenophobia of the Nationalist party and the Revolutionary League that the two groups constituted a serious threat both to internal order and to the March 6 Agreement, the French joined the Vietminh in police and military action against them; and some of their leaders fled to China. When the National Assembly met for its second session in October, the Vietnam Nationalist party filled only twenty of its fifty seats, the Vietnam Revolutionary League seventeen of its twenty. Having taken advantage of the months of relative peace ushered in by the March 6 Agreement, Vo Nguyen Giap had by this time strengthened and extended the Vietnamese army.

The National Assembly adopted a constitution at its fall session, declaring Vietnam to be a democratic republic that included Cochin China, Tonkin, and Annam. The constitution provided for a single-house legislature, cabinet government, and a president. It guaranteed democratic liberties to its citizens and paid special attention to the problems of the ethnic minorities inhabiting the country. But the Vietnamese had little respite from war in which to try out their constitution.

Report had it that Vo Nguyen Giap and an extremist wing of the Vietminh had taken over control of the country, imposing upon Ho, when he returned from France, a policy of more intransigent opposition to the French than the President would have liked. But there is little evidence that Ho at any time lost control of his government. Relations with the French worsened rapidly in the fall of 1946, and this situation was reflected in the new Vietnamese cabinet, announced in November 1946, in which the number of Communist seats was increased from two to five.

There was no mutual trust between the French and the Vietnamese, and the uneasy armistice inaugurated by the March 6 Agreement could not go on indefinitely. It was breached violently in November at Haiphong where the French had established their own customs control, in violation of the September *modus vivendi*. At first, the local

French and Vietnamese commanders achieved a peaceful settlement of the Haiphong incident, but this was upset on orders from the French high command, which decided to teach the Vietnam Republic a lesson. The French bombarded the city on November 23, killing thousands of Vietnamese. There was also a bloody incident at Langson the same month. In Cochin China there was still no sign of a referendum. When the first president of the Cochin Chinese "republic," Nguyen Van Thinh, hanged himself for lack of support and lack of power, the French replaced him with another puppet, Le Van Hoach. Tension and distrust of the French heightened among the Vietnamese, who in their turn attacked the French in Hanoi on December 19, 1946. War spread throughout Tonkin and north Annam, and flared up again in Cochin China.

In France, a government of Socialists, a party that sympathized with the aspirations of the Vietnamese, was in power; and it was Léon Blum, long an apostle of a liberal colonial policy, who found himself leading the war against Vietnam. Early in January 1947 Blum was succeeded by a coalition under Paul Ramadier, another Socialist. Although it included Socialists and Communists as well as members of the Popular Republican Movement (M.R.P.), this government—presumably because of its dependence on center and right-wing support—did not seem anxious to undertake negotiations with Ho. It discounted peace overtures that came almost immediately over the Vietnamese radio, and from the Vietnamese delegation in Paris. Late in December 1946 the Socialist minister for Overseas France, Marius Moutet, made a trip to Indochina which had been scheduled before the outbreak of hostilities, but he did not meet any members of the Ho government. Cabinet changes in 1947 oriented the Vietnamese government further to the right and Ho gave up the ministry of foreign affairs (which he had held himself) to a Socialist, Hoang Minh Giam. Only in April 1947 did the French government reply to a Vietnamese proposal for an armistice with a concrete offer of terms, brought secretly to Ho by Paul Mus, a noted scholar. This led to a brief but fleeting optimism among the Vietnamese until they discovered that it was a demand for capitulation.[3]

[3] *The Vietnamese were asked to lay down their arms, to permit French troops to circulate freely in Vietnamese territory and to*

Despite early French victories, it was soon evident that the French could not hope to win by military means alone in Vietnam; they found themselves at a military stalemate. Only by a political offensive could they hope to defeat Ho Chi Minh. In a memorandum to the Paris government soon after full-scale fighting broke out on December 19, d'Argenlieu proposed returning Bao Dai to the throne.[4] D'Argenlieu himself was replaced in March 1947; among French leftists and the Vietnamese, who blamed him for torpedoing the Franco-Vietnamese negotiations, he was regarded as a symbol of reaction and bad faith. But although d'Argenlieu was no longer in favor, his idea of using Bao Dai to checkmate Ho appealed to a number of influential people in France. It was left to d'Argenlieu's successor, Emile Bollaert—a Radical Socialist and long-time civil servant whose appointment seemed to promise a more conciliatory French attitude—to work out the Bao Dai policy.

Bao Dai, in name at least, was still an adviser to the Ho government, but he was no longer in Vietnam, having been sent by Ho in March 1946 on a mission to China from which he had not returned. His value to France depended upon the number of Vietnamese he could split away from Ho Chi Minh and persuade to accept terms less damaging to France's position in Vietnam than those demanded by Ho. But only if Bao Dai took a nationalist stand could he win over any of Ho's supporters. He had, in other words, to be nationalist enough to win friends among the Vietnamese, but not too nationalist to lose them among the French.

The ex-emperor, in 1947, was living in Hong Kong, where he laid the foundations of the reputation that caused critics to label him the "night-club emperor." He had little personal following in Cochin China or Tonkin. Even in Annam, the seat of the imperial dynasty, his support was not widespread. But Bao Dai seemed the one person around whom a number

---

surrender to the French all non-Vietnamese personnel in the Vietnamese army. Vietnamese troops were to be confined to zones designated by the French command, and French hostages were to be surrendered.

[4] *Journal Official de la République Française. Débats de l'Assemblé de l'Union Française, Séance du 19 Janvier, 1950,* p. 49.

of minor disaffected political groups might be rallied in opposition to Ho. Neither powerful nor popular, these groups formed a fluctuating series of coalitions that they called national union fronts.

Among them were the Vietnam Revolutionary League and the Vietnam Nationalist party, one favoring a consitutional monarchy, the other a republic. Large sections of both, however, supported Ho in the war against the French. Elements of the Cao Dai and the Hoa Hao,[5] which signed a pact in January 1948 setting up separate zones of action in Cochin China, also joined the Bao Dai camp. But theirs was

---

[5] With the Binh Xuyen, the three "sects" of Vietnam. John McDermott writes: "The Cao Dai, founded just after World War I, claim more than a million and a half adherents in the South, exercising their strongest influence in the Mekong delta region, particularly in the province of Tay Ninh, in other provinces bordering on Cambodia, and in Saigon itself. Their religion incorporates elements of local Buddhism, Christianity, Hinduism, and large doses of "spiritual science." Their clergy, headed by a "pope," is organized in a hierarchy modelled on that of the Roman Catholic Church. The extent of their borrowing is suggested by the fact that they count the French author Victor Hugo among their saints. Politically, the Cao Dai moved sharply in the direction of nationalism during the 1930's, organized their own militia, and fought sporadic actions against the French.

"In the late 1930's, a Buddhist bonze named Huynh Phu So began a reformation against the worldly and easy-going Buddhism then prevalent. His followers, whose ranks grew rapidly, called themselves Hoa Hao after the village where Phu So began his crusade. Intensely nationalistic and xenophobic, the Hoa Hao were under constant attack from the French and succeeded in establishing themselves only in the very south and west of Vietnam primarily along the Cambodian border. Like the Catholics, they tended to live apart in their own villages and hamlets. By 1945 they had recruited a militia of over 20,000. Today their overall membership stands at about one million." ("Profile of Vietnamese History," part I, *Viet-Report: Emergency News Bulletin on Southeast Asian Affairs*, I:1 [July, 1965], p. 21).

The Binh Xuyen originally operated from the swamps south of Cholon. They co-operated with the Vietminh in 1945–1946. In 1954 the Binh Xuyen, who controlled vice and crime in Saigon–Cholon, under circumstances that reeked of bribery, were also given control of the police! In 1955 they were crushed by Ngo Dinh Diem. (See Donald Lancaster, *The Emancipation of French Indo-China* [London/New York/Toronto, 1961], pp. 137-138, 307, 353n, 385-390.)—ed.

only a conditional and noncommittal promise of co-operation, which left their organizations free to do as they pleased. Their private armies provided the anti-Ho movement with a military force, but both were far more anti-French than pro-Bao Dai, and they could not be counted on for disciplined or reliable support for the ex-emperor. The two million Catholics of Vietnam, who might have been expected to join forces with any group offering an alternative to the Communists in the Vietminh, were nominally represented by the Catholic League, headed by Ngo Dinh Diem, formerly premier under Bao Dai. Diem was active in the Bao Dai movement only during its early stages, afterwards he took no part in it, and the majority of his co-religionists continued to support Ho. . . .

Although Bao Dai was in touch with the French early in 1947, he delayed making commitments to the various groups that appealed to him for leadership. He announced that he was neither for nor against the Vietminh and would not return home unless the people wanted him. Emile Bollaert favored a generous French gesture that would have permitted a truce with Ho Chi Minh and negotiations with him as well as with the Bao Dai groups, but the high commissioner was overruled by the French government. When Bollaert made what he called a final offer, at Hadong in September 1947, it envisaged such limited French concessions that Bao Dai's group, as well as the Republic, rejected it. But another part of Bollaert's speech was an appeal to all political, intellectual, and social groups in Vietnam, and to that Bao Dai responded more favorably. He announced that he was prepared to negotiate with France in the interest of unity and independence. In December 1947 he left for Europe for talks with the French government, which formally announced its intention henceforth to confine its negotiations to persons outside the Ho government.

In their political counter-offensive against the Republic, the French envisaged Bao Dai as a key figure, the majority of the country, however, still supported Ho. Despite the strong and entrenched Communist minority in the Republican government, by far the greater part of non-Communist Vietnamese nationalists regarded Ho as their only possible leader in the struggle against the French. Bao Dai appeared so much a creature of French policy as to make it extremely difficult for him to win support among his own people.

Bao Dai promised that the Vietnamese would decide their own regime as soon as peace and order were re-established. He was, he assured them, only a mediator and a negotiator, subordinating all lesser considerations to restoring peace. Unity by now had become so vital a part of any nationalist platform that the French reluctantly recognized that Bao Dai could not even hope to succeed unless he brought Cochin China back to Vietnam. On May 20, 1948 the pro-Bao Dai groups, with the ex-emperor's approval, set up what they called a Provisional Central Government of Vietnam, linking Tonkin, Annam, and Cochin China under the presidency of Nguyen Van Xuan. Bao Dai was on hand when, on June 5 aboard a ship in the Bay of Along, Xuan and the French signed an agreement recognizing "the independence of Vietnam [as an associated state within the French Union], whose task it is now fully to realize its unity."

The French had at last accepted the principle of unity for Vietnam. The problem was to translate that principle into practice, for Cochin China was still legally a French colony and its status could not be changed without the approval of the French parliament. The word "independence" appeared for the first time in a Franco-Vietnamese treaty, but it was an independence hedged about by qualifications. The French, it was true, had finally given up their insistence on creating a strong Indochinese Federation. The idea of federation had become so indistinguishable from French attempts to control the country that it had lost the little Indochinese support it may once have had. In the Bay of Along agreement, federation gave way to the concept of associated statehood within the French Union for each of the three states of Indochina. Only in August 1948 did the French premier, André Marie, endorse the agreement of June 5.

Negotiations with Bao Dai dragged on in 1949. By this time the victories of the Communists in China had brought them close to the northern frontier of Vietnam, and Ho Chi Minh would soon have powerful friends across the Chinese border. The French had to break up the nationalist-Communist alliance quickly if they were to break it up at all. They urged Bao Dai, who was then in France, to go home and rally his people around him. But no one would rally to

Bao Dai if he returned to Vietnam with empty hands; he refused to leave Europe without more generous terms than the French had yet been willing to offer with regard either to unity or independence. On March 8, 1949 he finally reached the Élysée agreements with France, which took the form of an exchange of letters between Bao Dai and Vincent Auriol, the French president. When ratified, they would bring Vietnam into the French Union as an associated state. . . .

Bao Dai had accepted the Élysée agreements only on condition that Cochin China be united with the rest of Vietnam. In March 1949 the French Assembly passed a law providing for a territorial assembly to meet in Cochin China and vote upon its future status, a procedure required by the French constitution. Only a strictly limited electorate was permitted to vote for members of this assembly and, of those qualified, less than twelve hundred French and Vietnamese actually voted. But even the assembly they elected favored union with Vietnam. On May 21, 1949 the French National Assembly voted to end the colonial status of Cochin China, which was to be "attached to the Associated State of Vietnam in accordance with the Joint Declaration of June 5, 1948 and the Declaration of the French Government of August 19, 1948."

With unity assured, Bao Dai departed for home, ending his three years of self-imposed exile on April 28, 1949. On June 14, at a ceremony in Saigon, he formally exchanged documents with Léon Pignon (who had replaced Bollaert as high commissioner the previous October), bringing the Élysée agreements into effect: they had still to be ratified, however, by the French government. There had been a time when Bao Dai had presented himself as a mediator between the Vietnamese people and the French, and there had even been speculation that he might make peace between France and Ho Chi Minh. But if Bao Dai ever actually had such ideas, he had clearly abandoned them. He acted as though he had never abdicated, announcing his intention to retain provisionally the title of emperor. The future constitution of Vietnam, he declared, would be decided by "the people [who] have fought heroically for the independence of their homeland." [6] In the meantime he proclaimed himself

[6] Bulletin d'Information de la France d'Outre-Mer (*Paris*), July 1949, p. 3.

chief of state. The ineffectual Xuan government, which had failed in its attempt to win popular support, resigned in his favor, and Xuan became Bao Dai's vice-president and minister of national defense. But the new cabinet seemed little better off than its predecessor. For a government that claimed to represent all Vietnam, it included an unduly large number of people from the area of South Vietnam. It was unable to attract many outstanding Vietnamese, no matter how opposed they might be to Ho; and, having few of the attributes of power, it did not wield any effective authority even over areas under French control.

Bao Dai was home at last but the struggle in Vietnam, contrary to French expectations, was slow in taking on the aspect of a civil war. The major antagonists were not Bao Dai and Ho Chi Minh and their respective followers, but the French army and the Democratic Republic of Vietnam, led by Ho Chi Minh. Some 150,000 soldiers were fighting on the French side in Vietnam (more than one quarter of the entire French army). They included not only Frenchmen, but also a number of Indochinese; there were Germans who had exchanged the swastika for the tricolor of the French Foreign Legion, and Moroccans and Senegalese from Overseas France. With these forces the French managed to control the centers of the major cities and the important lines of communication. But on the roads Frenchmen could travel only in convoys and then were not sure of reaching their destination. In the cities no French or Vietnamese opponent of the Republic was safe, particularly at night, and such a French stronghold as Saigon was honeycombed with Ho's supporters, who even collected taxes from the Chinese and Vietnamese inhabitants. The French were spending more than half of their military budget in Indochina, but still the guerrilla war went on, and by the end of 1949 the greater part of the country was in the hands of the Ho forces. The situation of the French in Indochina was grave, for neither by military force nor by political maneuver had they succeeded in bringing peace to the country.

As events laid bare the meagerness of France's resources, the war in Indochina became a major international concern because of the victories of the Communists in China. The French and the Vietnamese until then had fought their war in relative international obscurity. At the very time when the rights and wrongs of the Dutch and Indonesians were being hotly debated before the United Nations, a curtain of silence seemed to have dropped over Indochina. There were various reasons why the Democratic Republic of Vietnam could not find any champions during the first years of its existence. Unlike Indonesia, where both Americans and Englishmen had substantial investments, Indochina was almost exclusively a French economic preserve; no other nation had any serious stake to involve it in Indochinese affairs. But the United States did have a tremendous stake in France, which it regarded as a key to the defense and recovery of Western Europe. The State Department, as a result, despite American traditional opposition to colonialism, was sympathetic when Frenchmen argued that if they lost Vietnam, they would lose North Africa and most of their empire as well, with disastrous economic and military results to the mother country. Further, a "soft" policy toward Ho Chi Minh, according to French opponents of such a policy, would lead to the overthrow of any "Third Force" government in France and bring to power either General Charles de Gaulle or the Communists. When to this line of reasoning was added the fact that the Communists played a key role in the Vietnamese resistance, the American government was not inclined to be openly critical of French policy. It contented itself with expressing a wish for peace in Indochina.[7]

The Communist issue was generally played down by the Vietnam Republic, with the collaboration of the Communists, during the period of its negotiations with France. The Indochinese Communist party had been dissolved in November 1945 (in order to conciliate the Chinese Nationalists then in occupation of part of the country, as well as non-Communist international opinion generally) and had been replaced by an Association for the Study of Marxism. Ho Chi Minh refused to say whether or not he himself was still a Communist. His government was a broad coalition drawn from diverse groups which for a considerable period of time steered a middle course in its propaganda (its equivalent of more formal foreign relations) and was careful not to become identified either with the Soviet bloc or with the West.

[7] *In February 1947 Secretary of State George C. Marshall said that he hoped "a pacific basis of adjustment of the difficulties could be found." The New York Times, February 8, 1947.*

But the leading position of the Communists in Vietnam could hardly be denied. An emergent nationalist movement like the Indonesian, preoccupied with its struggle against the Dutch, was fearful of being tarred with the red brush and regarded the Vietnam Republic with official caution, as did other Asian governments. The Soviet Union also did not see fit to raise the Vietnamese question. The French Communist party, which belonged to the governing coalition in France, trod gingerly on political eggs after the outbreak of fighting in December 1946; it was critical of the war against Vietnam and yet it remained in the French government until May 1947. Even after that time it did not give up the hope of achieving a Communist government in France. For that reason the Communists were determined not to offend the nationalist sensibilities of the French electorate; they offered the Vietnamese little more than verbal support both during the 1946 negotiations and for some time afterwards; and they were anxious to keep Vietnam inside the French Union. Ho Chi Minh himself had asked for no more than membership in the French Union after the March 6, 1946 Agreement, but for the Vietnam Republic this was a retreat from the full independence it had expected in 1945.[8]

With no help from abroad, either from the Communists or from the Western powers, the Democratic Republic of Vietnam was thrown on its own resources. After the events of December 19, 1946 the Ho government found it more important than ever to have a noncontroversial program on which the different elements opposing the French could unite —whether they were Catholics or Communists, Socialists or Democrats, former members of the imperial court at Hué, peasants, or bourgeoisie. It was important also not to antagonize China and Thailand, both of which were friendly to the Vietnamese, or any other foreign country that one day might help the Republic. They therefore concentrated on the struggle with France, on growing food, combating illiteracy, and maintaining the dike system against the ever-present menace of floods.

As the war went on, the watchword in Vietnamese politics

---

[8] *Vietnamese Communists who had wanted independence in the fall of 1945 were bitterly critical of the failure of their French comrades to help them achieve it. See Harold R. Isaacs: No Peace for Asia (New York, 1947), pp. 173 ff.*

was national unity. The Vietminh was the principal party in the country, having units even at the village level and including widely diversified elements ranging from moderates to Communists, directed by the Tong Bo (the Vietminh Executive Committee). Some of its members were individuals and others were parties, like the Vietnam Democratic party founded in 1944 and the Vietnam Socialist party founded two years later, both of which held seats in the cabinet. The Vietminh extended its influence throughout Vietnam by means of a network of "national welfare" organizations of such groups as women, young people, workers, peasants, and soldiers, and also had political commissars in the army. It claimed a membership of nine million people. There were other groups, however, which did not belong to the Vietminh, and to bring them into the nationalist coalition, a new and more inclusive front, the League for the National Union of Vietnam (the Lien Viet) was set up in 1946 [9]

Within the framework of the Vietminh, the Communists continued in active leadership of the government. They followed a Popular Front line, collaborating with other parties in the nationalist resistance, although clashing sometimes with their ideological opponents, notably the Trotskyites.[10] The long struggle against the French strengthened the hold of the Communists within the Vietnam government, and to this was added the fact that a Communist regime would soon be in power in China. Disturbed at the spread of Communism in Asia, the United States began to show open sympathy for Bao Dai, while the Vietnam Republic, looking forward for the first time to having an ally on its frontier, promised its people a general and victorious counter-offensive. The Communists in the Vietminh increased their overt control over the country.[11] Vo Nguyen Giap, who had been dropped from his cabinet post, returned as minister of na-

[9] See p. 210n.–ed.

[10] *The Trotskyites had consistently opposed all concessions to the French, the March 6 Agreement as well as the September 14 modus vivendi.*

[11] *See in this connection Milton Sacks: "The Strategy of Communism in Southeast Asia," Pacific Affairs, September 1950, pp. 227–47; and J. R. Clémentin: "The Nationalist Dilemma in Vietnam," ibid., pp. 294–310.*

tional defense.[12] Ho Chi Minh sent a delegate to South Vietnam (Cochin China) to enforce party discipline. In Central Vietnam (Annam) Pham Van Dong, a Communist who had headed the Vietnamese delegation at Fontainebleau, performed a similar job and then, in 1949, became vice president of the government, second only to Ho. And Tran Van Giau, formerly Cochin Chinese general secretary of the Indochinese Communist party, assumed the important post of director of the Central Information Service of Vietnam. In France the Communist party dropped its insistence that Vietnam remain within the French Union and demanded that the French evacuate Vietnam as a preliminary to negotiations with Ho. "Peace with Vietnam" and "the dirty war" were old Communist phrases, but in 1950 the French Communists moved from words to action—the action that they had not chosen to take in 1947, 1948, or 1949—and started a campaign of strikes and demonstrations aimed at obstructing the transport of soldiers and war material to Indochina. When the Ho Chi Minh government sent out requests for recognition to a large number of countries early in 1950, the Chinese Communists recognized the Democratic Republic of Vietnam. The Soviet Union followed suit on January 31. The American Secretary of State, Dean Acheson, said that this "should remove any illusion as to the 'nationalist' character of Ho Chi Minh's aims and reveals Ho in his true colors as the mortal enemy of native independence in Indochina." [13]

The United States and Great Britain, now deeply concerned by Chinese Communist successes that threatened the balance of power throughout Southeast Asia, were anxious to stem the spread of Communism. The French recognized this and, hoping for help in their war against Ho, emphasized that they were not fighting a colonial war in Vietnam, but an anti-Communist war. They were the defenders of Western civilization in the Far East, they insisted, and as such were entitled to American aid, not only in Europe (where Marshall Plan dollars released francs for expenditures in the Vietnamese war), but also in Indochina.

[12] He continued to hold the post that he had held without interruption since 1945, that of commander-in-chief of the Vietnam army.

[13] Department of State Bulletin, February 13, 1950, p. 244.

The United States was far from unfriendly to Bao Dai.[14] In June 1949 the Department of State welcomed the formation of "the new unified state of Vietnam" and expressed its hope that the March 8 agreements would "form the basis for the progressive realization of the legitimate aspirations of the Vietnamese people." [15] And the following January, Philip C. Jessup, United States ambassador at large, delivered a message to Bao Dai in which Secretary of State Acheson wrote that the United States was looking forward to establishing closer relations with the Bao Dai government.

This was not the only encouragement Bao Dai had received from abroad. In October 1949 his government had been elected as associate member of the United Nations Economic Commission for Asia and the Far East. Malcolm MacDonald, the British high commissioner for Southeast Asia, had made a trip to Indochina and brought back an optimistic report on Bao Dai's position which had considerable influence on both British and American official opinion. At the Commonwealth conference in Colombo in January 1950, MacDonald stated that Bao Dai seemed to represent the wishes of the majority of the Vietnamese and was daily gaining new support.[16] Of all the delegates present, only Pandit Nehru of India refused to endorse this view. Bao Dai also achieved a diplomatic success at the Vatican. In 1948 French High Commissioner Bollaert had made an apparently unsuccessful attempt to persuade the Pope to call on Vietnamese Catholics to turn against Ho Chi Minh, but in November 1949 the Vatican announced that the Pope was praying for Bao Dai.

The need of the French for foreign aid had become urgent. But they could hardly ask the United States to support the Bao Dai government when the French Assembly itself had not yet given its support to Bao Dai by ratifying the Élysée agreements to which his government owed its existence. Delays by the French in implementing their promises,

---

[14] *Many Frenchmen attributed the origins of the Bao Dai policy at least in part to the influence of William C. Bullitt, former American ambassador to France, who, after a trip to Indochina in 1947, conferred with leading government people in France before he returned home to write an article for* Life *magazine (October 1947) proposing Bao Dai as an alternative to Ho.*

[15] Department of State Bulletin, *July 18, 1949, p. 75.*

[16] The Scotsman *(Edinburgh), January 15, 1950.*

so typical of the course of French-Vietnamese relations, served to weaken Bao Dai's position still further. Only on December 30, 1949 did the Bao Dai government sign a number of conventions with France to implement the March 1949 agreements. And finally, in January 1950, the treaties with the three associated states came up before the French Assembly.

The French Assembly debate on Indochina was a violent one, largely because of the Communists and some small left-wing groups who opposed the accords. One of the arguments offered by the government in favor of ratification was that it was a prerequisite to help from abroad. The Socialists proposed a motion calling for an armistice with Ho, but when that was defeated joined the majority of the Assembly in approving the three agreements on January 28 by 401 to 193. The agreements were ratified by the French government on February 2. On February 7 the United States and Great Britain both recognized Bao Dai.[17]

In Asia, it was difficult to find many friends for Bao Dai. Thailand, which under its present government was acutely fearful of Communism close to its borders, recognized Bao Dai, but only after a cabinet crisis. Other Asian states, like India and Indonesia, did not believe Bao Dai to be the legitimate representative of the Vietnamese people, and refused to recognize him.

American efforts to contain Communism in Asia led to American support of the French military effort in Vietnam. The United States did not desire this role. It tried rather to make a separate policy for Indochina, aimed at strengthening the Bao Dai government and using pressure on the French to grant it a more real independence. The French distrusted American policy toward the French empire generally, fearing American economic inroads into the French colonies. They also feared what they regarded as American anticolonialism and it was this fear that was uppermost in 1950 in regard to

---

[17] *The British government justified this act of recognition on the grounds that it regarded the Bao Dai regime as the only regime clearly controlling large areas of Vietnam, with a capital city and with a visible government. They were, however, "anxious that rather more independence should have been given to the Bao Dai Government than had, in fact, been given." House of Commons, Hansard, 5th Series, Vol. 475, p. 2099.*

Indochina. They insisted that if American economic aid was to be delivered directly to the Vietnamese, American military aid at least should go only to the French. General Marcel Carpentier, commander-in-chief of the French forces in Indochina, stated: "I will never agree to equipment being given directly to the Vietnamese. If this should be done I would resign within twenty-four hours. The Vietnamese have no generals, no colonels, no military organization that could effectively utilize the equipment. It would be wasted, and in China the United States has had enough of that." [18]

In May Secretary of State Acheson announced that the United States would grant military and economic aid to restore security and develop "genuine nationalism" in Indochina. He made a point of saying that this aid would go not simply to France but also to each of the associated states.[19] With the outbreak of war in Korea, President Truman on June 27 announced "acceleration in the furnishing of military assistance to the forces of France and the associated states in Indochina and the dispatch of a military mission to provide close working relations with these forces." [20]

But could the United States really distinguish between the assistance it was giving to France and that which was supposed to go directly to Bao Dai? His government was too unpopular and inefficient to make effective use of any aid it did receive. A few able men did rally to Bao Dai, like Nguyen Huu Tri, the governor of North Vietnam; they did so in the hope that they might yet transform the Élysée agreements into a more genuine independence. "The Vietnamese regard the March 8 agreements as only a stepping stone," Tri told a reporter. "We want full, complete independence." He said that there had been a considerable transfer of administrative functions from France to the Vietnamese in the North, in education, public welfare, agriculture, public health, public works, and some police powers, but "in every sphere, the French keep back something." [21]

The great majority of the intellectuals and the youth of Vietnam refused to have anything to do with Bao Dai. Ngo

---

[18] The New York Times, *March 9, 1950.*

[19] *See p. 89.—ed.*

[20] Department of State Bulletin, *July 5, 1950, p. 5.*

[21] The New York Times, *March 6, 1950.*

Dinh Diem turned down offers to head the new government.
He stated publicly his belief that "the national aspirations of
the Vietnamese people will be satisfied only on the day when
our nation obtains the same political regime which India
and Pakistan enjoy. . . . I believe it is only just to reserve
the best posts in the new Vietnam for those who have de-
served best of the country; I speak of those who resist." [22]
But appeals to resistance elements to join Bao Dai fell generally on deaf ears. Nguyen Phan Long, an influential editor
from South Vietnam who became Bao Dai's premier in January 1950, was dropped in May because of his efforts to ap-
pease the resistance. He was replaced by Tran Van Huu, who
had succeeded Xuan as governor of South Vietnam. The selection of Huu, because he was more amenable to the French
and less friendly to the resistance, did nothing to erase the
popular picture of the Bao Dai regime as a puppet government honeycombed with mediocrity and corruption.

Bao Dai, for his part, spent most of his time in retreat at
Dalat, remote from the day-to-day activities of his government. His behavior was not calculated to increase his following among the people. In June 1950, against the counsel of
his advisers and despite the displeasure of the French, he
left for France, presumably to see his family; there was
also vague talk of affairs of state that took him to Europe.
Premier Huu went to France the same month to join representatives of France, Laos, and Cambodia at Pau for discussions on the federal structure that was to be established
in Indochina. This conference was originally scheduled to
end in August but it dragged on into the fall. Huu and Bao
Dai remained in Europe, while their regime fell into still
greater disrepute at home. In Saigon the United States Military Mission, as well as the French, complained of their
absence. How could the Americans build up Bao Dai's army
when they could not even get final decisions from the Vietnamese officials in Saigon? Still more important, how could
the United States help Bao Dai toward greater independence
when he himself seemed so uninterested in achieving it?
Even Bao Dai's supporters were disquieted. There was talk in
some quarters of finding a possible replacement for Bao
Dai, and the names of Cuong De and Ngo Dinh Diem were

[22] L'Echo du Vietnam, *June 16, 1949.*

mentioned. The nationalism of both men was as unquestionable as their anti-Communism. Diem was much the younger, and was besides a prominent and widely respected Catholic. Neither man, however, seemed to have a following of any size within Vietnam.

The French had not been able to find a Vietnamese who could win over the mass of the nationalist resistance from Ho Chi Minh; and this fact was recognized by many non-Communists in France. In December 1949 a number of prominent French intellectuals, in a letter to President Auriol, had urged an immediate end to hostilities as a preliminary to free elections in Vietnam under international control and within the framework of the United Nations. The independent left-wing newspapers, *Combat* and *Franc-Tireur,* had long been critical of the government's refusal to negotiate with Ho, as had several magazines, notably the liberal Catholic *Esprit* and Jean-Paul Sartre's *Les Temps Modernes.* The French Socialist party had voted at successive party congresses for negotiations with Ho even though it was, until February 1950, a part of the government which led the war against him. At their congress in May 1950 the Socialists passed a resolution in favor of referring the Vietnamese situation to the United Nations. Demands for a French evacuation of Indochina were also heard from groups further to the right who believed it impossible for France to hold on to the country any longer. In the leading conservative newspaper, *Le Monde,* a writer pointed out that the Bank of Indochina, which had dominated so much of the Indochinese economy, had already turned in preference to other areas: "the realism of business circles precedes, alas, that of political circles." [23]

A sudden and victorious Vietnamese offensive in September and October 1950 focused French attention with renewed urgency on Indochina. With many of their units reportedly trained and equipped in Communist China, the Vietnamese succeeded in forcing the French to evacuate a series of key posts on the Chinese frontier. Tran Van Huu and Bao Dai hurried back to Vietnam; Jean Letourneau, the French minister for the associated states, and General Alphonse Juin, resident-general in Morocco, arrived to study the situation on the spot.

[23] *Le Monde, June 25–6, 1950.*

No sooner had Premier Huu returned home than he openly attacked France, alleging an attempt to impose continued French domination on Vietnam during the Pau conference. He demanded complete independence and a new and more equal treaty to supersede the Élysée agreements. "Many people are dying every day because Vietnam is not given independence," he said. "If we had independence the people would have no more reason to fight." [24]

In Paris the National Assembly debated on Indochina policy. Some members of the right criticized the government for its conduct of the war; the Communists once again urged withdrawal and negotiations with Ho Chi Minh; and a prominent member of the moderate Radical Socialist party also favored evacuation on the ground that contributing to the defense of Europe was more important than fighting a war in the Far East, and France could not do both. Letourneau who on his return from Asia was given sole responsibility for the direction of French policy in Indochina, ruled out the appeal to the United Nations favored by the Socialists. He told the French National Assembly that the government of Premier René Pleven intended to carry out the March 8, 1949 agreements with the greatest liberalism. Virtually all of the administrative machinery would be in Vietnamese hands by January 1, 1951, he promised, and the French would hand over power as rapidly as possible to a Vietnamese army. On November 23, 1950 the Assembly approved the government's Indochina policy by a vote of 337 to 187. General Jean de Lattre de Tassigny was installed as high commissioner and supreme commander the following month, replacing and combining the functions of Léon Pignon and General Carpentier.

Early in 1951 the French released official figures on the cost to France of the war with Vietnam. Some nineteen thousand European Frenchmen had been reported killed or missing (information on other nationalities in the expeditionary corps was not made public). And since 1947 the French had spent between $1,400,000,000 and $2,200,000,000 on the Indochinese War. [25]

By 1951 the French were no longer fighting alone in

[24] The New York Times, *October 20, 1950.*
[25] The New York Times, *January 4, 1951.*

Vietnam; they were receiving substantial aid from the United States.[26] The Democratic Republic of Vietnam, however, was also not alone. It had found powerful friends across the border in Communist China, which made it more hopeful than ever of victory. In August 1950 the Democratic Republic of Vietnam celebrated the fifth anniversary of its revolution. Five years before, the Vietnam radio had appealed jointly to Truman, Attlee, Stalin, and Chiang Kai-shek, declaring that its revolution stood above class or party. Ho Chi Minh had once been willing to join an Indochinese Federation and a French Union and to give priority to French capital and French technicians; later, he had insisted that Vietnam would be neutral in the cold war. But that was all in the past.

In 1950 the Republican radio called the Élysée agreements a treaty of treason and demanded a total French evacuation of Indochina. Ho said he was still willing to accept French capital, but "not on oppressive terms." Toward Laos and Cambodia he envisaged "fraternal relations based on absolute equality and mutual respect for independence." [27]

Ho Chi Minh told the people, "a few years of resistance have brought our country the greatest success in the history of Vietnam—recognition of the Democratic Republic of Vietnam as an equal in the world democratic family by the two biggest countries in the world—the Soviet Union and Democratic China—and by the new democratic countries. That means that we are definitely on the democratic side and belong to the anti-imperialistic block of 800 million people.

"Since the beginning of the war the Americans have tried to help the French bandits," Ho went on. "But now they have advanced one more step to direct intervention in Vietnam. Thus, we now have one principal opponent—the French bandits—and one more opponent—the American interventionists." [28] The Republican radio proclaimed: "Long live Marshal Stalin! Long live Chairman Mao Tse-tung! Long live President Ho Chi Minh!" No longer did the Republic mini-

---

[26] *By March of 1954 the U.S. was paying about 80% of total French military expenses in Indochina, in sum, over $1,400 million! (See Ellen J. Hammer,* The Struggle for Indochina *[Stanford Calif., 1954]. p. 313n, and R. Scheer's estimate, p. 244 of this volume).—ed.*

[27] *Radio Peking, August 5, 1950.*

[28] *Vietminh Radio, August 16, 1950.*

mize the role of the Communists in its affairs. The radio broadcast instructions to the country's propaganda services to acclaim the "Communist and Vietminh parties who led the victorious revolution" and to stress "the determined leadership of the proletariat. . . . If the Communist Party did not exist it is certain that there would be no August [1945] Revolution nor Democratic Republic of Vietnam." [29]

But how did the Communists and the Vietminh maintain their power in the areas ruled by the Republic? The element of force was not absent, but neither was it all-explanatory. Far more important was the fact that Ho Chi Minh stood for independence and that his government had an army in the field fighting the French. Vietnamese nationalists, who constituted the majority of the population of Vietnam, preferred to fight for independence under the leadership of their own compatriots, even if these happened to be Communists, rather than submit to French rule.

Onset of the First Indochina War for Independence (January 1947)*

The Vietnam Struggle for Independence. At a time when the democratic powers have just emerged from a long war against Fascism, Vietnam, victim of French colonial aggression, must still defend itself with arms. It is no longer necessary to emphasize the misdeeds and crimes of that particular form of colonialism, its constant and deliberate attempt to poison an entire people with alcohol and opium, its policy of exploitation, pressure, and obscurantism imposed upon Vietnam by a handful of colonialists and from which the French people themselves have derived no real benefit. Suffice it to recall that since the French conquest more than three-quarters of a century ago, the people of Vietnam have never ceased striving to regain their independence. The long list of uprisings and revolts, although harshly quelled, have marked this painful period without interruption and have demonstrated the invincible strength of our national spirit. . . .

* Declaration dated January 6, 1947, released by Vietnam News Service in Bangkok, January 25, 1947, translated in Harold R Isaacs, *New Cycle in Asia: Selected Documents on Major International Developments in the Far East, 1943-1947* (New York 1947) pp. 170-174. By permission of the American Institute for Pacific Affairs.

[29] *Vietminh Radio, August 10, 1950.*

Vietnam Appeals to the World. The era of colonial conquest and domination is over. Vietnam is firmly resolved to persevere to the very end in her struggle for her most sacred rights, viz., the territorial integrity of her country and her political independence. . . . The Vietnam Government in signing the agreement of March 6, 1946, offered France a policy of open door and co-operation. Yet the representatives of France in Indochina have sought to render this policy abortive in the hope of re-establishing over Vietnam the old regime of domination which was for them a veritable monopoly of exploitation. . . .

Vietminh Directives During the Resistance War (1946, 1948)*

APPEAL TO THE ENTIRE PEOPLE

Compatriots all over the country!

As we desired peace we made concessions. But the more we made concessions, the further the French colonialists went because they are resolved to invade our country once again.

No! We would rather sacrifice all than lose our country. We are determined not to be enslaved.

Compatriots! Rise up!

Men and women, old and young, regardless of creeds, political parties or nationalities, all the Vietnamese must stand up to fight the French colonialists to save the fatherland. Those who have rifles will use their rifles; those who have swords will use their swords; those who have no swords will use spades, hoes, or sticks. Everyone must endeavor to oppose the colonialists and save his country.

Army men, self-defense guards and militiamen!

The hour for national salvation has struck! We must sacrifice even our last drop of blood to safeguard our country.

Even if we have to endure hardship in the Resistance war, with the determination to make sacrifices, victory will surely be ours.

Long live an independent and unified Vietnam!

Long live the victorious Resistance!

December 20, 1946

---

* Both from Ho Chi Minh, *Selected Works* (4 vols., Hanoi, 1960–1962), III, pp. 81-82, 146-147.

TWELVE RECOMMENDATIONS

The nation has its root in the people.

In the Resistance war and national reconstruction, the main force lies in the people. Therefore, all the people in the army, administration, and mass organizations who are in contact or live with the people, must remember and carry out the following recommendations:

Six forbiddances:

1—Not to do what is likely to damage the land and crops or spoil the houses and belongings of the people.

2—Not to insist on buying or borrowing what the people are not willing to sell or lend.

3—Not to bring living hens into mountainous people's houses.

4—Never to break our word.

5—Not to give offense to people's faith and customs (such as to lie down before the altar, to raise feet over the hearth, to play music in the house, etc.).

6—Not to do or speak what is likely to make people believe that we hold them in contempt.

Six permissibles:

1—To help the people in their daily work (harvesting, fetching firewood, carrying water, sewing, etc.).

2—Whenever possible to buy commodities for those who live far from markets (knife, salt, needle, thread, pen, paper, etc.).

3—In spare time, to tell amusing, simple, and short stories useful to the Resistance, but not to betray secrets.

4—To teach the population the national script and elementary hygiene.

5—To study the customs of each region so as to be acquainted with them in order to create an atmosphere of sympathy first, then gradually to explain to the people to abate their superstitions.

6—To show to the people that you are correct, diligent, and disciplined.

Stimulating poem

The above-mentioned twelve recommendations
Are feasible to all.
He who loves his country,

Will never forget them.
When the people have a habit,
All are like one man,
With good army men and good people,
Everything will be crowned with success.
Only when the root is firm, can the tree live long,
And victory is built with the people as foundations.

April 5, 1948

The Origin of U.S. Military Involvement: Aid for the French (May 1950)*

The [French] Foreign Minister and I have just had an xchange of views on the situation in Indochina and are in neral agreement both as to the urgency of the situation n that area and as to the necessity for remedial action. We ave noted the fact that the problem of meeting the threat o the security of Vietnam, Cambodia, and Laos which now njoy independence within the French Union is primarily he responsibility of France and the Governments and peoles of Indochina. The United States recognizes that the soution of the Indochina problem depends both upon the resoration of security and upon the development of genuine ationalism and that United States assistance can and should ontribute to these major objectives.

The United States Government, convinced that neither naional independence nor democratic evolution exist in any rea dominated by Soviet imperialism, considers the situation o be such as to warrant its according economic aid and miliary equipment to the Associated States of Indochina and to France in order to assist them in restoring stability and pernitting these states to pursue their peaceful and democratic levelopment.

Opposition to the Spread of Communism "By Any Means": John Foster Dulles (March 1954)†

. . . If the Communist forces won uncontested control

---

* Statement of Secretary of State Dean Acheson at Ministerial Level meeting in Paris (May 8, 1950), *Department of State Bulletin,* (May 22, 1950), p. 821.

† Speech to The Overseas Press Club, New York City (March 29, 1954), in *Department of State Bulletin,* XXX (April 12, 1954), pp. 539–540.

over Indochina or any substantial part thereof, they would surely resume the same pattern of aggression against other free peoples in the area.

The propagandists of Red China and Russia make it apparent that the purpose is to dominate all of Southeast Asia. . . .

The United States has shown in many ways its sympathy for the gallant struggle being waged in Indochina by French forces and those of the Associated States.[1] Congress has enabled us to provide material aid to the established governments and their peoples. Also, our diplomacy has sought to deter Communist China from open aggression in that area.

President Eisenhower, in his address of April 16, 1953, explained that a Korean armistice would be a fraud if it merely released aggressive armies for attack elsewhere. I said last September that if Red China sent its own army into Indochina, that would result in grave consequences which might not be confined to Indochina.

Recent statements have been designed to impress upon potential aggressors that aggression might lead to action at places and by means of free-world choosing, so that aggression would cost more than it could gain.

The Chinese Communists have, in fact, avoided the direct use of their own Red armies in open aggression against Indochina. They have, however, largely stepped up their support of the aggression in that area. Indeed, they promote that aggression by all means short of open invasion.

Under all the circumstances it seems desirable to clarify further the United States position.

Under the conditions of today, the imposition on Southeast Asia of the political system of Communist Russia and its Chinese Communist ally, by whatever means, must be a grave threat to the whole free community. The United States feels that that possibility should not be passively accepted but should be met by united action. This might involve serious risks. But these risks are far less than those that will face us a few years from now if we dare not be resolute today.

The free nations want peace. However, peace is not had merely by wanting it. Peace has to be worked for and planned for. Sometimes it is necessary to take risks to win peace just as it is necessary in war to take risks to win victory. The

[1] The reference is to the struggle against the Vietminh.—ed.

chances for peace are usually bettered by letting a potential aggressor know in advance where his aggression could lead him.

I hope that these statements which I make here tonight will serve the cause of peace. . . .

Fear of Impending French Defeat: "Remarks Attributed to" Vice-President Richard Nixon (April 1954)*

. . . What is to be done [about the war in Indochina]? For one, the problem is not one of materials and wasn't four months ago. More men are needed and the question is where to get them. They will not come from France, for France is tired of the war, as we were tired of Korea. Therefore, additional man power must come from Vietnam, Cambodia, and Laos, particularly Vietnam. The French, however, while slow in training the native soldiers, resent the idea that the United States or others should send men to do the job.

More difficult is the job of spirit. Encouragement must be given to fight and resist. Some say if the French get out, the Vietnamese will fight with more spirit, because they would be fighting for their independence.

But the Vietnamese lack the ability to conduct a war by themselves or govern themselves. If the French withdrew, Indochina would become Communist-dominated within a month.

The United States as a leader of the free world cannot afford further retreat in Asia. It is hoped the United States will not have to send troops there, but if this government cannot avoid it, the Administration must face up to the situation and dispatch forces.

Therefore, the United States must go to Geneva and take a positive stand for united action by the free world. Otherwise it will have to take on the problem alone and try to sell it to the others.

French pressure will be exerted at the conference (beginning April 26) for negotiation and the end of the fighting. The British will take a similar position, because of mount-

* *New York Times* (April 17, 1954).

ing Labor Party pressure and defections in the Conservative ranks. The British do not want to antagonize Red China, which they have recognized.

This country is the only nation politically strong enough at home to take a position that will save Asia.

Negotiations with the Communists to divide the territory would result in Communist domination of a vital new area. Communist intransigence in Korea perhaps will teach the French and the British the futility of negotiation and bring them over to the plan of "united action" proposed by Secretary of State Dulles. . . .[1]

It should be emphasized that if Indochina went Communist, Red pressures would increase on Malaya, Thailand, and Indonesia and other Asian nations. The main target of the Communists in Indochina, as it was in Korea, is Japan. Conquest of areas so vital to Japan's economy would reduce Japan to an economic satellite of the Soviet Union. . . .

Southeast Asia Treaty Organization: Response to the Communist Threat (September 1954)*

The parties to this treaty,

Recognizing the sovereign equality of all the parties,

Reiterating their faith in the purposes and principles set forth in the Charter of the United Nations and their desire to live in peace with all peoples and governments,

Reaffirming that, in accordance with the Charter of the United Nations, they uphold the principle of equal rights and self-determination of peoples, and declaring that they will earnestly strive by every peaceful means to promote self-government and to secure the independence of all countries whose peoples desire it and are able to undertake its responsibilities,

Desiring to strengthen the fabric of peace and freedom

---

[1] The plan that eventually resulted in the Southeast Asia Treaty Organization (SEATO). See pp. 92–96.—ed.

* Background Information Relating to Southeast Asia and Vietnam (revised, June 16, 1965), Report of the U.S. Senate Committee on Foreign Relations [89the Congress; 1st Session] (Washington, D.C., 1965), pp. 62–66.

and to uphold the principles of democracy, individual liberty, and the rule of law, and to promote the economic well-being development of all peoples in the treaty area,

Intending to declare publicly and formally their sense of unity, so that any potential aggressor will appreciate that the parties stand together in the area, and

Desiring further to coordinate their efforts for collective defense for the preservation of peace and security,

Therefore agree as follows:

Article 1. The parties undertake, as set forth in the Charter of the United Nations, to settle any international disputes in which they may be involved by peaceful means in such a manner that international peace and security and justice are not endangered, and to refrain in their international relations from the threat or use of force in any manner inconsistent with the purposes of the United Nations.

Article 2. In order more effectively to achieve the objectives of this Treaty, the parties, separately and jointly, by means of continuous and effective self-help and mutual aid will maintain and develop their individual and collective capacity to resist armed attack and to prevent and counter subversive activities directed from without against their territorial integrity and political stability.

Article 3. The parties undertake to strengthen their free institutions and to co-operate with one another in the further development of economic measures, including technical assistance, designed both to promote economic progress and social well-being and to further the individual and collective efforts of governments towards these ends.

Article 4. 1. Each party recognizes that aggression by means of armed attack in the treaty area against any of the parties or against any State or territory which the parties by unanimous agreement may hereafter designate would endanger its own peace and safety, and agrees that it will in that event act to meet the common danger in accordance with its constitutional processes. Measures taken under this paragraph shall be immediately reported to the Security Council of the United Nations.

2. If, in the opinion of any of the parties, the inviolability or the integrity of the territory or the sovereignty or political independence of any party in the treaty area or of any other State or territory to which the provisions of paragraph 1 of

this Article from time to time apply is threatened in any way other than by armed attack or is affected or threatened by any fact or situation which might endanger the peace of the area, the parties shall consult immediately in order to agree on the measures which should be taken for the common defense.

3. It is understood that no action on the territory of any State designated by unanimous agreement under paragraph 1 of this Article or on any territory so designated shall be taken except at the invitation or with the consent of the government concerned. . . .

> [Certain Details of the Organization of the Pact are Omitted.—ed.]

Article 7. Any other State in a position to further the objectives of this Treaty and to contribute to the security of the area may, by unanimous agreement of the parties, be invited to accede to this Treaty. Any State so invited may become a party to the Treaty by depositing its instrument of accession with the government of the Republic of the Philippines. The Government of the Republic of the Philippines shall inform each of the parties of the deposit of each such instrument of accession.[1]

Article 8. As used in this Treaty, the "treaty area" is the general area of Southeast Asia, including also the entire territories of the Asian parties, and the general area of the Southwest Pacific not including the Pacific area north of 21 degrees 30 minutes north latitude. The parties may, by unanimous agreement, amend this Article to include within the treaty area the territory of any State acceding to this Treaty in accordance with Article 7 or otherwise to change the treaty area. . . .

> [Details of the Ratification Procedure are Omitted. —ed.]

Article 10. The Treaty shall remain in force indefinitely, but any party may cease to be a party one year after its notice of denunciation has been given to the government of the Republic of the Philippines, which shall inform the governments of the other parties of the deposit of such notice of denunciation. . . .

> [Discussion of English and French texts of this Treaty is Omitted.—ed.]

[1] No other state ever joined.—ed.

UNDERSTANDING OF THE UNITED STATES

The United States of America in executing the present Treaty does so with the understanding that its recognition of the effect of aggression and armed attack and its agreement with reference thereto in Article 4, paragraph 1, apply only to Communist aggression, but affirms that in the event of other aggression or armed attack it will consult under the provisions of Article 4, paragraph 2.

In witness whereof, the undersigned plenipotentiaries have signed this Treaty. Done at Manila, this eighth day of September 1954.

For Australia: R. G. Casey.

For France: G. La Chambre.

For New Zealand: Clifton Webb.

For Pakistan: Signed for transmission to my government for its consideration and action in accordance with the Constitution of Pakistan. Zafrulla Khan.

For the Republic of the Philippines: Carlos P. Garcia, Francisco A. Delgado, Tomas L. Cabili, Lorenzo M. Tañada, Cornelio T. Villareal.

For the Kingdom of Thailand: Wan Waithayakon Krommun Naradhip Bongsprabandh.

For the United Kingdom of Great Britain and Northern Ireland: Reading.

For the United States of America: John Foster Dulles, H. Alexander Smith, Michael J. Mansfield.

I certify that the foregoing is a true copy of the Southeast Asia Collective Defense Treaty concluded and signed in the English language at Manila, on September 8, 1954, the signed original of which is deposited in the archives of the government of the Republic of the Philippines.

In testimony whereof, I, Raul S. Manglapus, Undersecretary of Foreign Affairs of the Republic of the Philippines, have hereunto set my hand and caused the seal of the Department of Foreign Affairs to be affixed at the City of Manila, this 14th day of October, 1954.

[seal]

Raul S. Manglapus
Undersecretary of Foreign Affairs

PROTOCOL TO THE SOUTHEAST ASIA COLLECTIVE
DEFENSE TREATY

Designation of States and territory as to which provisions of
Article 4 and Article 3 are to be applicable:

The parties to the Southeast Asia Collective Defense
Treaty unanimously designate for the purposes of Article 4
of the Treaty the States of Cambodia and Laos and the free
territory under the jurisdiction of the State of Vietnam.

The parties further agree that the above-mentioned States
and territory shall be eligible in respect of the economic
measures contemplated by Article 3.

This protocol shall enter into force simultaneously with
the coming into force of the Treaty.

The Day We Didn't Go To War

BY CHALMERS M. ROBERTS*

Saturday, April 3, 1954 was a raw, windy day in Washington, but the weather didn't prevent a hundred thousand
Americans from milling around the Jefferson Memorial to see
the cherry blossoms—or twenty thousand of them from
watching the crowning of the 1954 Cherry Blossom Queen.

President Eisenhower drove off to his Maryland mountain
retreat called Camp David. There he worked on his coming
Monday speech, designed, so the White House said, to quiet
America's fears of Russia, the H-bomb, domestic Communists,
a depression. But that Saturday morning eight members of
Congress, five Senators and three Representatives, got the
scare of their lives. They had been called to a secret conference with John Foster Dulles. They entered one of the
State Department's fifth-floor conference rooms to find not
only Dulles but Admiral Arthur W. Radford, chairman of
the Joint Chiefs of Staff, Under Secretary of Defense Roger
Kyes, Navy Secretary Robert B. Anderson, and Thruston B.

* Chief, National News Bureau of the *Washington Post & Times-
Herald,* author of *Can We Meet The Russians Half Way?* (1958),
and many articles. The selection is from *The Reporter,* XI (September 14, 1954), pp. 31-35. By permission.

Morton, Dulles's assistant for Congressional Relations. A large map of the world hung behind Dulles's seat, and Radford stood by with several others. "The President has asked me to call this meeting," Dulles began.

The atmosphere became serious at once. What was wanted, Dulles said, was a joint resolution by Congress to permit the President to use air and naval power in Indochina. Dulles hinted that perhaps the mere passage of such a resolution would in itself make its use unnecessary. But the President had asked for its consideration, and, Dulles added, Mr. Eisenhower felt that it was indispensable at this juncture that the leaders of Congress feel as the Administration did on the Indochina crisis.

Then Radford took over. He said the Administration was deeply concerned over the rapidly deteriorating situation. He used a map of the Pacific to point out the importance of Indochina. He spoke about the French Union forces then already under siege for three weeks in the fortress of Dienbienphu.

The admiral explained the urgency of American action by declaring that he was not even sure, because of poor communications, whether, in fact, Dienbienphu was still holding out. (The fortress held out for five weeks more.)

Dulles backed up Radford. If Indochina fell and if its fall led to the loss of all of Southeast Asia, he declared, then the United States might eventually be forced back to Hawaii, as it was before the Second World War. And Dulles was not complimentary about the French. He said he feared they might use some disguised means of getting out of Indochina if they did not receive help soon.

The eight legislators were silent: Senate Majority Leader Knowland and his G.O.P. colleague Eugene Millikin, Senate Minority Leader Lyndon B. Johnson and his Democratic colleagues Richard B. Russell and Earle C. Clements, House G.O.P. Speaker Joseph Martin and two Democratic House leaders, John W. McCormack and J. Percy Priest.

What to do? Radford offered the plan he had in mind once Congress passed the joint resolution.

Some two hundred planes from the thirty-one-thousand-ton U.S. Navy carriers *Essex* and *Boxer,* then in the South China Sea ostensibly for "training," plus land-based U.S. Air Force planes from bases a thousand miles away in the

Philippines, would be used for a single strike to save Dien-bienphu.

The legislators stirred, and the questions began.

Radford was asked whether such action would be war. He replied that we would be in the war.

If the strike did not succeed in relieving the fortress, would we follow up? "Yes," said the chairman of the Joint Chiefs of Staff.

Would land forces then also have to be used? Radford did not give a definite answer.

In the early part of the questioning, Knowland showed enthusiasm for the venture, consistent with his public statements that something must be done or Southeast Asia would be lost.

But as the questions kept flowing, largely from Democrats, Knowland lapsed into silence.

Clements asked Radford the first of the two key questions: "Does this plan have the approval of the other members of the Joint Chiefs of Staff?"

"No," replied Radford.

"How many of the three agree with you?"

"None."

"How do you account for that?"

"I have spent more time in the Far East than any of them and I understand the situation better."

Lyndon Johnson put the other key question in the form of a little speech. He said that Knowland had been saying publicly that in Korea up to ninety per cent of the men and money came from the United States. The United States had become sold on the idea that that was bad. Hence in any operation in Indochina we ought to know first who would put up the men. And so he asked Dulles whether he had consulted nations who might be our allies in intervention.

Dulles said he had not.

The Secretary was asked why he didn't go to the United Nations as in the Korean case. He replied that it would take too long, that this was an immediate problem.

There were other questions. Would Red China and the Soviet Union come into the war if the United States took military action? The China question appears to have been sidestepped, though Dulles said he felt the Soviets could handle the Chinese and the United States did not think that

Moscow wanted a general war now. Further, he added, if the Communists feel that we mean business, they won't go "any further down there," pointing to the map of Southeast Asia.

John W. McCormack, the House Minority Leader, couldn't resist temptation. He was surprised, he said, that Dulles would look to the "party of treason," as the Democrats had been called by Joe McCarthy in his Lincoln's Birthday speech under G.O.P. auspices, to take the lead in a situation that might end up in a general shooting war. Dulles did not reply.

In the end, all eight members of Congress, Republicans and Democrats alike, were agreed that Dulles had better first go shopping for allies. Some people who should know say that Dulles was carrying, but did not produce, a draft of the joint resolution the President wanted Congress to consider.

The whole meeting had lasted two hours and ten minutes. As they left, the Hill delegation told waiting reporters they had been briefed on Indochina. Nothing more.

This approach to Congress by Dulles and Radford on behalf of the President was the beginning of three weeks of intensive effort by the Administration to head off disaster in Indochina. Some of those at the meeting came away with the feeling that if they had agreed that Saturday to the resolution, planes would have been winging toward Dienbienphu without waiting for a vote of Congress—or without a word in advance to the American people.

For some months now, I have tried to put together the bits and pieces of the American part in the Indochina debacle. But before relating the sequel, it is necessary here to go back to two events that underlay the meeting just described—though neither of them was mentioned at that meeting.

On March 20, just two weeks earlier, General Paul Ely, then French Chief of Staff and later commander in Indochina, had arrived in Washington from the Far East to tell the President, Dulles, Radford, and others that unless the United States intervened, Indochina would be lost. This was a shock of earthquake proportions to leaders who had been taken in by their own talk of the Navarre Plan to win the war.

In his meetings at the Pentagon, Ely was flabbergasted to

find that Radford proposed American intervention without being asked. Ely said he would have to consult his government. He carried back to Paris the word that when France gave the signal, the United States would respond.

The second event of importance is the most difficult to determine accurately. But it is clear that Ely's remarks started a mighty struggle within the National Security Council, [NSC] that inner core of the government where our most vital decisions are worked out for the President's final O.K. The argument advanced by Radford and supported by Vice-President Nixon and by Dulles was that Indochina must not be allowed to fall into Communist hands lest such a fate set in motion a falling row of dominoes.

Eisenhower himself used the "row-of-dominoes" phrase at a press conference on April 7. On April 15, Radford said in a speech that Indochina's loss "would be the prelude to the loss of all Southeast Asia and a threat to a far wider area." On April 16 Nixon, in his well-publicized "off-the-record" talk to the newspaper editors' convention, said that if the United States could not otherwise prevent the loss of Indochina, then the Administration must face the situation and dispatch troops.[1] And the President in his press conference of March 24 had declared that Southeast Asia was of the "most transcendent importance." All these remarks reflected a basic policy decision.

It is my understanding, although I cannot produce the top-secret NSC paper to prove it, that some time between Ely's arrival on March 20 and the Dulles-Radford approach to the Congressional leaders on April 3, the NSC had taken a firm position that the United States could not afford the loss of Indochina to the Communists, and that if it were necessary to prevent that loss, the United States would intervene in the war—*provided* the intervention was an allied venture and *provided* the French would give Indochina a real grant of independence so as to eliminate the colonialism issue. The decision may have been taken at the March 25 meeting. It is also my understanding that this NSC paper has on it the approving initials "D.D.E."

On March 29, Dulles, in a New York speech, had called for "united action" even though it might involve "serious risks," and declared that Red China was backing aggression

[1] See pp. 91-92.—ed.

in Indochina with the goal of controlling all of Southeast Asia. He had added that the United States felt that "that possibility should not be passively accepted but should be met by united action." [2]

The newspapers were still full of reactions to this speech when the Congressional leaders, at the April 3 secret meeting with Dulles and Radford, insisted that Dulles should line up allies for "united action" before trying to get a joint resolution of Congress that would commit the nation to war.

The Secretary lost no time. Within a week Dulles talked with diplomatic representatives in Washington of Britain, France, Australia, New Zealand, the Philippines, Thailand, and the three Associated States of Indochina—Vietnam, Laos, and Cambodia.

There was no doubt in the minds of many of these diplomats that Dulles was discussing military action involving carriers and planes. Dulles was seeking a statement or declaration of intent designed to be issued by all the nations at the time of the U.S. military action, to explain to the world what we were doing and why, and to warn the Chinese Communists against entering the war as they had done in Korea.

In these talks Dulles ran into one rock of opposition—Britain. Messages flashing back and forth between Washington and London failed to crack the rock. Finally Dulles offered to come and talk the plan over personally with Prime Minister Churchill and Foreign Secretary Anthony Eden. On April 10, just a week after the Congressional meeting, Dulles flew off to London and later on to Paris.

Whether Dulles told the British about either the NSC decision or about his talks with the Congressional leaders I do not know. But he didn't need to. The British had learned of the Congressional meeting within a couple of days after it happened. When Dulles reached London they were fully aware of the seriousness of his mission.

The London talks had two effects. Dulles had to shelve the idea of immediate intervention. He came up instead with a proposal for creating a Southeast Asia Treaty Organization (SEATO). Dulles felt this was the "united front" he wanted and that it would lead to "united action." He thought that some sort of *ad hoc* organization should be set up at once

[2] See pp. 89–90.

J

without waiting for formal treaty organization, and to this, he seems to have felt, Churchill and Eden agreed.

Just what the British did agree to is not clear, apparently not even to them. Dulles, it appears, had no formal SEATO proposal down on paper, while the British did have some ideas in writing. Eden feels that he made it plain that nothing could be done until after the Geneva Conference, which was due to begin in two weeks. But he apparently made some remark about "going on thinking about it" in the meantime.

At any rate, on his return to Washington Dulles immediately called a SEATO drafting meeting for April 20. The British Ambassador (who at this point had just read the Nixon off-the-record speech in the newspapers) cabled London for instructions and was told not to attend any such meeting. To cover up, the meeting was turned into one on Korea, the other topic for the Geneva Conference. Out of this confusion grew a thinly veiled hostility between Dulles and Eden that exists to this day. Dulles felt that Eden had switched his position and suspects that Eden did so after strong words reached London from Prime Minister Nehru in New Delhi.

A few days later, Dulles flew back to Paris, ostensibly for the NATO meeting with Eden, France's Georges Bidault, and others during the weekend just before the Geneva Conference opened.

On Friday, April 23, Bidault showed Dulles a telegram from General Henri-Eugene Navarre, then the Indochina commander, saying that only a massive air attack could save Dienbienphu, by now under siege for six weeks. Dulles said the United States could not intervene.

But on Saturday Admiral Radford arrived and met with Dulles. Then Dulles and Radford saw Eden. Dulles told Eden that the French were asking for military help at once. An allied air strike at the Vietminh positions around Dienbienphu was discussed. The discussion centered on using the same two U.S. Navy carriers and Philippine-based Air Force planes Radford had talked about to the Congressional leaders.

Radford, it appears, did most of the talking. But Dulles said that if the allies agreed, the President was prepared to go to Congress on the following Monday, April 26 (the day the Geneva Conference was to open) and ask for a joint resolution authorizing such action. Assuming quick passage by Congress, the strike could take place on April 28. Under Secretary of State Walter Bedell Smith, an advocate of intervention, gave the same proposal to French Ambassador Henri Bonnet in Washington the same day.

The State Department had prepared a declaration of intentions, an outgrowth of the earlier proposal in Washington, to be signed on Monday or Tuesday by the Washington ambassadors of the allied nations willing to back the venture in words. As it happened, there were no available British or Australian carriers and the French already were fully occupied. Hence the strike would be by American planes alone, presented to the world as a "united action" by means of the declaration of intentions.

Eden, on hearing all these details from Dulles and Radford, said that this was a most serious proposition, amounting to war, and that he wanted to hear it direct from the French. Eden and Dulles thereupon conferred with Bidault, who confirmed the fact that France was indeed calling desperately for help—though no formal French request was ever put forward in writing.

Eden began to feel like Horatius at the bridge. Here, on the eve of a conference that might lead to a negotiated end of the seven-year-old Indochina war, the United States, at the highly informal request of a weak and panicky French Government, was proposing military action that might very well lead to a general war in Asia if not to a third world war.

Eden said forcefully that he could not agree to any such scheme of intervention, that he personally opposed it. He added his conviction that within forty-eight hours after an air strike, ground troops would be called for, as had been the case at the beginning of the Korean War.

But, added Eden, he alone could not make any such formal decision on behalf of Her Majesty's Government. He would fly to London at once and put the matter before a Cabinet meeting. So far as I can determine, neither Dulles nor Bidault tried to prevent this step.

Shortly after Eden flew off that Saturday afternoon, Dulles sat down in the American Embassy in Paris with his chief advisers, Messrs. MacArthur, Merchant, Bowie, and McCardle, and Ambassador Dillon. They composed a letter to Bidault.

In this letter, Dulles told Bidault the United States could not intervene without action by Congress because to do so was beyond the President's Constitutional powers and because we had made it plain that any action we might take could only be part of a "united action." Further, Dulles added, the American military leaders felt it was too late to save Dienbienphu.

American intervention collapsed on that Saturday, April 24. On Sunday Eden arrived in Geneva with word of the "No" from the specially convened British Cabinet meeting. And on Monday, the day the Geneva Conference began, Eisenhower said in a speech that what was being sought at Geneva was a "modus vivendi" with the Communists.

All these events were unknown to the general public at the time. However, on Sunday the New York *Times* printed a story (written in Paris under a Geneva dateline) that the U.S. had turned down a French request for intervention on the two grounds Dulles had cited to Bidault. And on Tuesday Churchill announced to a cheering House of Commons that the British government was "not prepared to give any undertakings about United Kingdom military action in Indochina in advance of the results of Geneva" and that "we have not entered into any new political or military commitments."

Thus the Geneva Conference [3] opened in a mood of deepest American gloom. Eden felt that he had warded off disaster and that now there was a chance to negotiate peace. The Communists, whatever they may have learned of the behind-the-scenes details here recounted, knew that Britain had turned down some sort of American plan of intervention. And with the military tide in Indochina flowing so rapidly in their favor, they proceeded to stall.

In the end, of course, a kind of peace was made. On June 23, nearly four weeks before the peace, Eden said in the House of Commons that the British Government had "been reproached in some unofficial quarters for their failure to support armed intervention to try to save Dienbienphu. It is quite true that we were at no time willing to support such action. . . ."

This mixture of improvisation and panic is the story of how close the United States came to entering the Indochina

[3] See Part Four.—ed.

war. Would Congress have approved intervention if the President had dared to ask for it? This point is worth a final word.

On returning from Geneva in mid-May, I asked that question of numerous Senators and Representatives. Their replies made clear that Congress would, in the end, have done what Eisenhower asked, provided he had asked for it forcefully and explained the facts and their relation to the national interest of the United States.

Whether action or inaction better served the American interest at that late stage of the Indochina war is for the historian, not for the reporter, to say. But the fact emerges that President Eisenhower never did lay the intervention question on the line. In spite of the NSC decision, April 3, 1954, was the day we *didn't* go to war.

Dienbienphu: A Battle to Remember

BY BERNARD B. FALL*

On May 7, 1954, the end of the battle for the jungle fortress of Dienbienphu marked the end of French military influence in Asia, just as the sieges of Port Arthur, Corregidor, and Singapore had, to a certain extent, broken the spell of Russian, American, and British hegemony in Asia. The Asians, after centuries of subjugation, had beaten the white man at his own game. And today, ten years after Dienbienphu, Vietcong guerrillas in South Vietnam again challenge the West's ability to withstand a potent combination of political and military pressure in a totally alien environment.

On that day in May 1954 it had become apparent by 10 A.M. that Dienbienphu's position was hopeless. French artillery and mortars had been progressively silenced by murderously accurate Communist Vietminh artillery fire; and the monsoon rains had slowed down supply drops to a trickle and transformed the French trenches and dugouts

---

* Professor of International Relations, Howard University, author of *Le Viet Minh: La République Démocratique du Viet-Nam, 1945–1960* (Paris, 1960), *The Two Vietnams: A Political and Military Analysis* (rev. ed. New York/London, 1964), and many other works. The selection is from *The New York Times Magazine* (May 3, 1964). By permission.

nto bottomless quagmires. The surviving officers and men,
many of whom had lived for 54 days on a steady diet of
nstant coffee and cigarettes, were in a catatonic state of
exhaustion.

As their commander, Brig. Gen. Christian de la Croix de
Castries, reported the situation over the radiotelephone to
General René Cogny, his theater commander 220 miles
away in Hanoi in a high-pitched but curiously impersonal
voice, the end obviously had come for the fortress. De
Castries ticked off a long list of 800-man battalions which
had been reduced to companies of eighty men and of companies that were reduced to the size of weak platoons. All he
could hope for was to hold out until nightfall in order to give
the surviving members of his command a chance to break
out into the jungle under the cover of darkness, while he
himself would stay with the more than 5,000 severely
wounded (out of a total of 15,094 men inside the valley)
and face the enemy.

By 3 P.M., however, it had become obvious that the for-
ress would not last until nightfall. Communist forces, in
human-wave attacks, were swarming over the last remaining
defenses. De Castries polled the surviving unit commanders
within reach, and the consensus was that a breakout would
only lead to a senseless piecemeal massacre in the jungle.
The decision was made then to fight on to the end, as long
as the ammunition lasted, and let individual units be overrun after destruction of their heavy weapons. That course
of action was approved by the senior commander in Hanoi
at about 5 P.M., but with the proviso that "Isabelle," the
southernmost strongpoint closest to the jungle, and to friendly forces in Laos, should be given a chance to make a break
for it.

Cogny's last conversation with de Castries dealt with the
dramatic problem of what to do with the wounded piled up
under the incredible conditions in the various strongpoints
and in the fortress's central hospital—originally built to
contain forty-two wounded. There had been suggestions that
an orderly surrender should be arranged in order to save
the wounded the added anguish of falling into enemy hands
as isolated individuals. But Cogny was adamant on that
point:

"Mon vieux, of course you have to finish the whole thing

now. But what you have done until now surely is magnificent. Don't spoil it by hoisting the white flag. You are going to be submerged [by the enemy], but no surrender, no white flag."

"All right, *mon général,* I only wanted to preserve the wounded."

"Yes, I know. Well, do as best you can, leaving it to your [static: subordinate units?] to act for themselves. What you have done is too magnificent to do such a thing. You understand, *mon vieux.*"

There was a silence. Then de Castries said his final words: *"Bien, mon général."*

"Well, good-by, *mon vieux,*" said Cogny. "I'll see you soon."

A few minutes later, de Castries's radio operator methodically smashed his set with the butt of his Colt .45, and thus the last word to come out of the main fortress, as it was being overrun, came at 5:50 P.M. from the radio operator of the 31st Combat Engineer Battalion, using his regulation code name:

"This is 'Yankee Metro.' We're blowing up everything around here. *Au revoir.*"

Strongpoint "Isabelle" never had a chance. While the main defenses of Dienbienphu were being mopped up, strong Vietminh forces already had tightened their grip around the thousand Legionnaires, Algerians, and Frenchmen preparing their breakout. At 9:40 P.M., a French surveillance aircraft reported to Hanoi that it saw the strongpoint's depots blowing up and that heavy artillery fire was visible close by. The breakout had been detected. At 1:50 A.M. on May 8, 1954, came the last message from the doomed garrison, relayed by the watchdog aircraft to Hanoi:

"Sortie failed—Stop—Can no longer communicate with you —Stop and end."

The great battle in the valley of Dienbienphu was over. Close to 10,000 captured troops were to begin the grim death march to the Vietminh prison camps 300 miles to the east. Few would survive. About 2,000 lay dead all over the battlefield in graves left unmarked to this day. Only seventy-three made good their escape from the various shattered strongpoints, to be rescued by the pro-French guerrilla units awaiting them in the Laotian jungle. Eight thousand miles away, in Geneva, the North Vietnamese and Red Chinese delegations attending the nine-power conference which was supposed to settle both the Korean and the Indochinese conflicts toasted the event in pink Chinese champagne.

What had happened at Dienbienphu was simply that a momentous gamble had been attempted by the French High Command and had backfired badly. The Indochina War, which had broken out in December 1946 after Ho Chi Minh's Vietminh forces felt that France would not agree to Vietnam's eventual independence, had slowly bogged down into a hopeless seesaw.

Until Red China's victorious forces arrived on Vietnam's borders in December 1949, there had been at least a small hope that the French-supported Vietnamese nationalist government, headed by ex-emperor Bao Dai, could wean away from the Communist-led Vietminh the allegiance of much of Vietnam's population. But with the existence of a Red Chinese "sanctuary" for the Vietminh forces, that became militarily impossible. By October 1950 twenty-three regular Vietminh battalions, equipped with excellent American artillery coming from Chinese Nationalist stocks left on the mainland, smashed the French defense lines along the Chinese border and inflicted on France its biggest colonial defeat since Montcalm died before Quebec. Within a few weeks, the French position in North Vietnam had shrunk to a fortified perimeter around the Red River delta; a continuous belt of Communist-held territory stretched from the Chinese border to within 100 miles of Saigon. For all practical purposes the Indochina War was lost then and there.

What changed the aspect of the war for a time was the influx of American aid, which began with the onset of the Korean War. With Communism now a menace at both ends of the Far Eastern arc, the Indochina War, from a colonial war, became a "crusade"—but a crusade without a real cause. Independence, given too grudgingly to the Vietnamese nationalist regime, remained the catchword of the adversary.

But, militarily at least, disaster had temporarily been averted. The key Red River delta was more or less held by the French—at least during the daytime, for at night the enemy was everywhere—and the rice-rich Mekong delta in South Vietnam, where anti-Communist Buddhist sects were fighting on the French side, was held more solidly by Western forces in 1953-54 than in 1963-64.

In Laos the situation was just as grim then as it is now: the Laotian and French forces held the Mekong valley and the airfields of the Plain of Jars, and the enemy held the rest. Only Cambodia, then as now, was almost at peace: Prince Sihanouk (then King) had received independence from France in 1953 and galvanized his people into fighting against the guerrillas. They were so successful that, at the ensuing Geneva cease-fire conference, Cambodia did not have to surrender a province as a "regroupment area" for Communist forces.

This totally stalemated situation left the French with but one choice: to create a military situation of the kind that would permit cease-fire negotiations on a basis of equality with the enemy. To achieve this, the French commander-in-chief, General Henri Navarre, had to win a victory over the hard core of Communist regular divisions, whose continued existence posed a constant threat of invasion to the Laotian kingdom and to the vital Red River delta with its capital city of Hanoi and the thriving port of Haiphong. And to destroy those divisions and prevent their invasions into Laos, one had to, in American military parlance, "find 'em and fix 'em."

General Navarre felt that the way to achieve this was by offering the Communists a target sufficiently tempting for their regular divisions to pounce at, but sufficiently strong to resist the onslaught once it came. That was the rationale for the creation of Dienbienphu and for the battle that took place there.

There were other considerations also. Laos had signed a treaty with France in which the latter promised to defend it. Dienbienphu was to be the lock on the backdoor leading into Laos. Dienbienphu was also to be the test for a new theory of Navarre's. Rather than defend immobile lines, he wanted to create throughout Indochina "land-air bases" from which highly mobile units would sally forth and decimate the enemy in his own rear areas, just as the Vietminh guerrillas were doing in French rear areas. All that rode on Dienbienphu: the freedom of Laos, a senior commander's reputation, the survival of some of France's best troops and—above all—a last chance of coming out of that eight-year-long frustrating jungle war with something else than a total defeat. But Navarre, an armor officer formed on the European battlefields, apparently (this was the judgment of the French Government committee that later investigated the disaster) had failed to realize that "there are no blocking positions in country lacking European-type roads." Since the Vietminh relied largely on human porters for their front-line units, they could easily bypass such bottlenecks as Dienbienphu or the Plain of Jars while bottling up the forces contained in those strongholds at little expense to themselves.

The results were evident: soon after French forces arrived at Dienbienphu on Nov. 20, 1953, two of General Vo Nguyen Giap's regular 10,000-man divisions blocked the Dienbienphu garrison, while a third bypassed Dienbienphu and smashed deeply into Laos. On Christmas Day, 1953, Indochina, for the first time in the eight-year war, was literally cut in two. The offensive stabs for which Dienbienphu had been specifically planned became little else but desperate sorties against an invisible enemy. By the time the battle started for good on March 13, 1954, the garrison already had suffered 1,037 casualties without any tangible result.

Inside the fortress, the charming tribal village by the Nam Yum had soon disappeared along with all the bushes and trees in the valley, to be used either as firewood or as construction materials for the bunkers. Even the residence of the French governor was dismantled in order to make use of the bricks, for engineering materials were desperately short from the beginning.

Major André Sudrat, the chief engineer at Dienbienphu, was faced with a problem that he knew to be mathematically unsolvable: by normal military engineering standards, the materials necessary to protect a battalion against the fire of the 105-millimeter howitzers the Vietminh now possessed amounted to 2,550 tons, plus 500 tons of barbed wire. He estimated that to protect the 12 battalions there initially (five others were parachuted in during the battle) he would need 36,000 tons of engineering materials—which would mean using all available transport aircraft for a period of *five months.*

When he was told that he was allocated a total of about 3,300 tons of airlifted materials, Sudrat simply shrugged his shoulders. "In that case, I'll fortify the command post, the signal center, and the X-ray room in the hospital; and let's hope that the Viet has no artillery."

As it turned out, the Vietminh had more than 200 artillery pieces, reinforced during the last week of the siege by Russian "Katyusha" multitube rocket launchers. Soon, the combination of monsoon rains, which set in around mid-April, and Vietminh artillery fire smashed to rubble the neatly arranged dugouts and trenches shown to eminent visitors and journalists during the early days of the siege. Essentially, the battle of Dienbienphu degenerated into a brutal artillery duel, which the enemy would have won sooner or later. The French gun crews and artillery pieces, working entirely *in the open* so as to allow the pieces all-around fields of fire, were destroyed one by one; replaced, they were destroyed once more, and at last fell silent.

The artillery duel became the great tragedy of the battle. Colonel Piroth, the jovial one-armed commander of the French artillery inside the fortress, had "guaranteed" that his twenty-four 105-mm. howitzers could match anything the Communists had and that his battery of four 155-mm. heavy field howitzers would definitely muzzle whatever would not be destroyed by the lighter pieces and the fighter-bombers. As it turned out, the Vietminh artillery was so superbly camouflaged that to this day it is doubtful whether French counterbattery fire silenced more than a handful of the enemy's fieldpieces.

When, on March 13, 1954, at 5:10 P.M., Communist artillery completely smothered strongpoint "Beatrice" without noticeable damage from French counterbattery fire, Piroth knew with deadly certitude that the fortress was doomed. And as deputy to General de Castries, he felt that he had contributed to the air of overconfidence and even cockiness —had not de Castries, in the manner of his ducal forebears, sent a written challenge to enemy commander Giap?—which had prevailed in the valley prior to the attack.

"I am responsible. I am responsible," he was heard to murmur as he went about his duties. During the night of March 14-15, he committed suicide by blowing himself up with a hand grenade, since he could not arm his pistol with one hand.

Originally, the fortress had been designed to protect its main airstrip against marauding Vietminh units, not to withstand the onslaught of four Communist divisions. There never was, as press maps of the time erroneously showed, a continuous battle line covering the whole valley. Four of the eight strongpoints were from one to three miles away from the center of the position. The interlocking fire of their artillery and mortars, supplemented by a squadron of ten tanks (flown in piecemeal and reassembled on the spot), was to prevent them from being picked off one by one.

This also proved to be an illusion. Gen. Vo Nguyen Giap decided to take Dienbienphu by an extremely efficient mixture of 18th-century siege techniques (sinking TNT-laden mineshafts under French bunkers, for example) and modern artillery patterns plus human-wave attacks. The outlying posts which protected the key airfield were captured within the first few days of the battle. French losses proved so great that the reinforcements parachuted in after the airfield was destroyed for good on March 27 never sufficed to mount the counterattacks necessary to reconquer them.

From then onward the struggle for Dienbienphu became a battle of attrition. The only hope of the garrison lay in the breakthrough of a relief column from Laos or Hanoi (a hopeless concept in view of the terrain and distances involved) or in the destruction of the siege force through aerial bombardment of the most massive kind. For a time a U. S. Air Force strike was under consideration, but the idea was dropped for about the same reasons that make a similar attack against North Vietnam today a rather risky affair.[1]

Like Stalingrad, Dienbienphu slowly starved on its airlift tonnage. When the siege began, it had about eight days' worth of supplies on hand and required 200 tons a day to maintain minimum levels. The sheer magnitude of preparing that mass of supplies for parachuting was solved only by superhuman feats of the airborne supply units on the outside —efforts more than matched by the heroism of the soldiers inside the valley, who had to crawl into the open, under fire, to collect the containers.

But as the position shrunk every day (it finally was the size of a ball park), the bulk of the supplies fell into Communist hands. Even de Castries's general's stars, dropped to him by General Cogny with a bottle of champagne, landed in enemy territory.

The airdrops were a harrowing experience in that narrow

[1] *Less than a year after this article appeared the U.S. government took the risk.—ed.*

...lley which permitted only straight approaches. Communist ...tiaircraft artillery played havoc among the lumbering ...ansport planes as they slowly disgorged their loads. A few ...gures tell how murderous the air war around Dienbienphu ...as: of a total of 420 aircraft available in all of Indochina ...en, sixty-two were lost in connection with Dienbienphu ...d 167 sustained hits. Some of the American civilian pilots ...ho flew the run said that Vietminh flak was as dense as ...ything encountered during World War II over the Ruhr.

When the battle ended, the 82,926 parachutes expended in ...pplying the fortress covered the battlefield like freshly ...llen snow. Or like a burial shroud.

The net effect of Dienbienphu on France's military posture ... Indochina could not be measured in losses alone. It was to ...ttle avail to say that France had lost only 5 percent of its ...attle force; that the equipment losses had already been more ...an made good by American supplies funneled in while the ...attle was raging; and that even the manpower losses had ...een made up by reinforcements from France and new drafts ...f Vietnamese. Even the fact, which the unfortunate French ...ommander-in-chief, Navarre, was to invoke later, that the ...ttack on Dienbienphu cost the enemy close to 25,000 casual-...es and delayed his attack on the vital Red River delta by ...our months, held little water in the face of the wave of de-...eatism that swept not only French public opinion at home ...ut also that of her allies.

Historically, Dienbienphu was, as one French senior of-...cer masterfully understated it, never more than an "un-...ortunate accident." It proved little else but that an encircled ...orce, no matter how valiant, will succumb if its support ...ystem fails. But as other revolutionary wars—from Algeria ... the British defeats in Cyprus and Palestine—have con-...lusively shown, it does not take pitched "set-piece" battles ... lose such wars. They can be lost just as conclusively ...hrough a series of very small engagements, such as those ...ow fought in South Vietnam, if the local government and ...s population loses confidence in the eventual outcome of ...e contest—and that was the case of both the French and ...f their Vietnamese allies after Dienbienphu.

But as the French themselves demonstrated in Algeria, ...here they never again allowed themselves to be maneuvered ...nto such desperate military straits, revolutionary wars are

fought for *political* objectives, and big showdown battles ar
necessary neither for victory nor for defeat in that case
This now seems finally to have been understood in the Sout
Vietnam war as well, and Secretary of Defense McNamar
may well have thought of Dienbienphu when he stated in hi
major Vietnam policy speech of March 26 that "we hav
learned that in Vietnam, <u>political and economic progress ar</u>
the *sine qua non* of military success. . . ." One may only hop
that the lesson has been learned in time.

But on May 7, 1954, the struggle for Indochina was al
most over for France. As a French colonel looked out ove
the battlefield from a slit trench near his command post,
small white flag, probably a handkerchief, appeared on to
of a rifle hardly fifty feet away from him, followed by th
flat-helmeted head of a Vietminh soldier.

"You're not going to shoot anymore?" said the Vietmin
in French.

"No, I'm not going to shoot anymore," said the colonel.

"C'est fini?" said the Vietminh.

"Oui, c'est fini," said the colonel.

And all around them, as on some gruesome Judgmen
Day, soldiers, French and enemy alike, began to crawl out o
their trenches and stand erect for the first time in 54 days, a
firing ceased everywhere.

The sudden silence was deafening.

Part Four

THE CONFERENCE AT GENEVA

The French defeat at Dienbienphu in the spring of 1954 brought the First Indochinese War to an end. The prominence of the Vietminh [1] in this struggle and the preceding one against the Japanese laid the foundation for Communist leadership of modern Vietnamese nationalism. U. S. columnist Joseph Alsop lamented this fact in 1955. "Both the masses of peasants and great numbers of Vietnamese nationalists, political reformers, hopeful idealists, and the like firmly believe the Vietminh Communist leaders. . . ." [2] But the Conference at Geneva, called to settle major Asian problems left in the wake of the Korean and Indochinese wars, was unlike the jungles of Vietnam. Around the international conference table the military victories of the Vietminh were only one of the factors to be considered: international power politics, as Donald Lancaster shows, dictated the shape of the Agreements issuing from the Conference.

Lancaster's account of the Geneva Conference [3] should contain many surprises for American readers. For one thing, the role of the United States delegation did not quite conform to the picture of a peace-loving nation, seeking to enhance the international rule of law. In the end, the United States even refused to endorse the work of the Conference. [4] The reasons for American hostility were set forth rather explicitly in statements made by American political leaders before the Conference. [5] An American alternative to the settlement of Geneva emerged two months later in the form of the anti-Communist SEATO [6] alliance. The years after

---

[1] For clarification of this term, see p. 210n.

[2] Time, LXV (January 3, 1955), p. [19].

[3] See pp. 118–137.

[4] See pp. 156–157.

[5] See pp. 89–92.

[6] See pp. 92–95.

1954 would test this alternative and find it wanting. In early 1965 C. L. Sulzberger pronounced "the alliance structure devised by Secretary [of State John Foster] Dulles . . . valueless." [7]

Far more surprising should be Lancaster's shrewd account of the roles played by the Communist delegations at Geneva. Far from advocating relentless revolutionary struggle, both the Chinese and the Soviets actually put pressure on the Vietminh to accept far less territory than they had liberated by force of arms, and to drop claims on Cambodia and Laos. East-West cooperation, marred only by the behavior of the United States [8] and Bao Dai delegations, made the Geneva Conference a triumph of international "peaceful coexistence."

The four sets of Agreements that issued from the Conference deserve the most careful study,[10] for each of the parties to the current struggle has claimed that the Agreements justify its stand. President Lyndon B. Johnson has praised them as "a reliable agreement to guarantee the independence and security of all . . . Southeast Asia." [11] Secretary of State Dean Rusk has observed that "all that is needed [to bring peace to Vietnam] is compliance with

[7] Sulzberger, "The Loss of Options in Vietnam," The New York Times (January 11, 1965). See also O. Edmund Chubb, "Vietnam and the End of the SEATO Decade," The Correspondent no. 30 (Winter 1965), pp. 14-18.

[8] John Foster Dulles was reported to have ostentatiously turned his back on the outstretched hand of Chou En-lai at one point during the Conference (Edgar Snow, The Other Side of the River: Red China Today [New York, 1962], p. 695)

[9] This was the delegation from the French-sponsored "State of Vietnam." During the conference Emperor Bao Dai was persuaded (it is not yet clear how) to appoint Ngo Dinh Diem as Premier. This regime's protest against the Geneva Agreements appears on pp. 157, 159.

[10] Two of these, the cease-fire agreements relating to Laos and Cambodia, are not printed here. They are most easily accessible to American readers in Background Information Relating to Southeast Asia and Vietnam (revised, June 16, 1965), Report of the Committee on Foreign Relations, U.S. Senate [89th Congress, 1st Session] (Washington, D.C., 1965), Documents 10 and 11. This collection, edited to present only the American side is available free from the Senate Foreign Relations Committee, Washington, D.C.

[11] White House Statement (March 25, 1965), in Department of State Bulletin, LII (April 12, 1965), p. 527.

he agreements" of 1954.[12] And Secretary of Defense
Robert McNamara announced that the Geneva Agreements
of 1954 happily provided for the emergence of an "independent entity"—the state of South Vietnam.[13]

On the other hand Ho Chi Minh hailed the Agreements
as a "great victory for our diplomacy." [14] Radio Hanoi
commended them as "fully conform[ing] to the aspirations of the peoples of Vietnam, Laos, Cambodia, as well
as the other people in the world." [15] The National Liberation Front of South Vietnam has professed to be "aware
of the value of these Agreements." [16] Surely a document
so widely endorsed deserves close attention.

The Geneva Agreements consist of a detailed cease-fire
signed by the parties to the dispute—France and the Vietminh.[17] The State of Vietnam was considered negligible
in this arrangement, and protested accordingly.[18] A Final
Declaration of all Conference participants (except the United
States and the State of Vietnam) "took note" of the cease-
fire and amplified some of the political features of the settlement. The temporary nature of the demarcation line between the northern and southern zones, the eventual reunification of Vietnam, and the projected nation-wide elections were all stressed. In many respects it was an ad-
mirable conference. But in not containing adequate guarantees of its provisions, and in incurring the hostility of
the United States, the hopeful Agreements of 1954 did not
fulfill their promise of bringing peace to Vietnam.

[12] *Commencement Address, Williams College (June 14, 1965),*
in Department of State Bulletin, *LI (July 6, 1964), p. 5.*

[13] *News Conference (December 21, 1963), in Richard P. Steb-
bins (ed.),* Documents on American Foreign Relations, 1963
New York, 1964), p. 298.

[14] *"Appeal Made after the Successful Conclusion of the Geneva
Agreements" (July 22, 1954), in Ho Chi Minh,* Selected Works
4 vols., Hanoi, 1960–1962), IV, p. 17.

[15] *Radio Hanoi (April 23, 1955).*

[16] *NLFSV Central Committee's Statement (March 22, 1965), see
p. 411.*

[17] *See pp. 137–150.*

[18] *See pp. 157, 159.*

Power Politics At the
Geneva Conference 1954

BY DONALD LANCASTER*

PRELIMINARIES

John Foster Dulles, who was to lead the American delegation, left Washington on 20 April with the intention of first
attending a meeting of the North Atlantic Council which was
to take place in Paris on the 23rd.

On 23 April Dulles received an urgent appeal for help
from Bidault, the French Foreign Minister, who said that, unless a powerful air-strike by American carrier-based planes
was carried out within twelve hours, all hope of saving the
Dienbienphu garrison must be abandoned. That evening
Dulles cornered Eden and told him this grave news, adding
that, if Eden felt able to stand with him, he would advise the
President to ask Congress to approve a declaration of the
United States' intention to support France in Indochina: a
declaration which would apparently enable Eisenhower to
authorize an air-strike in support of the Dienbienphu garrison. But Eden questioned the effectiveness of an air-strike at
this late stage in the siege and discounted American fears
of an imminent and general collapse of French resistance.

On the following afternoon the two ministers met again to
discuss the situation. Dulles began by saying that the French
had warned him of their intention to abandon the struggle
unless assistance was forthcoming for the Dienbienphu garrison; and although he now admitted that the approval of Congress could not be obtained in time to save the situation, he
thought it essential to show that France had powerful allies,
who were prepared to stand by her in the emergency. Eden,
however, maintained his objections to Dulles's proposal,
pointing out that precipitate action might lead to a world
war. Finally, it was agreed that Bidault should be asked to

* Former official in the British legation, Saigon. The selection is
from *The Emancipation of French Indochina* (London/New
York/Toronto: Oxford University Press, 1961), pp. 313-326
332-337. By permission of the Royal Institute of International Af
fairs.

lear up the existing discrepancy between the American and
ne British assessment of the military situation. Accordingly
meeting took place later that afternoon at the Quai d'Orsay.
lere Eden's misgivings in regard to American intentions
vere increased still further, for not only did Dulles ap-
arently assume that the British Government was in some
vay committed to armed intervention, but he produced the
raft of a letter, which he proposed to send to Bidault of-
cially, announcing the readiness of his Government to move
American forces into Indochina if France and the other Al-
es so desired; and, although this offer appears to have taken
3idault aback, he agreed, after hesitating for some minutes,
o give the proposal official consideration. Faced with Dulles's
vident determination to enlist British support for armed in-
ervention, Eden decided to return to London immediately
nd consult with his colleagues.

Next day an emergency Cabinet meeting was held at which
t was agreed that no understanding should be given in re-
ard to military intervention before the Geneva Conference.
The Government decided, however, to join in guaranteeing
ny settlement reached, or in considering other forms of
oint action should the Conference fail to produce a settle-
nent. This decision was maintained despite a final *démarche*
›y the French Ambassador, René Massigli, who called on
3den in the afternoon and told him that if the United King-
lom would join with France's allies in immediately declaring
heir common determination to check the expansion of Com-
nunism in Southeast Asia, and to use "eventual military
neans" for that purpose, President Eisenhower, for his part,
vould seek Congressional approval for intervention: a step
vhich would be followed by an air-strike in support of the
Dienbienphu garrison on 28 April.[1]

Meanwhile the French Government, who may have wished
o allay suspicions that France might be tempted to purchase
he safety of the Expeditionary Corps in exchange for an
.greement with the Russians to abandon EDC,[2] had au-
horized Bidault to initial on its behalf the Convention on

Sir Anthony Eden. Full Circle: Memoirs . . . (London, 1960),
›. 106. [See the account of plans for U.S. support of the be-
eagued French by Chalmers Roberts, pp. 96–105.—ed.]

European Defense Community, a Western European military
lliance strongly opposed by the USSR.—ed.

Co-operation which had been drawn up by Great Britain and the six Governments participating in EDC and initialed by them on 12 April, and it was chiefly because a parliamentary decision in regard to EDC would increase the difficulties of the French delegation at the Geneva Conference and reduce the chances of peace in Indochina that the Government avoided a debate on all aspects of the EDC Treaty and allied matters at this stage.

On 24 April Dulles left Paris for Geneva, where he expressed the hope on his arrival that "the aggressors would come to the Conference in a mood to purge themselves of their 'aggression' ",[3] but the appearance of the burly, vigorous Chinese aggressor, in the person of Chou En-lai, who was greeted on the Geneva airfield next day by the even burlier General Nam Il, the head of the North Korean delegation, whose somewhat Napoleonic stance and broad and cheerful smile were noted by attendant journalists, seemed to belie the American Secretary of State's expectations.[4]

The Geneva Conference was virtually to become two conferences: one on the Korean question, and the other on Indochina. Moreover, although priority had officially been accorded to the Korean question, the interest of the Conference was to be centred on the possibility of restoring peace in Indochina since it was generally recognized that, whereas no progress could be expected toward the establishment of a united and independent Korea, an armistice based on the partition of Vietnam might be possible. Indeed, the French Foreign Minister's first concern on his arrival at Geneva was to request Russian assistance in arranging a truce to allow French wounded to be evacuated from Dienbienphu, but Molotov replied that he was unable to assist him and recommended that the French should discuss this matter directly with the Vietminh representatives, whose arrival at Geneva was reported to be imminent.

Similar tactics were adopted by the Soviet Foreign Minister when Bidault called a meeting of the representatives of the four powers to discuss the procedural difficulties which were threatening to delay the start of the Conference: Molotov who was evidently reluctant to attend a meeting to which his

[3] New York Times (25 April 1954).
[4] [London] Times (26 April 1954).

Chinese Communist colleague, Chou En-lai, had not been invited, declined the invitation on the pretext that he had "another engagement". These difficulties included the selection of a chairman to preside over the Indochinese phase of the Conference and the need for a decision in regard to the number of countries which should be invited to send representatives, and in particular to the capacity in which the Vietminh delegates should be asked to attend. The first of these difficulties was, however, solved by Dulles's reluctance to become personally involved in the work of the Conference, and his readiness to stand aside enabled Molotov to allow Chou En-lai's claims to be passed over in favour of an arrangement by which the chairmanship alternated between Eden and himself.

Indeed it was soon apparent that Dulles's position at the Conference was one of considerable delicacy since, whereas the French and British delegates were most anxious to reach a settlement, Dulles was precluded both by his personal convictions and by the attitude of Congress from taking part in negotiations which were likely to result in an armistice involving concessions to Asian Communists. Also it was now known that his proposals for an Asian Security Pact and for "united action" had again been rejected by the British Government on 25 April.

The decisive effect of this rejection was recognized by President Eisenhower, who announced at a press conference toward the end of the week that the American Government would take no action in Indochina pending the outcome of the Conference. This declaration is reported to have surprised and shocked Dulles, who seemed only partially mollified by a "warm personal message" from the President assuring him that the announcement of this decision was not designed to weaken the American position at the Conference; and he decided to return to Washington and leave the Under-Secretary of State, W. B. Bedell Smith, to lead the United States delegation.

His departure from a Conference of which he disapproved must have occasioned considerable relief to the representatives of the other participating powers, who were anxious to reach a settlement, and after a decision that the negotiations should be restricted to representatives of the four powers,

Communist China, the three Associated States,[5] and the Democratic Republic of Vietnam, measures were taken to hasten the arrival of the Indochinese delegations and to overcome Bao Dai's reluctance to agree to Nationalist representation.

On 28 April Marc Jacquet, the French Secretary of State for Indochinese Affairs, visited Bao Dai at Cannes to inform him of the wishes of the French Government, and on the 30th a joint message was addressed to him by Bidault, Dulles, and Eden expressing their desire to consult with a representative of the head of the state of Vietnam on the work of the Geneva Conference. At the same time, tendentious articles started to appear in the French press insinuating that the delay in evacuating the wounded from Dienbienphu was due to Bao Dai's refusal to allow Vietnamese representation at the Geneva Conference. Finally Bao Dai, whose conduct throughout the negotiations would seem to have been based on the belief that American opposition would prevent the conclusion of an armistice, agreed that the Minister for Foreign Affairs, Nguyen Quoc Dinh, who was engaged in negotiating with the French Government in Paris, should go to Geneva in order to discuss the question of Vietnamese representation with the three Foreign Ministers; during this discussion Dinh agreed to Nationalist and also to Vietminh participation in the Conference. He emphasized, however, that the presence of this last delegation would not constitute recognition of a Vietminh state or government, and that the Vietnamese Government reserved its right to refuse to subscribe to any decision prejudicial to national independence, liberty, or unity. On 3 May, therefore, a formal invitation was sent both to the Nationalist [Bao Dai] Government and to the Government of the Democratic Republic of Vietnam.

NEGOTIATING POSITIONS

The Government of the Democratic Republic seemed to have been anticipating such an invitation, and on the following day its delegation arrived from Berlin under the leadership of Pham Van Dong, who had been the principal Viet-

[5] *The Kingdoms of Laos and Cambodia, and the State of Vietnam. The latter was headed by Emperor Bao Dai, who at the time of the Geneva Conference, was vacationing on the French Riviera.—ed.*

minh representative at the Fontainebleau Conference.[6] Dong, who was now deputy Prime Minister and Minister for Foreign Affairs *ad interim*, soon revealed that neither the passage of years nor the hardships of life in the Vietminh zone had changed his somewhat truculent approach to a conference table, and bluntly declared on his arrival that a particularly important task facing the Conference would be the restoration of peace in Indochina on the basis of the recognition of the national rights of the peoples of Vietnam, the Khmer, and the Pathet Lao.[7]

Meanwhile the Laniel Government was under constant attack in the National Assembly, where a vigilant opposition under the leadership of Mendès-France were resolved that Bidault's pride and scruples should not be permitted to impede a settlement; after a debate on 9 May, it was generally recognized that the Government's survival now depended on the rapid progress of the impending negotiations.

On 8 May the Indochina phase of the Geneva Conference had opened under singularly unpropitious circumstances, the garrison at Dienbienphu having succumbed on the previous day.[8] At this session Bidault made a speech in which, after paying tribute to the heroism displayed by French Union troops at Dienbienphu, he put forward a number of proposals for an armistice. These were that the Vietminh regular and irregular forces which had invaded Cambodia and Laos should be evacuated, and that in Vietnam regular units of the opposing forces should regroup in predetermined areas, while irregular elements should be disarmed and prisoners of war and interned civilians liberated. Bidault also recommended that these troop movements should be supervised by international commissions and that the agreements should be guaranteed by the Governments participating in the Conference.

Pham Van Dong, whose brusque manner and embittered attitude did not appear to conceal diplomatic ability of a

[6] July 1946, *concerning French reluctance to grant significant autonomy to Vietnam under the Agreements of 6 March 1946. See* Lancaster, Emancipation of French Indochina, *pp. 157-163. —ed.*

[7] Figaro (5 May 1954).

[8] *See the account of the battle of Dienbienphu by Bernard Fall, pp. 105–114.—ed.*

high order, confined himself in his opening speech to repeating his demand that representatives of the Khmer and Pathet Lao resistance governments should be invited to take part in the work of the Conference. In spite of his insistence that the governments whose claims to recognition were thus advanced had "liberated vast areas of their national territory" and "exerted all their efforts in creating a democratic Power and in raising the living standard of the population in liberated areas",[9] the fallacious nature of these claims was promptly pilloried by Sam Sary, the head of the Cambodian delegation, who denied all knowledge either of a "Free Government of Free Khmer" or of the location of the vast if unspecified territories where its writ was alleged to run. Phoui Sananikone, the head of the Laotian delegation, after pointing out that the Lao Issara movement had dissolved itself voluntarily in October 1949, observed with equal vigour that "this so-called Pathet Lao", under the leadership of an expatriate prince, represented "absolutely nothing" and, indeed, that "it would be almost comic to recognize him as representing anybody."[10]

Dong, who was unabashed by the ridicule with which his pretensions had been treated, revealed two days later the Vietminh conditions for a cease-fire. These were the recognition by France of the sovereignty and independence of Vietnam over the whole national territory as well as the sovereignty and independence of Khmer and Pathet Lao, and an agreement for the withdrawal of all foreign troops from the territories of the three states, where free general elections would then be held under the supervision of local committees. The elections would be preceded by the convening of Advisory Conferences to discuss the necessary arrangements between representatives of the Governments of the two parties in Vietnam and of Khmer and Pathet Lao. These proposals were accompanied by a declaration of Vietminh readi-

[9] Documents Relating to the Discussion of Korea and Indochina at the Geneva Conference (Miscellaneous No. 16 [1954], Command Paper, 9186). London: Great Britain Parliamentary Sessional Papers, XXXI (1953/54), pp. 112-113.

[10] Ibid., pp. 114-116. [Later the Pathet Lao under Prince Souvanavong was admitted into a coalition government in Laos. See Roger M. Smith, "Laos," in George McTurnan Kahin (ed.), Government and Politics of Southeast Asia (2d ed. Ithaca, N.Y., 1964), pp. 538-563.—ed.]

ness to examine the question of the Democratic Republic of Vietnam's future association with the French Union and to recognize France's economic and cultural interests in Indochina.[11]

Dong's confused proposals caused surprise and dismay, but Anthony Eden, the British Foreign Secretary, who had already discussed with Molotov the implication of the Vietminh demand for Khmer and Pathet Lao representation, was sufficiently encouraged by the Soviet Foreign Minister's conciliatory attitude [12] to persist in his attempts to prevent the work of the Conference from being blocked by the Vietminh attitude. He therefore intervened in the debate on 10 May and, after refuting certain allegations which Dong had made in regard to American and French predatory designs, he recommended Bidault's plan to the attention of the delegates and proposed that the armistice should be based on the separation and subsequent concentration of the opposing forces within distinct and clearly defined zones under some supervisory organization. Two days later Eden again intervened during the third plenary session to discourage flights of dialectic materialistic fancy on the part of Chou En-lai and to urge the delegates to consider the French proposals.

Also during this session Nguyen Quoc Dinh, the Vietnamese Foreign Minister, whose delegation had symbolically established its residence outside Geneva at Saint-Julien-en-Genevois, submitted the proposals of his Government for an armistice. Dinh recognized that the restoration of peace would entail a political and a military settlement, but although he declared that the Vietnamese delegation would be prepared to examine any plan submitted in good faith, he stipulated that the military settlement must exclude any proposal that would lead either directly or indirectly to a permanent or temporary, *de facto* or *de jure*, partition of the national territory, and he insisted that provision must be made for international supervision of the execution of the cease-fire terms. Dinh also specified that the political settlement must accord recognition to the principle that the only state entitled to represent Vietnam legally was the state of which Bao Dai was the head; although he expressed willingness to

[11] Documents Relating to the Discussion of . . . Indochina . . . (Cmd., 9186), pp. 116-118.
[12] Roger Massip in Figaro (11 May 1954).

allow free elections to be held throughout the national territory as soon as the Security Council were satisfied that the Government's authority had been established and conditions of freedom were fulfilled, he insisted that these elections must be internationally supervised by representatives of the United Nations.[13]

MANEUVER AND COMPROMISE

At this stage in the Conference the negotiations appeared to have reached an impasse, but on 14 May Molotov, after a tirade against American aggressive designs in Southeast Asia, made an unexpected concession proposing that any agreement on the cessation of hostilities should include provisions for the setting up of a supervisory commission composed of representatives of neutral countries. If the credit for this concession was ascribed by the press to Eden,[14] Molotov's tirade appears to have been occasioned by Dulles's activities, for the divergences and uncertainties of the Western democracies perplexed and disquieted the Soviet representatives, who were inclined to suspect that some concerted plan of action must underlie such apparent incoherence.

However, on this occasion Soviet perplexity was fully shared by the French and British representatives. Whereas French morale had been adversely affected, on 12 May, by reports of a press conference in Washington at which Dulles was reported to have declared that the retention of Indochina was not essential to the defence of Southeast Asia, the British delegation, for their part, were astonished to read in the Swiss morning papers some days later that Franco-American discussions had taken place on the possibility of military intervention by the United States in Indochina. Moreover, inquiries about the truth of this report were met evasively, until Bidault's principal adviser, R. de Margerie, furtively produced a document setting out the conditions under which the United States would be prepared to intervene in Indochina either after the breakdown of the Conference, or earlier if the French so desired. Later that day the arrival of the *New York Herald Tribune*, giving full details of these negotiations, enabled Eden to raise the matter officially with the head of the American delegation, who deplored Washington's failure

[13] Documents Relating to the Discussion of . . . Indochina . . . (Cmd., 9186), pp. 123-124.
[14] Christian Science Monitor [Boston] (14 May 1954).

to keep the matter secret and sought to mollify Eden by assuring him that the discussions had been confined to the
provision of assistance with military training. Although
Bidault was to give an undertaking two days later that no
request for American intervention would be made while the
Conference was still in session, Eden discounted the American thesis that the threat of intervention would incline the
Chinese to compromise, and objected that the publicity given
to these "noises off" could prejudice the chances of a settlement.[15]

On 17 May the delegates met for the first time in restricted
session and decided that priority should be accorded to the
military aspects of the settlement, while the recommendation
was made that private discussions should take place between
the French and Vietminh delegations to solve the difficulties
that had arisen over the evacuation of the French wounded
from Dienbienphu.[16] These discussions in restricted session
again revealed an unexpectedly co-operative approach to the
problems confronting the Conference on the part of the
Soviet Foreign Minister. Nevertheless further proof of Washington's distrust of the proceedings was provided on 19 May,
when the French and British were shown a statement prepared by the United States' delegation proposing that restricted sessions should be brought to an end and plenary
sessions resumed; and only Eden's plea for patience and
Bidault's assurance that its adoption would lead to the fall
of the French Government stopped the United States delegation from putting this proposal to the Conference.[17] During
the ensuing discussions further progress was stopped by the
stubborn insistence of the Communist delegates that Pathet

---

[15] Eden, *Full Circle*, pp. 119-120.

[16] *The French refusal to establish non-official contacts with the
Vietminh delegation had been based on the consideration that
such contacts would represent the first step towards the* de facto
*recognition of the Democratic Republic. The evacuation of the
French wounded, which had been the subject of a local agreement between the two Commands, had been stopped following
Vietminh insistence that during the operation the road, Route
Provinciale 41, from Dienbienphu, which the Vietminh were
themselves using in order to move their forces back to the southeast fringe of the Red River delta, should not be subject to observation or attack by French aircraft.*

[17] Eden, *Full Circle*, p. 120.

Lao and Khmer should be recognized as *de facto* governments. Finally, a Soviet proposal was adopted toward the end of the week that discussions should be confined to a five-point plan. . . .[18]

Meanwhile the French Government continued to be harassed by interpellations in the National Assembly, and on 13 May its Indochinese policy was endorsed by the narrow majority of two votes. French uneasiness in regard to the outcome of the negotiations was increased, moreover, by press reports indicating that in spite of Molotov's conciliatory attitude, relations between the Soviet and French delegations were strained, as the Russians were perturbed by reports of Franco-American discussions on the Indochinese situation and resented Bidault's persistent refusal to contact the Vietminh delegation.[19]

On 29 May the deadlock was again broken by Eden, who had conferred privately with Molotov on the previous evening. After this meeting the Communist delegates waived their insistence on Khmer and Pathet Lao representation and agreed, during a restricted session, that contacts should be established between the two Commands in Indochina and that military discussion should take place in Geneva between French and Vietminh representatives to decide the location of the zones in which French Union and Vietminh troops should regroup after a cease-fire.

When these representatives met on 1 June, the Vietminh showed a marked reluctance to confine the discussions to the agenda and caused irritation by their tendency to lecture the French on their conduct in Indochina. However, private conversations between the French and Vietminh officers engaged in the discussions seemed to indicate some readiness on the part of the Vietminh to negotiate a cease-fire, a readiness which was ascribed to the losses that their regular forces had suffered at Dienbienphu, to the exhaustion of the population in the Vietminh zone, and also

[18] *Molotov's five-point plan covered the following aspects of a settlement: (1) the cease-fire, (2) the allocation of zones in which the hostile forces should be grouped, (3) measures to prevent the arrival of reinforcements after the cease-fire, (4) the creation of a supervisory body to control the execution of these arrangements, and (5), the form of guarantee required to ensure the implementation of a settlement* (Manchester Guardian [*22 May 1954*].)

[19] Le Monde (*18 May 1954*).

to the threat of direct and massive American intervention.

On the eve of another crucial debate in the French National Assembly one of the French military representatives who was in touch with a Vietminh officer was instructed to find out whether the Vietminh were in fact prepared to negotiate an armistice on the basis of partition. This approach was well received, and on the evening of 10 June an unofficial meeting took place, in the course of which Ta Quang Buu, the Vietminh Vice-Minister for National Defence, declared that his Government would be prepared to accept an armistice, on the basis of a regroupment of the opposing forces in North and South Vietnam respectively, and the partition of the country in the vicinity of Hué.[20]

Meanwhile the work of the Conference had again been impeded by failure to reach agreement on the composition of the International Commission which would be charged with supervising the execution of the terms of an armistice agreement and also by Communist insistence that decisions by this commission should be unanimous. At the beginning of June Molotov paid a brief visit to Moscow, and on his return the rumour became current that he intended to propose that a four-power conference should be held after the Geneva Conference, to discuss the organization of European security, acceptance of this proposal being the condition on which he would be prepared to restrain the Vietminh from launching an offensive on the Red River delta. This rumour, which was ascribed to the Russian desire to embarrass the French Government and to encourage the opposition in the French National Assembly in the impending debate on Indochina, led Bidault again to deny categorically that his Government would be prepared to trade French adherence to EDC against Russian assistance in securing acceptable terms for a cease-fire agreement in Indochina.[21]

On his return from Moscow Molotov had also proposed that a plenary session should be held, and in view of the procedure adopted in these sessions it was presumed that the Soviet Foreign Minister intended to make an announcement to which he wished maximum publicity to be given. At

[20] *Frédéric-Dupont, Mission de la France en Asie (Paris, 1956), pp. 154-156. [A glance at the map shows that the Vietminh eventually settled for a far less favorable partition line.—ed.]

[21] [London] Times (7 June 1954).

this plenary session, which was held on 8 June, the main interest therefore centred on Molotov's speech. The Soviet Foreign Minister soon revealed the motive that had prompted his proposal by making a virulent personal attack upon the French Foreign Minister, which was presumably designed to assist Mendès-France to overthrow the Laniel Government by persuading hesitant deputies that under the leadership of Bidault the French delegation would be incapable of reaching a settlement.[22]

Molotov's desire for a change of Government in France was fulfilled: after Mendès-France's attack on Bidault's conduct of Indochinese affairs and dilatory approach to the negotiations at Geneva the outcome of the debate in the National Assembly was unfavourable to the Government, which failed to carry a motion of confidence on 12 June. In accordance with French constitutional practice, Mendès-France was then charged by the President of the Republic with the task of forming a new Government, and on 17 June this Government was formally invested by a large majority.

During the speech in which he outlined his programme Mendès-France declared that his Government adhered to the Western Alliance, and undertook to submit definite proposals in regard to EDC to the National Assembly before the parliamentary recess. He also announced his intention of resigning if he should fail to conclude an honourable peace in Indochina by 20 July. This undertaking, which appeared to be a demagogic gesture designed to attract popular support, caused general surprise. Moreover in view of persistent Soviet inferences that such an armistice could only be arranged in exchange for a French undertaking to abandon EDC, the calculation that might underlie this wager was of a nature to arouse misgivings among the supporters of an integrated Europe, since the delicate balance between the supporters and opponents of EDC made it probable that an adroit Prime Minister, if he were not encumbered by excessive scruples, would be able to sabotage the ratification of the Paris Treaty. Mendès-France's confidence in his ability to secure an armistice must have been fortified, however, by Molotov's timely attack on his pred-

[22] *Ibid.* (*14 June 1954*); *Frédéric-Dupont, Mission de la France,* p. 153.

ecessor and also by the revelation of Vietminh readiness to agree to acceptable armistice terms.[23]

The news of Mendès-France's investiture was well received at Geneva where Chou En-lai had proposed, on 16 June, the evacuation of all foreign troops from Laos and Cambodia following bilateral military talks between the Vietminh and representatives of the two Governments concerned. This proposal, which represented the withdrawal of the Communist demand that a cease-fire agreement should be negotiated with Khmer and Pathet Lao representatives, was regarded as an important step forward. On 19 June the Conference reached agreement that representatives of the two Commands in Laos and Cambodia should study the questions relating to the cessation of hostilities in their territories, the talks to be held either in Geneva or in the country concerned. The military representatives taking part in these negotiations were instructed to report to the Conference on the progress that had been achieved in three weeks and during the interval the heads of the British, Soviet, and American delegations returned to their respective capitals.

Eden broke his journey to have luncheon with Mendès-France in Paris, where he urged the new Prime Minister to have an early meeting with Chou En-lai and also, if he felt able to do so, with Pham Van Dong. On his return to London Eden again set out, four days later, in company with Sir Winston Churchill, for Washington. Here he found Dulles in a somewhat chastened mood and apparently resigned to the partition of Vietnam, provided the French could be persuaded to abandon their economic stranglehold over the country, a prerequisite which he considered essential for the survival of a regime in the non-Communist part of the country; and although he considered that the United States would be most unlikely to guarantee any settlement reached at Geneva, he agreed nevertheless

[23] *Mendès-France was subsequently to deny in the National Assembly that he had been accurately informed, prior to his investiture, of the terms which the Vietminh had proposed on the night of 10–11 June. But this statement is challenged by Frédéric-Dupont, Minister for the Associated States in the Laniel Government, who claims to have personally given the Prime Minister designate particulars of the Vietminh proposals* (Mission de la France, *pp. 160-161, 167-171*).

that it would be useful for Mendès-France's guidance during the final negotiations, if the maximum concessions which the United States and the United Kingdom would be prepared to countenance were decided upon. . . .[24]

THE ARMISTICE AGREEMENTS

On the eve of the resumption of plenary sessions at Geneva there were indications that neither Dulles nor Bedell Smith, the Under-Secretary of State, would be returning to lead the American delegation, a decision which was ascribed to the fear that the presence of a member of the Government at Geneva might be interpreted as a sign of American readiness to ratify an agreement that formally recognized a territorial extension of Communist influence by force of arms. The absence of American ministerial representation at the concluding phase of the Conference was however viewed with misgivings by the French and British Governments on the grounds that the withdrawal of American support would be interpreted as evidence of basic disagreements among the members of the Western Alliance. But in spite of a *démarche* by the French Ambassador in Washington, on the eve of the resumption of the discussions Dulles publicly confirmed that neither he nor Bedell Smith would be returning to take part in the Conference unless some evidence of Communist goodwill were provided. This decision was discussed by Mendès-France and Eden, after the latter's return to Geneva on 12 July, and it was decided that the French Prime Minister should invite the American Secretary of State to fly to Paris for a tripartite meeting.

Dulles promptly accepted this invitation and left for Paris that evening. During the discussions Mendès-France managed to dispel his suspicions that there would inevitably be some departure from the conditions laid down in Washington, and a document setting out the position adopted by the French and United States Governments was then drawn up, signed, and exchanged, Eden expressing the general approval of the British Government in a separate letter. On his return to Washington, therefore, Dulles announced that a "formula for constructive Allied unity" had been found, [25] which would have a beneficial effect on the Conference

24 *Eden, Full Circle, pp. 131-133.*

25 New York Times (*16 July 1954*).

negotiations. The agreement on this formula also enabled him to recommend that Bedell Smith should return to Geneva.[26] His brief visit to Paris had likewise provided Dulles with an opportunity to discuss EDC with the French Prime Minister. He is reported to have expressed astonishment that the French Government should again have deferred the ratification of the Paris Treaty, but Mendès-France, who possessed a gift for lucid exposition, was able to persuade him that the American assumption that a majority existed for the ratification of the treaty was ill-founded, and that the French Government's decision to seek an acceptable compromise was entirely justified. Indeed so convincing did Mendès-France prove in his analysis of the state of French political opinion that Dulles is reported to have returned to Washington considerably incensed at the ineptitude of his advisers.[27]

This improvised tripartite meeting had, however, aroused the misgivings of the Soviet delegation, with the result that the Tass agency distributed among press correspondents in Geneva a statement in which Dulles's journey was described as another attempt by "aggressive circles in the United States" to wreck the Conference and to bring pressure to bear on France and Great Britain.[28] The suspicions aroused by Mendès-France's readiness not only to confer with Dulles but even, it was alleged, to discuss with him the ratification of the obnoxious Paris [EDC] Treaty were soon to be dispelled, however, by his patent anxiety to secure a settlement.

The Foreign Ministers who now returned to Geneva for the resumption of the plenary sessions included Dr. Tran Van Do, who held the portfolio of Foreign Affairs in the newly constituted Vietnamese Nationalist Government. Tran Van Do, who had long deplored the prevarication and subterfuge to which the French authorities had resorted in their attempts to prevent, and later to delay, the creation of a "Nationalist" state, was to play his thankless part in a manner which stressed the element of tragedy implicit in a Conference that the French Prime Minister is reported to have described with distasteful flippancy as a "stock-clear-

---

[26] Eden, *Full Circle*, pp. 138-139.
[27] *André Fontaine in* Le Monde *(17 July 1954).*
[28] [*London*] Times *(19 July 1954).*

ance sale". [29] Shortly after his arrival, prompted perhaps by the supposition that the head of the Vietminh delegation would share his objections to partition, Tran Van Do called on Pham Van Dong, but Dong, who had resigned himself to this solution, is reported to have confined the discussion to generalities. Indeed, the Vietminh leader appears to have been principally preoccupied at that time with obtaining, in return for his agreement to abandon the Khmer Resistance Movement, the establishment of an autonomous Pathet Lao regime in the Laotian provinces of Sam Neua and Phong Saly. However, on 18 July, after a homeric argument with Chou En-lai, Mendès-France obtained an understanding from the latter that he would cease to support these Vietminh claims. Chou En-lai's "betrayal" is reported to have reduced Dong to a state of suppressed fury and to have clouded subsequent relations between the Vietminh and Chinese delegations.[30]

Meanwhile the negotiations, which were conducted during the final stage of the Conference either in restricted sessions or by informal contacts between the delegates, continued to make good progress, but the somewhat furtive nature of these proceedings, which included frequent meetings between Mendès-France and Pham Van Dong, finally alarmed Tran Van Do, who had been left to wander disconsolately on the fringes of the Conference. On 17 July, therefore, he addressed a note to Mendès-France in which he complained that the French Command in Indochina had ordered the evacuation of zones vital to the defence and existence of a free Vietnam without fighting and despite protests, leaving the Vietnamese delegation at Geneva to discover from the newspapers and tardy communications that the French delegation had agreed to evacuate to the south all Vietnamese units stationed to the north of the 18th Parallel. This *démarche* merely evoked from the French delegation an expression of pained surprise at "this unexpected move." [31]

Next day the Vietnamese Foreign Minister intervened during a restricted session, and declared that his Government would refuse to subscribe to any cease-fire agreement

[29] *Fontaine in* Le Monde *(18–19 July 1954)*.
[30] *Roger Massip in* Figaro *(24-25 July 1954)*.
[31] Manchester Guardian *(19 July 1954)*.

partitioning the country, while he drew the attention of the delegates to the original Nationalist proposals, but on 20 July he informed the French Prime Minister with sorrowful dignity that his Government would not oppose the impending armistice, in spite of the fact that it considered such an armistice to be both catastrophic and immoral.

In the early hours of the 21st, Armistice Agreements covering the territory of Vietnam and Laos respectively were signed by General Deltiel on behalf of Ely, and by Ta Quang Buu, the Vietminh Vice-Minister for National Defence; the Armistice Agreement for Cambodia was signed some six hours later by Tep Phan, Cambodian Minister for Foreign Affairs, the delay being caused by his brusque decision to insist on his Government's retaining the right to establish bases on Cambodian soil for the military forces of foreign powers. After feverish discussions, however, in which Molotov displayed an amused tolerance, this demand was qualified by the restriction of this right to a situation in which Cambodian security was threatened.

The final plenary session was held that afternoon. At this session eight of the nine participating heads of delegations adopted by verbal assent a Final Declaration of intention, by which the Conference took note of the agreements which ended hostilities in Cambodia, Laos, and Vietnam and set up an international organization to supervise the execution of the provisions. The heads of delegations also agreed in the name of their Governments to consult one another on any question referred to them by the International Supervisory Commission in order to study such measures as might prove necessary to ensure the respect of the agreements.[32] Bedell Smith, representing the American delegation, made a unilateral declaration in which he stated that the Government of the United States took note of the Agreements and declared that it would refrain from the threat or the use of force to disturb them, and "would view any renewal of aggression in violation of the aforesaid Agreements with grave concern and as seriously threatening international peace and security." [33]

The session was marked by two further interventions by

[32] *See pp. 151–154.—ed.*
[33] *See pp. 156-157.—ed.*

the Vietnamese Foreign Minister, in which he protested "against the hasty conclusion of an Armistice by the French High Command alone" and proposed that the Vietnamese Government's objections and reservations should be incorporated in the Final Declaration. His protest was brusquely dismissed by Mendès-France and firmly overruled by Eden in his capacity as chairman of the plenary session. The Conference ended amid a flurry of mutual congratulations, while Molotov, giving further proof of the unusual amiability which had distinguished Soviet behaviour throughout the proceedings, paid a fulsome compliment to Eden, stressing the latter's outstanding services and role in the Conference, a role which Molotov insisted "cannot be exaggerated." [34]

In spite of the fact that the Conference had resulted in an armistice on terms which were unexpectedly favourable to France, the proceedings aroused misgivings among some observers, which Molotov's final tribute to the British Foreign Minister, with its hint of some undefined ironic undertone, did little to allay. This reaction appears to have been due to some suspicion that Mendès-France, in his patent desire to score a personal triumph, had been tempted to come to a tacit understanding with the Soviet representative by which, in return for Molotov's assistance in securing an armistice in Indochina on acceptable terms, he had given some understanding in regard to France's proposed participation in EDC, a *quid pro quo* which Bidault had stoutly rejected. The French Prime Minister's subsequent action in regard to the ratifications of the Paris Treaty did little to allay the suspicion that some understanding had, in fact, been given, for after the rejection, in August, at the Brussels meeting of the Defence Community of additional protocols which he had personally drafted, Mendès-France arranged for a debate on the Paris Treaty to take place in the National Assembly on 30 August; during this debate the proposed European Defence Community was implicitly and

[34] Further Documents Relating to the Discussion of Indochina at The Geneva Conference (*Miscellaneous, no. 20* [1954], *Command Paper, 9239*). London: *Great Britain Parliamentary Sessional Papers, XXXI* (1953/1954), p. 8 [See p. 159.—ed.]

ignominiously rejected on a mere question of procedure.[35]

Agreement on the Cessation
Of Hostilities In Vietnam
(July 20, 1954)*

CHAPTER I
PROVISIONAL MILITARY DEMARCATION
LINE AND DEMILITARIZED ZONE
Article 1

A provisional military demarcation line shall be fixed, on either side of which the forces of the two parties shall be regrouped after their withdrawal, the forces of the People's Army of Vietnam [P.A.V., or Vietminh, forces] to the north of the line and the forces of the French Union to the south. . . .[1]

It is also agreed that a demilitarized zone shall be established on either side of the demarcation line, to a width of not more than 5 kms. from it, to act as a buffer zone and avoid any incidents which might result in the resumption of hostilities.

Article 2

The period within which the movement of all forces of either party into its regrouping zone on either side of the provisional military demarcation line shall be completed shall

[35] *Mendès-France proposed seven amendments to the Paris Treaty, including the suspension of any clause of supra-nationality for eight years, the maintenance of a right to veto, and the limitation of the integration of the European Armies to the covering forces (i.e. to the forces stationed in Germany). "The protagonists of the European Defence Community never forgave M. Mendès-France what they called 'the crime of 30 August. Six months later they overthrew him, ostensibly on his North African policy, but in reality because they considered him responsible for the defeat of EDC." (Daniel Lerner and Raymond Aron*, France Defeats EDC [*New York, 1957*], pp. 162-163.)

* *Further Documents Relating to the Discussion of Indochina at the Geneva Conference* (Miscellaneous no. 20 [1954], Command Paper, 9239). London: Great Britain Parliamentary Sessional Papers, XXXI (1953/54), pp. 27-38.

[1] *The Provisional Demarcation Line was fixed as follows, from East to West: the mouth of the Song Ben Hat (Cua Tung) river, and the course of that river (known as the Rao Thanh in the mountains) to the village of Bo Ho Su, then the parallel of Bo Ho Su to the Laos-Vietnam frontier.—Ed.*

not exceed three hundred (300) days from the date of the present Agreement's entry into force.

Article 3

When the provisional military demarcation line coincides with a waterway, the waters of such waterway shall be open to civil navigation by both parties wherever one bank is controlled by one party and the other bank by the other party. The Joint Commission [1] shall establish rules of navigation for the stretch of waterway in question. The merchant shipping and other civilian craft of each party shall have unrestricted access to the land under its military control.

Article 4

The provisional military demarcation line between the two final regrouping zones is extended into the territorial waters by a line perpendicular to the general line of the coast.

All coastal islands north of this boundary shall be evacuated by the armed forces of the French Union, and all islands south of it shall be evacuated by the forces of the People's Army of Vietnam.

Article 5

To avoid any incidents which might result in the resumption of hostilities, all military forces, supplies, and equipment shall be withdrawn from the demilitarized zone within twenty-five (25) days of the present Agreement's entry into force.

Article 6

No person, military or civilian, shall be permitted to cross the provisional military demarcation line unless specifically authorized to do so by the Joint Commission.

Article 7

No person, military or civilian, shall be permitted to enter the demilitarized zone except persons concerned with the conduct of civil administration and relief and persons specifically authorized to enter by the Joint Commission.

Article 8

Civil administration and relief in the demilitarized zone on either side of the provisional military demarcation line shall be the responsibility of the Commanders-in-Chief of

---

[1] *This refers to a joint French-Vietminh Commission for supervising the details of the cease-fire (see Articles 10, 28-33), not the co-chairmen of the Geneva Conference (USSR and Great Britain).—ed.*

the two parties in their respective zones. The number of persons, military or civilian, from each side who are permitted to enter the demilitarized zone for the conduct of civil administration and relief shall be determined by the respective Commanders, but in no case shall the total number authorized by either side exceed at any one time a figure to be determined by the Trung Gia Military Commission or by the Joint Commission. The number of civil police and the arms to be carried by them shall be determined by the Joint Commission. No one else shall carry arms unless specifically authorized to do so by the Joint Commission.

Article 9

Nothing contained in this chapter shall be construed as limiting the complete freedom of movement—into, out of, or within the demilitarized zone—of the Joint Commission, its joint groups, the International Commission to be set up as indicated below, its inspection teams and any other persons, supplies, or equipment specifically authorized to enter the demilitarized zone by the Joint Commission. Freedom of movement shall be permitted across the territory under the military control of either side over any road or waterway which has to be taken between points within the demilitarized zone when such points are not connected by roads or waterways lying completely within the demilitarized zone.

CHAPTER II

PRINCIPLES AND PROCEDURE

GOVERNING IMPLEMENTATION OF

THE PRESENT AGREEMENT

Article 10

The Commanders of the Forces on each side, on the one side the Commander-in-Chief of the French Union forces in Indochina and on the other side the Commander-in-Chief of the People's Army of Vietnam, shall order and enforce the complete cessation of all hostilities in Vietnam by all armed forces under their control, including all units and personnel of the ground, naval, and air forces.

Article 11

In accordance with the principle of a simultaneous cease-fire throughout Indochina, the cessation of hostilities shall be simultaneous throughout all parts of Vietnam, in all areas of hostilities and for all the forces of the two parties. . . .

[*Section on precise timing of the cease-fire is omitted.
—ed.*]

From such time as the cease-fire becomes effective in
North Vietnam, both parties undertake not to engage in any
large-scale offensive action in any part of the Indochinese
theatre of operations and not to commit the air forces based
on North Vietnam outside that sector. The two parties also
undertake to inform each other of their plans for movement
from one regrouping zone to another within twenty-five (25)
days of the present Agreement's entry into force. . . .

Articles 12, 13

[*Further military details.—ed.*]

Article 14

Political and administrative measures in the two regrouping zones, on either side of the provisional military demarcation line:

(*a*) Pending the general elections which will bring about
the unification of Vietnam, the conduct of civil administration in each regrouping zone shall be in the hands of
the party whose forces are to be regrouped there in
virtue of the present Agreement.

(*b*) Any territory controlled by one party which is transferred to the other party by the regrouping plan shall
continue to be administered by the former party until
such date as all the troops who are to be transferred
have completely left that territory so as to free the
zone assigned to the party in question. From then on,
such territory shall be regarded as transferred to the
other party, who shall assume responsibility for it.

Steps shall be taken to ensure that there is no break in the
transfer of responsibilities. For this purpose, adequate notice
shall be given by the withdrawing party to the other party,
which shall make the necessary arrangements, in particular
by sending administrative and police detachments to prepare for the assumption of administrative responsibility. . . .
The transfer shall be effected in successive stages for the
various territorial sectors.

The transfer of the civil administration of Hanoi and
Haiphong to the authorities of the Democratic Republic of
Vietnam shall be completed within the respective time-limits
laid down in Article 15 for military movements.

(*c*) Each party undertakes to refrain from any reprisals

or discrimination against persons or organizations on account of their activities during the hostilities and to guarantee their democratic liberties.

(*d*) From the date of entry into force of the present Agreement until the movement of troops is completed, any civilians residing in a district controlled by one party who wish to go and live in the zone assigned to the other party shall be permitted and helped to do so by the authorities in that district.

Article 15

The disengagement of the combatants, and the withdrawals and transfers of military forces, equipment, and supplies shall take place in accordance with the following principles:

(*a*) The withdrawals and transfers of the military forces, equipment, and supplies of the two parties shall be completed within three hundred (300) days, as laid down in Article 2 of the present Agreement;

(*b*) Within either territory successive withdrawals shall be made by sectors, portions of sectors, or provinces. Transfers from one regrouping zone to another shall be made in successive monthly installments proportionate to the number of troops to be transferred;

(*c*) The two parties shall undertake to carry out all troop withdrawals and transfers in accordance with the aims of the present Agreement, shall permit no hostile act, and shall take no step whatsoever which might hamper such withdrawals and transfers. They shall assist one another as far as this is possible;

(*d*) The two parties shall permit no destruction or sabotage of any public property and no injury to the life and property of the civil population. They shall permit no interference in local civil administration;

(*e*) The Joint Commission and the International Commission shall ensure that steps are taken to safeguard the forces in the course of withdrawal and transfer; . . .

CHAPTER III

BAN ON THE INTRODUCTION OF FRESH TROOPS, MILITARY PERSONNEL, ARMS, AND MUNITIONS. MILITARY BASES

Article 16

With effect from the date of entry into force of the present Agreement, the introduction into Vietnam of any troop reinforcements and additional military personnel is prohibited.

It is understood, however, that the rotation of units and groups of personnel, the arrival in Vietnam of individual personnel on a temporary duty basis, and the return to Vietnam of the individual personnel after short periods of leave or temporary duty outside Vietnam shall be permitted under the conditions laid down below:

(*a*) Rotation of units (defined in paragraph (*c*) of this Article) and groups of personnel shall not be permitted for French Union troops stationed north of the provisional military demarcation line laid down in Article 1 of the present Agreement during the withdrawal period provided for in Article 2.

However, under the heading of individual personnel not more than fifty (50) men, including officers, shall during any one month be permitted to enter that part of the country north of the provisional military demarcation line on a temporary duty basis or to return there after short periods of leave or temporary duty outside Vietnam.

(*b*) "Rotation" is defined as the replacement of units or groups of personnel by other units of the same echelon or by personnel who are arriving in Vietnam territory to do their overseas service there.

(*c*) The units rotated shall never be larger than a battalion —or the corresponding echelon for air and naval forces.

(*d*) Rotation shall be conducted on a man-for-man basis, provided, however, that in any one quarter neither party shall introduce more than fifteen thousand five hundred (15,500) members of its armed forces into Vietnam under the rotation policy.

(*e*) Rotation units (defined in paragraph (*c*) of this Article) and groups of personnel, and the individual personnel mentioned in this Article, shall enter and leave Vietnam only through the entry points enumerated in Article 20 below.

(*f*) Each party shall notify the Joint Commission and the International Commission at least two days in advance of any arrivals or departures of units, groups of personnel, and individual personnel in or from Vietnam. Reports on the arrivals or departures of units, groups of personnel, and individual personnel in or from Vietnam shall be submitted daily to the Joint Commission and the International Commission.

All the above-mentioned notifications and reports shall indicate the places and dates of arrival or departure and the number of persons arriving or departing.

(g) The International Commission, through its Inspection Teams, shall supervise and inspect the rotation of units and groups of personnel and the arrival and departure of individual personnel as authorized above at the points of entry enumerated in Article 20 below.

Article 17

(a) With effect from the date of entry into force of the present Agreement, the introduction into Vietnam of any reinforcements in the form of all types of arms, munitions and other war material, such as combat aircraft, naval craft, pieces of ordnance, jet engines and jet weapons, and armored vehicles, is prohibited.

(b) It is understood, however, that war material, arms, and munitions which have been destroyed, damaged, worn out, or used up after the cessation of hostilities may be replaced on the basis of piece-for-piece of the same type and with similar characteristics. Such replacements of war material, arms, and ammunitions shall not be permitted for French Union troops stationed north of the provisional military demarcation line laid down in Article 1 of the present Agreement, during the withdrawal period provided for in Article 2.

Naval craft may perform transport operations between the regrouping zones.

(c) The war material, arms, and munitions for replacement purposes provided for in paragraph (b) of this Article, shall be introduced into Vietnam only through the points of entry enumerated in Article 20 below. War material, arms, and munitions to be replaced shall be shipped from Vietnam only through the points of entry enumerated in Article 20 below.

(d) Apart from the replacements permitted within the limits laid down in paragraph (b) of this Article, the introduction of war material, arms, and munitions of all types in the form of unassembled parts for subsequent assembly is prohibited.

(e) Each party shall notify the Joint Commission and the

International Commission at least two days in advance
of any arrivals or departures which may take place of
war material, arms, and munitions of all types.

In order to justify the requests for the introduction into
Vietnam of arms, munitions, and other war material
(as defined in paragraph (*a*) of this Article) for replacement purposes, a report concerning each incoming shipment shall be submitted to the Joint Commission and
the International Commission. Such reports shall indicate the use made of the items so replaced.

(*f*) The International Commission, through its Inspection
Teams, shall supervise and inspect the replacements permitted in the circumstances laid down in this Article.

Article 18

With effect from the date of entry into force of the
present Agreement, the establishment of new military bases
is prohibited throughout Vietnam territory.

Article 19

With effect from the date of entry into force of the present
Agreement, no military base under the control of a foreign
State may be established in the regrouping zone of either
party; the two parties shall ensure that the zones assigned
to them do not adhere to any military alliance and are not
used for the resumption of hostilities or to further an aggressive policy.

Article 20

The points of entry into Vietnam for rotation personnel
and replacements of material are fixed as follows:

—Zones to the north of the provisional military demarcation line: Laokay, Langson, Tien-Yen, Haiphong, Vinh,
Dong-Hoi, Muong-Sen;

—Zones to the south of the provisional military demarcation line: Tourane, Quinhon, Nhatrang, Bangoi, Saigon,
Cap St. Jacques, Tanchau.

CHAPTER IV

PRISONERS OF WAR

AND CIVILIAN INTERNEES

Article 21

The liberation and repatriation of all prisoners of war and
civilian internees detained by each of the two parties at the
coming into force of the present Agreement shall be carried
out under the following conditions:

(*a*) All prisoners of war and civilian internees of Vietnam, French, and other nationalities captured since the beginning of hostilities in Vietnam during military operations or in any other circumstances of war and in any part of the territory of Vietnam shall be liberated within a period of thirty (30) days after the date when the cease-fire becomes effective in each theater.

(*b*) The term "civilian internees" is understood to mean all persons who, having in any way contributed to the political and armed struggle between the two parties, have been arrested for that reason and have been kept in detention by either party during the period of hostilities.

(*c*) All prisoners of war and civilian internees held by either party shall be surrendered to the appropriate authorities of the other party, who shall give them all possible assistance in proceeding to their country of origin, place of habitual residence, or the zone of their choice.

CHAPTER V
MISCELLANEOUS
Article 22

The Commanders of the Forces of the two parties shall ensure that persons under their respective commands who violate any of the provisions of the present Agreement are suitably punished.

Article 23

In cases in which the place of burial is known and the existence of graves has been established, the Commander of the Forces of either party shall, within a specific period after the entry into force of the Armistice Agreement, permit the graves service personnel of the other party to enter the part of Vietnam territory under their military control for the purpose of finding and removing the bodies of deceased military personnel of that party, including the bodies of deceased prisoners of war. The Joint Commission shall determine the procedures and the time limit for the performance of this task. The Commanders of the Forces of the two parties shall communicate to each other all information in their possession as to the place of burial of military personnel of the other party.

Article 24

The present Agreement shall apply to all the armed forces of either party. The armed forces of each party shall respect the demilitarized zone and the territory under the military control of the other party, and shall commit no act and undertake no operation against the other party and shall not engage in blockade of any kind in Vietnam.

For the purposes of the present Article, the word "territory" includes territorial waters and air space.

Article 25

The Commanders of the Forces of the two parties shall afford full protection and all possible assistance and co-operation to the Joint Commission and its joint groups and to the International Commission and its Inspection Teams in the performance of the functions and tasks assigned to them by the present Agreement.

Article 26

The costs involved in the operations of the Joint Commission and joint groups and of the International Commission and its Inspection Teams shall be shared equally between the two parties.

Article 27

The signatories of the present Agreement and their successors in their functions shall be responsible for ensuring the observance and enforcement of the terms and provisions thereof. The Commanders of the Forces of the two parties shall, within their respective commands, take all steps and make all arrangements necessary to ensure full compliance with all the provisions of the present Agreement by all elements and military personnel under their command.

CHAPTER VI

JOINT COMMISSION AND INTERNATIONAL COMMISSION FOR SUPERVISION AND CONTROL IN VIETNAM

Article 28

Responsibility for the execution of the agreement on the cessation of hostilities shall rest with the parties.[2]

Article 29

An International Commission shall ensure the control and supervision of this execution.

Article 30

In order to facilitate, under the conditions shown below, the execution of provisions concerning joint actions by the two parties, a Joint Commission shall be set up in Vietnam.

[2] *French Union Forces and Vietminh Forces—ed.*

Article 31

The Joint Commission shall be composed of an equal number of representatives of the Commanders of the two parties.

Article 32

The Presidents of the delegations to the Joint Commission shall hold the rank of General.

The Joint Commission shall set up joint groups the number of which shall be determined by mutual agreement between the parties. The joint groups shall be composed of an equal number of officers from both parties. Their location on the demarcation line between the regrouping zones shall be determined by the parties whilst taking into account the powers of the Joint Commission.

Article 33

The Joint Commission shall ensure the execution of the following provisions of the Agreement on the cessation of hostilities:

(a) A simultaneous and general cease-fire in Vietnam for all regular and irregular armed forces of the two parties.

(b) A regroupment of the armed forces of the two parties.

(c) Observance of the demarcation lines between the regrouping zones and of the demilitarized sectors.

Within the limits of its competence it shall help the parties to execute the said provisions, shall ensure liaison between them for the purpose of preparing and carrying out plans for the application of these provisions, and shall endeavor to solve such disputed questions as may arise between the parties in the course of executing these provisions.

Article 34

An International Commission shall be set up for the control and supervision over the application of the provisions of the agreement on the cessation of hostilities in Vietnam. It shall be composed of representatives of the following States: Canada, India, and Poland.

It shall be presided over by the Representative of India.

Article 35

The International Commission shall set up Fixed and Mobile Inspection Teams, composed of an equal number of officers appointed by each of the above-mentioned States. The Fixed Teams shall be located at the following points: Laokay, Langson, Tien-Yen, Haiphong, Vinh, Dong-Hoi, Muong-Sen,

Tourane, Quinhon, Nhatrang, Bangoi, Saigon, Cap St. Jacques, Tanchau. These points of location may, at a later date, be altered at the request of the Joint Commission, or of one of the parties, or of the International Commission itself, by agreement between the International Commission and the command of the party concerned. The zones of action of the Mobile Teams shall be the regions bordering the land and sea frontiers of Vietnam, the demarcation lines between the regrouping zones and the demilitarized zones. Within the limits of these zones they shall have the right to move freely and shall receive from the local civil and military authorities all facilities they may require for the fulfillment of their tasks (provision of personnel, placing at their disposal documents needed for supervision, summoning witnesses necessary for holding inquiries, ensuring the security and freedom of movement of the Inspection Teams, etc.) . . . They shall have at their disposal such modern means of transport, observation, and communication as they may require. Beyond the zones of action as defined above, the Mobile Teams may, by agreement with the command of the party concerned, carry out other movements within the limits of the tasks given them by the present agreement.

Article 36

The International Commission shall be responsible for supervising the proper execution by the parties of the provisions of the agreement. For this purpose it shall fulfill the tasks of control, observation, inspection, and investigation connected with the application of the provisions of the agreement on the cessation of hostilities, and it shall in particular:

(a) Control the movement of the armed forces of the two parties, effected within the framework of the regroupment plan.

(b) Supervise the demarcation lines between the regrouping areas, and also demilitarized zones.

(c) Control the operations of releasing prisoners of war and civilian internees.

(d) Supervise at ports and airfields as well as along all frontiers of Vietnam the execution of the provisions of the agreement on the cessation of hostilities, regulating the introduction into the country of armed forces, military personnel and of all kinds of arms, munitions, and war material.

Article 37

The International Commission shall, through the medium of the Inspection Teams mentioned above, and as soon as possible either on its own initiative, or at the request of the Joint Commission, or of one of the parties, undertake the necessary investigations both documentary and on the ground.

Article 38

The Inspection Teams shall submit to the International Commission the results of their supervision, their investigation, and their observations; furthermore, they shall draw up such special reports as they may consider necessary or as may be requested from them by the Commission. In the case of a disagreement within the teams, the conclusions of each member shall be submitted to the Commission.

Article 39

If any one Inspection Team is unable to settle an incident or considers that there is a violation or a threat of a serious violation the International Commission shall be informed; the latter shall study the reports and the conclusions of the Inspection Teams and shall inform the parties of the measures which should be taken for the settlement of the incident, ending of the violation, or removal of the threat of violation.

Article 40

When the Joint Commission is unable to reach an agreement on the interpretation to be given to some provision or on the appraisal of a fact, the International Commission shall be informed of the disputed question. Its recommendations shall be sent directly to the parties and shall be notified to the Joint Commission.

Article 41

The recommendations of the International Commission shall be adopted by majority vote, subject to the provisions contained in Article 42. If the votes are divided the chairman's vote shall be decisive.

Article 42

The International Commission may formulate recommendations concerning amendments and additions which shou'd be made to the provisions of the Agreement on the cessation of hostilities in Vietnam, in order to ensure a more effective execution of that Agreement. These recommendations shall be adopted unanimously.

Article 43

When dealing with questions concerning violations, or threats of violations, which might lead to a resumption of hostilities, namely:

(a) Refusal by the armed forces of one party to effect the movements provided for in the regroupment plan;

(b) Violation by the armed forces of one of the parties of the regrouping zones, territorial waters, or air space of the other party;

the decisions of the International Commission must be unanimous.

Article 44

If one of the parties refuses to put into effect a recommendation of the International Commission, the parties concerned or the Commission itself shall inform the members of the Geneva Conference.

If the International Commission does not reach unanimity in the cases provided for in Article 42, it shall submit a majority report and one or more minority reports to the members of the Conference.

The International Commission shall inform the members of the Conference in all cases where its activity is being hindered.

Article 45

The International Commission shall be set up at the time of the cessation of hostilities in Indochina in order that it should be able to fulfill the tasks provided for in Article 36.

Articles 46, 47

[Discussion of co-operation of International Commission with similar groups in Laos and Cambodia is omitted. —ed.]

Done in Geneva at 2400 hours on the 20th of July, 1954, in French and in Vietnamese, both texts being equally authentic.

For the Commander-in-Chief of the French Union Forces in Indochina:

[Henri] DELTIEL,

Brigadier-General.

For the Commander-in-Chief of the People's Army of Vietnam:

TA QUANG BUU,
Vice-Minister of National Defense
of the Democratic Republic of Vietnam.

Final Declaration of the Geneva Conference (July 21, 1954)*

Nations taking part in the Conference: Kingdom of Cambodia, Democratic Republic of Vietnam, France, Kingdom of Laos, People's Republic of China, State of Vietnam, Union of Soviet Socialist Republics, United Kingdom (Great Britain), United States of America. —ed.

1. The Conference takes note of the agreements ending hostilities in Cambodia, Laos, and Vietnam and organizing international control and the supervision of the execution of the provisions of these agreements.

2. The Conference expresses satisfaction at the ending of hostilities in Cambodia, Laos, and Vietnam; the Conference expresses its conviction that the execution of the provisions set out in the present declaration and in the agreements on the cessation of hostilities will permit Cambodia, Laos, and Vietnam henceforth to play their part, in full independence and sovereignty, in the peaceful community of nations.

3. The Conference takes note of the declarations made by the Governments of Cambodia and of Laos of their intention to adopt measures permitting all citizens to take their place in the national community, in particular by participating in the next general elections, which, in conformity with the constitution of each of these countries, shall take place in the course of the year 1955, by secret ballot and in conditions of respect for fundamental freedoms.

4. The Conference takes note of the clauses in the agreement on the cessation of hostilities in Vietnam prohibiting the introduction into Vietnam of foreign troops and military personnel as well as of all kinds of arms and munitions. The Conference also takes note of the declarations made by the Governments of Cambodia and Laos of their resolution not

* *Further Documents Relating to the Discussion of Indochina at the Geneva Conference* (Miscellaneous no. 20 [1954], Command Paper, 9239). London: Great Britain Parliamentary Sessional Papers, XXXI (1953/54), pp. 9-11.

to request foreign aid, whether in war material, in personnel, or in instructors except for the purpose of the effective defense of their territory and, in the case of Laos, to the extent defined by the agreements on the cessation of hostilities in Laos.

5. The Conference takes note of the clauses in the agreement on the cessation of hostilities in Vietnam to the effect that no military base under the control of a foreign State may be established in the regrouping zones of the two parties, the latter having the obligation to see that the zones allotted to them shall not constitute part of any military alliance and shall not be utilized for the resumption of hostilities or in the service of an aggressive policy. The Conference also takes note of the declarations of the Governments of Cambodia and Laos to the effect that they will not join in any agreement with other States if this agreement includes the obligation to participate in a military alliance not in conformity with the principles of the Charter of the United Nations or, in the case of Laos, with the principles of the agreement on the cessation of hostilities in Laos or, so long as their security is not threatened, the obligation to establish bases on Cambodian or Laotian territory for the military forces of foreign powers.

6. The Conference recognizes that the essential purpose of the agreement relating to Vietnam is to settle military questions with a view to ending hostilities and that the military demarcation line is provisional and should not in any way be interpreted as constituting a political or territorial boundary. The Conference expresses its conviction that the execution of the provisions set out in the present declaration and in the agreement on the cessation of hostilities creates the necessary basis for the achievement in the near future of a political settlement in Vietnam.

7. The Conference declares that, so far as Vietnam is concerned, the settlement of political problems, effected on the basis of respect for the principles of independence, unity, and territorial integrity, shall permit the Vietnamese people to enjoy the fundamental freedoms, guaranteed by democratic institutions established as a result of free general elections by secret ballot. In order to ensure that sufficient progress in the restoration of peace has been made, and that all the necessary conditions obtain for free expression of the

national will, general elections shall be held in July, 1956, under the supervision of an international commission composed of representatives of the Member States of the International Supervisory Commission, referred to in the agreement on the cessation of hostilities. Consultations will be held on this subject between the competent representative authorities of the two zones from July 20, 1955, onward.

8. The provisions of the agreements on the cessation of hostilities intended to ensure the protection of individuals and of property must be most strictly applied and must, in particular, allow everyone in Vietnam to decide freely in which zone he wishes to live.

9. The competent representative authorities of the North and South zones of Vietnam, as well as the authorities of Laos and Cambodia, must not permit any individual or collective reprisals against persons who have collaborated in any way with one of the parties during the war, or against members of such persons' families.

10. The Conference takes note of the declaration of the Government of the French Republic to the effect that it is ready to withdraw its troops from the territory of Cambodia, Laos, and Vietnam, at the request of the Governments concerned and within periods which shall be fixed by agreement between the parties except in the cases where, by agreement between the two parties, a certain number of French troops shall remain at specified points and for a specified time.

11. The Conference takes note of the declaration of the French Government to the effect that for the settlement of all the problems connected with the re-establishment and consolidation of peace in Cambodia, Laos, and Vietnam, the French Government will proceed from the principle of respect for the independence and sovereignty, unity and territorial integrity of Cambodia, Laos, and Vietnam.

12. In their relations with Cambodia, Laos, and Vietnam, each member of the Geneva Conference undertakes to respect the sovereignty, the independence, the unity, and the territorial integrity of the above-mentioned States, and to refrain from any interference in their internal affairs.

13. The members of the Conference agree to consult one another on any question which may be referred to them by the International Supervisory Commission, in order to study such measures as may prove necessary to ensure that the

agreements on the cessation of hostilities in Cambodia, Laos, and Vietnam are respected.

[*This section of the Geneva Agreements was not signed by any nation, but rather agreed to by voice vote.—ed.*]

The Close of the Geneva Conference (July 21, 1954)*

The Chairman (Mr. Eden): As I think my colleagues are aware, agreement has now been reached on certain documents. It is proposed that this Conference should take note of these agreements. I accordingly propose to begin by reading out a list of the subjects covered by the documents, which I understand every delegation has in front of them.

First, agreement on the cessation of hostilities in Vietnam; second, agreement on the cessation of hostilities in Laos; third, agreement on the cessation of hostilities in Cambodia. I would draw particular attention to the fact that these three agreements now incorporate the texts which were negotiated separately concerning the supervision of the Armistice in the three countries by the International Commission and the joint committees.

I should also like to draw the attention of all delegations to a point of some importance in connexion with the Armistice Agreements and the related maps and documents on supervision. It has been agreed among the parties to each of these Agreements that none of them shall be made public for the present, pending further agreement among the parties. The reason for this, I must explain to my colleagues, is that these Armistice terms come into force at different dates. And it is desired that they should not be made public until they have come into force.

The further documents to which I must draw attention, which are in your possession, are: fourth, declaration by the Government of Laos on elections; fifth, declaration by the Government of Cambodia on elections and integration

* *Further Documents Relating to the Discussion of Indochina at the Geneva Conference* (Miscellaneous no. 20 [1954], Command Paper, 9239). London: Great Britain Parliamentary Sessional Papers, XXXI (1953/54), pp. 5-9.

of all citizens into the national community; sixth, declaration by the Government of Laos on the military status of the country; seventh, declaration by the Government of Cambodia on the military status of the country; eighth, declaration by the Government of the French Republic on the withdrawal of troops from the three countries of Indochina.

Finally, gentlemen, there is the Draft Declaration by the Conference, which takes note of all these documents. I think all my colleagues have copies of this Draft Declaration before them. I will ask my colleagues in turn to express themselves upon this Declaration.

M. Mendès-France (France): Mr. Chairman, the French Delegation approves the terms of this Declaration.

Mr. Phoui Sananikone (Laos): The Delegation of Laos has no observations to make on this text.

Mr. Chou En-lai (People's Republic of China): We agree.

The Chairman: On behalf of Her Majesty's Government in the United Kingdom, I associate myself with the final Declaration of this Conference.

M. Molotov (U.S.S.R.): The Soviet Delegation agrees.

Mr. Tep Phan (Cambodia): The Delegation of Cambodia wishes to state that, among the documents just listed, one is missing. This is a Cambodian Declaration which we have already circulated to all delegations. Its purport is as follows: Paragraphs 7, 11 and 12 of the final Declaration stipulate respect for the territorial integrity of Vietnam. The Cambodian Delegation asks the Conference to consider that this provision does not imply the abandonment of such legitimate rights and interests as Cambodia might assert with regard to certain regions of South Vietnam. . . .

In support of this Declaration, the Cambodian Delegation communicates to all members of this Conference a note on Cambodian lands in South Vietnam.

The Chairman: If this Declaration was not inscribed on the agenda on the list of documents I have read out, it is because it has only at this instant reached me. I do not think it is any part of the task of this Conference to deal with any past controversies in respect of the frontiers between Cambodia and Vietnam.

Mr. Pham Van Dong (Democratic Republic of Vietnam): Mr. Chairman, I agree completely with the words pronounced by you. In the name of the Government of the Democratic

Republic of Vietnam we make the most express reser
regarding the statement made by the Delegation of Can
just now. I do this in the interests of good relations ar
derstanding between our two countries.

The Chairman: I think the Conference can take no
the statements of the Delegation of Cambodia just circu
and of the statement of the Representative of the De
cratic Republic of Vietnam.

I will continue calling upon countries to speak on the s
ject of the Declaration. I call upon the United States of
America.

Mr. Bedell Smith (United States): Mr. Chairman, Fellow
Delegates, as I stated to my colleagues during our meeting
on July 18, my Government is not prepared to join in a
Declaration by the Conference such as is submitted. However, the United States makes this unilateral declaration of
its position in these matters:

The Government of the United States being resolved to
devote its efforts to the strengthening of peace in accordance
with the principles and purposes of the United Nations

Takes Note of the Agreements concluded at Geneva on
July 20 and 21, 1954, between (*a*) the Franco-Laotian Command and the Command of the People's Army of Vietnam;
(*b*) the Royal Khmer Army Command and the Command
of the People's Army of Vietnam; (*c*) the Franco-Vietnamese
Command and the Command of the People's Army of Vietnam, and of paragraphs 1 to 12 of the Declaration presented to the Geneva Conference on July 21, 1954.

The Government of the United States of America

Declares with regard to the aforesaid Agreements and
paragraphs that (i) it will refrain from the threat or the use
of force to disturb them, in accordance with Article 2 (Section 4) of the Charter of the United Nations dealing with
the obligation of Members to refrain in their international
relations from the threat or use of force; and (ii) it would
view any renewal of the aggression in violation of the aforesaid Agreements with grave concern and as seriously threatening international peace and security.

In connexion with the statement in the Declaration concerning free elections in Vietnam, my Government wishes to
make clear its position which it has expressed in a Declaration made in Washington on June 29, 1954, as follows:

"In the case of nations now divided against their will, we shall continue to seek to achieve unity through free elections, supervised by the United Nations to ensure that they are conducted fairly." [1]

With respect to the statement made by the Representative of the State of Vietnam, the United States reiterates its traditional position that peoples are entitled to determine their own future and that it will not join in an arrangement which would hinder this. Nothing in its declaration just made is intended to or does indicate any departure from this traditional position.

We share the hope that the agreement will permit Cambodia, Laos and Vietnam to play their part in full independence and sovereignty, in the peaceful community of nations, and will enable the peoples of that area to determine their own future.

The Chairman: The Conference will, I think, wish to take note of the statement of the Representative of the United States of America.

Mr. Tran Van Do (State of Vietnam): Mr. Chairman, as regards the final Declaration of the Conference, the Vietnamese Delegation requests the Conference to incorporate in this Declaration after Article 10, the following text:

"The Conference takes note of the Declaration of the Government of the State of Vietnam undertaking:

"to make and support every effort to re-establish a real and lasting peace in Vietnam;

"not to use force to resist the procedures for carrying the cease-fire into effect, in spite of the objections and reservations that the State of Vietnam has expressed, especially in its final statement."

The Chairman: I shall be glad to hear any views that my colleagues may wish to express. But, as I understand the position, the final Declaration has already been drafted and this additional paragraph has only just now been received; indeed, it has been amended since I received the text a few minutes ago. In all the circumstances, I suggest that the best course we can take is that the Conference should take note of the Declaration of the State of Vietnam in this respect. If any of my colleagues has a contrary view, perhaps they would be good enough to say so. (None.) If none of my

[1] From Eisenhower-Churchill joint "Potomac Declaration."—ed.

colleagues wishes to make any other observations, may I pass to certain other points which have to be settled before this Conference can conclude its labours?

The first is that, if it is agreeable to our colleagues, it is suggested that the two Chairmen should at the conclusion of this meeting address telegrams to the Governments of India, Poland, and Canada to ask them if they will undertake the duties of supervision which the Conference has invited them to discharge. Is that agreeable? (Agreed.) Thank you.

The last is perhaps the least agreeable chapter of all our work. Certain costs arise from the decisions which the Conference has taken. It is suggested that it should be left here to your Chairmen as their parting gift to try to put before you some proposal in respect of those costs. I only wish to add in that connexion that, as this Conference is peculiar in not having any Secretariat in the usual sense of the term, the two Chairmen with considerable reluctance are prepared to undertake this highly invidious task. The costs to which I refer are not our own but those of the International Commission.

Does any delegate wish to make any further observation? (None.)

Gentlemen, perhaps I may say a final word as your Chairman for this day. We have now come to the end of our work. For a number of reasons it has been prolonged and intricate. The co-operation which all delegates have given to your two Chairmen has enabled us to overcome many procedural difficulties. Without that co-operation, we could not have succeeded in our task. The Agreements concluded to-day could not, in the nature of things, give complete satisfaction to everyone. But they have made it possible to stop a war which has lasted for eight years and brought suffering and hardship to millions of people. They have also, we hope, reduced international tension at a point of instant danger to world peace. These results are surely worth our many weeks of toil. In order to bring about a cease-fire, we have drawn up a series of agreements. They are the best that our hands could devise. All will now depend upon the spirit in which those agreements are observed and carried out.

Gentlemen, before we leave this hospitable town of Geneva I'm sure you would wish your Chairmen to give a message of gratitude to the United Nations and its able staff who have housed and helped us in our work.

And lastly let me express our cordial thanks to the Swiss Government and to the people and authorities of Geneva who have done so much to make our stay here pleasant as well as of service to the cause of peace.

Mr. Bedell Smith (U.S.A.): If I presume to speak for my fellow delegates, it is because I know that they all feel as I do. I hope that they join me in expressing our thanks to the two Chairmen of this Conference. Their patience, their tireless efforts, and their goodwill have done a great deal to make this settlement possible. We owe them our sincere thanks.

M. Molotov (U.S.S.R.): Mr. Chairman, as one of the Chairmen at the Geneva Conference, I would like to reply to the remarks just made by Mr. Bedell Smith, who spoke highly of the work done by the Chairmen. Naturally I must stress the outstanding services and the outstanding role played by our Chairman of to-day, Mr. Eden, whose role in the Geneva Conference cannot be exaggerated. And I would also like to reply and thank Mr. Bedell Smith for his warm words of to-day.

The Chairman: Has any other delegate anything else they want to say?

Mr. Tran Van Do (State of Vietnam): Mr. Chairman, I expressed the view of the Delegation of the State of Vietnam in my statement and I would have this Conference take note of it in its final act.

The Chairman: As I think I explained, we cannot now amend our final act, which is the statement of the Conference as a whole, but the Declaration of the Representative of the State of Vietnam will be taken note of.

Any other observations? (None.)

I would like to be allowed to add my thanks for what General Bedell Smith has said and also to thank M. Molotov for his words. Both were undeserved, but even if things are not true, if they are nice things it's pleasant to hear them said.

But I do want to close this Conference with this one sentence: I'm quite sure that each one of us here hopes that the work which we have done will help to strengthen the forces working for peace.

Part Five

The Fate of the Geneva Agreements:
Testimony of the International Commission
for Supervision and Control in Vietnam

The Geneva Agreements of July 1954 marked the end of an epoch in the history of Indochina. French imperialism in the area was to give way to the forces of indigenous nationalism, and the independent nations of Laos, Cambodia, and Vietnam were to emerge. The appearance of a unified Vietnam, free of colonial control, was to be deferred, however, until 1956. The interim period was to be spent preparing for eventual reunification under the conditions clearly laid down in the Geneva Agreements.[1]

The responsibility of ensuring that the Agreements were carried out rested first of all with the parties—France and the Vietminh. Although the latter accepted the terms at Geneva reluctantly (under Soviet and Chinese prodding)[2] thereafter Vietminh hopes were pinned on strict observation of what President Lyndon Johnson later called "the essentials of the Agreements of 1954."[3] To the Vietminh these "essentials" meant that after more than a decade of war, the struggle for control of Vietnam would be transferred to the political plane, where they felt certain of victory. Therefore it was in their interest to observe the Agreements, and the data set forth in the pages that follow constitute the most reliable body of evidence on which to judge whether or not they did so.

The responsibility of the other side—the French—was not discharged, much to the surprise and dismay of the Vietminh. "It was with you, the French, that we signed the Geneva Agreements," declared Premier Pham Van Dong of

---

[1] See pp. 152–153.

[2] See p. 134.

[3] Department of State Bulletin, LI (April 12, 1965), pp. 527–528.

the Democratic Republic of Vietnam, "and it is up to you to see that they are respected." [4] But in one of the most curious of modern imperialist maneuvers, the French *withdrew* their forces just before the deadline for nationwide elections. And, of course, no such elections were held.

The Geneva Agreements anticipated such an occurrence. If the responsibility "for ensuring [their] observance and enforcement" was not fulfilled by either of the original signatories, it was to devolve on "their successors." [5] The successor to French power in South Vietnam was the State of Vietnam, ruled until October 1955 by Emperor Bao Dai and his Premier, Ngo Dinh Diem. This government was bitterly hostile to the Agreements from the very outset, declaring that an " 'agreement' with such an adversary [as the Vietminh] could only be a fool's bargain." [6]

This attitude of hostility to the Agreements reached at Geneva was fully shared by the United States. As the deadline for elections neared, Assistant Secretary of State Walter S. Robertson lined up the American government fully behind Diem's decision not to hold them. In a speech delivered to the American Friends of Vietnam [7] Robertson offered the two standard arguments, embellished by lurid tales of the "crimes against suffering humanity" committed by the North Vietnamese, who were charged with having "sold their country to Peking." First, the Communists were held to have violated the Geneva Agreements by the incorporation of guerrilla forces brought up from the South into the military establishment of the Democratic Republic of Vietnam. Second, to Mr. Robertson, the provision for elections in the Geneva Agreements was meaningless unless "conditions which preclude intimidation or coercion of the electorate" were guaranteed beforehand to the satisfaction of the Saigon authorities. [8]

The first argument was a masterpiece of subtlety, for the reason why the armed forces in the North were augmented was none other than the scrupulous Vietminh observation

[4] See p. 217.

[5] *Cessation of Hostilities, Article 27, p. 146.*

[6] *Embassy of Vietnam, Washington, D.C.,* Vietminh Violations of the Geneva Armistice Agreement *(Washington, D.C. [1955]), p. 1.*

[7] *On this important organization see pp. 250–251.*

[8] Department of State Bulletin, *(June 11, 1956).*

of the regroupment provisions of the Geneva Agreements.[9] Presumably if the Vietminh forces had remained in the South, the U.S. and the Saigon government would have charged violation of the Agreements. In that case the Vietminh would have committed a violation no matter what it had done. (This argument finds no support in the Reports of the International Control Commission, excerpts from which are reprinted below).

Mr. Robertson's second argument conveniently overlooked a key provision of the Final Declaration of the Geneva Conference. It provided for, not immediate elections, but elections in July 1956, to be preceded by consultative conferences.[10] At these conferences the parties could set their conditions, iron out difficulties, and arrange for impartial international supervision of the elections. The Saigon regime *refused to participate in these consultative conferences*, although they could have used them to insist on the most rigid conditions for free elections. The clear implication is that they feared a Vietminh electoral victory no matter how carefully prepared and supervised the elections were.[11] This would have been intolerable to the Southern regime and its American supporters, both of whom could claim if pressed that they had not "signed" the Agreements anyway.[12] Under

[9] See pp. 137–141.

[10] See pp. 250–251.

[11] Incidentally, the record of the Saigon government on its own elections in the South is, to put it mildly, not free from blame. In 1959 Phan Quang Dan, an opponent of the Diem regime, won election to the South Vietnamese assembly. He was placed under house arrest and not allowed to take his seat. (Lennox A. Mills, Southeast Asia: Illusion and Reality in Politics and Economics) (Minneapolis, Minn., 1964), p. 88.

[12] A minor point is that the sequence of events in Article 7 of the Final Declaration (pp. 152–153) makes the elections antecedent to, and a necessary condition for, "fundamental freedoms, guaranteed by democratic institutions." The key phrases, when quoted out of order, can justify refusal to hold elections because of absence of "democratic institutions," etc. The provisions for elections in Laos and Cambodia are of a different form. See George McT. Kahin and John W. Lewis, "The United States in Vietnam," Bulletin of the Atomic Scientists, XXI (June 1965), note 7, p. 29.

such justification the successors to French power in Vietnam circumvented the Geneva Agreements.[13]

A distinctly lesser responsibility to see that the Geneva Agreements were not flouted rested with Great Britain and the Soviet Union, Co-Chairmen of the 1954 Geneva Conference. But once having made an effort to bring peace to Indochina in 1954, neither power cared to exert itself thereafter in an area not of major strategic concern to either. The Co-Chairmen became very little more than the persons to whom complaints about alleged violations of the Agreements could be sent, with assurance that little would then be done.

A lesser degree of responsibility yet fell to the International Commission for Supervision and Control in Vietnam, created at the 1954 Conference.[14] The Control Commission, consisting of Indian, Canadian, and Polish representatives, was unlike the international peace-keeping forces patrolling Cyprus or the borders of Israel. It had no police powers. In cases of violation it could do little more than issue Reports. The following pages contain generous portions of these Reports from 1954 to 1965. It will be seen that the powerlessness of the Commission prevented it from enforcing peace, but its records and deliberations serve the cause of truth, and that is the reason for their inclusion here. They provide ample data to refute the contentions of both sides that only the other has violated the Geneva Agreements.[15]

[13] *It would seem that President Eisenhower explicitly acknowledged the U.S. responsibility. "Our direct interest in" the Geneva negotiations, he wrote, "arose out of the assumption that the United States would be expected to act as one of the guarantors of whatever agreement should be achieved."* Mandate for Change, *(New York, 1963), p. 357.*

[14] *See pp. 146–150*

[15] *Compare Wilfred G. Burchett's claim* (The Furtive War: The United States in Vietnam and Laos *[New York, 1963], p. 56) that up to 1961 "no violations had been registered by the ICC against the North. . . ." with the statement of President Lyndon B. Johnson: "For ten years, through the Eisenhower Administration, the Kennedy Administration, and this Administration, we have had one consistent aim—observance of the 1954 [Geneva] Agreements. . . ." He went on to say that these "Agreements guaranteed the independence of South Vietnam." Of course they did no such thing, but rather laid the groundwork for unification of the Northern and Southern zones. Address to the American Bar Association (August 12, 1964), in* Department of State Bulletin, *LI (August 31, 1964), p. 299.*

Nevertheless there were significant differences in the compliance granted to the Commission's teams. The South Vietnamese government was actively hostile at first, and refused to co-operate with the Commission on the grounds that it was not a signatory to the Geneva Agreements. A climax of sorts was reached in July 1955, when, instead of initiating the consultative conferences, the Diem regime staged an attack on the hotel in which Commission members were staying.[16] The Vietminh regime in the North, for its part, eagerly welcomed the Commission,[17] and as the documents in this section show, generally co-operated. One exception to the compliance of the Vietminh was the occasional harassment of refugees who wished to go South.[18] But in light of subsequent events, the surreptitious introduction into South Vietnam of immense amounts of U.S. arms, military personnel, and war material constituted a far more serious violation of the Geneva Agreements.[19] In its sixth Interim Report the Control Commission candidly stated that "[w]hile the Commission has experienced difficulties in North Vietnam the major part of its difficulties has arisen in South Vietnam."[20] This imbalance between Northern observance and Southern defiance of the Control Commission persisted long

[16] New York Times (July 21, 22, 23, 28, 1955). The story became newsworthy in the U.S. partly because the American hostess, Perle Mesta, and other American dignitaries were turned out of the hotels by the rioters. Responsibility is inferred from the South Vietnamese governments' subsequent willingness to pay damages, and from eyewitness reports that Catholic refugees made up the mob. Diem, of course, blamed the riot on the Communists.

[17] See Ho Chi Minh, "Welcome to the International Commission for Supervision and Control" (August 13, 1954), in Ho Chi Minh, Selected Works (4 vols., Hanoi, 1960–1962), IV, pp. 21–24.

[18] The Vietminh claimed that this was not always a free choice, but was often brought about by claims that "the Virgin Mary has gone South," etc. See La Vérité sur l'affair des "Réfugiés" au Vietnam (Hanoi, 1955), passim. On the importance of the Refugee Program, see Robert Scheer's analysis, pp. 244–249.

[19] An eye-witness observer saw "U.S. warplanes being landed on an aircraft carrier in sight of Saigon's main thoroughfare while a handsomely turbaned Indian ICSC officer said: 'Yes—but officially we have not been informed of the presence of the aircraft carrier.'" (Bernard B. Fall, "That Geneva Agreement," New York Times Magazine [May 2, 1965]).

[20] See p. 172.

after the deadline for elections had passed and the guerrilla war in the South had begun.

Although the Commission has left posterity a valuable record of events in Vietnam, it could not itself escape the intense cold war pressures focused on Vietnam. Internal dissension in the Commission began in 1960 when the South Vietnamese government, in a sudden burst of respect for the Commission began to allege "subversion" by Vietminh agents.[21] This allegation was made in the Commission's Report in 1961. A wedge was driven between the Canadian and Indian representatives on the one hand, and the Polish on the other. The entire dispute was aired in the Special Report of 1962.[22] The escalation of 1965 saw a different line-up of members of the Commission on the question of air strikes by the United States against North Vietnam, with Canada the lone defender of American policy.[23] The disputes among Commission members, far from diminishing the value of the Reports, enhance them by showing yet another dimension of the cold war tragedy of Indochina. The deliberations of the International Commission for Supervision and Control in Vietnam,[23] too often cited out of context for purposes of special pleading,[24] deserve to be rescued from library shelves, and gain wider circulation. The following pages intend to do just that.

[21] *The first mention of "subversion" is in* The Tenth Interim Report of the International Commission for Supervision and Control in Vietnam *(Vietnam no. 1 [1960], Command Paper, 1040). London: Great Britain Parliamentary Sessional Papers, XXXVI (1959/60), p. 13.*

[22] *See pp. 185–188.*

[23] *The Reports of Commissions operating in Laos and Cambodia under the same dispensation are available in any research library in the Great Britain Parliamentary Sessional Papers, which are admirably indexed.*

[24] *See an example on pp. 187–188.*

The First Six Months of the International Commission for Supervision and Control In Vietnam (February, 1955)*

118. Despite difficulties of communication, frayed tempers due to eight years of strife, and differences in the degrees of effectiveness of administration in various parts of Vietnam, the provisions of the Agreement which are of a military or semi-military nature have on the whole been carried out according to the time schedules and directions given in the Agreement. . . . As regards prisoners of war and civilian internees. . . , by and large, the parties have and are carrying out the directions under Article 21 [1], and the bulk of the exchanges have been completed, though the time schedule has not been maintained mainly due to administrative difficulties.

119. The two parties in the Joint Commission [2] have on occasions been unable to arrive at mutually satisfactory arrangements to execute the Agreement. On such occasions, the International Commission has been approached for intervention. The International Commission has consistently appealed to the parties to approach problems arising out of the Agreement in a practical spirit and not in a narrow formalistic manner. The Commission feels that a practical approach would be in the long run the most effective way of ensuring that the provisions of the Agreement are properly carried out, and it is only in this spirit that the two parties can jointly fulfill the obligations which they have accepted at Geneva.

120. It is obvious from the review that there is room for improvement in the implementation by both parties of the

* First and Second Interim Reports of the International Commission for Supervision and Control in Vietnam (Vietnam No. 1 [1955], Command Paper. 9461). London: Great Britain Parliamentary Sessional Papers, XIX (1954/55), pp. 29-30.

[1] This, and the many similar references that follow are to the Agreement on the Cessation of Hostilities in Vietnam. See pp. 137-150.—ed.

[2] That is, France and the Vietminh.—ed.

Articles of the Agreement dealing with democratic free-doms. . . . The Commission realizes that in a climate of suspicion and fear engendered by eight years of strife, and with administrative difficulties of some magnitude which the parties have had to face, effective implementation of the provisions of the Agreement dealing with democratic free-doms is bound to be a difficult matter, but the Commission feels that, while difficulties exist, both sides have been sadly lacking in a sense of purpose and urgency in dealing with these matters. . . .

122. Similarly, the High Command of the People's Army of Vietnam, while they did co-operate with the Commission and took measures to secure freedom of movement in the case of about 8,000 Phat Diem refugees, have so far done little to develop adequate administrative arrangements, with the result that complaints continue to pour in. . . .

124 . . . [B]oth sides have preferred narrow legalistic interpretation of the Articles of the Agreement regarding the tasks and the spheres of movement of the Commission's teams. The Commission is taking up the matter with both sides on the basis of experience of the last few months, but it must be stated that our Fixed and Mobile Teams have dis-played considerable patience and perseverance in the face of restrictions and obstacles they have met in the form of in-efficiency of local administration, the narrowness of local of-ficials, or general misunderstanding regarding their tasks. . .

126. The Commission is satisfied that, on the whole, the specific points noted in the Final Declaration of the Geneva Powers dated the 21st of July, 1954, have been borne in mind by both sides and that they have made and continue to make efforts to implement the Agreement on the Cessation of Hostilities in Vietnam signed on the 20th of July, 1954.

Vietminh Compliance With the Geneva Agreements (May-June, 1955)*

The manner in which the withdrawals and transfers were effected satisfied both parties to the agreement and improved

* *Fourth Interim Report of the International Commission for Supervision and Control in Vietnam* (Vietnam No. 3 [1955], Command Paper, 9654). London: Great Britain Parliamentary Ses-sional Papers, XLV (1955/56), pp. 6-7.

the general atmosphere of co-operation and goodwill between the P.A.V. and the French High Commands. The following extracts speak for themselves:

Extract from General Vo Nguyen Giap's speech made at a tea party on May 17, 1955, organised by the High Command of the P.A.V.

"On May 16, 1955, that is three days before the time-limit fixed by the Geneva Agreement, the last units of the Vietnam People's Army left South Vietnam to regroup into the North. Simultaneously, the Vietnam People's Army in the North completed the taking-over of newly liberated regions and towns, including Haiphong perimeter.

"We ought to mention here the efforts made by both signatories to the Agreement and by the International Commission for Supervision and Control in Vietnam.

"I also take this opportunity to express my thanks to the members of the International Commission for their efforts in the past and their notable contribution to the achieving of regroupment and transfer of military forces of the two parties.

"The completion of the regroupment and transfer of military forces has laid foundation for the continuation of the execution of the Geneva Agreement and for the strengthening of peace in the days to come."

Extract of letter No. 5882/Cab/CD dated Saigon, June 2, 1955, from General [Paul H.R.] Ely, Le Général d' Armée Commissaire Général de France et Commandant en Chief en Indochine to His Excellency Mr. Ambassador Desai, Chairman of the International Commission for Supervision and Control, Hanoi.

"Before I leave, I should like to express to you my deep appreciation for the work you have done here.

"Indeed, it is thanks to the conciliatory work of the International Commission which you have been leading with such authority and tact that an important part of the Decisions of the Geneva Agreement, despite innumerable difficulties, has been executed in a practical manner.

"For my part, I shall never forget that it is your efforts which have allowed the clarification of the problem of prisoners, have allowed a great many people to benefit from the rights given by Article 14 (d), and have, finally, allowed the transfer of territories and the regroupment of forces in favourable conditions.

"Above all, in the course of an experiment which I am sure will constitute a remarkable precedent on the international plane, you have succeeded in creating, in particularly difficult circumstances, a climate of *détente.*"

Differences In Compliance With the Geneva Agreements North and South (1955)*

CHAPTER VIII

The Commission was able, by making strong representation to the High Command concerned [P.A.V.], and without resort to Article 22, to get the obstructions [to free movements of population] removed in most cases[,] though delays that occurred could not be remedied. Recommendations were made to the High Command of the P.A.V. to take action against Liaison Officers or local authorities who were obstructing the work of the Commission's teams, and reports of the remedial action were sent by the P.A.V. High Command in three cases out of five. In the case of the zone of the French Union High Command [south of the temporary demarcation line], however, the independent attitude of the Government of the State of Vietnam, which controlled the civil administration and which had not signed the Geneva Agreement, made the obstructions and difficulties progressively more serious[,] and the French High Command could not take adequate remedial action [under Article 22].

* *Fourth Interim Report of the International Commission for Supervision and Control in Vietnam* (Vietnam No. 3 [1955], Command Paper, 9654). London: Great Britain Parliamentary Sessional Papers, XLV (1955/56), p. 16.

Differences In Compliance With the Geneva Agreements North and South (1956)*

CHAPTER VI
CO-OPERATION OF THE PARTIES
TO THE AGREEMENT
Difficulties in South Vietnam

Cases where the Commission's Activities are being hindered

71. Another major difficulty is the time notice restrictions placed by the authorities in South Vietnam on the Commission's Fixed Teams. . . .

The Commission had made it clear that the existence of such time notices makes it impossible for its teams to carry out all their duties effectively. . . .

72. The provisions of Articles 16 and 17 . . . have not been fully implemented by the French High Command. The notifications which the parties have undertaken to give under the provisions of these Articles were not received regularly by the Commission. Thirty-six cases have been recorded where no notifications have been received by the Commission's team in Saigon and on fourteen occasions the team actually saw military personnel deplaning at Saigon airfield. The Commission has repeatedly taken serious objection to the failure of the French High Command to give the required notifications under Articles 16 and 17. On April 25, 1956, the French High Command informed the Commission that the Government of the Republic of Vietnam had indicated its consent to give the required notifications.

73. The Commission has been unable to conduct reconnaissance and control of . . . airfields in South Vietnam . . . The Commission had asked that immediate arrangements should be made for the reconnaissance and control of the airfields as the case may be. Because of this lack of co-operation, the Commission has not been able to supervise all airfields in the discharge of its statutory duties under Article 36 (d). . . .

* Sixth Interim Report of the International Commission for Supervision and Control in Vietnam (Vietnam No. 1 [1957], Command Paper, 31). London: Great Britain Parliamentary Sessional Papers, XXXIII (1956/57), pp. 26-31.

Cases of Non-Implementation of Recommendations of the Commission

76. Apart from the hindrances in South Vietnam mentioned above, there are cases where specific recommendations of the Commission have not been implemented by the French High Command or where implementation has been delayed. The majority of cases concern recommendations made by the Commission regarding release of civilian internees from prisons in South Vietnam. . . .

In spite of repeated requests, twenty-one recommendations regarding release of civilian internees have not been implemented. In nineteen cases, the authorities of the Republic of Vietnam have rejected the Commission's recommendations on the ground that the persons concerned were former members of the [Vietminh] armed forces. . . . [T]he Commission gave very careful consideration to the legal aspect of the matter and confirmed its recommendations. In spite of this, the recommendations have not been implemented. . . .

77. The Commission conveyed on February 24, 1956, its recommendations that notifications of import of war material and introduction of military personnel should be given in writing to the Central Joint Commission as laid down in Articles 16 and 17 and for this purpose a Central Secretariat should be set up. The French High Command has not accepted these recommendations.

DIFFICULTIES IN NORTH VIETNAM

Cases where the Commission's Activities are being hindered

79. There also exist cases in North Vietnam where the Commission's activities are being hindered. The case of Mobile Team F-44 . . . [in which] the Commission has been experiencing a major difficulty, has been pending with the Commission since April 1955, and the Commission's repeated efforts to complete the investigation have not been successful so far. Various reasons have been given by the P.A.V. High Command for not arranging for the interview of the seminarists, including the reason of the reluctance of the religious authorities to allow the team to interview the seminarists inside the seminary. . . . [W]ith a view to expediting the matter, the Commission has decided to interview the persons concerned at Vinh and has made a recommendation to that effect. This recommendation has not been implemented

Case of Non-implementation of Recommendation of the Commission

83. One difficulty of a serious nature where the Commission's recommendation has not been implemented has been the withdrawal of the Commission's mobile team from Phuc Hoa. . . .

84. Under the Cease-Fire Agreement the parties have, apart from the obligation to implement all the Articles fully, accepted the obligation to afford full protection and all possible assistance and co-operation to the International Commission and its inspection teams in the performance of functions and tasks assigned to them by the Agreement. Neither party has fulfilled in their entirety these obligations. As has been revealed in the preceding paragraphs, the degree of co-operation given to the Commission by the two parties has not been the same. While the Commission has experienced difficulties in North Vietnam, the major part of its difficulties has arisen in South Vietnam.

The Geneva Agreements After the Deadline for Elections Has Passed (1957)*

CHAPTER VI

CO-OPERATION OF THE PARTIES TO THE AGREEMENT

59. . . . [T]he Commission recorded a violation under Article 14 (c) (which is also reported under Article 43) and a few violations under Articles 16 and 17 of the Agreement by the French High Command and the Government of the Republic of South Vietnam, and none by the Democratic Republic of Vietnam. The violations of Articles 16 and 17 mentioned above concern introduction into South Vietnam of United States military personnel in five United States military aircraft, a few aircraft wheel tires, 1,000 revolvers, and 610 cases of revolver ammunition.

60. As the Government of the Republic of Vietnam did not

* *Seventh Interim Report of the International Commission for Supervision and Control in Vietnam* (Vietnam No. 2 [1957], Command Paper, 325). London: Great Britain Parliamentary Sessional Papers, XXX (1957/58), pp. 18-19.

afford the necessary assistance and co-operation to the Commission in cases under Article 14 (*c*) and, in particular, decided not to send any more replies to the Commission's communications and not to permit the deployment of any Mobile Teams for investigation of complaints under this Article in South Vietnam, the Commission addressed a special letter to the Co-Chairmen on April 11, 1957 . . . and expressed its grave concern to the Government of the Republic of Vietnam.

61. . . . [T]he Commission has not been able to decide the cases of 122 alleged civilian internees/prisoners-of-war under Article 21 in South Vietnam, as the Government of the Republic of Vietnam failed to produce the relevant documents and dossiers in the manner required by the Commission.

62. In North Vietnam, the Commission has not been able to supervise continuously, under Article 36 (*d*) of the Agreement, the Phuc Hoa section of the land frontier through its Mobile Team set up under Article 35 . . ., as the P.A.V. High Command did not co-operate with the Commission in this matter. . . .

63. The Government of the Republic of Vietnam did not, in all cases, give the Commission advance notification under Articles 16 (*f*) and 17 (*e*) of the arrival of military personnel and war materials respectively. The said Government did not ask for the Commission's approval, as required . . . in any case concerning war material.

64. The situation described . . . in the Sixth Interim Report [1] showed no improvement during the period under review. As will be seen from previous paragraphs, the Commission encountered further difficulties in the exercise of its functions, in particular, a major difficulty with respect to the implementation of Article 14 (*c*) of the Agreement by the Government of the Republic of Vietnam.

CHAPTER VII
CONCLUSIONS

65. In . . . the Sixth Interim Report . . . the Commission had referred to the situation which arose as a consequence of the withdrawal of the French High Command from Vietnam. As was mentioned in the Commission's message, the

[1] *See pp. 172–174.—ed.*

Government of the Republic of Vietnam had stated that it was prepared to offer effective co-operation to the Commission but that it was not prepared to assume responsibility for the implementation of the Geneva Agreements in Vietnam. While this major development had its origin during the period of the Sixth Interim Report, it was during the period under review that its effects on the work of the Commission were felt fully.

The Joint Commission, which is an important part of the machinery for the implementation of the Geneva Agreements, has not resumed its activities since May, 1956.

The Commission had requested the Co-Chairmen to give urgent consideration to the situation mentioned in its letter of September 14, 1956. There has been no progress toward a solution of those difficulties. In fact they have further increased.

66. A major difficulty facing the Commission arises from the failure to hold consultations between the two parties and free nation-wide elections with a view to reunification of Veitnam. . . . The Commission is naturally anxious about the duration of its stay in Vietnam which is conditioned by the political settlement in this country, as envisaged in the Final Declaration of the Geneva Conference.

Airfields and U. S. Arms In South Vietnam: The Problems of Inspection (1958)*

25. The Commission completed reconnaissance of the airfields in South Vietnam referred to in . . . the Seventh Interim Report and decided, Polish Delegation dissenting, that it was not necessary to control any of them. As regards the new airfields referred to in . . . that Report, the Government of the Republic of Vietnam informed that while some of these were not fit for use, the others were damaged.

27. During the period under review, the Commission requested the P.A.V. High Command to make necessary ar-

* Eighth Interim Report of the International Commission for Supervision and Control in Vietnam (Vietnam No. 1 [1958], Command Paper, 509). London: Great Britain Parliamentary Sessional Papers, XXX (1957/58), pp. 10-13.

rangements for a visit of the Air Advisers to the Bach Mai airfield, with a view to ascertaining the need for reviewing its previous decisions to control the airfield, as the P.A.V. High Command stated that the airfield is not in use. The reply of the P.A.V. High Command is awaited.

30. In . . . the Seventh Interim Report reference was made to the alleged factual materialization of a military alliance between the Republic of Vietnam and the member countries of SEATO. A new complaint of the P.A.V. High Command concerning the presence of the representatives of the Republic of Vietnam at the SEATO Conference held at Manila in March, 1958, as observers, has been sent to the Government of the Republic of Vietnam for comments.

31. In . . . the Seventh Interim Report, references were made to the American Military Missions called TERM (Temporary Equipment Recovery Mission), MAAG (Military Assistance Advisory Group), TRIM (Training Reorganization and Inspection Mission) and CATO (Combat Arms Training Organization).

32. The Government of the Republic of Vietnam submitted a report on TERM personnel up to September 30, 1957, and a statement of damaged or worn-out material of American origin shipped out of Vietnam up to May 31, 1957. Monthly reports asked for by the Commission have been submitted, thereafter, though not on time, and no change in TERM personnel has been reported. . . . Regarding the question when this Mission, which is claimed to be temporary, would be completing its task and leaving Vietnam, the Government of the Republic of Vietnam has replied that it is impossible to forecast when TERM will cease its activities. The matter is under consideration.

As regards MAAG and other organizations referred to above, the Government of the Republic of Vietnam did not supply information on all the points requested by the Commission and the Commission expressed grave concern that all assistance and co-operation in this matter had not been offered in terms of Article 25 and asked the Mission in charge of relations with the Commission to supply the necessary information. The Canadian Delegation dissented from this decision citing Article 25 because it held that the essential information had already been supplied. Indian and Polish Delegations would like to point out that the Commission had unanimously decided earlier that the information furnished was inadequate and unsatisfactory. . . .

34. As regards the question of physical control of the cargo of the incoming aircraft at Saigon airport . . . the Republic of Vietnam informed the Commission that military planes transporting military personnel or war material would stop at the civilian parking area in order to allow physical control after unloading, but not of the material inside the planes. Since the receipt of this letter there have, however, been some instances where incoming planes have proceeded directly to the military parking area to which the Commission's team has no access and in some cases no manifest concerning personnel or cargo were produced. . . .

35. The Commission's teams have been experiencing difficulties in the matter of having access to the control tower registers at airfields and registers at sea ports. The P.A.V. High Command has, "as an exception," agreed to make available for inspection these registers, when required by the Commission's teams, where the control is not daily. Since November 1957, the teams in the North have had access to control tower registers at Gia Lam airport and to port registers at Campha, the only two places where the Commission has asked for these registers. The Government of the Republic of Vietnam has not so far acceded to the Commission's request. The Commission has directed its Senior Military Advisers to explain to the party the Commission's point of view and the necessity and requirements of the teams having access to these registers, and recommend what action should be taken to meet the requirements of the Commission. Their report is under consideration.

38. The foregoing chapters set forth, in brief, the performance of the parties with respect to the implementation of the provisions of the Geneva Agreements.

It will be seen from these chapters that while in North Vietnam the Commission generally continued to receive the necessary co-operation, it did not . . . receive the required co-operation in keeping a team at Phuc Hoa for continuous control.

In South Vietnam the Commission received during the period under review an increased measure of co-operation from the Government of the Republic of Vietnam with re-

spect to the supplying of copies of documents concerning
civilian internees, though the implementation of the Commission's recommendations to release some civilian internees
in which the party maintained its own interpretation of
Article 21 did not show any improvement. There has been
an increased measure of co-operation from the Government
of the Republic of Vietnam with regard to notifications
under Articles 16 and 17, but . . . there have been some
cases of procedural contravention of Articles 16 (*f*) and 17
(*e*) and some lack of necessary co-operation in respect of
physical control of incoming aircraft. The Commission did
not receive . . . full information regarding MAAG within
the time specified . . .

*Violations of the Geneva Agreements by the Republic of [South] Vietnam (1960)**

[T]he Government of the Republic of Vietnam reiterated its stand that for security reasons the Commission
should agree to the time notices required by the party in
respect of every movement by the Commission's teams and
stated that, in the event of the Commission insisting on the
observance of time notices prescribed by it, the Government
of the Republic of Vietnam should be absolved of all responsibility for security. The Commission drew the attention
of the Government of the Republic of Vietnam to its responsibility for ensuring security under Article 35 of the
Geneva Agreement and stated that the Commission could
not take this responsibility upon itself. The Commission once
again recommended to the Government of the Republic of
Vietnam that all the control restrictions imposed by it on the
Commission's teams be removed. . . .

47. Subsequent to the issue of the communication in regard
to the American military mission called TERM (Temporary
Equipment Recovery Mission), referred to in . . .
the Ninth Interim Report, the Government of the Republic of Vietnam intimated that large additional quantities

* *Tenth Interim Report of the International Commission for
Supervision and Control in Vietnam* (Vietnam No. 1 [1960],
Command Paper, 1040). London: Great Britain Parliamentary Ses-
sional Papers, XXXVI (1959/60), pp. 18-21.

of war material had been discovered and that it was materially impossible to forecast when the activities of TERM would cease. This position was not acceptable to the Commission and the party was asked to furnish final information in this regard. . . .

48. In regard to the American military mission called the Military Assistance Advisory Group (MAAG), referred to in . . . the Ninth Interim Report, the Commission, having considered the reply received from the Government of the Republic of Vietnam, reiterated its concern and informed the party that it had not furnished full information and specific answers to queries raised by the Commission . . .

50. The Commission continued to receive complaints from the P.A.V. High Command, during the period under report, in regard to the alleged increase in the strength of American military personnel in the Republic of Vietnam. The Government of the Republic of Vietnam furnished its explanation for the excess figure of 759 of arrivals over departures of American military personnel in the Republic of Vietnam for the period January 7, 1956, to December 28, 1957. . . The Commission, having considered this reply, informed the party that it had not shown cause why violation of Article 16 of the Geneva Agreement should not be recorded.

51. . . . There were 86 cases in the Republic of Vietnam wherein aircraft either arrived without prior notification or in respect of which manifests or other documents were not produced by the party during the period under report. The Commission is examining these cases and will take appropriate action in the matter. . . .

During the period under report, the Commission considered a case which occurred in North Vietnam of a Liaison Officer refusing to approach the captain of a ship for permission for the Commission's team to board the ship when requested by the team. This incident occurred prior to the period under review. The party has been requested to issue suitable instructions to its liaison staff to avoid a recurrence of such incidents.

1 *The vigorous dissent of the Polish Delegation is recorded in Appendix B of this [Tenth] report, omitted here.—ed.*

Achievements and Setbacks of the Commission (1960)*

57. A complaint was received from the Government of the Republic of Vietnam regarding the alleged introduction of war material into North Vietnam at Haiphong by s.s. *Lidice*. The Commission informed the party that this ship visited the port of Haiphong in June 1959 and was controlled by the Commission's team which did not report the introduction of any war material. The case was, therefore, closed. . . .

CHAPTER VI

CO-OPERATION OF THE PARTIES TO THE AGREEMENT

62. It will be observed that while in North Vietnam the Commission continued to receive, in general, the necessary co-operation, it did not . . . receive the required co-operation in regard to its decision to carry out a reconnaissance of the Bach Mai airfield.

63. The Commission did not receive the required co-operation from the Government of the Republic of Vietnam in the matter of removal of time notice restrictions on the movement of the mobile elements of the Commission's Fixed Teams, as mentioned in paragraph 45. The Commission, therefore, continues to be forced to restrict its supervision and control in South Vietnam to the extent permitted by the party.

. . . Another difficulty [of] the Commission in South Vietnam, during the period under report, concerns the reconnaissance and control of airfields. The Government of the Republic of Vietnam afforded facilities to the Commission to carry out the reconnaissance of the airfields at Ban Me Thuot and Tourane but in all other cases raised the question of parity. . . .

The Commission has, therefore, been unable to carry out the reconnaissance in these cases so far. The Government

* *Tenth Interim Report of the International Commission for Supervision and Control in Vietnam* (Vietnam No. 1 [1960], Command Paper, 1040). London: Great Britain Parliamentary Sessional Papers, XXXVI (1959/60), pp. 22-25.

of the Republic of Vietnam did not implement the Commission's recommendation in respect of the control of Bienhoa airfield. . . .

There was no change, in principle, in the stand taken by the Government of the Republic of Vietnam in regard to Article 14 (c), although the party sent replies to the Commission's communications in several cases under this Article. However, the Commission was unable to investigate . . . complaints . . . since it did not receive the necessary assistance and co-operation from the party. During the period under review, the Government of the Republic of Vietnam maintained its position as regards the interpretation of Article 21 and did not implement the Commission's recommendations. . . .

CHAPTER VII
CONCLUSIONS

66. The Commission has referred in some of its earlier Interim Reports to the lacuna created in the machinery for implementation of the Geneva Agreement as a result of the withdrawal of the French High Command and the consequent non-functioning of the Joint Commission. . . .

[Thus] there is no possibility of the Joint Commission being revived to resume its activities so long as the Government of the Republic of Vietnam maintains its attitude. The efforts made by the Commission to find a practical solution to this difficulty with the co-operation of the two parties have not, so far, been successful. The Commission has already informed the Co-Chairmen that it is faced with a major difficulty which it cannot resolve on the spot and has urged them to give it their urgent consideration for such action as they may consider necessary.

67. The tendency of the parties to differ from the Commission's interpretation of some of the provisions of the Geneva Agreement and to refuse to accept and implement the Commission's recommendations and decisions, maintaining their respective stands, has continued during the period under report. The Commission feels concerned since the effectiveness of the Commission in carrying out its tasks of supervision and control under the Geneva Agreement requires that the parties accept its interpretation as final and comply with its recommendations and decisions in all cases. The Commission hopes that, in view of the importance

of maintaining peace in Vietnam, the parties will give the Commission all possible assistance and co-operation to which it is entitled under Article 25 of the Geneva Agreement.

68. During the period under report, there has been no progress in regard to the political settlement envisaged in the Final Declaration. The parties have not held consultations with a view to holding free nation-wide elections leading to the reunification of Vietnam and thereby facilitating early fulfillment of the tasks assigned to this Commission and the termination of its activities. The Commission is confident that this important problem is engaging the attention of the Co-Chairmen and the Geneva Powers and that they will take whatever measures they deem necessary to resolve it.

*"Democratic Freedoms" in 1961**

CHAPTER III

DEMOCRATIC FREEDOMS UNDER ARTICLES 14 (C) AND 14(D)

13. During this period the Commission received 239 complaints under Article 14 (*c*) from the P.A.V. High Command against the Government of the Republic of Vietnam. Ninety complaints out of these 239 covering the period from February 1, 1960 to June 30, 1960, and 17 complaints carried over from November 1, 1959 to January 31, 1960, were forwarded to the Government of the Republic of Vietnam for comments within a period of seven months, Polish Delegation dissenting on the extension of the time-limit from six to seven months.

14. A reference was made in . . . the Tenth Interim Report to the case of alleged food poisoning and shooting resulting in deaths of a large number of former resistance members detained in Phu Loi concentration camp. A number of fresh complaints in this regard has been received from the P.A.V. High Command. A reply from the South Viet-

* *Eleventh Interim Report of the International Commission for Supervision and Control in Vietnam* (Vietnam No. 1 [1961], Command Paper, 1551). London: Great Britain Parliamentary Sessional Papers, XXXIX (1961/62), pp. 8-9.

namese Mission to the original complaints has also been received. These are under consideration. . . .

16. Replies of the P.A.V. High Command have been received with regard to the 16 remaining cases referred to in . . . the Tenth Interim Report which concerned petitions under Article 14 (c) against the North. The P.A.V. High Command's comments on th[ese] . . . cases . . . are still under consideration.

17. During the period under report the Commission further considered the complaint from the P.A.V. High Command alleging that the passing of Law 10/59 by the National Assembly of South Vietnam [1] constituted a violation of Article 14 (c) of the Geneva Agreement. The Commission decided, Polish Delegation dissenting, that the Law does not contain any provision specifically designed to discriminate against, or subject to reprisals, persons or organizations on account of their activities during the hostilities, and therefore, Law 10/59 as such does not attract Article 14 (c) or any other Article of the Geneva Agreement. However, the Commission also noted that certain provisions of this Law are of such a nature that they may in specific cases be applied in a manner which may be incompatible with Article 14 (c) of the Geneva Agreement. . . .

Military Operations in Vietnam (1961)*

CHAPTER V

BAN ON THE INTRODUCTION OF FRESH TROOPS, MILITARY PERSONNEL, ARMS, AND MUNITIONS——MILITARY BASES IN VIETNAM . . . .

. . . [T]he Government of the Republic of Vietnam, in a subsequent note, alleged that the airfield of Thai Nguyen in North Vietnam had been repaired and put into service again and that the planes, forming part of the Peo-

---

[1] See pp. 256–262.–ed.

* Eleventh Interim Report of the International Commission for Supervision and Control in Vietnam (Vietnam No. 1 [1961], Command Paper, 1551). London: Great Britain Parliamentary Sessional Papers, XXXIX (1961/62), pp. 13-25.

ples' Republic of China's aid, were hidden in the workshops of the Corps of Engineers of this area. In October 1960, the Commission requested the P.A.V. High Command to offer its comments. The party in reply stated that this airfield has remained unserviceable to date and that the allegations of the Republic of Vietnam are unfounded. The case is under consideration by the Commission. . . .

[*Various allegations of violations by both parties—ed.*]

49. In paragraph 47 of the Tenth Interim Report, it was stated that the Commission recommended to the Government of the Republic of Vietnam that the Temporary Equipment Recovery Mission (TERM) complete its work and all its personnel be withdrawn from Vietnam by December 31, 1960. During December 1960 and January/February 1961 the Commission received three communications from the P.A.V. High Command alleging that TERM has not ceased to exist in South Vietnam and instead was extending the scope of its activity under the assumed name of the Logistics Section of the Military Assistance Advisory Group (MAAG). Meanwhile, the Government of the Republic of Vietnam informed the Commission in January 1961 that TERM had ceased its activities and was disbanded on December 31, 1960. The party further stated that out of the total strength of 350 personnel, 261 had left South Vietnam during the course of 1960 and the remaining 89 were transferred on the spot to MAAG on account of their technical ability. They also stated that this transfer of 89 personnel to MAAG was within the authorized quota of MAAG. The Commission considered the communications from the Government of the Republic of Vietnam and the P.A.V. Liaison Mission and asked the Government of the Republic of Vietnam to furnish more detailed information regarding the evacuation of TERM personnel from Vietnam and distribution by numbers of officers and enlisted men within MAAG; the party's reply is awaited. . . .

The Polish Delegation holds the view that the communication of the Government of the Republic of Vietnam dated January 11, 1961, informing the Commission, among other things, that 89 personnel of TERM have been transferred on the spot to MAAG amounts to non-implementation of the Commission's decision under which this mission had to cease its activities and its entire personnel had to leave Vietnam by December 31, 1960.

The concern of the Polish Delegation is all the stronger in the light of an allegation made by the P.A.V. High Command that not 89 but—in fact—the whole TERM continues to operate in the Republic of Vietnam incorporated into MAAG mission under an assumed name of the Logistics Section of MAAG. In this connection the Polish Delegation holds the view that this fact amounts to a violation of Articles 16 and 25 of the Geneva Agreement.

With regard to the above sub-paragraph the Indian and Canadian Delegations consider that as this matter is still under consideration and no decision has been taken, any conclusions are not justified. . . .

In the view of the Polish Delegation the existence and activity of MAAG in the Republic of Vietnam after the signing of the Geneva Agreement are inconsistent with its provisions and they contravene Articles 16 and 19 of the Agreement as well as paragraphs 4, 5, and 10 of the Final Declaration.

The MAAG mission, whose activities have never been subjected to the Commission's control despite the Commission's efforts, should have been withdrawn from this country along with the French Expeditionary Corps.

In the opinion of the Polish Delegation the Commission's decision allowing the party to double the strength of the personnel of MAAG is contradictory with the letter and spirit of the Geneva Agreement and particularly with its Article 16 and paragraph 4 of the Final Declaration. For these reasons the Polish Delegation voted against this decision. . . .

61. During the period under report the Commission received complaints from the Government of the Republic of Vietnam accusing the Government of the Democratic Republic of Vietnam of open and direct aggression in Kontum and Pleiku provinces during October 1960 from North Vietnam through the territory of Laos. The Commission received three communications from the Government of the Republic of Vietnam in this regard, two in November 1960 and one in December 1960. The Commission considered this matter twice, once in December 1960 and again in January 1961. The Commission at the latter meeting decided to forward these allegations made by the Government of the Republic

of Vietnam to the Government of the Democratic Republic of Vietnam for their comments, with the Polish Delegation not participating in the vote. The reply from the party is awaited.

The Polish Delegation did not participate in the voting since, in its view, the South Vietnamese complaint did not constitute a *prima facie* case. The Polish Delegation considered that this complaint could not be entertained by the Commission as it is entirely groundless.

The Indian and Canadian Delegations believe it is the responsibility of the Commission to investigate if necessary all allegations covered by the Geneva Agreement made by either party, including those of aggression, without attempting to prejudge the merits of the case. As this complaint is still under investigation the Indian and Canadian Delegations are of the view that to pronounce an advance judgment on it is inappropriate. . . .

66. During the period covered by the Report, the Commission recorded three contraventions of the procedure contained in point (*f*) of Article 16 and 34 contraventions of the procedure contained in point (*e*) of Article 17 of the Geneva Agreement by the Government of the Republic of Vietnam. No contravention of Articles 16 and 17 of the Geneva Agreement was recorded in the period under report against the Democratic Republic of Vietnam.

During the same period, the Commission received from the Government of the Republic of Vietnam six complaints alleging violations of Article 17 by the P.A.V. and from the P.A.V. High Command against the Republic of Vietnam 122 and 132 complaints alleging violation of Articles 16 and 17 respectively. . . .

Aggression, Subversion, and a Divided Commission (1962)*

4. Since the presentation of the 11th Interim Report, the situation in Vietnam has shown signs of rapid deterioration.

* *Special Report . . . of the International Commission for Supervision and Control in Vietnam* (Vietnam No. 1 [1962], Command Paper, 1755). London: Great Britain Parliamentary Sessional Papers, XXXIX (1961/62), pp. 4-11, 21-22.

The Commission is obliged to make this Special Report to the Co-Chairmen with regard to the serious allegations of aggression and subversion on the part of the Democratic Republic of Vietnam against the Republic of Vietnam and the serious charges of violation of Articles 16, 17, and 19 of the Geneva Agreement by the Republic of Vietnam, in receiving military aid from the United States of America.

The Polish Delegation dissents from the views expressed in this Special Report. The Statement of the Polish Delegation is forwarded herewith.

Mention was . . . made in paragraph 61 of the 11th Interim Report to the complaints, which the Commission had received from the Government of the Republic of Vietnam, accusing the Government of the Democratic Republic of Vietnam of aggression in the Kontum and Pleiku provinces during October 1960. Complaints of this nature continued to increase during 1961. In June 1961, the Commission made known its stand regarding its competence to entertain and examine complaints of this nature in terms of specific Articles of the Geneva Agreement.

6. The Commission also received several complaints from the High Command of the People's Army of Vietnam (P.A.V.) making serious allegations with regard to the increased introduction of U.S. military personnel into South Vietnam, along with substantial quantities of war material, in contravention of Articles 16 and 17. All these allegations were forwarded to the South Vietnamese Mission for comments. The party in most cases denied these allegations. But the Commission was not in a position to make a precise assessment as to the correctness or otherwise of these allegations, as the Commission's teams at most points of entry have not been able to carry out effective inspections and controls. However, the South Vietnamese Mission did state in July 1961, that whatever American aid its Government was receiving was meant to fight Communist subversion in South Vietnam, and in support of this contention it had also referred to the text of the communiqué published after the visit of the U.S. Vice-President Johnson to Saigon, in May 1961.[1]

7. While the Commission continued to function in this difficult atmosphere, a communication was received on September 9, 1961, from the Liaison Mission of the Republic of

[1] See pp. 204–205.—ed.

Vietnam, alleging that the P.A.V. forces had launched another action in the Kontum region on September 1, 1961. The letter containing these allegations was forwarded to the Liaison Mission of the P.A.V. High Command for its comments. In its reply . . . dated December 11, 1961, the Mission stated that "the P.A.V. High Command will resolutely reject all decisions taken by the International Commission relating to the so-called 'subversive activities' in South Vietnam, a question which has no relevance to the Geneva Agreement." It further informed the Commission that "henceforth the Mission would find itself constrained to resolutely reject all possible requests for comments of this kind . . ."

9. The Legal Committee has made a careful examination of the various allegations and the evidence produced to support them, in the form of documents and other material evidence, and has made the following report, with the Polish Member dissenting . . . :

> (2) Having examined the complaints and the supporting material sent by the South Vietnamese Mission, the Committee has come to the conclusion that in specific instances there is evidence to show that armed and unarmed personnel, arms, munitions, and other supplies have been sent from the zone in the North to the zone in the South with the object of supporting, organizing, and carrying out hostile activities, including armed attacks, directed against the Armed Forces and Administration of the zone in the South. These acts are in violation of Articles 10, 19, 24, and 27 of the Agreement on the Cessation of Hostilities in Vietnam.
>
> (3) In examining the complaints and the supporting material, in particular documentary material sent by the South Vietnamese Mission, the Committee has come to the further conclusion that there is evidence to show that the P.A.V. has allowed the zone in the North to be used for inciting, encouraging, and supporting hostile activities in the zone in the South, aimed at the overthrow of the Administration in the South. The use of the zone in the North for such activities is in violation of Articles 19, 24, and 27 of the Agreement on the Cessation of Hostilities in Vietnam. . . . [2]

[2] *The U.S. Government has quoted this part of the* Special Report *in* Department of State Bulletin, *XLVII (July 16, 1962),*

11. Concurrently with the developments referred to in paragraphs 7 and 8 above, and subsequently, the Commission received communications from the P.A.V. High Command and its Liaison Mission alleging direct military intervention in South Vietnam by the Government of the United States of America, and ever-increasing import of war material and introduction of military personnel in violation of the Geneva Agreement. . . .

12. Since December 1961 the Commission's teams in South Vietnam have been persistently denied the right to control and inspect, which are part of their mandatory tasks. Thus, these teams, though they were able to observe the steady and continuous arrival of war material, including aircraft carriers with helicopters on board, were unable, in view of the denial of controls, to determine precisely the quantum and nature of war material unloaded and introduced into South Vietnam. . .

20. Taking all the facts into consideration, and basing itself on its own observations and authorized statements made in the United States of America and the Republic of Vietnam, the Commission concludes that the Republic of Vietnam has violated Articles 16 and 17 of the Geneva Agreement in receiving the increased military aid from the United States of America in the absence of any established credit in its favor. The Commission is also of the view that, though there may not be any formal military alliance between the Governments of the United States of America and the Republic of Vietnam, the establishment of a U.S. Military Assistance Command in South Vietnam, as well as the introduction of a large number of U.S. military personnel beyond the stated strength of the MAAG (Military Assistance Advisory Group), amounts to a factual military alliance, which is prohibited under Article 19 of the Geneva Agreement. . . .

[The Commission issued no reports between 1962 and 1965—ed.]

---

pp. 109-110, and in Aggression From the North: The Record of North Vietnam's Campaign to Conquer South Vietnam [Department of State Publication 7839; Far Eastern Series 130] (Washington, D.C., [February], 1965), p. 30. But the rest of this Special Report was not referred to.—ed.

The Control Commission in the Midst of Escalating War (February, 1965)*

. . . On February 7, 1965, a joint communiqué was issued by the Acting Premier of the Republic of Vietnam (RV), acting under the authority of the National Security Council, and the Ambassador of the United States, acting under the authority of his Government. This communiqué announced that military action had been taken against military installations in the Democratic Republic of Vietnam (DRV). . . .

> [The communiqué reads: "The Acting Prime Minister of the Republic of Vietnam, acting under the authority of the National Security Council, and the United States Ambassador, acting under the authority of the United States Government, announced this evening that military action has been taken today against military installations in North Vietnam.
>
> "These installations had been employed in the direction and support of those engaged in aggression in South Vietnam, such as the attacks earlier this morning against installation and personnel in the areas of Pleiku and Tuy Hoa."—ed.]

On the same day, the Liaison Mission of the People's Army of Vietnam (P.A.V.) transmitted the text of a communiqué which was issued by the Ministry of Defense of the Government of the Democratic Republic of Vietnam referring to the bombing and strafing of the DRV; subsequently the Government of the Democratic Republic of Vietnam issued on February 8, 1965 a communiqué on these events, which was communicated by the P.A.V. Liaison Mission in their letter to the International Commission. The Liaison Mission of the P.A.V. brought to the notice of the International Commission that again on February 8, 1965, bombing and strafing of a number of places had taken place and requested the International Commission "to consider and condemn without delay these violations of utmost gravity

* *Special Report . . . of the International Commission for Supervision and Control in Vietnam* (Vietnam No. 1 [1965], Command Paper, 2069), [unbound], pp. 4-9, 12-15.

and report them to the Co-Chairmen of the Geneva Conference on Indochina." . . .

[These communiqués read, in part:
"Telegram dated February 8, 1965.

"FROM: COL HA VAN LAU CHIEF OF THE
        LIAISON MISSION OF VIETNAM
        PEOPLES ARMY HIGH COMMAND

"TO: THE AMBASSADOR M. A. RAHMAN CHAIRMAN ICSC VIET-
STATEMENT BY THE GOVERNMENT OF THE DEMOCRATIC RE-
PUBLIC OF VIETNAM DATED FEBRUARY 8, 1965 REGARDING THE
BOMBING AND STRAFING OF A NUMBER OF PLACES IN NORTH
VIETNAM BY THE U.S. AIR FORCE ON FEBRUARY 7, 1965

"With a view to carrying out their scheme of sabotaging the
1954 Geneva Agreements on Indochina the U.S. imperialists
have unleashed a special war in South Vietnam. But they
have come up against the resolute and vigorous struggle of
the South Vietnamese people and have sustained heavy defeat. In an attempt to retrieve their defeat they have been
endeavoring to step up the dirty war in South Vietnam while
increasing provocation and acts of sabotage against North
Vietnam . . . The Vietnamese peoples who are fighting for
their sacred national rights will certainly not be cowed by the
U.S. attempt at intimidation, instead they will increase their
forces, will step up the struggle, and are confident that their
just cause will elicit stronger support from the world's peoples
and that the vile acts of aggression of the U.S. imperialists
will be even more strongly condemned by the opinion of
progressive mankind. Victory will certainly belong to the
Vietnamese people. U.S. imperialists are doomed to ignominious defeat."—ed.]

On February 8, 1965, it was officially announced that
further military action on the territory of the DRV had
been undertaken by RV and U.S. aircraft. . . .

These documents point to the seriousness of the situation
and indicate violations of the Geneva Agreement.

M. A. RAHMAN   R. B. STAWICKI
Representative of India   *Acting Representative of the*
                                 Polish People's Republic

SAIGON:
February 13, 1965.

Part Six

The Reign of Ngo Dinh Diem

One of Ngo Dinh Diem's earliest supporters wrote of him in 1959 as the prophet of an indigenous Asian form of democracy.[1] Much later, after Diem's policies had generated great strife in Vietnam, after Diem and his family had been overthrown and the Premier himself assassinated with his brother, the same writer made a timely reevaluation of the philosophy of Ngo Dinh Diem and found it to be nothing less than "peasant-based, revolutionary fascism."[2]

The change in Fishel's outlook doubtless had something to do with the passage of time, but it may have also been related to the fact that when he wrote the first piece Fishel was an intimate adviser to Diem, and when he wrote the second he was back in the academic environment of East Lansing, Michigan. Wesley Fishel's strange metamorphosis suggests a number of interesting questions about Ngo Dinh Diem and his American champions. First, what was the nature of the alternative they sought to a Communist-dominated Vietnamese nationalism? How did an obscure Asian politician gain so many American friends? What did these valuable contacts mean to Diem? Why, with such high-placed friends and the initial backing of the United States, did Diem fall?

The readings in this section provide a number of different perspectives on these questions. The distinguished French authority on Vietnam, Philippe Devillers, recounts the stages by which Diem alienated potential sources of support in Vietnam and brought upon himself a massive, indigenous insurgency. Robert Scheer unfolds the stages in the generation of the pro-Diem lobby in America, in which Professor Fishel played a central role. Finally, a succession of official statements retrace the course of U.S. military, financial, and political support for Diem. From all three perspectives, there emerges a grim record of failure.

So momentous a failure as the fall of Diem had many causes. One was the American tendency to view Communism

[1] *Wesley Fishel in* The New Leader, *pp. 195–204.*

[2] *Wesley R. Fishel, "Vietnam: Is Victory Possible?" Foreign Policy Association,* Headline Series, *no. 163 (February 1964), p. 16.*

everywhere as an evil so monstrous that any measures taken to suppress it are justified. It was this intellectual rigidity about Communism, and the imperatives of the cold war that President Kennedy was referring to in the address delivered at American University, Washington, D.C. a few months before his death. At that time he called for a reexamination of cold war attitudes in the interest of intellectual honesty and mutual survival.[3] But the man who made this appeal in the summer of 1963 has also been responsible for the decision in 1961 to step up the war upon the insurgents, whom Diem collectively referred to by the pejorative term "Vietcong."[4] It was possible that in the last months of his Administration Kennedy was indeed groping toward a new kind of peace.

Another factor in the American failure during the reign of Diem was a certain ambiguity about who was the enemy. Certainly the guerrillas were the most obvious enemies, but the military drive against them was continuously hampered by the internal political system in Saigon. Diem and his family used the army as a political tool, promoted or demoted officers on political or personal (not military) grounds, kept key regiments out of the war zones in order to protect Saigon from a coup.[5] But the war against the "Vietcong" went badly, and a dedicated group of American newsmen reported what they saw. The Ngo family began to use their influence to harass the U.S. press corps, and received help in this from the American diplomatic mission and the American military establishment. President Kennedy gently suggested to the publisher of the New York Times that its young reporter in Vietnam, David Halberstam, be given a vacation.[6] The Times resisted the pressure, and Halberstam

[3] John F. Kennedy, "What Kind of Peace," reprinted in Hillman M. Bishop and Samuel Hendel (eds.), Basic Issues of American Democracy (5th ed., New York, 1965), pp. 585-591.

[4] See p. 39.

[5] A huge literature documenting these phenomena is readily available. See John Mecklin, Mission in Torment: An Intimate Account of the U.S. Role in Vietnam (Garden City, N.Y., 1965), chap. III; Malcolm W. Browne, The New Face of War (Indianapolis/Kansas City/New York, 1965), esp. chap. IX; David Halberstam, The Making of a Quagmire (New York, 1964). A defender of Diem—as Anthony T. Bouscaren, The Last of the Mandarins: Diem of Vietnam (Pittsburgh, Penn., 1965)—is obliged simply to ignore this evidence.

[6] Halberstam, "Getting the News in Vietnam," Commentary XXXIX (January, 1965).

stayed on, closely covering the Buddhist crisis and the coup that brought about Diem's fall and death. For this reporting Halberstam won a Pulitzer prize.

The failure in Vietnam that was clearly marked by the overthrow and death of Ngo Dinh Diem in November 1963 was not wholly an American failure. There was an aura of Greek tragedy about the aloof, doctrinaire Catholic who proclaimed a republic in South Vietnam in 1955. His tendency to build a family dictatorship, despite the needs of his country and the wishes of his American supporters, raises the interesting question of whether Diem was an American puppet or vice versa. In any case, by the fall of 1963 he had proved his inability to preside over a country of such ethnic, religious, and political diversity as Vietnam. His overthrow had immense significance for the future of Vietnam and for the possibilities of world peace.

Ngo Dinh Diem on Elections in Vietnam
(July 16, 1955)*

The National Government has emphasized time and time again the price it has paid for the defense of the unity of the country and of true democracy. We did not sign the Geneva Agreements. We are not bound in any way by these Agreements, signed against the will of the Vietnamese people. Our policy is a policy of peace, but nothing will lead us astray from our goal: the unity of our country—a unity in freedom and not in slavery.

Serving the cause of our nation more than ever, we will struggle for the reunification of our homeland. We do not reject the principle of free elections as peaceful and democratic means to achieve that unity. Although elections constitute one of the bases of true democracy, they will be meaningful only on the condition that they are absolutely free.

Faced now with a regime of oppression as practiced by the Vietminh, we remain skeptical concerning the possibility of fulfilling the conditions of free elections in the North. We shall not miss any opportunity which would permit the unification of our homeland in freedom, but it is out of the question for us to consider any proposal from

* Embassy of Vietnam, Washington, D.C., Press and Information Service, Vol. I, no. 18 (July 22, 1955).

the Vietminh if proof is not given that they put the superior interests of the national community above those of Communism, if they do not cease violating their obligations as they have done by preventing our countrymen of the North from going South or by recently attacking, together with the Communist Pathet Lao, the friendly state of Laos.

The mission falls to us, the Nationalists, to accomplish the reunification of our country in conditions that are most democratic and most effective to guarantee our independence. The free world is with us. Of this we are certain. I am confident that I am a faithful interpreter of our state of mind when I affirm solemnly our will to resist Communism.

To those who live above the 17th Parallel, I ask them to have confidence. With the agreement and the backing of the free world, the National Government will bring you independence in freedom.

South Vietnamese Policy On Reunification
(August 9, 1955)*

In a radio broadcast of last July 16, the Government of the State of Vietnam clearly defined its position regarding the problem of territorial reunification.

The Government does not consider itself bound in any way by the Geneva Agreements which it did not sign. It affirms once again that placing the interests of the nation as its first consideration it is determined, in any circumstances, to reach the obvious goal of its policy—the unity of the country in peace and freedom.

The Vietminh authorities sent a letter dated July 19 to the Government in which they asked for a pre-election consultation conference, thus, for propaganda purposes, seeking to give credence to the false idea that they would be defenders of territorial unity.

It is recalled that last year at Geneva, the Vietminh claimed a viable economic zone while recommending the partition. At the same time, the delegation of the State of Vietnam proposed an armistice, even though provisional, without partitioning Vietnam in order to safeguard the sacred right of the Vietnamese people to territorial unity, national independence, and freedom.[1] Through the voice of its dele-

* Embassy of Vietnam, Washington, D.C., Press and Information Service, Vol. I, no. 20 (August 19, 1955)

[1] See pp. 157–159.—ed.

ation, the Government affirmed that it hoped to fulfill the
aspirations of the Vietnamese people by every means at its
disposal resulting from the independence and sovereignty
solemnly recognized by France toward the State of Vietnam
which is the only legal State.[2]

The policy of the Government remains unchanged toward
the partitioning of the country accomplished against its will.
Serving the cause of true democracy, the Government is
anxious that all Vietnamese throughout the entire country
may live without fear, and that they be totally free from all
dictatorship and oppression. The Government considers the
principle of essentially free elections as a democratic and
peaceful institution, but believes that conditions of freedom
of life and of voting must be assured beforehand. From
this point of view, nothing constructive will be done as long
as the Communist regime of the North does not permit
each Vietnamese citizen to enjoy democratic freedoms and
the basic fundamental rights of man.

Vietnam's Democratic One-Man Rule

BY WESLEY R. FISHEL*

"When I use a word," Humpty Dumpty said, in rather a
scornful tone, "it means just what I choose it to mean
either more nor less."

"The question is," said Alice, "whether you *can* make
words mean so many different things."

"The question is," said Humpty Dumpty, "which is to be
master, that's all."

Every age has its shibboleths, every people its fetishes
and phobias. The color words which express our fears and
hopes, our likes and dislikes, constitute a semantic corset
which we bind ourselves as we march bravely along in a
world populated by scientific goblins, technological sprites,
and ideological angels and demons.

Our angels today are "democrats" and "anti-Communists";
our demons are "dictators" and "Communists." These crea-
tures come in many shapes, varied sizes, and diverse forms.

* Professor of Political Science at Michigan State University,
and former head of the MSU Advisory Group in Vietnam, 1956-
1958. This selection is from *The New Leader*, XLII (November
1959), pp. 10-13. By permission.

[2] *But see the Declaration of Abdication of Emperor Bao Dai
(pp. 59-61) which would seem to establish in 1945 the legitimacy
of the Democratic Republic of Vietnam.—ed.*

And when we stop every now and then to think about our "friends" and our "foes" we feel more than a little confused. For we are living in a world that has suddenly changed and expanded. The family of nations is no longer a comfortably small club of European "Powers," more or less Christian in character (with Japan holding "alternate membership"). No, now it includes all sorts of heathens—many of them brown, still others black, and most of them non-Christian!

In tropical West Africa, out of the loins of the British Commonwealth, is born a "constitutional" "democratic" state named Ghana. And before the ink is dry on its birth certificate, its elected leader is imprisoning his opponents and castigating his country's constitution in a most disconcerting manner. And on the ruins of the Dutch empire in the farthermost Indies, an elected President who talks a good game of Jefferson has created what sounds like a contradiction in terms: a "guided democracy."

If things seem a bit confusing to us, it is because we are truly prisoners of our political vernacular. Even as our cultures haven't managed to keep pace with developments in technology, our languages have failed to stay abreast of political change. Recently, one articulate observer shrugged his verbal shoulders in annoyance over the inadequacies of the English language. He recognized the emotional trap involved in the word "dictatorship," and he explained that when he talked about the political systems of Asia he was referring to "Hamiltonian rather than Jeffersonian principles." At the same time, he concluded, let's be "more blunt and use the word dictatorship, in spite of its associations." The essential point, as he sees it, is "whose dictators" are going to rule Asia. But is this a valid conclusion? Are we faced only with a choice between—to use the horrible term once more dictators of different complexions? Let us examine here his prime example: Vietnam.

For ninety years Vietnam was a colony of France, kept subjugated by force. By their occupation of French Indochina from 1940 to 1945, the Japanese ended for all time the legend of white invincibility. After V-J Day, the attempted restoration of full French control over Vietnam was never successful. And after the disaster at Dienbienphu in 1954, the French regime of Pierre Mendès-France "simplified" France's costly involvement in the peninsula: he turned over the northern half of Vietnam to the Communist Viet-minh—and gave them a promissory note on the southern half, collectable after elections which presumably would take place two years later.

As we now know—much to our satisfaction and to the confusion of our enemies—things just didn't work out the way the negotiators at Geneva in July 1954 thought they would. And the principal reason for this surprising develop-ment has been the leadership given the free remnant of Vietnam since 1954 by Ngo Dinh Diem.

Is Ngo Dinh Diem a "dictator" or a "democrat"? As one examines the structure of the Republic of Vietnam and the behavior of President Ngo, he learns that (a) Ngo Dinh Diem has all the authority and all the power one needs to operate a dictatorship, but (b) he isn't operating one! Here is a leader who speaks the language of democracy, who holds the powers of a dictator, and who governs a Republic in accordance with the terms of a Constitution. The Con-stitution was written at his request by a National Assembly which he caused to be elected by the people of the Republic.

Ngo Dinh Diem did not *have* to do this. His authority and power at that moment were so absolute that he could have ruled for many years as a dictator, had he chosen to do so. But he chose instead the path of limited govern-ment, out of a long-standing and unshakable belief, which he had enunciated publicly time and again even before he came to power, that the keys to the restoration of Vietnam's stature were "the independence of the nation and the liberty of the people."

He came to power on July 7, 1954, having been selected by the Emperor Bao Dai—a lifelong political opponent—and with French approval, to be the "fall guy" when the terms of the Geneva accords would be announced. For it was a foregone conclusion as early as the first week in May 1954 that France was going to have to give up Indo-china, unless it was willing to take its chances on a further expansion and extension of a war which had already cost it fantastic treasure in both lives and material wealth. France was not willing. The new French Premier, Mendès-France, set himself a time limit for the settlement of the Indochina problem. And he understood that the settlement would offer France, at best, a period of grace before the end.

Ngo took office as Prime Minister with "full powers,

civil and military." This extraordinary grant of authority was his price for accepting the task of attempting the impossible: holding his country together in the face of a devastating flood of Communist military victories. Within three weeks, his country was cut in two and he was left with an incredible set of problems to resolve. True, the shooting war apparently was ended, at least for the time being. But under the provisions of the Geneva agreements, he had to repatriate his military forces from the now-Communist north and resettle whatever civilians might choose to move from the north to his zone of Vietnam. His representatives at Geneva had refused to sign the accords; nevertheless, his Government was regarded by its French sponsors and many other powers as responsible under them.

During the next 300 days (the time allotted for free movement between the two zones), Ngo's Government, aided by the U.S. and France, received and temporarily resettled—without a single untoward incident or an epidemic of disease—some 850,000 refugees from the Communist zone. And today virtually all these people are self-supporting citizens, truly a record to remember when one thinks of the tragedy that has marked similar refugee movements elsewhere in the world.

But this was not all. The new Prime Minister learned quickly enough that his "full powers, civil and military," existed principally on paper. He could not control the police: They were the *property*—bought and paid for—of the Binh Xuyen, a gang of thugs and racketeers who also had a well-trained and well-equipped army, and who controlled gambling, narcotics, and prostitution in the capital city of Saigon. The National Army was commanded by an opportunistic Chief of Staff, General Nguyen Van Hinh, who held a commission simultaneously as a major in the French Air Force, and who thought he could make a better Prime Minister than Ngo Dinh Diem.

Vast sections of real estate in South Vietnam were ruled in feudal fashion by leaders of the Cao Dai and Hoa Hao religious sects, which also maintained their own armies (subsidized by the French) and set a high price on their cooperation with the new Prime Minister. The Communists, after partition, withdrew their main fighting forces to the north, but left behind several thousand cadres, who were instructed to await "the day" when their leaders would move back in and take over. And the French, who regarded Ngo as anti-French, not only expected him to fall momentarily; they even made occasional unofficial efforts to assist him out of office.

Finally there were the bureaucrats. France had never permitted the Vietnamese to run their own government and administration, notwithstanding many highly publicized promises to that effect. Vietnamese cabinet ministers before Ngo's time were surrounded by French "advisors"; Duong-tan-Tai, a former Minister of Finance in one of the earlier "independent" cabinets of Bao Dai, likes to tell how the next nearest Vietnamese in his administrative hierarchy was some four levels below him. So Ngo inherited a civil service which had had virtually no experience in decision-making positions.

Ngo managed to survive. He ousted the Chief of Staff without a fight, drove the Binh Xuyen armies from the capital in a series of bloody encounters, won over or vanquished the military forces of the Cao Dai and the Hoa Hao, resettled the refugees, and reduced the Communist capability in South Vietnam from that of mounting a coup against him to one of sheer nuisance activity.

Naturally, this all required strong leadership and considerable political flexibility and manipulative skill. Nevertheless, it was rather difficult for our journalists on the scene (or on the rewrite desks back in New York) and for our political commentators to make up their minds about him. During his first 300 days Ngo was described variously as: weak, strong, monklike or ascetic, friendly, stern, inefficient, honest, corrupt, anti-French, anti-American, America's puppet, sectarian (a reference to the fact that he is a Roman Catholic), Cardinal Spellman's choice, indecisive, strong-minded, slow-acting, decisive, clumsy, skillful, conservative, liberal, and heaven only knows what else.

As a matter of fact, the only thing on which thoughtful pundits agreed during Ngo's first year in office was that his administration would fold at any moment; its failure was inevitable. And yet Ngo is with us today, and his regime now is assuredly one of the most stable and honest on the periphery of Asia. He has made highly acclaimed state visits to Washington, Manila, New Delhi, Rangoon, and Bangkok, and his Government is recognized by forty-five members of the

United Nations. Surely here is an unusual man—and a frequently misunderstood one.

He is a devout Roman Catholic, holding the reins of government in a state whose people are largely Taoist and Buddhist in their religious and philosophical outlook. Perhaps 10 percent of the population is Catholic, but the Vietnamese are notable for their spirit of religious toleration. It is worth observing that although President Ngo destroyed the political and military power of the two native religions of Vietnam, Cao Dai and Hoa Hao, they reportedly have gained thousands of new adherents in the past three years. And yet, during the critical days of 1954-55, rumors of impending religious warfare circulated through the diplomatic colony in Saigon. What was not generally recognized was that most of these rumors originated with Europeans, or with ax-grinding Vietnamese who understood that religious issues are often extremely important in European and American politics.

Indeed, this is the heart of our problem. We see Asian situations through Western eyes and in terms of Western traditions and Western situations. We persist in attempting to apply our standards, 1959-style, to peoples and situations where they have little or no direct relevance. That our Asian friends and enemies understand this habit of ours is clear, as witness the burbling praise of American democratic thought and institutions that issued from the lips of President Achmed Sukarno of Indonesia during his state visit to the United States three years ago; and compare those words with his later remarks (and acts) after his return to his own country.

In Vietnam, as in the other new states of Asia that have burst forth like popping corn in the years since World War II, independence could not have been achieved and cannot be maintained, under prevailing world conditions, without strong leadership. And strong leadership implies the possession of great power. As Sebastian Chamfort remarked to Marmontel, who was deploring the excesses of the French Revolution: "Do you suppose, then, that revolutions are made with rose water?"

As one travels through these newly born countries, he comes to realize that from the standpoint of the history of thought, the peoples of Southeast Asia are not, generally speaking, sufficiently sophisticated to understand what we mean by democracy and how they can exercise and protect their own political rights. And even though the leaders of the new states are making efforts to increase their peoples understanding of democratic concepts, their consciousness will be many years in awakening. With literacy rates that range from a low of perhaps 10 percent to a high of possibly 50 percent, the peoples of Southeast Asia should not be expected to understand, let alone embrace, the difficult articles of our democratic faith and practice. Furthermore, we often forget that our principles, stemming from Judaic-Christian Hellenic traditions, are a far cry from "The Way" of Taoism or the orderly, correct society preached by Confucius.

This is not to say that the stirring principles of the Declaration of Independence do not exercise a magnetic attraction on many Asians. It is rather to caution that the articulate few in Southeast Asia who understand, accept, and even preach the gospel of democracy are still *the few*. The unlettered majority, while they too may find the sound of the words appealing, are far more interested in the more immediate and tangible issues of securing and guarding their independence, increasing their standard of living, and developing their countries. That individual human rights may often be neglected or sacrificed in this period of national infancy should not be surprising. We may find much consolation, however, in the fact that many of the new leaders in Southeast Asia are thinking and planning in terms of enlarged areas of freedom for individual citizens, when such developments will be possible without endangering "the independence of the nation and the liberty of the people."

We do ourselves and our Asian neighbors a distinct disservice when we insist on stretching them or shrinking them to fit our particular semantic bed. Implicit in this Procrustean semantics is the assumption of the superiority of our ideas and our ways of doing things. Not only is this in itself a rather undemocratic (or, at least, unegalitarian) assumption, but it brands us as ideologically blind and inflexible. We are unlikely to win many friends or campaigns in Asia if we continue to proceed from this snobbish base.

Ngo Dinh Diem, for example, rejects both absolute individualism and absolute state power. Whether or not we agree with his interpretation of history and his view of the ends of government, they are at the very least worthy of consideration. Transmitting to the National Assembly his ideas

n what the then-projected Constitution of the Republic
nould contain, he wrote:

> We affirm that the sole legitimate end and object of
> the State is to protect the fundamental rights of the
> human person to existence and to the free development
> of his intellectual, moral, and spiritual life.
>
> We affirm that democracy is neither material happi-
> ness nor the supremacy of numbers. Democracy is es-
> sentially a permanent effort to find the right political
> means for assuring to all citizens the right of free de-
> velopment and of maximum initiative responsibility and
> spiritual life. . . .
>
> Citizens are born free and equal before the law. The
> State should assure them equal conditions for the exer-
> cise of their rights and the accomplishment of their
> duties. It owes aid and protection to the family so that
> harmonious family life can develop. Citizens have the
> right to a secure and peaceful life, to justly remunerated
> work, to sufficient individual property to assure a dig-
> nified and free life, to democratic freedoms, and to the
> full development of their personalities.
>
> They have the duty of developing the national herit-
> age for the Common Good and for universal peace, of
> safe-guarding freedom and democracy, of defending the
> Nation and the Republic against all those who seek to
> destroy the foundation of the common life and the Con-
> stitution.

This Asian leader, who in four years' time has steered his
ittle country from the edge of chaos to peace, stability,
nd a gradually increasing tempo of development, under-
tands well the problems involved in establishing and main-
aining a "democratic" state. He is a man of few illusions. He
as studied the writings of Western theorists, and he has
bserved the tendency toward the development of the "wel-
are state" in the Western democracies. He has also witnessed
he failure of parliamentary institutions in many of those
ountries. And so, in inaugurating the first session of the
National Assembly (March 15, 1956), he said:

> The most urgent task before us is to organize political
> power in such a fashion as to make it manifest and ap-
> propriate for giving shape to long-range general policy,
> and at the same time preserving the fundamental rights
> of the Nation and of the individual human personality.
> . . . [We must balance] the requirements of ever-
> unifying power against the growing pressures of life.
> For a country as exposed as ours is from within and

without, the possibilities of realizing the democratic ideal are of necessity limited. But we would betray the people were we incapable of responding to their ardent desire for a government of true freedom.

The living and unconquerable faith which sustained us through the last two years of heavy trials, the watchful intelligence which kept us from giving in to despair and as a consequence turning to fascism, these must also furnish us with the resourcefulness and concentration to foster the growth of the permanent orientation of free men toward a democratic structure suited to the conditions and possibilities of the moment, but built out of a genuine respect for the dignity of the individual, from an ideal conception of community life where the common good takes precedence over the good of the individual, from a pluralism which does not represent either social conservatism or a collection of anarchical contradictions.

No one who has known Ngo Dinh Diem well can fail to be impressed by his determination to keep his country alive and bring increasing benefits, happiness, and freedoms to his countrymen. That he is criticized is sure. But then, as Disraeli said, "the depository of power is always unpopular." It may seem paradoxical to some that out of strong governmental power may come individual freedom. But considering the context in which Vietnam exists, can one think of a more dependable method of assuring it?

We ought also to remember that while we put great store in "government by law," the Confucian ideal of "government by virtue" has for 2,500 years been a guiding principle in those Asian lands which felt the influence of Chinese political thought. Ngo was brought up in this tradition. His speeches and his writings reflect his debt to it. He would agree with Confucius that government by virtue, by moral influence, and by personal example is of paramount importance. At the same time, he was educated by the West and spent more than three years in the U. S. (1950-53), examining what we had to offer. Perhaps we can learn from this man who is endeavoring to create an acceptable synthesis of East and West in Vietnam.

There is little percentage in continuing to try to force these (or any other) Asians into categories of our own making, which reflect only our own experience and wisdom. One of these days our political theorists will come up with a new vocabulary which will enable us to describe more satisfactorily the new orders in Asia. Until then, we should do well to attempt to understand what is taking place in these countries, and to remember that politics is not geometry and that arbitrary definitions do not render its conclusions indisputable.

President Eisenhower Offers Aid to Ngo Dinh Diem With Conditions*

[October 23, 1954]

Dear Mr. President:

I have been following with great interest the course of developments in Vietnam, particularly since the conclusion of the conference at Geneva. The implications of the agreement concerning Vietnam have caused grave concern regarding the future of a country temporarily divided by an artificial military grouping, weakened by a long and exhausting war, and faced with enemies without and by their subversive collaborators within.

Your recent requests for aid to assist in the formidable project of the movement of several hundred thousand loyal Vietnamese citizens away from areas which are passing under a *de facto* rule and political ideology which they abhor, are being fulfilled. I am glad that the United States is able to assist in this humanitarian effort.

We have been exploring ways and means to permit our aid to Vietnam to be more effective and to make a greater contribution to the welfare and stability of the Government of Vietnam. I am, accordingly, instructing the American Ambassador to Vietnam [Donald R. Heath] to examine with you in your capacity as Chief of Government, how an intelligent program of American aid given directly to your Government can serve to assist Vietnam in its present hour of trial, provided that your Government is prepared to give assurances as to the standards of performance it would be able to maintain in the event such aid were supplied.

The purpose of this offer is to assist the Government of Vietnam in developing and maintaining a strong, viable state, capable of resisting attempted subversion or aggression through military means. The Government of the United States expects that this aid will be met by performance on the part of the Government of Vietnam in undertaking needed re-

* *Department of State Bulletin*, XXXI (November 15, 1954), pp. 735-736.

forms. It hopes that such aid, combined with your own continuing efforts, will contribute effectively toward an independent Vietnam endowed with a strong Government. Such a Government would, I hope, be so responsive to the nationalist aspirations of its people, so enlightened in purpose and effective in performance, that it will be respected both at home and abroad and discourage any who might wish to impose a foreign ideology on your free people.

Sincerely,

DWIGHT D. EISENHOWER

Joint Declaration by U. S. Vice-President Johnson and Ngo Dinh Diem (May 13, 1961) *

[Saigon]

. . . The United States . . . is conscious of the determination, energy, and sacrifices which the Vietnamese people under the dedicated leadership of President Ngo Dinh Diem have brought to the defense of freedom in their land.

The United States is also conscious of its responsibility and duty, in its own self-interest as well as in the interest of other free peoples, to assist a brave country in the defense of its liberties against unprovoked subversion and Communist terror. It has no other motive than the defense of freedom.

The United States recognizes that the President of the Republic of Vietnam, Ngo Dinh Diem, who was recently re-elected to office by an overwhelming majority of his countrymen despite bitter Communist opposition, is in the vanguard of those leaders who stand for freedom on the periphery of the Communist empire in Asia.

Free Vietnam cannot alone withstand the pressure which this Communist empire is exerting against it. Under these circumstances—the need of free Vietnam for increased and accelerated emergency assistance and the will and determination of the United States to provide such assistance to those willing to fight for their liberties—it is natural that a large measure of agreement on the means to accomplish the joint purpose was found in high-level conversations between the two Governments.

* *Department of State Bulletin* (June 19, 1961), pp. 956-957.

Both Governments recognize that under the circumstances guerrilla warfare now existing in free Vietnam, it is necessary to give high priority to the restoration of a sense of security to the people of free Vietnam. This priority, however, in no way diminishes the necessity, in policies and programs of both Governments, to pursue vigorously appropriate measures in other fields to achieve a prosperous and happy society. . . .

Augmented U.S. Support for Ngo Dinh Diem: Correspondence With John F. Kennedy (December 1961)*

President Diem to President Kennedy

DECEMBER 7, 1961.

DEAR MR. PRESIDENT: Since its birth, more than six years ago, the Republic of Vietnam has enjoyed the close friendship and co-operation of the United States of America.

Like the United States, the Republic of Vietnam has always been devoted to the preservation of peace. My people know only too well the sorrows of war. We have honored the 1954 Geneva Agreements even though they resulted in the partition of our country and the enslavement of more than half of our people by Communist tyranny. We have never considered the reunification of our nation by force. On the contrary, we have publicly pledged that we will not violate the demarcation line and the demilitarized zone set up by the Agreements. We have always been prepared and have on many occasions stated our willingness to reunify Vietnam on the basis of democratic and truly free elections.

The record of the Communist authorities in the northern part of our country is quite otherwise. They not only consented to the division of Vietnam, but were eager for it. They pledged themselves to observe the Geneva Agreements and during the seven years since have never ceased to violate them. They call for free elections but are ignorant of the very meaning of the words. They talk of "peaceful reunification" and wage war against us.

From the beginning, the Communists resorted to terror in their efforts to subvert our people, destroy our government,

* *Department of State Bulletin,* XXXVII (January 1, 1962), pp. 13-14.

and impose a Communist regime upon us. They have attacked defenseless teachers, closed schools, killed member of our anti-malarial program, and looted hospitals. This i coldly calculated to destroy our government's humanitarian efforts to serve our people.

We have long sought to check the Communist attack from the North on our people by appeals to the International Control Commission. Over the years, we have repeatedly published to the world the evidence of the Communist plot to overthrow our government and seize control of all of Viet nam by illegal intrusions from outside our country. The evidence has mounted until now it is hardly necessary to rehearse it. Most recently, the kidnapping and brutal murder of our Chief Liaison Officer to the International Control Commission, Colonel Noang Thuy Nam, compelled us to speak out once more. In our October 24, 1961 letter to the ICC, we called attention again to the publicly stated determination of the Communist authorities in Hanoi to "liberate the South" by the overthrow of my government and the imposition of a Communist regime on our people. We cited the proof of massive infiltration of Communist agents and military elements into our country. We outlined the Communist strategy, which is simply the ruthless use of terror against the whole population, women and children included.

In the course of the last few months, the Communist assault on my people has achieved high ferocity. In October they caused more than 1,800 incidents of violence and more than 2,000 casualties. They have struck occasionally in battalion strength, and they are continually augmenting their forces by infiltration from the North. The level of their attacks is already such that our forces are stretched to the utmost. We are forced to defend every village, every hamlet, indeed every home against a foe whose tactic is always to strike at the defenseless.

A disastrous flood was recently added to the misfortunes of the Vietnamese people. The greater part of three provinces was inundated, with a great loss of property. We are now engaged in a nationwide effort to reconstruct and rehabilitate this area. The Communists are, of course, making this task doubly difficult, for they have seized upon the disruption of normal administration and communications as an opportunity to sow more destruction in the stricken area.

In short, the Vietnamese nation now faces what is perhaps the gravest crisis in its long history. For more than 2,000 years my people have lived and built, fought and died in this land. We have not always been free. Indeed, much of our history and many of its proudest moments have arisen from conquest by foreign powers and our struggle against great odds to regain or defend our precious independence. But it is not only our freedom which is at stake today, it is our national identity. For, if we lose this war, our people will be swallowed by the Communist bloc, all our proud heritage will be blotted out by the "Socialist society" and Vietnam will leave the pages of history. We will lose our national soul.

Mr. President, my people and I are mindful of the great assistance which the United States has given us. Your help has not been lightly received, for the Vietnamese are proud people, and we are determined to do our part in the defense of the free world. It is clear to all of us that the defeat of the Vietcong demands the total mobilization of our government and our people, and you may be sure that we will devote all of our resources of money, minds, and men to this great task.

But Vietnam is not a great power and the forces of international Communism now arrayed against us are more than we can meet with the resources at hand. We must have further assistance from the United States if we are to win the war now being waged against us.

We can certainly assure mankind that our action is purely defensive. Much as we regret the subjugation of more than half of our people in North Vietnam, we have no intention, and indeed no means, to free them by use of force.

I have said that Vietnam is at war. War means many things, but most of all it means the death of brave people for a cause they believe in. Vietnam has suffered many wars, and through the centuries we have always had patriots and heroes who were willing to shed their blood for Vietnam. We will keep faith with them.

When Communism has long ebbed away into the past, my people will still be here, a free united nation growing from the deep roots of our Vietnamese heritage. They will remember your help in our time of need. This struggle will then be a part of our common history. And your help, your friendship, and the strong bonds between our two peoples will be a part of Vietnam, then as now.

President Kennedy to President Diem

DECEMBER 14, 1961.

DEAR MR. PRESIDENT: I have received your recent letter in which you described so cogently the dangerous condition caused by North Vietnam's efforts to take over your country. The situation in your embattled country is well known to me and to the American people. We have been deeply disturbed by the assault on your country. Our indignation has mounted as the deliberate savagery of the Communist program of assassination, kidnapping, and wanton violence became clear.

Your letter underlines what our own information has convincingly shown—that the campaign of force and terror now being waged against your people and your Government is supported and directed from the outside by the authorities at Hanoi. They have thus violated the provisions of the Geneva Accords designed to ensure peace in Vietnam and to which they bound themselves in 1954.

At that time, the United States, although not a party to the Accords, declared that it "would view any renewal of the aggression in violation of the Agreements with grave concern and as seriously threatening international peace and security." We continue to maintain that view.

In accordance with that declaration, and in response to your request, we are prepared to help the Republic of Vietnam to protect its people and to preserve its independence. We shall promptly increase our assistance to your defense effort as well as help relieve the destruction of the floods which you describe. I have already given the orders to get these programs underway.

The United States, like the Republic of Vietnam, remains devoted to the cause of peace and our primary purpose is to help your people maintain their independence. If the Communist authorities in North Vietnam will stop their campaign to destroy the Republic of Vietnam, the measures we are taking to assist your defense efforts will no longer be necessary. We shall seek to persuade the Communists to give up their attempts of force and subversion. In any case, we are confident that the Vietnamese people will preserve their independence and gain the peace and prosperity for which they have sought so hard and so long.

Ngo Dinh Diem and the Struggle for Reunification In Vietnam

BY PHILIPPE DEVILLERS*

For many years, many thousands of Vietnamese patriots have sacrificed themselves for a double objective—the unity and independence of Vietnam—and it was in pursuit of these aims, immediately after the Second World War, that first the Vietminh,[1] then the anti-Communist Nationalists, brought into operation all the means at their disposal, both military and diplomatic. The Geneva Agreements of July 1954 confirmed the independence of Vietnam at the international level. Yet at the same time the country's unity, which for several years had no longer constituted a problem, was destroyed.

In fact, by splitting the country along the 17th Parallel,[1a] the Geneva Agreements made geographic a cleavage which had formerly been in evidence over the whole national territory, since it was by nature ideological and not racial or regional.

A military arrangement, the Geneva Agreement put an end to an armed conflict, and was solely concerned with fixing the limits of zones of regroupment for the two opposing forces after the cease-fire. The demarcation line was to be purely provisional; the principle of Vietnamese unity was not questioned, and the idea of partition was officially rejected with indignation by both sides. When military forces were regrouped and administrative divisions laid down, national political unity would be restored by free general elections—the only well-tested instrument for measuring public

* French scholar and writer who lived in Vietnam during the First Indochinese War. His *Histoire du Vietnam de 1940 à 1952* (Paris, 1952) and *La fin d'une guerre: Indochine 1954* (Paris, 1960), written with Jean Lacouture, are standard works. The selection is from "The Struggle for Unification of Vietnam," *The China Quarterly* [London], no. 9 (January–March, 1962), pp. 2–23. By permission.

[1] The term *Vietminh* is used in this article to designate not only this organization which lasted ten years (1941–51), but also those which took over after it (the Lienviet, 1951–55, and the Patriotic Front). *Vietminh* is a useful and well-known term, even when it is not strictly accurate.

[1a] This is not quite accurate; see p. 137n.—ed.

pinion. The Final Declaration at Geneva had provided for
ections to be held at the latest by July 1956, and for au-
orities from the two zones to make contact in order to
rganize them before July 1955.[2]

During the conference, French diplomatic strategy with
eference to this problem had been wholly inspired by the
dea that if the elections took place quickly, while the ef-
ects of what appeared to be a great success for the Vietminh
ere still apparent, Ho Chi Minh* and his followers would
merge triumphant. On the other hand, given a reasonable
elay, the prestige of the Resistance would have waned, the
eople, given time to recover, would be more aware of their
est interests, more conscious of ideological affinities and an
tmosphere of freedom, thus providing an opportunity for
ne non-Marxist parties (Liberals, Democrats, etc.), to step in.

THE PROSPECTS IN 1954

he majority of Western observers had undoubtedly few il-
isions about the non-Marxists' chances of "recovery." The
olitical cliques which had formerly existed in Nationalist
ietnam merely represented scattered bourgeois elements,
hose political ideology was of the vaguest, or groups of
ivil servants, all of whom had practically no contact with
ne people. It was most probable, therefore, that they would
ll be carried away in the powerful stream of the wind blow-
ag from the Vietminh. There were still, of course, the
aore coherent groups, such as the politico-religious sects in
ne South, the Catholics in the North, and the national army.
ut would they be able to remain standing, supposing the
aasses in the countryside and the towns were stirred up and
orked upon by the Vietminh?

The disproportion between the monolithic power of the
ietminh, armed and with the halo of victory, and the al-
aost derisory weakness of the so-called Nationalist Vietnam
as such that in the summer of 1954 almost no one thought
nat the two years' delay won by M. Mendès-France at Ge-
eva could be anything but a respite in which to salvage as
auch as possible from the wreck. At the end of the period,
nity would certainly be restored, this time to the benefit
f the Vietminh, the basic hypothesis. then acknowledged by
l being that the Geneva Agreements would definitely be im-
emented.

See pp. 152–153.—ed.

In actual fact—though this was ignored at the time—the peak hour had passed, and a more balanced state of affairs was beginning to take shape. The DRV (Democratic Republic of [North] Vietnam), exhausted but still very strong, had been forced by its allies to agree to a less advantageous compromise than the one it might have hoped for (to go any further would doubtless have involved it in open war with the United States). The result was that for the moment it could no longer exercise force south of latitude 17°, but it was relying on the prestige of its leaders, its own political dynamism, and well-tried methods of warfare to bring about the desired outcome within the period laid down.

Its chances of victory were, however, linked to two factors:

(a) the implementation of the Geneva Agreements;
(b) the possibility of preventing the consolidation of the South by preserving the initial unequal situation, and maintaining the crushing political progress which it had been making at the time of the Geneva Conference.

Nevertheless, the Hanoi government was to realize very quickly that in both respects the situation was evolving in a way disturbing to it, without it being able to exercise any influence whatsoever on the process.

(a) As far as the legal aspect was concerned, who could guarantee that the Agreements would be respected and implemented? South Vietnam, which was not a signatory, was already declaring that it was not bound by them. The United States had stated that it would not oppose the carrying out of the agreements, either by force or by the threat of force, but it had not identified itself with them. Where did France stand? The Geneva Agreements (on military regroupment and a cease-fire) had linked the commands of the Popular Army and the forces of the French Union, but the latter had not entered into any *political* agreement, certainly not in the name of a country like Vietnam whose full and complete sovereignty and independence France had just recognized. Thus, neither South Vietnam nor its two allies, France and the United States, upon whom depended the implementation of the agreements, appeared to be really committed by them.

(b) The consolidation of the South was to take shape fairly rapidly. In the first place, American support contributed to stemming the wave of discouragement which followed the disaster and reminded South Vietnam that it was neither alone nor abandoned.

For months the United States had been anxious to establish a line of resistance to Communism in Southeast Asia. For Washington, the Geneva Agreements represented a cutting of losses—the amputation of the gangrenous part of Vietnam. It was now necessary to save the healthy part at any price, and transform it into a "bastion of the free world." The setting up of SEATO and the Treaty of Manila (September 1954) gave the states of Indochina a guarantee on the part of the Western powers against external aggression and even subversion.[3] This was a pointer that the United States would not sit by quietly if faced with the prospect that South Vietnam might go Communist, even perhaps as a result of free elections. The threat of a Vietminh victory (brought about by pre-electoral maneuvers) was offset for the time being by this American guarantee.

As early as September 1954 it became clear that the Americans' desire to hold on to the 17th Parallel at all costs would constitute a serious obstacle to the reunification of Vietnam. The latter was in danger of being sacrificed to the demands of Pentagon world strategy. The DRV did not fail to realize this. It protested immediately, naturally without eliciting any response. It was open to query whether this American resolution would continue to hold if international tension were relaxed. For the moment, under the shelter of the American umbrella, South Vietnam had time to recover.

The second element acting in a way detrimental to the interests of the North was the progressive coagulation of the still fluid mass of the South around a hard core.

THE RISE OF NGO DINH DIEM

M. Diem, the anti-Communists' last card, which they played at the eleventh hour and in the worst conditions, had found himself, just after the armistice, practically without means of action and isolated in the midst of the hangers-on of the French administration (the politicians, sects, army, police, etc.). His personal prestige could not, on its own, make up for the absence of a faithful party and political cadres.

The Americans, having decided to place their stakes, had already reached the conclusion that South Vietnam could not reasonably be held and preserved without the help of anti-Communist Nationalism as proclaimed by Diem and his

[3] *See pp. 92–95.*

family. As early as October 1954, a letter from President Eisenhower assured M. Diem of the unconditional support of the United States. On their side, the Nationalists, who suspected the French either of gambling on a rapprochement with Hanoi, or of seeking to prolong the colonial regime by putting their friends in power, considered that, for themselves, the only hope of resistance was to stake everything on the American alliance.

The North at this time underestimated the importance of the fact that for the first time it was not confronted by people linked in one way or another to discredited colonial authorities, but by a man whose past testified to his patriotism and integrity, and whose uncompromising anti-Communism did not stem from calculated self-interest, but from deep religious convictions.

Furthermore—and to the detriment of the North again—military regroupment was accompanied by an important political "regroupment." Hundreds of thousands of people from all walks of life escaped southward from the victorious Vietminh—and by their exodus showed that a great many Vietnamese (like the people of East Germany) preferred to risk everything rather than to live under Communist law.

The South was thus increased in numbers, reinforced, and revitalized by a flood of refugees, the majority of whom were Catholic—people who had not fled from the North to risk finding themselves two years later under the Communist rod of iron, or obliged to flee elsewhere yet again. These people would inevitably be hostile to reunification so long as it would seem that the Vietminh would profit by it. Knowledge of their experiences contributed greatly to reinforcing the potential moral resistance of the South, and spread among the people a lasting repulsion toward a regime so often based on the arbitrary authority of brutal, narrow-minded, and sectarian *can-bo* (cadres). It was among these refugees from the North that M. Diem recruited his guards and the cadres faithful to his regime.

It was now that Diem began to assert himself, to overcome the veiled resistance of the generals, and to ensure that the army over which he exercised control should be primarily devoted to the Nationalist ideal. At the beginning of 1955, Diem, strong this time in American support [4] (the French

4 See Robert Scheer's account, pp. 235–253.

had just agreed to this shift of responsibilities), tackled the sects. South Vietnam was emerging from chaos. The Southern nebula was solidifying.

But the North still held a master trump: fear—based on the conviction of the majority of people in the South that the elections of 1956 would result in a victory for the Vietminh—a fear which encouraged each one not to compromise himself. It was Hanoi's interests to prevent fear being dispelled.

NORTH VIETNAMESE POLICY

It was not long before the DRV revealed its hand. As of February 4, 1955, it proposed the restoration of normal relations (for posts, roads, railways, air and sea traffic, etc.), between the two zones, and declared itself ready to carry this out immediately.

This was the first volley fired in a diplomatic shooting-match which has practically never stopped for seven years, over the two questions on which the DRV has chosen to concentrate: (a) the restoration of normal relations between the two zones, (b) the implementation of the Geneva "decisions" concerning pre-electoral consultations and general elections.

As far as the first question is concerned, the proposal of February 4, 1955, was to be repeated many times, in particular on March 7, 1958, and October 4, 1960, each time with no more success than previously, with the result that in 1962 the frontier of the 17th Parallel is one of the most closely sealed in the world. There is still no regular communication through any medium at all between North and South Vietnam. As for postal exchanges, these were and still are restricted simply to interzonal letters.

The Diem regime, to justify its refusal, has never ceased to assert that the North, in proposing this resumption of "normal relations," had no other aim than to infiltrate agents or propaganda into the Southern zone. It cannot be denied that there is a grain of truth in this, but it is possible to wonder whether the anti-Communists' lowering of this iron curtain (revealing a singular inferiority complex on their part) has not ultimately caused much injury to the Vietnamese nation, and has not made the ordeal of the whole people more difficult.

The intransigence of the South has, in fact, destroyed any

hopes which the North might have had of putting its reconstruction policy and its economic development upon a "pan-Vietnamese" footing, and has forced it to seek the aid necessary to it exclusively in the Communist bloc. Instead of relying on the South to make good its food deficits, the North has had to intensify agricultural production at a costly price and in difficult conditions. The South's decision has probably contributed toward pushing the North into the arms of China, has been a justification for the pre-eminence of pro-Chinese elements in the inner councils of the Lao Dong Party (the Communists), and has certainly made it more difficult for the DRV to turn toward Southeast Asia, as certain elements would have liked it to do. Has not the South, by its refusal, condemned itself to an ever-increasing state of dependence in relation to its great protectors?

Nor were the Geneva "decisions" implemented, and the strong position which the DRV believed itself to be in was ultimately of no use to it.

The first date-line fixed by Geneva—for July 1955—passed without incident. The South, urged by Hanoi to take part in the consultative conference provided for, gave a negative reply (August 9, 1955), invoking the totalitarian nature of the Northern regime, the absence of guarantees, and the multiple violations of the agreement of which it had been guilty. It also requested that those held in the North against their will should be allowed to leave. Hanoi could only protest to the co-chairmen of the Geneva Conference, and ask them to intervene.

To make an impression on the South, and, doubtless, to "attenuate" the totalitarian nature of the regime, the DRV employed time-honored methods of deception: a new party was formed in September at Hanoi—the Patriotic Front which absorbed the Lien Viet. The aim was to unite in one immense organization (which would be manipulated by the Lao Dong Party) all those who were working only for the independence and the unity of the country.

But the appeals made by the North fell on deaf ears in the South, where Diem, having secured army support, compelled the sects to go into hiding, and forced the Liberal and Demo-

---

[5] See pp. 194–196.—ed.
[6] On the question of prerequisites for elections in Vietnam under the Geneva Agreements, see p. 152–153.—ed.

cratic politicians into exile, was now launching an attack upon corruption and the last vestige of the *ancien régime* in the person of Bao Dai himself. Following a hastily organized referendum in October 1955, Diem replaced Bao Dai as the head of the Vietnamese state, and proclaimed the "Republic of Vietnam" of which he became President. Once again Hanoi could only protest against this "separatist" action.

The constitution of the South, which was largely inspired by American models, contained, certainly, a reference to the unity of Vietnam. But what it did in fact was to sanction the division of this unfortunate country and turn it into another Korea, another Germany. Saigon had fallen into line with Seoul, Taipei and Bonn. In the same way as Hanoi, the Saigon regime (the only one recognized by the West as "free" and "untainted") felt itself called upon to bring about (to its advantage, of course) the unification of the country.

It would seem that for a long time the DRV relied upon the powers that had signed the Geneva agreements to make the authorities in the South respect the provisions made. Here again the Hanoi government was to travel a long road of rebuffs and disappointments.

THE FRENCH WITHDRAWAL

It was on France that Hanoi was relying most heavily. This was emphasized by M. Pham Van Dong when he declared on January 1, 1955: "It was with you, the French, that we signed the Geneva Agreements, and it is up to you to see that they are respected." France was, in fact, the only great power which was both bound by the agreements and at the same time capable of action in South Vietnam, thanks to the important effectives still at her disposal there. Hanoi built certain hopes on the pressure which the "democratic" forces might be able to exert in Paris in a direction favorable to her. The presence and the attitude of the Sainteny mission in Hanoi had, for a certain time, encouraged Ho Chi Minh and his followers to hope that France, disappointed or exasperated by the affronts offered them by the followers of Diem, might change partners and gamble on unification (in agreement with the North) in order to maintain her presence in Vietnam.

This was the same grave misunderstanding of the "balance of strength" as had been shown in 1946. For one thing, the so-called "democratic elements" were no longer in a position in France to impose any policy whatsoever, and certainly not on the question of Indochina, concerning which there was a growing and widespread desire for disengagement, at a time when the events in North Africa were increasingly claiming attention. In addition to this, Hanoi was overestimating the amount of influence wielded by those French who supported the idea of a change of policy, for in political circles in Paris they were of small importance compared with the adherents of a policy of loyalty toward the "free world" (the U.S.A.) and toward their former Vietnamese comrades-in-arms. Moreover, in a somewhat tragic reappraisal of her foreign policy, France was, in fact, in the process of abandoning her political responsibilities in Asia to the Americans.

But what Hanoi had not foreseen was that France would disengage her forces so quickly. In withdrawing the Expeditionary Force at the end of April 1956, that is, three months before the deadline fixed for the elections, France was undoubtedly fulfilling her engagements toward Vietnam (*i.e.*, to respect the independence of the country and the promises made) but at the same time she was placing herself in the situation predicted by M. Pineau, where, as a guarantor of the Geneva Agreements, she no longer had the means of seeing that they were carried out.

This somewhat premature withdrawal of the French forces, on the eve of the date fixed for the elections, brought about a timid intervention on the part of the powers. The occasion was a lesson to the DRV on the importance which the great powers attached to the problems of their small allies.

The government of the South having reasserted that it did not consider itself bound by the Geneva Agreements and that it would refuse not only to assume in the mixed commissions the responsibilities formerly held by the French but also to take part in pre-electoral consultations or in general elections, the great powers began to fear a rapid renewal of tension along the 17th Parallel. It was to guard against this danger, and for that purpose alone, that they took action, and it was brought home to the DRV on this occasion how feeble was the support given to it by its great allies during this period of *détente* based on the status quo. China had asked that a new conference should meet in Geneva. The

Co-chairmen of the first conference (English and Russian) agreed simply to extend *sine die* the functions of the International Control Commission beyond the term initially fixed (July 20, 1956). Concerning the elections, which it was recognized would not be held within the stipulated period, the two parties were merely enjoined to advise the Co-chairmen when they had agreed on a date to begin consultations and to hold the elections.

BURIAL OF THE GENEVA AGREEMENTS

This was, in fact, the occasion for the great powers to bury the Vietnamese problem. With the consent of the other signatories to the Agreements, unification by elections was to all intents and purposes postponed *sine die,* at least until Saigon, without which they could not be organized, had modified its attitude. If the United States had exerted pressure on M. Diem, it was not so much in order to soften his intransigence over the basic issue as to persuade him to present his views in a more intelligent manner: henceforward, M. Diem would no longer question the very principle of elections; he would simply refuse to consider the problem as long as the Northern zone remained under Communist control or at least did not give way to a free multiple-party system.

Repeatedly, in May and June 1956, in July 1957, in March 1958, and in July 1959 and 1960, the DRV returned to the charge, suggesting to Diem that the pre-electoral consultative conference should be held, and offering to negotiate on the basis of "free general elections by secret ballot." Each time it met with scornful silences or stinging replies. Each time Soviet and Chinese support was restricted to kind words, warm gestures of solidarity, and propaganda campaigns.

There was a similar lack of support for the DRV among the nations of the Bandung group; neither India, Burma, nor Indonesia made any effective gesture—not even one merely intended to facilitate what Nehru and Ho Chi Minh's joint communiqué of February 1958 called "understanding between the two zones of Vietnam," and one may suppose that none of these powers, even today, is particularly anxious to see the red flag with the yellow star floating over Saigon.[7]

[7] *The reference is to the DRV flag.—ed.*

By taking up the Communist challenge, by coldly refusing to lend himself to the electoral game, provided for at Geneva, Diem had clearly freed the Southern populace from the fear complex which had been Hanoi's master card. The dangerous cape of the summer of 1956 was weathered calmly, without incident, to the astonishment of almost everyone. Diem's position was further consolidated the following autumn by the public revelation of the terror reigning in the North, by Giap's own recognition of the "errors" committed in the course of agrarian reform, and of the cruelties which had accompanied it. Coming immediately after the events in Budapest, the small peasant revolt of Nghe An, crushed in November 1956, was highly exploited by Diem's propaganda machine. The whole South vibrated at this time to tales of the brutalities suffered by "our brothers of the North," and there was a further revulsion from Communism. The mistakes of the Lao Dong Party and the successes of M. Diem seemed to be slowly immunizing the South against contagion from the North. Better still, Saigon, with growing assurance, now spoke of "liberating" the North.[8]

From this time onward, it would seem that Hanoi became painfully resigned to the situation. It was recognized in the course of the sixth session of the National Assembly (January 1957) that "the struggle for unity would be long and difficult," and that a prerequisite would be the "consolidation" of the already-liberated North; to disguise the failure of the campaign for reunification, they fell back on the building of "Socialism within one country."[9]

[8] *A Saigon daily paper at this time said: "In the North, the fall of the illegitimate regime is near. . . . As soon as the people's hatred of the Communist dictatorship is sufficiently mature for it to succeed in overthrowing it, then general elections which are really free will take place in the whole of Vietnam, and will peacefully bring about the reunification of the country.*

"If he refuses to have recourse to force in order to liberate the North, while yet realizing the dearest aspirations of the people, the supreme head of the Republic of Vietnam does so solely in order to avoid bloodshed and undesirable fratricidal strife." (Cong Nhan *quoted by* Vietnam Press, *the official agency,* November 9, 1956.)

[9] *It is to be noted that at this time (the beginning of 1957) the U.S.S.R., showing small regard for Vietnamese national sentiments, proposed at the United Nations the simultaneous admission of the two Vietnams.*

After this there were merely patently ineffectual attempts to keep alive "the desire of the Southern compatriots to achieve unification," attempts to procrastinate and keep the case open, and, before long, to canalize the grievances of the Southerners. The enemy was all the tougher because he depended only on himself and the Americans, and not on public opinion, so that there was no way of getting a grip on him. But Hanoi could reasonably hope for good dividends from a propaganda campaign which put the blame for the division of the country on the Americans, and denounced Vietnamese allies of the Americans as puppets and lackeys. This was a line which at one and the same time gained the favor of the Communist bloc and created the psychological conditions for a North-South rapprochment; anti-Americanism, that latest of national binding-forces, would permit the question of Communism to be relegated to a less prominent position. From 1956 on, American intervention in the South was constantly denounced as the principal obstacle existing in the way of reunification. But such denunciations were for long of a purely negative character. International *détente,* until 1959, operated entirely in favor of Ngo Dinh Diem.

Apart from the United States, from which South Vietnam had obtained real protection and support, it seemed that nobody henceforward had the slightest hope of securing any softening of the rigid position which the Saigon oligarchy had taken up, fully realizing what it was doing. In these conditions, it seemed likely that the division of Vietnam would last long. The North would have had little hope of setting the wheels of reunification in motion if the South had been able to forge itself into a real nation, that is to say, if the Saigon government had succeeded with its internal policies and had received the full support of the people. But the wheel was soon to turn, and the North was to find itself with trump cards in its hand, for M. Diem had begun to dig his own grave.

MISTAKES OF THE DIEM GOVERNMENT

The best is often the enemy of the good. The "mistakes" of the South from 1957 onwards, were to furnish opportunities to Communism and to the movement for reunification which operated under its aegis.

As if not satisfied with the reestablishment of calm and

ecurity, the Diem regime, haunted by a strange desire to
bring back into being the society of former days, when
there were no sects and no Communists, and reckoning that
would itself be safe in the future, accentuated its authori-
arian and repressive character. There are serious reasons for
supposing that it was encouraged along this path by certain
American activists who were alarmed by the agreement
reached over Laos (the entry of the Pathet Lao into the
government) and by the continued existence in rural areas
in the South of certain cells and centers of Communist
llegiance. The *de facto* integration of South Vietnam within
the American military defense structure implied that the
region ought to be secure, and hence ought to be purged of
anything which might, however remotely, serve the Red cause.

Men who fought for the Vietminh (insultingly termed Vietcong) have since this date been to all intents and purposes
outlaws. The Diem government, profiting from the wave of
emotion aroused by the putting down of the Hungarian revolution, and the events at Nghe An, launched out in 1957 into
what amounted to a series of man-hunts. The population was
called upon to redouble its vigilance and to denounce all
Communist activity. The organization of the police, which was
already elaborate, was yet further strengthened. Guided by informers, "mopping-up operations" became only too frequent,
especially in the center, where the President's brother, Ngo
Dinh Can, had recourse to the toughest of methods.

A considerable number of people were arrested in this
way, and sent to concentration camps, or political re-education camps, as they were euphemistically called, under
conditions which, to be sure, reflected no credit on a state
that proclaimed itself to be a respecter of the human person.

This repression was in theory aimed at the Communists.
In fact it affected all those, and they were many—Democrats,
Socialists, Liberals, adherents of the sects—who were bold
enough to express their disagreement with the line of policy
adopted by the ruling oligarchy, which was now relying for
its support upon two parties, the *Cach Manh Quoc Gia*
(National Revolutionary Movement) and the *Can Lao Nhan
Vi.* Often too (in error!) people of no political affiliations
found themselves subjected to the repression.

It soon became evident to many Western observers, and
to the most clear-sighted and best-informed among the Viet-

namese themselves, that this policy was playing into the hands of the Communists, and warnings were frequently announced to this effect.[10]

In 1958 the situation grew worse. Round-ups of "dissidents" became more frequent and more brutal. The enemy (those suspected of Communist activities or of being affiliated with the sects) were difficult to apprehend. The areas where they took refuge . . . were not favorable for operations by government forces. Moreover, the way in which many of the operations were carried out very soon set the villagers against the regime. A certain sequence of events became almost classical: denunciation, encirclement of villages, searches and raids, arrest of suspects, plundering, interrogations enlivened sometimes by torture (even of innocent people [11], deportation, and "regrouping" of populations suspected of intelligence with the rebels, etc.

Diem never succeeded in winning the peasants and tenant farmers over to his side. His policy of agrarian reform, an extremely timid one in the first place, became bogged down before very long, and, what is more, the tenant farmers were afraid that the benefits which had been conceded to them during the war would be called in question by the

[10] *At the beginning of 1958 the press of Saigon and the National Assembly itself (in the sessions of January 3–4, 1958) gave voice to the serious popular unrest provoked by the way the police were acting; the brutal behavior of the prison authorities was mentioned in forthright terms. The semi-governmental newspaper* Tu Do *wrote (March 4, 1958) "We must have done with arbitrary arrests and imprisonment. The citizens of a free and independent country have the right to be protected in accordance with the spirit of the Constitution." Some days earlier, on March 18, the National Democratic Movement of South Vietnam launched an appeal to the French and American peoples in which it stated, "We enjoy neither justice nor freedom of the press nor free speech nor freedom to travel and meet together. A revolt is simmering."*

But the regime had prepared in advance weapons to deal with such a situation. Ordinance No. 6, dated January 11, 1956, authorized the arrest or imprisonment of "any person considered to be a danger to the defense of the state or to national interests," and their detention until order and security were fully restored. By Article 98 of the Constitution, the President was empowered provisionally to suspend all liberties in case of danger.

[11] *Cf. the case of Ng. Xuan Hieu and Lam Van Nanh heard by the Saigon Court of Appeal in January 1961.*

andlords. For so long as it did keep order the regime could
get certain measures accepted, even when they were unpopular; but now disorder and insecurity were returning, and
the villagers, exposed to the depredations of foraging parties
sent out by both the Communists and the sects, suffered
even more from the reprisals and operations organized by
the police and the army.

RESISTANCE BY COMMUNISTS IN SOUTH VIETNAM

As early as 1958 the cycle of events, so well described by
the Vietminh theoretician, Truong Chinh,[12] was set in motion in Cochin China. The Communists, finding themselves
hunted down, began to fight back. Informers were sought
out and shot in increasing numbers, and village chiefs who
had presided over the denunciations, village notables, and
members of the militia who took part were frequently treated
in the same way. The people of the villages, thus intimidated, fell silent. Diem's police and army saw their sources
of information drying up one after another. To make good
the lack, they resorted to worse barbarity, hoping to inspire
an even greater terror among the villagers than that inspired
by the Communists. And in that fateful year of 1958 they
overstepped all bounds. The peasants, disgusted to see Diem's
men acting in this way, lent their assistance to the Communists and even to the sects, going so far as to take up arms
at their side. The opposition (and deserters) found it increasingly easier to find hide-outs; they were able to set up
more and more supply dumps and outposts, and even to
fortify villages according to well-tried methods, transforming
them into bases for their operations.

In December 1958, the death of some 20 Vietcong detainees in the Phu Loi concentration camp served to fan
the flames of anger of the guerrillas—and gave Hanoi an
opportunity for propaganda—and to bring them to the point
where they decided to answer force by force. In the course
of that December and the following January armed bands
sprang into being almost everywhere. The ground was well
prepared; many villages fell under their control and were
immediately transformed into bases. To mark the festival
of *Têt* 1959, the Resistance put on a large-scale raid, and
a group attacked the outpost of Trang Sup near Tay Ninh
in strength.

[12] *Cf. Truong Chinh, La Résistance Vaincra, 1947, Chap. XV.*

Keenly alive to the danger, the Diem government tried to re-establish its administrative hold over the lost villages. It launched against dissident regions (in the Plaine des Joncs and Eastern Cochin China) what amounted to a series of full-scale military operations, bringing infantry, artillery, paratroops, and aircraft to bear. But this time the forces of Diem met with resistance from the inhabitants themselves in many places. At the end of March 1959, M. Diem told the correspondent to *Figaro* that "at the present time Vietnam is a nation at war."

Under the pressure of the rising tide of terrorism and sabotage, the Saigon government passed the celebrated Law 10/59,[12a] which provided for the "repression of acts of sabotage, of infringements of national security, and of attacks upon the life or property of citizens." Special military tribunals were convened which could only pass sentences of death or of hard labor for life, with no provisions for appeal against their decision. In an effort to wrest the population from the grip of the rebels, the Diem government made various attempts to set up villages on new sites in groupings at key points, imitating the policy the French had tried in Tonkin in 1953 (Hanoi-belt experiment, especially Hoa My), only to find that it had played into Vietminh hands.

And indeed, in the course of 1959 the battle spread and became more intense. From the stage of scattered guerrilla operations it passed gradually into partisan warfare. Caught between two fires, and in a state of terror, the population witnessed tragic man-hunts. The power of the Diem government, in spite of American aid, was, it is true, on the ebb, but no village could feel that it was yet safe from the danger of "reprisal" operations.

REACTION OF DRV GOVERNMENT

What did the authorities of the Democratic Republic of [North] Vietnam do in the face of these sad circumstances? They protested in diplomatic notes. The members of the Vietminh cadre in the south, who had been promised by Hanoi that unification would be rapidly achieved, had to listen to the bitter remarks that were made to them about the inability of the North to do anything about the Diem dictatorship. The overriding needs of the world-wide strategy of the Socialist camp meant little or nothing to guerrilla

12a See pp. 256–262.—ed.

fighters being hunted down in Nam-bô.[13] It was in such a climate of feeling that, in 1959, responsible elements of the Communist Resistance in Indochina came to the conclusion that they had to act, whether Hanoi wanted them to or not. They could no longer continue to stand by while their supporters were arrested, thrown into prison, and tortured, without attempting to do anything about it as an organization, without giving some lead to the people in the struggle in which it was to be involved. Hanoi preferred diplomatic notes, but it was to find that its hand had been forced.

In March 1960 the "Nam-bô Veterans of the Resistance Association" published a long declaration. After describing the reign of terror to which the country was submitted by the Diem regime, it declared that the government had "driven the people of South Vietnam to take up arms in self-defense." The Veterans of the Resistance thus called upon the people to intensify their struggle to oblige the authorities to change their policies: to put an end to the bloody rounding-up operations, to repression, to the pillaging of crops, to the moving of villages. They almost certainly did not believe that the regime could be reformed, for they declared that in all this, they were fighting "to put an end to the Fascist dictatorship of the Ngo family" and to "set up a democratic government of National Union in South Vietnam . . . in order to realize national independence and democratic liberties and to guarantee a decent life to the people." But they added (and it is here that one can see the tip of the devil's ear poking out) that this should be "in full and energetic implementation of the terms of the Geneva agreement by entering into talks with North Vietnam with a view to the peaceful reunification of the Fatherland. This government shall base itself on the principles of the Bandung Conference and institute a foreign policy of Peace and Friendship." A little after the date of this manifesto,[14] a People's Liberation Army of South Vietnam appeared in Nam-bô. From this time forward it carried on incessant guerrilla operations against Diem's forces.

It was thus by its *home* policy that the government of the South finally destroyed the confidence of the population,

---

[13] *Vietminh term for South Vietnam.—ed.*
[14] *Declaration of the Veterans of the Resistance on the current situation in South Vietnam, March 1960.*

which it had won during the early years, and practically drove them into revolt and desperation. The non-Communist (and even the anti-Communist) opposition had long been aware of the turn events were taking. But at the beginning of 1960 very many elements, both civilian and military, in the Nationalist camp came to a clear realization that things were moving from bad to worse, and that if nothing were done to put an end to the absolute power of Diem, then Communism would end up by gaining power with the aid, or at least with the consent, of the population. If they did not want to allow the Communists to make capital out of the revolt, then they would have to oppose Diem actively. In a manifesto dated April 26, 1960, eighteen well-known personalities of varying political affiliations demanded that Diem should liberalize his regime. If not, they added, a revolution would follow. On August 1, the Bloc of Liberty and Progress launched a petition to the same effect. Neither of these approaches elicited any response from the government. But among the Nationalist opposition the tone grew more bitter month by month. At the beginning of November an influential Nationalist journal, after indicating that the government would have in all probability to deal with a popular insurrection, wrote:

> This rising is justified: in a country where the most elementary rights of the people are ignored, where the legality of the actions of the government has become an empty expression, the will of the people can only make itself felt by means of force, that is to say, by means of a revolution and the taking-over of the government. . . . We Nationalists, all of us, know that there is a race against the clock taking place between the Vietminh and ourselves.[16]

Even in the army the mood of the staff officers became hostile to the regime. But the abortive military coup d'état of November 11, 1960, followed as it was by a large-scale purge, of which the principal victim was brave Dr. Phan Quang Dan, leader of the "legal" opposition, was to show that the ruling oligarchy had made up its mind to hang onto its power and privileges at all costs.

After the spectacular failure of this first right-wing Nationalist plot, the initiative passed to the Communist Party and its allies once more. But it would be as well to analyze

[16] *Pour le Viêt-Nam, Paris, No. 2, November 1960.*

n a little more detail the background to this development.

When it decided to take up arms against the Diem regime, the Resistance movement in the South placed the leaders of Communism in Vietnam in an embarrassing situation. In the field of international relations the Democratic Republic of Vietnam had in all essentials kept to the Soviet line of peaceful co-existence, taking great care not to give, through the slightest provocation, any pretext to M. Diem or to the Americans. But could the Lao Dong Party stick to this policy of "peaceful co-existence" when its result was, in effect, to allow the Diem police to proceed with impunity to take their toll of the best elements in the Party?

Whereas the leading group of the Lao Dong Party seemed to be afraid that they would be dragged, behind the "adventurism" of members from the South, into a series of international complications likely to hinder the diplomacy of the Socialist camp, some "activist" elements came out in favor of a bolder policy of effective support for Southern comrades. This tendency had already appeared at the meeting of the Central Committee of the Lao Dong Party in May 1959, and had made itself felt in the field in the shape of the aid given at the beginning of 1960 to the *maquis* of the High Plateaus (Pleiku-Kontum region).

These hesitations, and the divergence between the two tendencies, had an international bearing. And in the light of what happened at the Twenty-second Party Congress at Moscow (the Russo-Albanian dispute) we can better understand what was at stake in Hanoi during the Third Congress of the Lao Dong Party held there in September 1960. The question of national reunification was then at the heart of the debate, along with the question of support to be given to compatriots in the South. We have every reason to think that Moscow counselled prudence. It is interesting to note that the chief Soviet delegate, Mr. Mukhitdinov, stressed on that occasion that "peaceful co-existence was the only line which was in complete accord with the ultimate aim of Communism," [17] while the chief Chinese delegate, Mr. Li

---

[17] *The Soviet-Vietnamese talks which followed after the Congress, according to the communiqué issued, served to bring out "the complete identity of the points of view" of the two governments as regards "the essential aspects" of the problems discussed (among which was the international situation).*

Fu-ch'un, reminded the Congress of the importance of Lenin's teaching "when one is struggling against Imperialists," and went on to denounce those revisionists who set about blackening the name of those who gave firm support to the Marxist-Leninist standpoint.

The prudent (and pro-Soviet) tendency finally won the day, but the "activist" faction scored many points. Ho Chi Minh demanded that "greater efforts" should be made to achieve unification, and it was a former guerrilla leader in Nam-bô, Le Duan, who was elected Party Secretary. In this way closer liaison with the South was assured: the situation was deteriorating there, and the Lao Dong Party was afraid that the situation would slip from its control.

THE "NATIONAL LIBERATION FRONT"

It is against this background that we must estimate the importance of the setting up in December 1960 "somewhere in Cochin China" of the National Liberation Front of South Vietnam (*Mat-Tran dan-toc giaiphong*). The weakening of Diem's regime which resulted from the coup of November 11 made it at once the principal political force in South Vietnam. How effective its armed struggle was and how serious a threat to the Diem regime it represented are now facts known to the whole world.

In the space of two years the Liberation Front of the South gained control of the greater part of the countryside in Cochin China and also of a large zone between the Fourteenth and Seventeenth Parallels. It built up a strong organization by setting up at the various administrative levels (provinces, *huyen* and villages) committees which have already assumed governmental powers over whole regions, and then provided itself with effective means of action by attacking government positions, by desertions,[18] through accomplices in Diem's army, by setting up factories to manufacture arms, and also through outside aid of by no means negligible extent which furnished arms, ammunition, medical supplies and money. Its propaganda is skillful, and hits its mark. The growing power of the Front is shown by its very ubiquitousness and by the increasing tendency of the forces of Diem to fall back on the main lines of communications and on the principal centers of population.

[18] *At the beginning of 1961 for example, Diem forces discovered near the Khmer frontier a hide-out where 400 deserters had taken refuge.*

If it maintains and extends its hold over the countryside, the Front will be in an increasingly stronger position, and able to determine the policy of South Vietnam. Already it constitutes there a factor which cannot be ignored.

To what extent have the successes of the Front and the weakening of the Diem regime increased the chances of unification coming about? The situation is complex. The point of view of most foreign governments, in the West especially, is that the fighting going on in South Vietnam is simply a subversive campaign directed from Hanoi. The DRV, unable to get the better of Diem by means of diplomacy, and not daring to resort to direct action, has chosen to attempt to overthrow him from within, sapping tirelessly the foundations of the regime and spreading terror.

The hypothesis is certainly a plausible one [19] (and to formulate it serves the purposes of Communist propaganda); but it leaves out of account the fact that the insurrection existed before the Communists decided to take part, and that they were simply forced to join in. And even among the Communists, the initiative did not originate in Hanoi, but from the grass roots, where the people were literally driven by Diem to take up arms in self-defense.

We do not at the moment know the composition of the Liberation Front of the South, or its leading elements, but it seems likely that it reflects the checkerboard variety of the political forces within the opposition (even if the delegates are not all representative). Now the majority of the opponents of M. Diem are still anti-Communist and the inhabitants of the South feel as yet only a slight sympathy for Communism. It is for this reason that the Communists, even though they do play a preponderant part in the National Front, are in no position to comport themselves as if they were the dominant force, and indeed have to proceed with great caution.

For the people of the South unification is not an essential problem. Peace, security, freedom, their standard of living, the agrarian question—these are far more important questions to them. The strong hold of the sects over certain regions remains one of the factors of the situation, as is also, in a general fashion, the distrustful attitude of the

[19] *Leading articles like that of April 3, 1961, in the* Nhan Dan *of Hanoi make it seem very likely.*

Southerner toward the Northerner, who is suspected of a tendency to want to take charge of affairs.

The Communists, whatever the extent of their loyalty toward Hanoi, have had to take this national or regional sentiment of the South into account. This is evident from the program of the Front,[20] which by and large transposes on the level of internal politics the manifesto of the Veterans of the Resistance. While it does call for the overthrow of the government and the setting up of a government of national and democratic union, nevertheless the points most stressed are those concerning the establishment of a democratic regime guaranteeing peace for all and a decent standard of living, the giving of land to the peasants and political autonomy to ethnic minorities. Efforts have been made to give a "Southern" slant to the movement. The flag chosen by the Front is not that of the Democratic Republic of Vietnam: it is not red, but red and blue. As for the Front's attitude toward reunification, it is defined as follows in its program:

> The National Liberation Front of South Vietnam advocates the progressive reunification of the country by peaceful means on the basis of negotiations between the two zones with the object of finding by common agreement what measures and practical steps towards reunification can be taken in conformity with the interests of the people and of the Fatherland.

> In the period before the reunification of the country, the governments of the two zones will meet to negotiate and will engage themselves not to undertake any propaganda activities likely to lead to division and war, and will also pledge themselves not to use military force against the other party, also to encourage economic and cultural exchanges between the two zones, and to allow the inhabitants of the two zones full liberty to travel, trade, and carry on correspondence between the two zones.

All this is prudent and restrained enough. A simple matter of tactics, one might object: the Vietminh is out to gain the confidence of the population and to get itself accepted in order to win key positions, and to set up its private army which will later enable it to lay down its own law. When it is master, it will oust its rivals one by one. Indeed, one ob-

[20] *Program published in the* Echo du Viêt-Nam, *No. 4, Paris, May 1961.* [*See pp. 253–256.–ed.*]

serves that wherever it can it eliminates those men of recognized competence or of wide political influence who might prove awkward: certain rural agitators won over to the Nationalist opposition, for example.

PROSPECTS FOR THE FUTURE

Yet the problem of reunification must be considered without overdramatizing it, In the present international context the Government of Hanoi knows quite well that it is impossible to realize this policy of unification without risking open war with the United States. It will try nothing in that direction, for it follows the "Khrushchev line." The only solution conceivable by Hanoi is to take advantage of the mistakes committed by the Americans in order to gain acceptance for a "Laos-type" solution: that is to say, within the framework of a given nation where American policy has provoked an open conflict between Right and Left, to obtain, through military pressure, the overthrow of a reactionary dictatorship and its replacement by a democratic and neutralist government benevolently disposed toward them.

We should be quite frank with ourselves: this is the solution toward which we are heading directly. Month by month the forces of Diem are losing their hold on the countryside: before long there will only be a few pockets and bridgeheads left, and these they will probably be able to hold on to indefinitely with American aid. One thinks of Hué-Tourane [Danang], Nhatrang, the region of Saigon, and of perhaps one or two scattered "hedgehog-type" defensive positions. But what can be the outcome of this? Neither side can allow such an impasse to continue for long, and sooner or later it will be necessary to come to the point of negotiating a political settlement re-establishing for this country the unity of the cities and the country regions. It is when this inevitable meeting takes place that we will be able to estimate what chances there are of speedy reunification.

At that moment everything will depend, on the one hand, on the balance of forces existing between the Liberation Front and its enemies (among whom one must include the Americans), and on the other hand, on the balance of forces within the Front itself, exactly as in Laos. It is obvious that the stronger the Communists are when the moment comes, the greater the chances will be of a speedy reunification taking place (and to the extent that Hanoi is able at that time to furnish proof that it is truly independent, it is not certain that fundamental obstacles would be met with on the international plane).

This is the prospect that faces us. As things are at the moment, one can hardly see how the Diem Government, discredited and detested as it is, could restore its authority in South Vietnam. Its enemies will henceforward be strong enough both to resist any plans it may undertake and also to deny it the exercise of power in the countryside. The Americans are themselves aware of this situation. In May 1961, the Secretary of State, Mr. Dean Rusk, emphasized that it was no longer possible to oppose Vietminh threats by purely military means.[21] The recent Taylor-Rostow mission has confirmed this point of view. Profound reforms are necessary, and the first thing to make sure of is that the Saigon Government is capable of inspiring confidence, which, under the Ngo family, it is no longer able to do.

The problem of the nature of the regime is thus at the present moment underlying all others in South Vietnam. Whether the process of unification is speedy or slow depends on whether it is solved or not. The methods and the nature of M. Diem's regime are indeed such that with every month that goes by the grip of the Communists in Vietnam grows firmer over the forces of the Resistance. The process which, under the French regime between 1930 and 1954, operated in favor of the Communist Party, operates still today, for the fact is that the people of Vietnam have always been caught between Communism and a form of anti-Communism which they could not accept. In the days of the French, they had to choose between Communism and a hated colonial regime; today the Americans give them a choice between Communism and a dictatorship of a type which is at one and the same time fascist and medieval. Everything leads one to think that "if they had at all costs to choose between Communism and reaction, the masses of Vietnam would opt for the former." [21]

The longer Diem's regime lasts, the more enemies it has, and the stronger Communist and anti-American influences

---

[21] *Cf. Nguyen Ngoc Huy, "Open letter to Mr. Kennedy," in* Pour le Viêt-Nam, *No. 6, March 1961.*

become within the Resistance. This development could doubtless be stemmed and reversed, but to do so would require
a way out to be found from the terrible choice "either
Diem or the Vietminh." It would require the emergence of
another pole of influence. A change of government in Saigon,
with the advent to power of a popular and democratic Nationalist regime resolved to have done, once and for all, with
the use of terror as an instrument of government and to
follow an advanced economic and social policy would in all
probability help toward the relaxation of tension, and would
bring about the progressive sterilization of the ground which
now acts as a seedbed for Communism and Communist
sympathizers. In the same way, if such a government abandoned the purely negative attitude adopted by the Diem
regime toward relations with the North, the *détente* which
would result, both in the minds of the people and throughout Southeast Asia, would destroy many of the most cherished
debating points of Northern propaganda.

For the die is not irrevocably cast, and the situation remains fluid. That part of the Nationalist movement in Vietnam which is not identified with Marxism has still a few
good cards up its sleeve, but, unfortunately, it has very
little time left in which to play them. It would be possible
for it to play them to some advantage, perhaps even win
back the sympathy of the population, and this without abandoning its ideological references, truly democratic attitude,
or its Western friends and the support they bring. But even
if it ought to preserve a healthy suspicion of reunification for
so long as it seems likely to be achieved to the advantage
of the Communists alone, one can see no reason why it
should fear contact with the North. After all, there are not
two peoples nor two nations in Vietnam, and if certain
regional interests diverge, if families and individuals look
upon themselves as being for or against such and such a
social system, this does not mean that they all want to live
as strangers and enemies to each other. When one represents freedom (which ought to be the *raison d'être* of the
South) one can, if one wishes, work effectively toward the
mutual understanding and coming-together of the two Vietnams, and to that end put forward confederal solutions

which would serve both the interests of the present time and the opportunities of the future.

The Liberation Front of the South constitutes, on the other hand, an unknown factor. The bigger it grows, the more non-Communist adherents it contains. If there were a *détente* in Saigon, could the Communists remain dominant or preponderant in it? [22] The risk now for Hanoi is that the Front, which is essentially a Southern movement, should remain open to non-Marxist influences coming from powers which, for example, considering the victory of the Front as a virtual certainty, might wish in this way at least to make some provision for the future.

These are merely conjectures. But can what happened in South Korea happen again in South Vietnam? The blindness displayed over Laos by the Western powers, and by the United States in particular, leads one to think that for Hanoi the risks of failure are not large this time either, and that, as Ho Chi Minh has said, "Reunification is now only a question of time." At this very moment a process of osmosis is taking place between the North and the country districts of the South through that open sieve, the Laotian border, and it is taking place to the advantage of the Communists alone. The situation is thus evolving toward the tragic ranging of city against countryside to which allusion has been made above. Who is still able, at the present time, to make a new deal?

The Genesis of United States Support for Ngo Dinh Diem

BY ROBERT SCHEER[*]

[Ngo Dinh] Diem had been destined, by family posi-

---

[22] *The creation in January 1962 of a "People's Revolutionary Party" (a "party of the working class") within the framework of the Liberation Front is probably designed as an insurance against the risk that they could not. It would be interesting to know whether this new move was made on the advice of the Chinese that it was essential to have in the South an ideologically solid core to ensure that the Front maintained a correct line. It was certainly the Chinese who advocated a similar relationship between the Vietminh and the Lien Viet in 1951.*

[*] Foreign correspondent for *Ramparts* magazine, author of "A View from Phnompenh," *Ramparts*, IV (July 1965), pp. 25-31, and co-author (with Maurice Zeitlin) of *Cuba: Tragedy in Our Hemisphere* (New York, 1963). The selection is from *How*

tion and training, for service in the Mandarinite, the feudal administrative apparatus that had always governed Vietnam and that the French bent to their own purposes. He belonged to that group of officials who believed in the traditional Vietnamese monarchy and the Mandarin hierarchy that served it. They hoped for eventual independence, but sought the moderate path of reform from within the French colonial hierarchy.

At the time Diem had been part of the French colonial government, other nationalists, including Communists, Trotskyites, and pro-Kuomintang groups, had chosen the path of violent opposition to the French. In the early 1930's the Indochinese Communists, led by Ho Chi Minh, had played the most prominent role in this movement and the "terror" unleashed by the French broke against them. Ho was arrested in Hong Kong and the situation inside Vietnam was disastrous to his cause. As Ellen Hammer described it in *The Struggle for Indochina,*

> The French Legion terrorized north and central Annam. The prisons were filled and thousands were killed. The year 1931 was a time of terror in which perished not only many Communists, but Nationalists and liberals, and many others, innocent victims of French action.

In September of 1933, at the age of thirty-three, Diem abandoned the possibilities of reform from within and left the French administration to go into retirement. But he did not, and never was to, take up active opposition to the French. His decision was determined by a style of political life that he had retained from his Mandarin background. Diem believed in intercession by Providence and his politics were marked by an extreme fatalism. He felt that if one upheld one's personal integrity, remained dedicated, and issued a clear and courageous call to the powers of this world, it would be answered. He had first addressed his call to the French. When that failed, he turned to the Japanese when they occupied Vietnam in 1940. After the war, he tried again with the French, and when that showed little promise, he turned to the Americans.

This last turn came in 1950 when Diem, who was then

the United States Got Involved in Vietnam (Report to the Center for the Study of Democratic Institutions [Santa Barbara, California,] 1965), pp. 13-16, 20-44. By permission of the Fund for the Republic.

in Japan, encountered Wesley Fishel, a young assistant professor of political science at the University of California at Los Angeles. In an interview with this author Fishel said that he later persuaded Diem to travel to the United States to plead his case and convinced Michigan State University, to which Fishel had moved, to sponsor the trip. Diem was to spend a considerable part of the next three years in the United States. His brother, Bishop Can, was an important contact with the American Catholic Church, and Diem lived for some time in the Maryknoll seminaries in New Jersey and New York State. The latter school was under the jurisdiction of Cardinal Spellman, and Diem soon developed a close relationship with this important American Catholic. The Cardinal became one of Diem's most influential backers in the United States, and there is no doubt that this support was crucial, for, among other things, it certified Diem as an important anti-Communist—no small matter during the McCarthy period.

Diem was thus launched upon a career as a lobbyist, which was perhaps the most successful role in his political life. He managed to enlist in his cause not only the sympathy of Spellman but also that of liberal and sophisticated political figures who were ordinarily at odds with the conservative prelate.

Supreme Court Justice William O. Douglas was one of the first of this group to champion Diem, in his book *North from Malaya,* published in 1952. Douglas had traveled in Vietnam and was convinced that the French could not win against the popular support of the Communist-led Vietminh. This posed a dilemma for Douglas, which he thought was resolved when he met Diem in Washington upon his return from Vietnam. Diem represented the third force Douglas believed the United States could back: "Ngo Dinh Diem is revered by the Vietnamese because he is honest and independent and stood firm against the French influence." At the same time Douglas admitted that "there is little doubt that in a popularity contest Ho Chi Minh would still lead the field."

Douglas told this author that he arranged a breakfast meeting at which he introduced Diem to Senators Mike Mansfield and John F. Kennedy. Mansfield was to become the Senate's leading authority on Vietnam and as Majority Leader was an important architect of the Kennedy Administration's Vietnam policy some seven years later. During this earlier period, 1951-54, Mansfield and Kennedy became arch-critics of the French role in Vietnam and proponents of an independent nationalist alternative. To them, Diem appeared as that alternative. . . .

The installation of Diem as the Premier of Vietnam helped focus U.S. policy in Southeast Asia. Diem was committed to the remaking of Vietnamese society according to a not always lucid, but always anti-Communist and anti-French, model that required for its enactment the concentration of total power in the hands of a small trusted group. According to Bernard Fall, in *The Two Vietnams*, Diem, unlike some of his advisers, never had any doubts about the necessity for tight central control to divert the Nationalist revolution from Communist objectives. Ho and Giap, the Communist leaders of the Vietminh, were heroes of the resistance to the French. Diem understood that changing the course of their revolution required the liquidation of the Vietminh and the "re-education" of the majority of the population that supported the movement. It was a formidable task for a regime that had arisen late in the day and by grace of a foreign power.

Diem in his first year in office moved to consolidate his control by crushing all sources of opposition—the religious sects and Nationalist but anti-Diem politicians, along with the cadres left behind by the Vietminh. These came to be called the Vietcong. It was soon clear that Diem would refuse to provide for the popular mandate called for in the Geneva Agreements. Each step to that end required American support and conflicted with the interests of the French, who wanted to limit Diem's power, keep the situation fluid, and maintain whatever influence they could.

Eisenhower was sympathetic to the French position, as his later writings make clear. He recognized not only Ho's popularity but the high cost of any effort to crush his movement. He resisted grandiose schemes for building up Diem's regime as a Western-style alternative to the Vietminh, and the man he chose as his Special Ambassador to Vietnam, General Lawton Collins, shared these sentiments. But the Eisenhower Administration was particularly vulnerable to political pressure, and it was during this unsettled period that Diem's pre-Geneva lobbying began to bear fruit. One of the first voices raised publicly on behalf of a "hard line" of all-out support for Diem was that of Cardinal Spellman. In a speech before the American Legion Convention on August 31, 1954, he was quoted by *The New York Times:*

> If Geneva and what was agreed upon there means anything at all, it means . . . Taps for the buried hopes of freedom in Southeast Asia! Taps for the newly betrayed millions of Indochinese who must now learn the awful facts of slavery from their eager Communist masters! Now the devilish techniques of brainwashing, forced confessions, and rigged trials have a new locale for their exercise.

Spellman emphasized the essential theses of the cold war containment policy: ". . . Communism has a world plan and it has been following a carefully set-up time table for the achievement of that plan . . ." ". . . the infamies and agonies inflicted upon the hapless victims of Red Russia's bestial tyranny. . . ." A show of strength was required, ". . . else we shall risk bartering our liberties for lunacies, betraying the sacred trust of our forefathers, becoming serfs and slaves to Red rulers' godless goons." The danger lay in the illusion of peace with the Communists:

> Americans must not be lulled into sleep by indifference nor be beguiled by the prospect of peaceful coexistence with Communists. How can there be peaceful coexistence between two parties if one of them is continually clawing at the throat of the other . . . ? Do you peacefully coexist with men who thus would train the youth of their godless, Red world . . . ?

The Cardinal demonstrated his support of Diem by going to Vietnam to deliver personally the first check for Catholic Relief Services funds spent in Vietnam. Others of Diem's early supporters followed suit. Wesley Fishel, the Michigan State University professor who had originally induced Diem to come to the United States, turned up in Vietnam as one of his chief advisers, with residence in the presidential palace. Another American inhabitant of the palace was Wolf Ladejinsky, a New Dealer who had stayed on in the Department of Agriculture only to be fired under pressure from Senator Joseph McCarthy for alleged (but never proved) radical connections. Ladejinsky had worked on the Japanese land reform program, and Diem hired him to work on land problems in Vietnam—proof to many American liberals of Diem's commitment to serious social reform.

Another visitor to Diem was Leo Cherne, who had helped to found the Research Institute of America, one of the first of the management-research firms designed to help American corporations cope with the expanding government of the post-1930's. It also supplied its 30,000 business clients with general political information. Cherne was also president of the International Rescue Committee, an organization aimed at helping refugees from Communism.

Cherne went to Vietnam in September 1954 and spent two and a half weeks there, becoming very interested in Diem's potentialities as a democratic, nationalist alternative to the Communists. In a cable he sent back to the subscribers to his Research Institute he reported:

> . . . have been talking intimately with American officials here, including Ambassador Heath. Conferred at length yesterday with Vietnam Premier Ngo Dinh Diem . . . success of effort to hold Vietnam from Communists depends on whether all non-Communist Vietnamese can unite for struggle. U.S. Embassy, strongly supporting Diem, views him as key to the whole situation. Political and financial instability . . . unless Vietnamese Government can organize important forces and U.S. continues pouring in substantial help and money. . . . If free elections held today, all agree privately Communists would win . . . situation not hopeless . . . future depends on organizing all resources to resettle refugees, sustain new bankrupt government, give people something to fight for, and unite them to resist Communism. . . . West can't afford to lose from now on.

Upon returning to the United States, Cherne sent his second-in-command in the International Rescue Committee, Joseph Buttinger, to set up an office in Vietnam. At this time Buttinger was involved in Socialist politics as an editor of *Dissent* magazine; during the mid-Thirties, under the name of Gustave Richter, he had been the leader of the underground Social Democratic Party in Austria. This had been a bitter experience. His one accomplishment, as he writes about it in his memoirs, *In the Twilight of Socialism*, had been to stop the growth of the Communists.

A year after this book was published, a CIA agent named Edward Lansdale introduced Buttinger to the men around Ngo Dinh Diem, and after some three months in Vietnam Buttinger believed Diem to be the answer to the Communist revolution. As Buttinger remarked to this author, "He was strong and shrewd and determined to stay in power and would stay in power."

During the late fall of 1954, while Buttinger was in Vietnam, a serious split was developing among Americans concerned with Vietnam. As Cherne's telegram indicated, U.S. missions in Saigon were strongly backing Diem. For example, an abrupt halt was called to the revolt of General Hinh, the head of the Vietnamese army and an officer in the French army as well. When General Collins arrived in mid-November 1954, as Eisenhower's Special Ambassador, he made it clear that the United States would not pay the army if Diem was overthrown. In a matter of days Hinh was sent out of the country and dismissed as head of the army.

However, from the very beginning Diem displayed that tendency toward autocracy and family rule for which the mass media of the United States would belatedly condemn his administration eight years later. In early 1955, when he moved to crush the religious sects, whose military forces rivaled his power, some influential Americans began to side with the French against him. The most important of these was General Collins, and his view was shared by other American observers. Among them was the newspaper columnist Joseph Alsop, who contended that Diem's base of support was too narrow to rival that of the Vietminh. (Both men were later to renew their support of Diem after he defeated the sects.)

At this juncture, when it looked as if the United States might dispose of Diem, his reservoir of support, his "lobby," proved decisive. In the ensuing struggle the curious alliance of Lansdale, the CIA agent, Buttinger, the ex-Austrian Socialist, and Cardinal Spellman won the day.

On the official level, Lansdale convinced his Director, Allen Dulles, of Diem's efficiency, and the latter convinced his brother, who, as Secretary of State, talked with the President. The recent book on the CIA, *The Invisible Government,* by David Wise and Thomas B. Ross, places the total responsibility for swinging U.S. support to Diem at this stage on Lansdale, but the private political pressures were important. Buttinger returned from Vietnam excited about Diem but fearful that the United States was not totally committed to him. He turned to the group around the International Rescue Committee, one of the most useful of them being the public relations counsel for the organization, Harold Oram. Oram knew the head of the Catholic Relief Services in Washington and that gentleman introduced Buttinger to Cardinal Spellman. The Cardinal was still an enthusiastic believer in Diem, and Buttinger alerted him to the impending crises in Diem's fortunes.

Spellman sent Buttinger back to Washington to meet with Joseph P. Kennedy and finally, according to Buttinger in an interview with this author, these two powerful men, in a long-distance telephone conversation, decided to whom Buttinger should tell his story. In Washington, Kennedy introduced him to Senator Mike Mansfield and to Kenneth Young of the State Department. John F. Kennedy was in California at the time but Buttinger had a long conversation with his administrative assistant.

Meanwhile, Cardinal Spellman had arranged meetings with the editorial board of the New York *Herald Tribune*, the chief editors of *Life* and *Time*, and several editors of *The New York Times*. On January 29, 1955, two days after Buttinger's visit to the *Times*, that paper carried an editorial which closely paralleled Buttinger's arguments on Diem's behalf. Buttinger also elaborated his position in *The Reporter* of January 27, 1955 and *The New Republic* of February 28, 1955.

From the spring of 1955 on, the U.S. commitment to Diem was complete. This meant that the United States would ignore any French protestations and the Geneva Accords—including the provisions calling for reunification through free elections, which, as even Diem's most ardent supporters conceded, would bring the Communist-oriented Vietminh to power. A cardinal, a CIA agent, and an ex-Austrian Socialist seemed to have carried the day against the instincts of a general turned President.

One provision of the Geneva Accords, it will be remembered, had specified that during a 300-day period following the signing of the Accords "any civilians . . . who wish to go and live in the zone assigned to the other party shall be permitted and helped to do so. . . ." This led to a great flow of refugees between spring 1954 and spring 1955. The bulk of the movement was from the Vietminh area in the North to the South and eventually involved close to a million people. (According to Bernard Fall, only about 150,000 refugees went North to the Vietminh.)

These statistics were interpreted in the United States as a repudiation of Vietminh rule by the Vietnamese people —a mass flight to freedom. But the interpretation ignored two facts: (1) the number of people going North was held to a small total by order of the Vietminh, which wanted its sympathizers to remain in the South to prepare for the elections; (2) the bulk of those going South fell into two groups—dependents of the colonial native army (200,000) and Catholics (679,000).

The Catholics were a by-product of the French rule, members of a minority religion which had been brought by Portuguese and French missionaries into a predominantly Buddhist population. The Catholic communities in the North had enjoyed a protected status under the French and they had raised militia units that fought beside the French against the Vietminh. With the collapse of the French, these communities feared reprisals, or at least grave restrictions on their activities, under the new Vietminh rule.

One American who did much to blur the distinction between the Catholic minority and the rest of the population in the North was Tom Dooley, a young navy doctor turned writer, whose book *Deliver Us from Evil* had a great impact on the American public. Dooley had gone to Vietnam as part of the U.S. Navy's program of aid in transporting the refugees to the South. He witnessed the great suffering of an uprooted people. As a Catholic, he was particularly impressed with their religious opposition to Communism and the fact that they fled with the physical symbols of that religion in hand:

> . . . recognizing us as friends and not as foes, they hoisted, on a broken spar, their own drenched flag; a flag they had hidden for years . . . their symbol, their emblem, their heraldry . . . a yellow and gold flag displaying the Pope's tiara and the keys of Saint Peter.

Working among the Catholic refugees, Dooley took no account of the fact that 90 percent of the Vietnamese population would be indifferent to the yellow and gold flag, even in the unlikely event that they understood its symbolism.

To Dooley, even aside from the religious aspect, these people were on the side of the "free world" in opposition to the total evil of Communism: ". . . how, outside expanding Russia, do you go about being an imperialist nowadays?" "Ho Chi Minh has been a Moscow-trained puppet from the start." "The Godless cruelties of Communism. . . ."

The Vietminh was indicted:

> They preached hatred against the institutions, traditions, and customs of colonial Vietnam. Everything "feudal" or "reactionary" was to be destroyed . . .

Dooley combined his anti-Communism with a strenuous belief in an American-style economic system as the basis of any country's prosperity and freedom:

> . . . we continually explained to thousands of refugees, as individuals and in groups, that only in a country which permits companies to grow large could such fabulous charity be found. . . . These companies [that sent drugs] . . . responded with the enthusiasm of great corporations in a great country.

With this ideological background, it becomes easier to understand Dooley's rather extensive rewriting of history. No act attributed to the Communists was dismissed as unbelievable or as requiring factual substantiation. All of them fitted the "devil theory" and were passed on to the millions who read his book, heard his lectures, and saw the film based on *Deliver Us from Evil.*

Dooley's account of the American effort begins not with the $2.6 billion spent in support of the French between 1950-54, but rather with the mission to aid the refugees. "We had come late to Vietnam, but we had come. And we brought not bombs and guns, but help and love."

The 17th Parallel that divided the refugees from the free world was "the rim of Hell" with "the demons of Communism stalking outside and now holding the upper half of the country in their strangling grip." Those who fought the "devils" were, by definition, heroes. . . .

It is unfair to treat Dooley's book as history, although it may have served as such for many of its readers. Its significance was to provide a vocabulary of Communist horror that found its way into the speeches of presidents and was, for many ordinary Americans, their only significant emotional encounter with Communism in Asia. According to Dooley, Ho Chi Minh had begun his war against the French in December 1946, "by disembowelling more than 1,000 native women in Hanoi" who were associated with the French. There had been rumors about this, but no factual evidence is provided in any of the standard accounts of that period. An authoritative refutation is supplied by the French writer, Paul Mus:

> I am today in a position to state and to prove that four-fifths of the stories or reports of awful atrocities inflicted by the Vietnamese on our compatriots in Hanoi, December 19, 1946, are either made up or in error.

Dooley lent highly emotional support to the goals of American foreign policy in Vietnam, but he sharply criticized inefficiency in execution. America proved receptive to this type of criticism and Dooley became a folk hero. In 1960 the Gallup Poll found him to be one of the ten most admired Americans.

Dooley believed in his work and his writing, and was deeply moved, as he said, when President Diem gave him the highest award of his land. It attests to his innocence that he did not know that the choice for the award had been inspired by the CIA's man in Vietnam, Colonel Edward Lansdale.

On January 25, 1955, *Look* carried an impressive photostory of the flight of the refugees. The article was by Leo Cherne and it combined a poignant description of the plight of the refugees with a political message. The subheading stated the theme: "Battered and shunted about by war, they are too weary to resist the Reds without us." The United States had a responsibility to become involved further in Vietnam because the South is "still free but will fall under Red control if Communists win elections set for July of 1956." And this was the likely event, said Cherne, for "if elections were held today, the overwhelming majority of Vietnamese would vote Communist." But if the South Vietnamese might be indifferent to the Communist menace, others were not: "Asians are convinced that U.S. prestige and influence in Asia cannot survive another defeat. Europe wants to see whether the Communists will be stopped here or will grow into an irresistible force. . . ."

Cherne stated the U.S. predicament: "No more than eighteen months remain for us to complete the job of winning over the Vietnamese before they vote. What can we do?"

The answer was for the United States to "mobilize democratic leadership," which could be found among the Catholic refugees. The International Rescue Committee was helping to do this by ferreting out the educated men among the refugees and funneling them into the government administration.

It was later to be charged by many in the United States that Diem's regime floundered on his pro-Catholic prejudice. But the heavy use of Catholic refugees as administrators was natural, because they were certified opponents of the Vietminh who also were educated. As Cherne said of the Catholic refugees, "There is an army of 400,000 Vietnamese ready and anxious to convince their countrymen that they must choose freedom." By embracing the refugees, Diem helped maintain his administration in power, but he also planted seeds for the anti-Catholic demonstrations that led to the fall of his government in 1963.

There is no doubt that the movement and resettlement of 900,000 refugees from North to South Vietnam was the most successful program of the Diem administration. It was also the first immediate result of massive American aid, which laid out about $89 for each refugee (in a country with an $85 per year per capita income). The U.S. Seventh Fleet joined the French navy to move the refugees, and private agencies (Catholic Relief Services, International Rescue Committee, Red Cross, Junior Chamber of Commerce, Michigan State University, etc.) poured in to assist the large numbers of French and American government personnel in Saigon.

Once the refugees had been transported, the paramount task was to see to their permanent well-being by integrating them into the economy. The South was under-populated and this facilitated the provision of land to the refugees. Usually, the refugees had moved as whole villages, with their hierarchies and leadership generally intact. During the first two years of the program, most of these were supported by a U.S. relief program of dollar aid and surplus agricultural food distributed by the Catholic Relief Services. In his book, *The Two Vietnams,* Bernard Fall concluded, "Obviously most of these refugees were then still living from handouts rather than from the fruits of their labor." A good portion of the land cleared for them was in the Cai San project, where 90,000 were settled in an area formerly sparsely populated. This was the showplace for government tours by visitors to Vietnam. The land was cleared by 100 tractors ordered by the United States Operations Mission, which also brought in technicians and representatives of the tractor firms from the United States to train native operators.

This was an effective crash program of American aid; it had little to do with the ability of the Diem government to develop the economy as a whole. In fact, the refugee program had a negative impact on the Vietnamese not so favored. An essentially "welfare" movement tailored to the needs of a minority group by a minority leader was bound to grate on the non-Catholic majority. The religious problem in Vietnam had some of its roots in this program. In the final analysis, the refugees were *not* integrated into South Vietnamese society.

The "flight to freedom" of the refugees provided an important public relations basis for continued U.S. involvement in Vietnam and was used as such by those Americans concerned about Diem's future. The U.S. government had helped Diem over the hurdles posed by the rival sects, the opposition elements, the Vietminh, and the "non-elections." [1] But if Diem as Chief of State, an office he assumed on October 26, 1955, was to continue to hold off the Vietminh, he would have to develop a governmental structure, provide political stability, and carry out a program of economic development. All of this would require massive American aid, both economic and technical. The flight of the refugees and the wide publicity given to it in the United States made the American public receptive.

At this point, the various individuals committed to the development of Vietnam as a showcase of democracy began to draw together as an unofficial "Vietnam lobby." The founding of the American Friends of Vietnam in the fall of 1955 provided the "lobby" with a formal organization. This group led the fight on Diem's behalf during the next six years.

The announced purpose of the American Friends of Vietnam was "to extend more broadly a mutual understanding of Vietnamese and American history, cultural customs, and democratic institutions." In actuality, it was concerned with the political objective of committing the United States to a massive aid program on Diem's behalf. In pursuit of that policy, the organization cited the alleged success of the program to date in creating an "economic and political miracle" in Vietnam.

The Friends was primarily an organization of the liberal center. Its founding members as listed on its letterhead included Senators Kennedy and Neuberger, Max Lerner, Arthur Schlesinger, Jr., Representatives Edna Kelly and Emmanuel Celler, with the Socialist Norman Thomas and the "right wing" Governor J. Bracken Lee. This provided an attractive

---

[1] *The reference is to the nationwide elections scheduled under the Geneva Agreements for 1956, but never held because of Diem's and the United States' opposition. See pp. 159–160.–ed.*

political balance. Power in the organization resided in a fourteen-member executive committee, some of whose members were also on the board of directors of the International Rescue Committee, including Leo Cherne and Joseph Buttinger. Cardinal Spellman and the Church's program in Vietnam were represented on the board by Monsignor Harnett, head of the Catholic Relief Services.

Two members of the executive committee, Norbert Muhlen and Sol Sanders, were on the staff of *The New Leader*, and the political philosophy of that magazine, militant anti-Communism plus sympathy for government-inspired social reform, best summarizes the philosophy of most of the executive committee members. Another member of the executive committee was Elliot Newcomb, who was later to become the treasurer of the organization. Newcomb and Harold Oram, were partners in a public relations firm, Newcomb-Oram, which two months before the formation of the American Friends of Vietnam had signed a contract with Diem's government to handle its public relations in the United States. Newcomb subsequently left the firm, but Oram continued to be registered with the Justice Department as a foreign agent acting for the Diem government until June 30, 1961. The Diem government paid the Oram firm a $3,000 monthly fee plus expenses, with a third of it earmarked for a full-time campaign director. This position was held from 1956 to the end of the contract in 1961 by Gilbert Jonas, who had been executive secretary of the American Friends of Vietnam and later became its secretary and assistant treasurer.

Up to this point Vietnam had not been a popular subject for American scholarship or journalism. There were few "experts" on the area in the universities or the press. The vastly expanded American role in the period following the Geneva Accords produced a great demand for knowledge about the country. As a result, those who were most intimately involved in the American program there generally blossomed as the chief sources of information and opinion. This was natural, but most of them were committed protagonists and their writing soon became propaganda for the cause. This was particularly true of university participation. The one group of social scientists most informed about the area was pulled in to work on a U.S.-sponsored program that came to typify American political involvement in Vietnam. This was the group sent out by Michigan State University.

In 1955, '56, '57, even '58, President Ngo Dinh Diem and his entire government had a fantastically complete and almost naive, confidence in Americans, per se.

Especially "on the in" in those days was the Michigan State University Group, paid by the U.S. Government under a contract to "advise" the Vietnamese Government in a number of fields of activity. Among their "advisory" duties was the formation of what is now referred to by "foreign adventurers" and the foreign press as "the secret police of Mr. Ngo Dinh Nhu."

The MSU group proceeded with "training" for several years. The head of the MSU group was considered the most "in" man among the foreigners and many considered him more "in" than the President's own ministers.

The MSU group enjoyed an extraordinary power based on this confidence. Not only did they "train" but they also "controlled" in large measure the now famous "secret police."

The most "in" man of 1955 referred to in this 1963 editorial from *The Times of Vietnam,* a Diem-controlled paper, was Wesley Fishel, the young professor who had persuaded Diem to come to the United States to line up American support for his cause. Fishel first went to work for the Diem government in 1954 as an "advisor on government reorganization." He was also a member of the personal staff of Special Ambassador Collins and, in Fishel's words to this author, "I was the only contact that he [Collins] had with Diem that was at all effective for many months. . . . After two years I surfaced—to use a CIA term—to become head of the MSU program."

In addition to Fishel's and Diem's interest the decision to formally associate Michigan State involved higher policy considerations. The National Security Council in the spring of 1955 had decided on continuing all-out U.S. support for Diem. No less a personage than Vice-President Nixon called John Hannah, the president of Michigan State, to elicit his support. Hannah was told, according to Fishel, that Vietnam had been declared top priority and that it was in the national interest for his university to become involved. Officially, the project would be part of the International Cooperation Administration program of assistance to underdeveloped countries. It was in fact the largest operation and would involve 54 professors and 200 Vietnamese assistants. It was also to fill a special need.

The Geneva Accords had prohibited increases in the

rength of either side through the introduction of "all
ypes of arms" or build-ups in troop strength. The presence
f the International Control Commission (made up of na-
onals of Canada, Poland, and India) offered the prospect
f unfavorable publicity to the United States if its Military
Assistance Advisory Group, United States Operations Mis-
ion, or CIA agents operated openly. The Michigan group
yould serve as "cover."

Diem, as a minority figure in his own country, required a
trengthened police power. The Diem government had reason
o expect an attack from segments of the armed forces hostile
o it or from police units under the control of the bandit
3inh Xuyen sect. It was for this reason, according to Fishel,
hat Art Brandstatter, head of the Michigan State University
chool of Police Administration and ex-Colonel of M.P.s,
began training Diem's Palace Guard. As part of this training
program, described in MSU monthly reports, the Palace
Guard was supplied with guns and ammunition the Michigan
State professors obtained from the U.S.-MAAG.

Bao Dai, when he had been Chief of State, had placed the
national police and security services under the control of the
Binh Xuyen, and they were hostile to the Diem government.
By April of 1955, Diem could call upon army troops whose
oyalties had been ensured by Ambassador Collins' statement that the United States would only meet the payroll of an
army committed to the Diem government. These were employed to crush the Binh Xuyen. The Michigan State professors decided to concentrate their energies on the reconstitu-
tion of the police apparatus. Their monthly report for July
1955, stated:

> It has been generally agreed and the Ambassador has
> specifically asked that we concentrate almost ex-
> clusively on the police and field administration projects
> until the elections of next July. . . . It is now felt by
> the MSU team that in order to be in accord with
> U.S. policy locally it is necessary to engage almost ex-
> clusively in immediate impact programs until after the
> elections in July 1956 and that the immediate impact
> programs in our program are the field administration
> and the police projects.

By November 1955, the professors were able to state in their
monthly report:

> During the month of October we received a notice of
> Washington's approval of the recommended expanded
> police program submitted August 29. We started imme-

diately to implement this program. Conferences were
held at USOM on October 10 and the Embassy on
October 23 and 24, trying to coordinate Internal Security operations in Vietnam, in which our government
has an interest.

With Washington's sanction, the professors reorganized the
old French-sponsored Sureté into a new "Vietnamese Bureau of Investigation," which was modeled upon the FBI but
would "also be responsible for the many other enforcement
duties that are peculiar to this part of the world, such as information and postal control, etc." The police force was
turned into a paramilitary unit, trained in particular to deal
with uprisings on the part of the citizenry. Once Saigon was
secured, it became essential to pacify the countryside, and
so the Civil Guard, a rural-based militia of 40,000 men, was
organized. The immigration authorities were trained to fin-
gerprint the Chinese population, which was distrusted by the
Diem government, and all agencies of government were
trained in maintaining security dossiers. The monthly records
of the project list a wide variety of guns, ammunition, vehicles, grenades, handcuffs, and tear-gas equipment that the
Michigan State team passed on from "official U.S. agencies"
to their Vietnamese protégés. From 1955 to 1960, the
Michigan team had the major responsibility for training,
equipping, and financing the police apparatus for Diem's
state.

The MSU team, of course, had other responsibilities for
building a governmental structure. The professors worked on
the constitution, redesigned parts of the bureaucracy, developed a school of public administration and the beginnings of
a civil service. In their attempts to gear the government to a
solution of the serious social problems confronting it, the
MSU project published many studies. They were couched in
the jargon of public administration and were aimed at increasing the efficiency of Diem's operations. These documents never mentioned the facts of the dictatorship under
which the Diem family consistently stood in the way of the
reforms suggested. The MSU team constructed a beautiful
paper government that never was translated into reality.

The failure of the MSU project may have resulted in part
from that "in-ness" to which *The Times of Vietnam* referred.
President Hannah was an important Republican figure and
had been an Assistant Secretary of Defense. Interviews with
some members of the project revealed that involvement in a

igh priority government program gave them a heady feeling
f glamour and prestige. As one member frankly states, "I
aw the job in Vietnam primarily from the standpoint of my
wn career development. I had taught public administration
nd I saw this as a job with experience, with an entrée back
nto the academic world."

The project favored a technical approach to social prob-
ems. This "scientific style" provided a justification for aca-
demics functioning in a strange land as controlled agents of
heir government and permitted them to perform tasks that
vould otherwise have run contrary to the personal ethics of
nany of them. The interviews this author had with various
nembers of the MSU team revealed a strong sensitivity to
he titles, positions, awards, and other attentions of the in-
titutions with which they had contact. Later, their attitudes
vere to range from the rather cynical view of one project
ead who stated: "Knock it out of your head that 99 percent
f university guys are educators—they are all operators," to
hose who became tormented by the moral implications of
heir work in Vietnam. In this category was one economist
vho thought that the economic program of the Diem gov-
rnment was an almost total failure and concluded that the
easants might have been better off with the other side. But
ilthough he was to write about Vietnam, he did not express
uch thoughts, and his reasons for not doing so were de-
cribed as follows:

> If you are an ordinary person you will be listened to
> insofar as it sounds right. Otherwise you're considered
> a deviant. Only if you have high status will a deviant
> be listened to. . . . I suppose people would most likely
> figure that I was a crackpot who lacks good judg-
> ment—not cashiered for this but always a question
> mark—wouldn't say you're subversive—but would in-
> fluence their judgment about my judgment.

If they were reticent while in Vietnam, some of the professors became highly prolific on paper after their return to the
United States at the end of their tours of duty. Much of our
public expertise on Vietnam has come from alumni of the
MSU project; they are the authors of many of the articles
about Vietnam not only in scholarly journals but in the mass
media. In this writing, they have concerned themselves with
the many social and political problems facing Vietnam, but
nowhere have they engaged in a critical analysis of the MSU
project itself. They had played a vital role in building the
governmental apparatus for the Diem Administration, but
much of their work was irrelevant and self-defeating, and
many of them came to feel that a good part of it was, in an
old-fashioned sense, immoral.

In 1957, after three years in power, Diem traveled to the
United States for an official visit. By then he had crushed

the rival power of religious sects and opposition politicians and had won the commitment of the United States to finance his regime and supply it with a large force of Americans to implement the aid program.

It was during this trip that the celebration of the "Miracle of Vietnam" began in earnest. Diem was "handled" by the Oram public relations firm and the American Friends of Vietnam. He received the red-carpet treatment in official circles and in the press. He was flown in on President Eisenhower's personal plane, the "Columbine," and the President met him at the airport. . . .

The "miracle" thesis formulated by the lobby was accepted by most of the mass media during the first five years of Diem's regime. It was generally accepted that aid to Vietnam had produced a success story: the Diem government had turned back the threat of Communism by initiating vast programs of economic and political reform and greatly improving the lives of the people. American aid and advice had helped to develop a "nationalist alternative" to the Vietminh and the country was making rapid strides toward political stability and economic independence.[3]

Program of the National Liberation Front of South Vietnam*

I. *Overthrow the camouflaged colonial regime of the American imperialists and the dictatorial power of Ngo Dinh Diem, servant of the Americans, and institute a government of national democratic union.*

The present South Vietnamese regime is a camouflaged colonial regime dominated by the Yankees, and the South Vietnamese Government is a servile government, implementing faithfully all the policies of the American imperialists. Therefore, this regime must be overthrown and a government of national and democratic union put in its place composed of representatives of all social classes, of all nationalities, of the various political parties, of all religions; patriotic, eminent citizens must take over for the people the control of economic, political, social, and cultural interests and thus bring about independence, democracy, well-being, peace, neutrality, and efforts toward the peaceful unification of the country.

II. *Institute a largely liberal and democratic regime.*

1. Abolish the present constitution of the dictatorial powers of

[3] *In this valuable study Scheer also discusses the agrarian reform program under Diem, the press campaign on behalf of the South Vietnamese regime, and the general economic situation. By 1959, he concludes, "the 'miracle' bubble of Vietnam burst; it had been nothing more than a miracle of public relations." (p. 54.) Scheer also points out that another precondition for the "stability" of the Diem regime (besides U. S. support) was North Vietnam's willingness to abide by the Geneva Agreements, a willingness that lasted until about 1959. He also discusses the policy of the Kennedy Administration toward Vietnam. Scheer's study is available from the Center for the Study of Democratic Institutions, Box 4068, Santa Barbara, California 93103—ed.*

* From Liberation Radio/South Vietnam (Feb. 13, 14, 1961).

Ngo Dinh Diem, servant of the Americans. Elect a new National Assembly through universal suffrage. 2. Implement essential democratic liberties: freedom of opinion, of press, of assembly, of movement, of trade-unionism; freedom of religion without any discrimination; and the right of all patriotic organizations of whatever political tendency to carry on normal activities. 3. Proclaim a general amnesty for all political prisoners and the dissolution of concentration camps of all sorts; abolish fascist law 10/59 and all the other antidemocratic laws; authorize the return to the country of all persons persecuted by the American-Diem regime who are now refugees abroad. 4. Interdict all illegal arrests and detentions; prohibit torture; and punish all the Diem bullies who have not repented and who have committed crimes against the people.

III. Establish an independent and sovereign economy, and improve the living conditions of the people.

1. Suppress the monopolies imposed by the American imperialists and their servants; establish an independent and sovereign economy and finances in accordance with the national interests; confiscate to the profit of the nation the properties of the American imperialists and their servants. 2. Support the national bourgeoisie in the reconstruction and development of crafts and industry; provide active protection for national products through the suppression of production taxes and the limitation or prohibition of imports that the national economy is capable of producing; reduce customs fees on raw materials and machines. 3. Revitalize agriculture; modernize production, fishing, and cattle raising; help the farmers in putting to the plow unused land and in developing production; protect the crops and guarantee their disposal. 4. Encourage and reinforce economic relations between the city and country, the plain and the mountain regions; develop commercial exchanges with foreign countries, regardless of their political regime, on the basis of equality and mutual interests. 5. Institute a just and rational system of taxation; eliminate harassing penalties. 6. Implement the labor code: prohibition of discharges, of penalties, of ill-treatment of wage earners; improvement of the living conditions of workers and civil servants; imposition of wage scales and protective measures for young apprentices. 7. Organize social welfare: find work for jobless persons; assume the support and protection of orphans, old people, invalids; come to the help of the victims of the Americans and Diemists; organize help for areas hit by bad crops, fires, or natural calamities. 8. Come to help of displaced persons desiring to return to their native areas and to those who wish to remain permanently in the South; improve their working and living conditions. 9. Prohibit expulsions, spoliation, and compulsory concentration of the population; guarantee job security for the urban and rural working populations.

IV. Reduce land rent; implement agrarian reform with the aim of providing land to the tillers.

1. Reduce land rent; guarantee to the farmers the right to till the soil; guarantee the property right of accession to fallow lands to those who have cultivated them; guarantee property rights to those farmers who have already received land. 2. Dissolve "prosperity zones," and put an end to recruitment for the camps that are called "agricultural development centers." Allow those com-

patriots who already have been forced into "prosperity zones" and "agricultural development centers" to return freely to their own lands. 3. Confiscate the land owned by American imperialists and their servants, and distribute it to poor peasants without any land or with insufficient land; redistribute the communal lands on a just and rational basis. 4. By negotiation and on the basis of fair prices, repurchase for distribution to landless peasants or peasants with insufficient land those surplus lands that the owners of large estates will be made to relinquish if their domain exceeds a certain limit, to be determined in accordance with regional particularities. The farmers who benefit from such land distribution will not be compelled to make any payment or to submit to any other conditions.

V. Develop a national and democratic culture and education.

1. Combat all forms of culture and education enslaved to Yankee fashions; develop a culture and education that is national, progressive, and at the service of the Fatherland and people. 2. Liquidate illiteracy; increase the number of schools in the fields of general education as well as in those of technical and professional education, in advanced study as well as in other fields; adopt Vietnamese as the vernacular language; reduce the expenses of education and exempt from payment students who are without means; resume the examination system. 3. Promote science and technology and the national letters and arts; encourage and support the intellectuals and artists so as to permit them to develop their talents in the service of national reconstruction. 4. Watch over public health; develop sports and physical education.

VI. Create a national army devoted to the defense of the Fatherland and the people.

1. Establish a national army devoted to the defense of the Fatherland and the people; abolish the system of American militray advisers. 2. Abolish the draft system; improve the living conditions of the simple soldiers and guarantee their political rights; put an end to ill-treatment of the military; pay particular attention to the dependents of soldiers without means. 3. Reward officers and soldiers having participated in the struggle against the domination by the Americans and their servants; adopt a policy of clemency toward the former collaborators of the Americans and Diemists guilty of crimes against the people but who have finally repented and are ready to serve the people. 4. Abolish all foreign military bases established on the territory of Vietnam.

VII. Guarantee equality between the various minorities and between the two sexes; protect the legitimate interests of foreign citizens established in Vietnam and of Vietnamese citizens residing abroad.

1. Implement the right to autonomy of the national minorities: found autonomous zones in the areas with a minority population, those zones to be an integral part of the Vietnamese nation. Guarantee equality between the various nationalities: each nationality has the right to use and develop its language and writing system, to maintain or to modify freely its mores and customs; abolish the policy of the Americans and Diemists of racial discrimination and forced assimilation. Create conditions permitting the national minorities to reach the general level of progress of the population: development of their economy and culture; formation of cadres of

minority nationalities. 2. Establish equality between the two sexes; women shall have equal rights with men from all viewpoints (political, economic, cultural, social, etc.). 3. Protect the legitimate interests of foreign citizens established in Vietnam. 4. Defend and take care of the interests of Vietnamese citizens residing abroad.

VIII. *Promote a foreign policy of peace and neutrality.*

1. Cancel all unequal treaties that infringe upon the sovereignty of the people and that were concluded with other countries by the servants of the Americans. 2. Establish diplomatic relations with all countries, regardless of their political regime, in accordance with the principles of peaceful coexistence adopted at the Bandung Conference. 3. Develop close solidarity with peace-loving nations and neutral countries; develop free relations with the nations of Southeast Asia, in particular with Cambodia and Laos. 4. Stay out of any military bloc; refuse any military alliance with another country. 5. Accept economic aid from any country willing to help us without attaching any conditions to such help.

IX. *Re-establish normal relations between the two zones, and prepare for the peaceful reunification of the country.*

The peaceful reunification of the country constitutes the dearest desire of all our compatriots throughout the country. The National Liberation Front of South Vietnam advocates the peaceful reunification by stages on the basis of negotiations and through the seeking of ways and means in conformity with the interests of the Vietnamese nation. While awaiting this reunification, the governments of the two zones will, on the basis of negotiations, promise to banish all separatist and war-mongering propaganda and not to use force to settle differences between the zones. Commercial and cultural exchanges between the two zones will be implemented; the inhabitants of the two zones will be free to move about throughout the country as their family and business interests indicate. The freedom of postal exchanges will be guaranteed.

X. *Struggle against all aggressive war; actively defend universal peace.*

1. Struggle against all aggressive war and against all forms of imperialist domination; support the national emancipation movements of the various peoples. 2. Banish all war-mongering propaganda; demand general disarmament and the prohibition of nuclear weapons; and advocate the utilization of atomic energy for peaceful purposes. 3. Support all movements of struggle for peace, democracy, and social progress throughout the world; contribute actively to the defense of peace in Southeast Asia and in the world.

Repression In the South: Law 10/59*

Article 1—Sentence of death, and confiscation of the whole or part of his property, with loss of rank in the case of army men, will be imposed on whoever commits or attempts to com-

* From Pham Van Bach, *et al.* [Members of the Juridical Studies Section of the National Scientific Research Board of the Democratic Republic of Vietnam], *Fascist Terror in South Vietnam: Law 10/59* (Hanoi, 1961), pp. 71-77. [*Although I have seen no other text of Law 10/59, I am confident that this North Vietnamese source is accurate. I conclude this from the references to the law in the writings of such Western scholars as Philippe Devillers (see p. 225).—ed.*]

mit one of the following crimes with the aim of sabotage, or of infringing upon the security of the State, or injuring the lives or property of the people: 1—Deliberate murder, food poisoning, or kidnapping; 2—Destruction, or total or partial damaging of one of the following categories of objects by means of explosives, fire, or any other means:

a) Dwelling-houses, whether inhabited or not, churches, pagodas, temples, warehouses, workshops, farms and all out-buildings belonging to private persons; b) Public buildings, residences; offices, workshops, depots, and, in a more general way, all constructions of any kind belonging to the State, and any other property, movable or immovable, belonging to, or controlled by the State, or which is under the system of concession, or of public management; c) All air, land, and water means of transport, all kinds of vehicles; d) Mines, with machines and equipment; e) Weapons, military material and equipment, posts, buildings, offices, depots, workshops, and constructions of any kind relating to defense or police forces; f) Crops, draft animals and farm implements, forests of any kind; g) Installations for telecommunications, postal service, broadcasting, the production and distribution of electricity and water, as well as all buildings, constructions, instruments used in connection with the above; h) Dikes, dams, roads, railways, airfields, seaports, bridges, channels, or works relating to them; i) Waterways, large or small, and canals.

Article 2—Sentence of hard labor for life, and confiscation of the whole or part of his property, with loss of rank in the case of army men, will be imposed upon whoever commits or attempts to commit one of the following crimes with the aim of sabotage, or of infringing upon the security of the State, or if injuring the lives or property of the people: 1—Robbery, either armed or committed by two or more persons; 2—Interruption of land or water traffic by terrorist acts, threats to use arms, or any other means; 3—Threats of assassination, of arson of houses and crops, or of kidnapping, either direct or indirect; 4—Hindrance to the holding of a market on the usual day; 5—Any act of destruction or sabotage not mentioned in the above provisions.

Article 3—Whoever belongs to an organization designed to help to prepare or to perpetrate crimes enumerated in Articles 1 and 2, or takes pledges to do so, will be subject to the sentences provided for in the said articles.

Article 4—Offenders, accomplices, and instigators of the crimes coming within the competence of the special military courts, as provided for in the second part of the present law, will not benefit from extenuating circumstances.

Article 5—Any person charged with a crime falling within the competence of the special military courts who is the first person to give information to the Government or the military, administrative, or judicial authorities before such a crime is committed or attempted, and while no legal proceedngs have yet opened, or, in case of legal proceedings having already been opened, helps to arrest the authors or accomplices, will not be subject to the sentence provided for and will be able to enter a plea of extenuating circumstances.

However, the accused who enjoys non-application of sentence may be subject to forced residence, or prohibition from remaining in certain specified areas, for a period to be determined by the court.

Article 6—Three special military courts are set up and based in Saigon, Ban Me Thuot, and Hué.

The jurisdiction of the Saigon special military court extends over the southern provinces, that of Ban Me Thuot special military court over the provinces of the central High Plateaus, that of the Hué special military court over the provinces of the central plains.

As the need arises, other special military courts may be set up by decree, which will also determine their respective jurisdictions vis-à-vis the courts already existing.

Any change in the jurisdiction of the special military courts will be the subject of a subsequent decree.

The special military courts will be established in the seat of the courts of appeal, courts of first instance, or courts of the peace with extended powers, in case they have no separate seat of their own. They will sit there, or can sit away from their usual seats, if the need arises.

Article 7—Each special military court will consist of:

—A field or general officer graduated in law: president;

—The mayor of the town, or the chief of the province in which the court is sitting or a representative: counsellor;

—A field or general officer: counsellor.

The president or counsellors of the court will be appointed by decree of the Minister for Defense or the Assistant Secretary of State for Defense for a term of six months. In case of lack of field officers, company officers will be chosen where possible.

If need be, substitutes may also be immediately appointed according to the above procedure.

Article 9—A chief clerk, assisted by a number of clerks and typists, will be responsible for the clerk's office.

This personnel will be appointed by decree of the Minister for Defense or the Assistant Secretary of State for Defense.

Article 10—All personnel of the court shall take a written oath before the High Court before assuming their functions.

Article 11—The following categories of offenses fall within the competence of the special military courts:

1—The offenses enumerated in articles 1, 2, and 3 of the present law, without regard to the civilian or military status of the accused.

2—The crimes of espionage and treason determined by ordinance No. 47 dated August 21, 1956.

3—The crimes of speculation, and sabotage of the economy and finances of the State, as determined by ordinance No. 61 dated October 3, 1955.

4—Crimes expressly stated by law to come within the competence of the special military courts.

Article 12—When a case comes within the competence of a special military court, the Minister for Defense or the Assistant Secretary of State for Defense will serve an order on the accused to appear before the court, without preliminary inquiry.

Article 13—The public prosecutor shall read the bill affirming the competence of the court and giving the details of the charges made.

Article 14—The public prosecutor is empowered to use the agents of public order in the pursuit of an offender coming within the competence of the special military court.

Article 15—The special military court is to sit within three days of receipt of the order of the Minister for Defense, or the Assistant Secretary of State for Defense, mentioned in Article 12.

The summons of the public prosecutor will be communicated to the accused twenty-four hours before the sitting of the special military court.

Article 16—The accused has the right to have his case conducted by counsel. In case he has none, the public prosecutor or the president of the court shall appoint counsel for him.

Article 17—The decisions of the special military court are not subject to appeal, and no appeal is allowed to the High Court.

Article 18—The decisions of the special military court will be acted upon in accordance with the procedure provided for in articles 93 to 98 of the military penal code.

Article 19—Sentence of death will only be acted upon

after the appeal for mercy has been rejected.

Article 20—If need be, the methods of application of the present law will be determined by decree.

Article 21—All legal provisions which are contrary to the present law are hereby repealed.

The present law will be published in the Official Journal of the Republic of Vietnam.

Saigon, May 6, 1959   NGO DINH DIEM

"The Policy of the Government of the Republic of [South] Vietnam With Regard to Former Resistance Members" *

It is necessary to review all the organizations of the Vietcong or other organizations set up by them, and proceed with a classification of persons belonging to the following organizations:

The Vietcong founded the "Vietminh League," the "Democratic Party," and the organizations of the youth, women, peasants, and workers "for national salvation," etc. In the Nam Phan [1] they made use of the Vanguard Youth Organization to their own benefit.

In 1946, the Vietcong founded the "Lien Viet Front," the Socialist Party, the General Confederation of Labor (member of the World Trade Unions of the Communist International), and innumerable organs of the civil and military power such as the administrative committees, the people's councils, the liberation army, the relieving troops[2], etc.

During the war period, from 1946 to 1954, the Vietcong established many other organizations under the various signboards "for national salvation," "for the Resistance," "for the revolution," "for peace," such as the "Administrative and Resistance Committees," the "Committee for the Defense of Peace," the "Cultural Association for National Salvation,"

---

* Excerpts from Saigon newspaper *Cach Manh Quoc Gia*, various issues from August 25 to September 2, 1959, in *Fascist Terror in South Vietnam: Law 10/59* (Hanoi, 1961), pp. 78-81.

[1] *Cochin China, or Nam Bo.*

[2] *They were the Vietnamese units which relieved Chiang Kai-shek's troops, along with the units of the French Expeditionary Corps, in accordance with the March 6, 1946 Preliminary Agreement.* [See p. 61—ed.]

the "Association of Resistant Catholics," the "Association of Buddhists for National Salvation," the "Association of the Fighters' Mothers;" and such military and para-military formations as "the People's Army," the "Guerrilla fighters," the "Self-Defense Corps," the "Shock Youth," the "White-haired Fighters," the "Death Volunteers," etc.[3]

With regard to persons belonging to the above-mentioned organizations founded by the Vietcong before 1945, the Government will verify, differentiate, and adopt the following attitude:

All the members, cadres, and leaders of the Indochinese Communist Party and the Vietnam Workers' Party (i.e. the Vietcong) cannot be considered as former Resistance members. The reason is that they have not pursued the fulfillment of the objectives of the Resistance, as has been said previously. On the contrary, they pursued Communist objectives, and sought to turn Vietnam into a colony and the Vietnamese into the slaves of Red imperialism. They are Communists, traitors, and agents of Russia and China.

It is impossible to admit the arguments advanced by a number of Communist Party members for their defense, saying that they have adhered to this party for the purpose of an ideological resistance. This is precisely the argument most often used by the Vietcong to conceal the other schemes of the Communist Party and to monopolize the title of Resistance member for them. . . .

With regard to families having their members re-grouped to the North and those entertaining relations with the cadres and members of the Communist Party and the Workers' Party, the government and the people will compel them to cut off any political relations with the latter (that is to say to abstain from supplying them with food, money, medicine, and daily necessities, from giving them information and from sustaining the Vietcong, etc.) and, on the basis of the personal activity of each of them, will determine who is a Resistance member and a patriot, who is a Vietcong saboteur . . .

Those who adhere to the illegal organizations secretly left behind in South Vietnam by the Vietcong or set up by

[3] *Thus the term "Vietcong" designates all artisans of the revolution, all the Government of the Democratic Republic of Vietnam, and all Resistance members, civilian and military.—ed.*

them after the signing of the Geneva Agreements are, without exception, elements who deliberately help the Vietcong and work for the interests of foreign Communist imperialists, Russian or Chinese, carrying out activities of subversion, espionage, and betrayal. They are not Resistance members and patriots. The illegal and treacherous organizations secretly left behind or created by the Vietcong in the Southern zone after the conclusion of the Geneva Agreements are: the "Workers' Party," the "Fatherland Front," the "Peace Movement," the "Liberation Front," the "Labor Youth," the "Religious Sects League," the "Religious Sects Alliance," and the various armed formations of the Vietcong.

—To severely punish the Vietcong who profit by the title of former Resistance members to carry out sabotage.

The Buddhist Crisis In Vietnam:
A Pulitzer Prize-Winning Report

BY DAVID HALBERSTAM*

The scene has changed sharply in South Vietnam since the conflict between the Government and the Buddhists erupted four months ago.

Last May, when Buddhist protests were beginning, a Vietnamese professor told a foreigner: "You Americans look around and see the Vietnamese orderly and quiet, and you think everything is all right here. But this is not so. We Vietnamese have been living under oppression for centuries. When the time is right, the people express themselves in one way or another."

"Today," the professor added, "they dare not make outright political protests. So they express their feeling through religion."

Few Americans would now consider Vietnam calm. Out of a seemingly orderly state a crisis exploded—first as a religious quarrel, then as a political dispute, then as a national emergency. Finally it grew into an international conflict reducing to hostility the Vietnamese Government's relations with its foremost ally, the United States.

* Former correspondent for the West Point, Mississippi *Daily Times-Leader* and Nashville *Tennessean* before joining the staff of *The New York Times* in 1960. He became *The Times*' correspondent in South Vietnam in the fall of 1962, replacing Homer Bigart. The selection is from *The New York Times* (September 11, 1963).

In these four months unknown Buddhist priests rose to power and then went to jail. The President's brother and sister-in-law, Mr. and Mrs. Ngo Dinh Nhu, long considered powers behind the scenes, came into full public view and accomplished what some observers consider a palace coup against President Ngo Dinh Diem. Finally, some United States civilian officials fear that the present Government can no longer wage a successful war against the Communist guerrillas of the Vietcong.

What caused the Buddhist crisis? How political was it? What were the issues? What went wrong? Through months of protests, statements, and demonstrations, two political aspects of the crisis have stood out.

First, the Buddhist protest, observers say, could not have taken place unless the climate for some sort of dissent had been ripe, unless there had been deep and latent dissatisfaction in many areas of the country.

Second, the lasting impact of the crisis will stem not from who was right and who was wrong, not from the merits of the Buddhist demands, but from how the Government handled events. Most observers say the key question centers on the regime's ability to unite the population at a time when it is engaged in a shooting war with a real enemy.

That there was any trouble at all between Buddhists and the Roman Catholic leadership of Vietnam came as a surprise to most Americans stationed here. Americans, preoccupied with the guerrilla war, their reason for being in Vietnam, had rarely seen evidence of religious discrimination. Even politically alert foreigners had had little contact with the Buddhists.

Yet, as most Americans knew, Vietnam is a predominantly Buddhist country. The Asia Foundation, a nonprofit American group that has devoted considerable research to the country, estimates that ten or eleven million of South Vietnam's 14.5 million people consider themselves Buddhists. Of these, five or six million are practicing Buddhists. The rest, particularly the poor and the peasants, are closer to simple ancestor worshipers, but their sects profess Buddhism.

Catholics number close to 10 per cent, including many who fled from North Vietnam in 1954, when the country was partitioned. Many of the most cultured and best-educated people here are Catholics. They include the powerful and aristocratic Ngo family, which governs the country. Though there had been no great religious outburst in Vietnam before May 8, many observers felt that beneath the surface there was considerable unrest and growing dissatisfaction. In recent years, some observers felt, the Government, which had made a popular start here, had become increasingly isolated from the people and increasingly repressive. Many observers believed that the changes coincided with the growing power of Mr. and Mrs. Ngo Dinh Nhu and that the President saw events more and more through their eyes.

High American officials had seen these same omens and had suggested that the Government become more responsive. Although there was little change, American aid continued. Some observers suspected that the aid was being used to make the Government's security and police network more powerful and less dependent on the backing of the people. These warnings were voiced by many visitors, including Western correspondents and a Senate committee headed by Mike Mansfield, Democrat of Montana, who cited his long friendship with President Ngo Dinh Diem.

As recently as last March a high State Department official on a visit said, "The thing that bothers me about this Government is that the only people who are for it are Americans."

In this atmosphere the Buddhist question arose. It started with the Buddhists' wish to fly their patchwork flag in Hué on the Buddha's birthday, reckoned here as the 2,587th. The Government, citing an old regulation, replied that only Government flags were permitted in public. Thousands of Buddhists demonstrated, and the Government broke up the demonstration by firing into the crowd and killing nine.

Why did the Buddhists suddenly demonstrate and choose the flag issue?

"This," said Thich Tri Quang, a Buddhist leader, "was the last straw. Whatever happens now, we will stand no more."

Most observers believe the Buddhist affair began as a religious protest with primarily religious objectives. Symbolically its birthplace was Hué, the central coastal city where religious feeling is particularly strong.

Hué is the see of Archbishop Ngo Dinh Thuc, a brother of the President. There Catholicism has become closely identified with the Government. The city was also the imperial capital of the old state of Annam, a center of Buddhist learning and a symbol of a time when Buddhism was the favored religion of Vietnam.

In Hué religious feeling is strong on both sides. This is

atypical in Vietnam. Where Buddhist leaders were often to find their Saigon followers sympathetic but cautious, Hué was to be a center of militant feeling. Buddhist leaders there often had to run hard to stay in front of the parade. Most observers believe that if the Government had moved quickly, acknowledging responsibility for the May 8 incident and paying reparations, the entire issue would have ended then and there. Had President Ngo Dinh Diem made a dramatic gesture at a pagoda, they say, or delivered a few warm and magnanimous words, he could have emerged stronger than ever.

One foreigner, recalling the episode, said he had suggested to high Saigon officials that reparations of 500,000 piasters (about $7,000), plus a quick public statement, would settle the affair. His friend, a high Vietnamese official, said quickly: "The money is all right, but we can't admit we did it. We can't have the admission."

So in spite of eyewitness accounts and photographic evidence, the Government stuck resolutely to its story: nine died at the hands of the Vietcong.

When a delegation of Buddhist high priests visited the President at this time, he told them they were "fools" to ask for religious freedom since it was guaranteed in the Constitution. At this point, the outlines of the Government's attitude began to take shape. The Buddhist protest was regarded as an affront to the Ngo family, and the kind of dramatic reply that Americans were urging on the Government was seen as a sign of weakness.

The Ngo Dinh Diem of earlier years, many observers believe, would have been able to move toward a quick settlement of the dispute. Throughout Vietnam he is known for toughness, courage, and strong anti-Communism. But the Ngo Dinh Diem of today is considered an isolated man, removed further and further from the population, hearing finely sifted reports about his people.

One officer who had been traveling through the country found himself being questioned by Ngo Dinh Diem about popular feeling. Again and again the President asked what the people were thinking. Several times the officer, sensing trouble, hedged. Finally Ngo Dinh Diem asked again: "What do the people think?"

"Well, Mr. President," the officer said, "the people are very unhappy."

At this point, according to the officer, Ngo Dinh Diem

became enraged, charged out of his chair and said, "It is all Communist propaganda."

Ngo Dinh Diem does not see himself as the type of leader Americans envision. He sees himself representing God to the people and believes that it is the duty of the population to honor him. In this situation, observers say, the President's hand was tied by his family. There were times, it is said, when he would have liked to see the entire issue settled. But the Ngo Dinh Nhus opposed a conciliatory approach, as did Archbishop Ngo Dinh Thuc.

The President is not considered anti-Buddhist as such. Most observers agree that Buddhists were persecuted in some areas of the central coastal region and that in these areas the Catholic Church and the Government had become entwined. Some sources believe that the Ngo family did not consider Buddhism a serious religion and that the Buddhists sensed this. There is no doubt that Ngo Dinh Diem, an extremely suspicious man, trusted primarily Catholics and in particular Catholics from the central region. Once he told a high officer, forgetting that he was a Buddhist: "Put your Catholic officers in sensitive places. They can be trusted."

At vital centers of the Government, power was held by Catholics—positions in the secret police and the command of troops in areas around Saigon. Thus, on purely religious grounds, the Buddhists could document their claims, although many of the claims were vague and some were exaggerated. Though the Buddhist movement was not always political, observers assert, it was, to the Government, political from the start. The Government's political flaws, and not its religious beliefs, would later haunt it.

By June the protest born in Hué began to spread to other cities in the central coastal region and to Saigon. Buddhist demonstrations continued. In Hué one student demonstration was stopped by Government forces throwing gas grenades. Sixty-seven persons went to the hospital with blister-gas burns. Slowly the protest began to take form. Priests became adept at calling correspondents, and mimeograph machines began to reproduce Western press coverage. Priests also began to show increased organizational ability; warned in Saigon that they would not be able to assemble, they quietly hired four buses, filled them with monks, pulled the shades down, and drove around the city until precisely 2 P.M. Then all the buses arrived in front of the National

Assembly. The priests filed out and began a sitdown hunger strike.

Early in June the Government began to worry about the implications of the Buddhist movement. People in Saigon and in other cities were becoming aware of a new force in Vietnam, a force standing up to the Government as no one had in years. It appeared that the Buddhists were becoming a spearhead for other dissident elements.

At this point, the United States Embassy here became concerned over the potential effect of the crisis on United States and world opinion, and on the anti-Communist war effort. The war was costing the United States $1.5 million a day. The embassy began to pressure Ngo Dinh Diem to settle the issue and to settle it quickly. Then, on June 8, Mrs. Ngo Dinh Nhu's Women's Solidarity Movement issued a bitter statement implying that the Buddhists were infiltrated by Communists. Embassy officials were stunned. "If that statement is policy, it's a disaster," one official said. "Otherwise it's simply an aberration."

Americans then let the Government know that if the matter was not settled the United States might have to dissociate itself. Americans also suggested that silence from Mrs. Ngo Dinh Nhu might be welcome. Later she was to describe this suggestion as a State Department attempt to blackmail her into silence.

Then, on June 11, an aged Buddhist priest, Thich Quang Duc, sat down at a major intersection, poured gasoline on himself, took the cross-legged "Buddha" posture and struck a match. He burned to death without moving and without saying a word. Thich Quang Duc became a hero to the Buddhists in Vietnam, and he dramatized their cause for the rest of the world. "When pictures of Quang Duc burning himself to death went around the world," an American said, "if this Government was not discriminating against Buddhists it might just as well have been."

Under considerable United States pressure, the Government and the Buddhists negotiated a five-point settlement. On June 16 they signed a joint communiqué, a strange statement of the views of both sides. It gave in to the Buddhists on some points, but it did not admit Government responsibility for the Hué incident. Instead, it appointed an all-Government committee to investigate it. The joint communiqué pleased neither side, and it radically changed the complexion of the contesting forces.

Reliable palace sources say Mrs. Ngo Dinh Nhu was furious when she heard that her brother-in-law was about to sign the communiqué. "You are a coward," she is reported to have told him.

Witnesses recall that Ngo Dinh Diem answered: "You do not understand this affair. It has international implications. We must settle it."

At almost the same moment, in Xa Loi pagoda, a young priest was threatening: "If I tell some of the other Buddhists what has been signed they will be very angry."

In days, there were reports that the Government, and particularly the Ngo Dinh Nhus, had no intention of carrying out the accord. On June 26 Ngo Dinh Nhu issued a secret memorandum to his Cong Hoa (Republican) Youth, calling the Buddhists rebels and urging the Cong Hoa to tell the Government not to accept the joint communiqué. According to diplomats and other sources, reliable reports from the palace said the Government planned to wait until interest and attention had slackened and then seize some Buddhist leaders. Early in July Vice-President Nguyen Ngoc Tho, a Buddhist, announced that a preliminary investigation of the Hué incident showed that the Vietcong were responsible for the deaths.

To the Buddhists, this and continued attacks from a newspaper supporting Ngo Dinh Nhu had an ominous sound. They were partly responsible, observers say, for a major change in the Buddhist leadership. Up to then, the leaders had been conservative; though there were powerful young members, the older leadership had managed to control them.

Some observers believe that at this point the younger priests, realizing that they were probably in the movement too deep for an easy retreat, that they were marked men, took over. They represented a new force in Vietnamese politics, for by now they were deep in politics. These priests are in their thirties and early forties, men clearly affected by thirty years of political revolution and political war in Vietnam.

At first these new leaders, essentially political in their instincts, seemed to represent vague Buddhist political ideas: better education for their people, more recognition for their religion. Later, as the lines became more sharply drawn, they became increasingly open in their attacks on the Government and the leading family. Soon they were clearly trying to create an atmosphere in which the Government would fall. Most observers say they very nearly accomplished this. Were they Communists? The Government has repeatedly charged that they were. Some, like Tri Quang, had participated in the nationalist fight against French rule. These had had some contact with the Communists. But the analysis of high American political officers was that the movement was anti-Communist as well as anti-Government. Some leaders would probably have been more susceptible to a neutralist solution than to partition a few years ago, but the general feeling of observers now was that Buddhism had had a difficult time in North Vietnam and that Buddhists were no longer apathetic about Communism.

As a climax to the crisis drew near, the protest was a complicated force. It was in small part Buddhist against Catholic; it was in much larger part the protest of a large segment of the people who happened to be Buddhist against an authoritarian Government that happened to be Catholic-dominated. It was also, in small part, have-nots protesting against haves; it was in much larger part twentieth-century Asians protesting against older Asians molded from a mandarin past.

Weeks passed, and the Buddhist protests seemed endless. Always formidable in the major cities and in the central coastal region, the dissension was seeping by August into the army and into the countryside. An American survey, carried out by Vietnamese, showed that the people in the countryside were aware of the crisis, were worried by it, were more sympathetic to the Buddhists than to the Government and had little confidence in the Government's ability to solve the dispute.

Similarly the army showed growing unrest and a growing consciousness of religion, particularly among young officers. Some officers had believed before that the way to get ahead was to be converted to Catholicism, and the Buddhist crisis had underlined this feeling. Though American military officials said the crisis had not affected the war effort, private Vietnamese readings were sharply different: that it was affecting morale and having an effect on individuals' efficiency.

In the countryside, there was acute consciousness, even in smaller communities in the coastal region. By August the word had reached the Mekong delta, where the Vietcong were making a major propaganda effort. Voice of America broadcasts were carrying Western news reports on the events.

Now the Buddhists hoped to provoke the Government into rash acts. "We will throw the banana peels for them to slip on," one Buddhist leader said. Now, too, the protest leaders were storing up human resources for demonstrations to impress the new United States Ambassador, Henry Cabot Lodge, when he arrived. The Government, while less repressive than it had been earlier, appeared to have lost its initiative.

Ngo Dinh Diem was caught between powerful and conflicting forces. One was Mr. and Mrs. Ngo Dinh Nhu, who wanted to crush the movement and get the matter over with. The other was the United States, urging as strongly as it could a conciliatory approach. Yet the steps Americans were urging were alien to the Government, which felt that concessions now would be a sign of weakness. The result satisfied neither side. The Americans were able to urge Ngo Dinh Diem into a radio address, heralded in Washington by State Department spokesmen but ignored in Saigon. His brief, cold statement added little new to the situation.

The protests were clearly out of control, and there were reliable reports that at least two groups were moving toward a coup. A general fear of disintegration gripped the country. Into the vacuum Ngo Dinh Nhu moved on Wednesday, August 21. Just how much President Ngo Dinh Diem knew of the plans is a matter of controversy. On Tuesday night, Buddhists were alerted by friends that a raid was imminent. They tipped off reporters that the combat police were coming.

At the headquarters of the operation, a high official received a telephone call shortly before midnight. Then he put his head in his hands and said, "The priests have been alerted. They know we are coming."

But for some reason, most of the priests decided to stay in their pagodas. Only Tri Quang, it appears, left. Why they remained is not certain—perhaps they thought the Americans could still protect them, and perhaps they thought Ngo Dinh Nhu would fall. Reporters were already in the area when the strike came about at 12:30. Due Nghiep managed to call one newspaper office. Usually Due Nghiep speaks English to reporters, but this time his voice was shrill and terrified, a reporter recalls, and he spoke in Vietnamese.

His message was repeated again and again like a phonograph record with the needle stuck: "The combat police are breaking into Xa Loi! The combat police are in Xa Loi!"

It was, in a sense, the end of the Buddhist affair and the beginning of an international crisis.

The Coup In South Vietnam:
A Pulitzer Prize-Winning Report

BY DAVID HALBERSTAM*

Plot and counterplot in a complex pattern of intrigue culminated in the military coup d'état in South Vietnam Friday.[1]

The vanity of an ambitious young general, Ton That Dinh, appears to have been a key factor in the train of events that led to the overthrow of the Ngo family regime and the deaths of President Ngo Dinh Diem and his brother Ngo Dinh Nhu.

Buddhist dissatisfaction with the Ngos, which had long been simmering, erupted into demonstrations and violence during the summer and the climate was ripe for a coup. Generals who had been considering a coup at various times began to plan seriously. One of the first allies they needed was Ton That Dinh.

Ton That Dinh, at thirty-eight years of age, had risen meteorically to the rank of brigadier general. He owes much of his success to the fact that the Ngo family trusted him as it trusted only one other general, Huynh Van Cao.

The family gave Ton That Dinh a command to the north of Saigon so that it could block any attempt to overthrow the Government from that direction. Defense to the south of Saigon was in the hands of Huynh Van Cao in the Mekong delta area. Thus, when other generals who were disaffected with the Ngo family persuaded Ton That Dinh to join the plot, the Ngo family's carefully planned system of self-protection was left with a big hole. The Ngos did not know the hole was there, so great was their faith in Ton That Dinh.

Ton That Dinh shows the marks of vanity and driving ambition. He likes to wear a tightly tailored paratrooper's uniform, a red beret at a jaunty angle, and dark glasses. Behind him there usually is a tall, silent Cambodian bodyguard. Newspaper photographers who take pictures of Ton That

---

* Former managing editor of the Harvard *Crimson,* winner of the Pulitzer Prize for international news reporting (1964), author of *The Making of a Quagmire* (New York, 1965), presently *The New York Times* correspondent in Warsaw. The selection is from *The New York Times* (November 6, 1963).

[1] This dispatch appeared in the next Wednesday's Times.—ed.

Dinh have always been warmly treated. The dissident generals played upon his vanity to bring about his defection.

What follows is a recapitulation, as complete as can be obtained today, of what actually went on at the secret meetings of the plotters and the secret meetings of Government officials from the beginning of the critical period.

The Buddhists' discontent with the Ngo family, which is Roman Catholic, became overt in the spring when the Government forbade the Buddhists to fly their religious banners along with the national flag. The Buddhists drew up a list of demands to remedy what they considered the Government's repressions. The Government promised action, but there was none. . . .

Three generals began to plot in June, when the Buddhist crisis began to grow from a religious dispute into a full-scale political crisis.

One of the three was Duong Van Minh, known as Big Minh, who had a distinguished record as a combat leader, but who had been shunted aside because of Ngo Dinh Nhu's jealousies. The second was Tran Van Don, a suave, aristocratic graduate of St. Cyr, the French West Point. The third was Le Van Kim, virtually an unemployed general who was called by one military man the shrewdest of generals.

These men felt that the Government was provoking a major crisis and that its refusal to meet some of the Buddhist demands was arrogant and self-defeating. They brought in other key officers step by step. In all this early planning, Duong Van Minh's prestige gave the plot respectability.

The officers moved slowly and gained the consent of Gen. Nguyen Kanh of the II Corps, and Gen. Do Cao Tri of the I Corps. They had no set plan and too few troops. Their main problem would be to get troops into Saigon.

The Ngos, however, had prepared a military structure to guard against such threats. Great emphasis was placed on loyalty among the high officers, particularly those in and directly north and south of Saigon.

There were two reasons for this:

First, a disloyal commander could turn his troops around and head up the highway and storm the Presidential Palace. Second, if other troops rebelled, then Ngo Dinh Diem and Ngo Dinh Nhu could call in their loyal commanders. This had happened in the past.

In 1960, when paratroopers had all but scored a coup d'état, they began negotiating with Ngo Dinh Diem only to find that the President had moved in tanks and loyal units from the Seventh Division. The palace also depended on two elite units. These were the Special Forces and the Presidential Guard, with about twenty-four tanks. Their main job, if there was a rebellion, was to hold off rebel units until a loyal force could arrive. Such loyal forces were the troops under the command of Ton That Dinh to the north and Huynh Van Cao to the south of Saigon. The latter, perhaps the most vigorous prosecutor of the war against the Communist guerrillas, the Vietcong, was known as the most political of the generals. He also had advanced quickly in the military because of his personal loyalty to Ngo Dinh Diem.

In August the secretly dissident generals hatched a plot to circumvent the careful protection set up by the regime. They suggested to Ngo Dinh Diem and Ngo Dinh Nhu that martial law be declared and that troops be moved into the town from the distant areas where the three had supporters.

The three generals planned to stage the coup the moment the troops were in the city.

Ngo Dinh Nhu, however, had been planning to raid the pagodas with his Special Forces and the police. When he heard the generals' suggestions, he decided to work it into his plan. He went ahead with the raid, but he declared martial law to make it look as if the army had forced him to take action and to make it appear that the anti-Buddhist move had enjoyed wide popular support.

Ngo Dinh Nhu brought his trusted general, Ton That Dinh, to Saigon and let him plan the raids on the pagodas. They were carried out August 21, with international repercussions. The raids were violent and they scarred Saigon's relations with the United States—the chief support of South Vietnam in the war against the Communists. The military, which had been growing progressively uneasy about the progress of the war, was angered further by the fact that the army had been used as a front for violent attacks on civilians.

After the pagoda raids, however, Ton That Dinh felt that he was the hero of the republic. In private he told other officers that he had "defeated" the United States Ambassador, Henry Cabot Lodge, who had arrived to take up his post just as the raids occurred. "He came here to hold a coup," Ton That Dinh said, "but I, Dinh, have conquered him and saved the country."

Soon afterward, Ton That Dinh held a news conference. That conference, in effect, sealed the doom of the Ngo regime by opening the way for the dissident generals to woo Ton That Dinh. The generals played upon his vanity. At the news conference, Ton That Dinh spoke of plots by "foreign adventurers," indirectly called the United States Central Intelligence Agency "crypto-Communist," and assailed the Buddhists as Communists.

Ton That Dinh was questioned sharply. He is a man with a quick temper and he became angry. On several occasions newsmen—including Vietnamese reporters for Government-controlled newspapers—broke into laughter at some of the general's accusations. This added to the general's fury.

This was just what the three dissident generals wanted—an angry Ton That Dinh. The three generals did not have troops in positions from which a successful attack could be staged, but Ton That Dinh did. They needed him. So they began to play on his wounded pride.

The plotters decided to try to discredit the regime in Ton That Dinh's eyes, undermine his loyalty to Ngo Dinh Diem and Ngo Dinh Nhu, and convince him that he had been used. They told him that he was a great national hero and that the country looked up to him. They said he was being badly treated by Ngo Dinh Nhu. They told him that his military moves against the pagodas were a good start but that political moves must follow, that the tired, ineffectual cabinet of the Ngo family was unable to do these things and that young, active military men were needed in the cabinet.

The generals said they needed to get up momentum in the war against the guerrillas to maintain the morale of the troops. They suggested that Ton That Dinh talk with Ngo Dinh Diem and use his influence. For he, after all, the advice continued, was now the foremost hero of the republic.

The generals believed that these ideas would outrage Ngo Dinh Diem and Ngo Dinh Nhu, and that the brothers would turn on Ton That Dinh. Ton That Dinh believed the generals and went to see Ngo Dinh Diem. He demanded new roles for the military officers, and the Ministry of the Interior for himself.

Ngo Dinh Diem, extremely sensitive both about police control and about the role of the military, was stunned. The last thing he wanted was members of the military in the Cabinet, and in particular Ton That Dinh as Minister of the Interior. The President gave Ton That Dinh a blunt rejection and lectured him angrily. He told him he was, in effect, temporarily relieved and to go to Dalat and rest. "Stay out of politics and leave the politics to me," Ngo Dinh Diem said. Ton That Dinh left the office and went to Dalat, humiliated now in front of the other generals, too.

He did not follow Ngo Dinh Diem's order to leave politics to the palace. He became a plotter.

When Ngo Dinh Diem inadvertently turned Ton That Dinh into a dissident, he destroyed the arrangement for the protection of the palace. And he did it at a time when he already had too many enemies, when he and Ngo Dinh Nhu were in what amounted to a twilight struggle for survival.

Junior officers were becoming disaffected. "The police techniques of the Ngos," one Vietnamese officer said, "which used to reach mostly into the homes of people we considered political, were more and more reaching into our own homes."

There was, as one officer said privately at the time, a strong feeling that the regime had become so preoccupied with its own survival that the war against the Communists had become secondary. The army, the plotters believed, was increasingly being twisted into something that fitted the Ngo family's requirements for loyalty first. Ironically, it was the Ngo family's preoccupation with possible plotters that turned still loyal soldiers like Duong Van Minh and Tran Van Don into plotters.

When a rebellion was decided upon by the generals and these young officers were approached, it was almost as if the generals had to run to catch up with the parade. "We handed the generals a ready-made coup on a platter," one young major said.

The United States policy in South Vietnam, which had never been clear to the military leaders, was becoming clear, along new lines. President Kennedy indicated that he felt South Vietnam would be a happier place without Mr. and Mrs. Ngo Dinh Nhu. John Richardson, the CIA chief in South Vietnam, who was believed by the Vietnamese military to be close to Ngo Dinh Nhu, was recalled to Washington.

It was known in South Vietnam that the new United States Ambassador neither admired the Ngo family nor thought it could win the war. Large amounts of American aid to South Vietnam were suspended.

Then the Americans told Ngo Dinh Nhu that the Special Forces led by Col. Le Quang Tung, would receive no more United States aid if they remained on security duty instead of fighting the Vietcong.

For a time, in September and early October, the dissidents

became frightened and disorganized. The Government made mass arrests in Saigon and tightened its control of the troops. The plotters, fearing discovery, became confused and stopped their planning. But the Government's repressions began to let up in mid-October and the dissidents resumed their work. According to extremely reliable sources, about two weeks before the coup, after several weeks of working on Ton That Dinh, the generals said to him, in effect, "You should carry out the coup. It is time to save your country."

Ton That Dinh began to draw up plans, discarding many before finally settling on one. The generals then set about recruiting units to join them. Three days before the coup, Ton That Dinh sent his deputy, Nguyen Huu Co, to My Tho to talk to some officers. My Tho is a key city, forty miles south of Saigon, along a main highway. It is the seat of the Seventh Division, which sent the tanks up the highway in 1960 to break up the paratroopers' coup.

Nguyen Huu Co, according to reliable sources, talked to the deputy divisional commander, to two regimental commanders, the armored unit commander, and the My Tho province chief. He told them that the army should overthrow the Ngo family, citing many reasons including possible loss of the war against the Vietcong.

Nguyen Huu Co said that all the generals had joined in the plan except Huynh Van Cao. He said that Ton That Dinh had not yet joined but was expected to. The entire episode was reported to the President.

The next day the President called in Ton That Dinh. Reliable sources believe that at this point Ngo Dinh Diem and Ngo Dinh Nhu did not entirely trust Ton That Dinh but felt he could be used against the other generals because he was not yet fully committed. Ngo Dinh Diem showed Ton That Dinh the report of the conversation in My Tho.

According to the story, Ton That Dinh put on a show of weeping. "This is my fault," the general was reported to have said. "Because you have suspected me. I have not really gone to work for the last fifteen days but have stayed at home because I was sad. But I am not against you. I was sad because I thought I was discredited with you. So Nguyen Huu Co profited from my absence to make trouble."

Then Ton That Dinh was reported to have suggested that he arrest his deputy and have him shot. Ngo Dinh Nhu was against this; he wanted him arrested and interrogated to find the names of the other plotters. The President and his brother said they had not really distrusted Ton That Dinh, but had been preoccupied with other matters. Indeed, Ngo Dinh Nhu said, he had been thinking of promoting Ton That Dinh to major general, and would take care of it quickly. Then the three men decided they must have a plan for a counter-coup.

Ton That Dinh suggested they make a massive show of force, moving troops and tanks into Saigon to crush the plotters. Ngo Dinh Nhu agreed and suggested that Ton That Dinh get together "with the other two members of the party," Lieut. Col. Nguyen Ngoc Khol, commander of the Presidential Guard, and Col. Le Quang Tung.

The next day Ton That Dinh met with two other officers and told them a major show of force must be made, and tanks must be used "because armor is dangerous." The two others, who are considered by many Vietnamese officers to be armchair soldiers, readily agreed. According to the account, Ton That Dinh said that if they brought in all the reserves, the Americans would become angry and charge that the Vietnamese were not prosecuting the war.

"So we must deceive the Americans," Ton That Dinh said, ordering Le Quang Tung to send his four Special Forces companies out of Saigon and ordering him to tell the Americans that the forces were going into combat.

The following day, the day before the coup, Le Quang Tung moved the four companies out with the approval of the President and his brother. Ton That Dinh then drew up plans that were presented to Ngo Dinh Diem as plans for Operation Bravo, a show of force, and that were to the other generals the start of moves for the coup. When he signed and approved the plans for Operation Bravo, Ngo Dinh Diem legalized the groundwork for a coup d'état.

Reliable sources here believe that some of the generals privately saw some key Americans before the coup and let them know that a coup might take place. All they were reported to have told the Americans was that they wanted no interference. The insurgents' plans involved three main task forces. The first consisted of two marine battalions and a company of M-113 armored personnel carriers. The marines were brought in from Binh Duong Province and two battalions of airborne troops considered loyal to the President were moved out to take their places.

This first task force was the spearhead of the coup.

The second task force consisted of the Sixth Airborne Battalion from Vung Tau and a battalion from a training

amp, assisted by twelve armored vehicles from the school at
ong Hai.

The third task force consisted of the Second Battalion of
he Seventh Regiment of the Fifth Division and the Second
Battalion of the Ninth Regiment of the Fifth Division.

These were the troops that occupied various parts of the
ity, and guarded the four 155 howitzers and the headquar-
ers of Col. Nguyen Van Thieu, who directed the attack on
he Presidential Guard barracks. Some troops from the
Quang Trung training camp were used to occupy the security
police headquarters. These troops were commanded by Mai
Huu Xuan, who is now director general of the national police.

Ton That Dinh also had twenty tanks brought to his headquarters at Camp Le Van Duyet. Fifteen were used during the
coup. All told, the plotters had more than forty tanks and
armored personnel carriers and they were a decisive factor in
the showdown around the palace. When these movements began, the security police called Ngo Dinh Diem and Ngo Dinh
Nhu. They were reassured by Ngo Dinh Nhu that the movements were legal and part of a palace plan.

The coup came shortly before noon on Friday when the
navy commander, Capt. Ho Tan Quyen, was assassinated
while he was driving along the Bien Hoa Highway. At 1:30
marines began occupying the central police headquarters, the
radio station and the post office. Shortly afterward, the central police called Ngo Dinh Diem and told him the marines
were there and they were not friendly.

Ngo Dinh Diem immediately ordered his military aide to
call Ton That Dinh's headquarters. An aide to Ton That Dinh
answered and the President took the phone at his end. The
President said that the marines were at the police station and
told the aide to tell Ton That Dinh to send troops there immediately. The aide said Ton That Dinh was not in.

In the meantime, a group of high-ranking military men
were having luncheon at the officers club of the general staff.
The luncheon had been called nominally for a discussion of
changes in corps boundaries. At 1:30, Gen. Tran Van Don
announced that a coup was on and arrested all of those at the
lunch.

At about this time, there was some fighting between some
of the Special Forces and troops from General Headquarters.
The plotters forced Col. Le Quang Tung to get on the phone
and tell his troops to surrender.

Half an hour after his first call, the President's aide again called Ton That Dinh's headquarters, and was again told that Ton That Dinh was not there. In the background, according to the report, President Ngo Dinh Diem could be heard saying that Gen. Ton That Dinh must have been arrested by the other generals.

At this point, the President and his brother began broadcasting on a palace transmitter. The first broadcast called on all division commanders and province chiefs to send troops to protect the President. The message asked for acknowledgment and there was none. As time passed, the palace receiver got messages from division commanders pledging loyalty to the military leaders.

The Presidential Palace became lonelier and lonelier. Ngo Dinh Nhu began calling the provincial chiefs to send irregular units to protect the President. The last of these messages, at four o'clock the next morning, called on the Republican Youth and paramilitary women's groups to move into Saigon to save the Government.

One of the insurgents' vital goals was to keep the Seventh Division from attempting to save Ngo Dinh Diem as it had before. This division was to be transferred on Friday to the III Corps under Ton That Dinh's command. Ngo Dinh Diem had ordered Col. Lam Van Phat to take command of this division Thursday, but according to tradition, he could not assume command until he had paid a courtesy call on Ton That Dinh, his new corps commander. Ton That Dinh refused to see him and told him to come back at 2 P.M. Friday.

In the meantime Ton That Dinh got Gen. Tran Van Don to sign orders transferring the command of the Seventh Division to Nguyen Huu Co, his deputy. Nguyen Huu Co went to My Tho by helicopter, locked the staff officers in a room and took command.

Then Nguyen Huu Co called Huyhn Van Cao, who, like Lam Van Phat, is a Southerner. Nguyen Huu Co is from the central region and he was afraid Huyhn Van Cao would detect the difference in accent, but he did not.

Word of what was happening in Saigon reached Huyhn Van Cao in midafternoon, but he told the Seventh Division officers that Ngo Dinh Nhu had assured him this was a false coup and that the idea was to turn against the dissident elements before they could act. Huyhn Van Cao, however, ordered one regiment and some armor to prepare to move if necessary.

By early Saturday, Huyhn Van Cao realized it was a real coup. When he radioed My Tho, Nguyen Huu Co identified himself and taunted him, "Didn't you recognize my accent?" Nguyen Huu Co then told Huyhn Van Cao that he had pulled all the ferry boats to the Saigon side of the Mekong River and that Huyhn Van Cao should not attempt to cross the river unless he wanted to die.

This left no one to help the President and his brother.

By this time the coup was going by clockwork; the radio station, the telephone office, and police headquarters were sealed off. After Col. Le Quang Tung was captured, most of his Special Forces were through. Then the insurgents moved to seal off the Presidential Guard's barracks. The fighting there was heavy and there was stiff resistance. The barracks were heavily mortared for several hours and then surrounded by tanks. At midnight the barracks fell.

Then Ton That Dinh began to plan the attack on the palace itself. During the entire evening, the generals kept asking the President and his brother to surrender to save Vietnamese lives. If they surrendered, the generals pledged, the two brothers would be protected and sent out of the country, but if they did not, they would be killed. The President asked the commanders to send a delegation to the Palace to talk. The rebels feared this was a repetition of 1960 and did not agree.

It was reported that at 4 A.M. Ngo Dinh Diem called Ambassador Lodge. Mr. Lodge was reported to have told the President that he was concerned for the President's safety and would do all he could to insure that he and his family were honorably treated.

The coup, in the view of one observer, went slowly because the rebels made every effort to talk troops into surrendering to avoid killing Vietnamese.

In the early morning, civilians watching the struggle from roofs noted the flashes of double flares that can be used in gauging artillery fire. At 4 A.M. the President's military aide called Ton That Dinh for the last time and asked for troops to save the palace. This time, according to the story, Ton That Dinh came on the phone "and cursed, using insulting phrases to describe the family." According to one source, he told the brothers, "You are finished. It is all over."

"I saved them on August 21, but they are finished now," he said after the conversation.

Most of the real fighting was done around the palace by

opposing armored units. One observer described the maneuvering as "two boxers fighting in a closet."

Atop the United States Embassy a cluster of staff members watched. Early in the morning one decided to go downstairs and tell Thich Tri Quang, the Buddhist protest leader who had taken refuge there.

"Reverend," the American said, "there is a coup d'état taking place."

The priest replied: "Do you think I am deaf?"

When the rebels brought in flamethrowers, the issue was decided. For the rest of the early morning, the tanks blasted at the palace. At 6 A.M. the firing ceased and then marines stormed and took the palace.

But Ngo Dinh Diem and Ngo Dinh Nhu were gone.

There are said to be three main tunnels leading from the palace but the rebels knew and guarded the exit of only one. According to one report, Ngo Dinh Diem and Ngo Dinh Nhu escaped through a tunnel leading to a park north of the palace where they were picked up by a vehicle.

The vehicle, reported to have been a Land-Rover, took the brothers to a church in suburban Cholon where they apparently hoped to wait for rescue.

Armored vehicles were sent to the church where the brothers were arrested. It was reported that they had a large sum of money with them. They were placed in an armored personnel carrier.

When the news was telephoned that they were dead, Ton That Dinh grabbed the phone and made the officer repeat what he had said. Then Ton That Dinh slowly let his arms fall.

At this point the others contended that the Ngos had committed suicide. One of Ton That Dinh's aides demanded how they could have committed suicide. The officer answered that they had grabbed a rifle from an enlisted man. Then Ton That Dinh's aide asked why only one officer was guarding them. "Someone was careless," was the answer.

Then all was over. Duong Van Minh became chairman of the committee. Tran Van Don became Minister of Defense and Ton That Dinh became, as he had wanted, a major general and the Interior Minister.

The Government had fallen, the Ngos were dead, and the military leaders had won all they had sought.

The war with the Vietcong, the questions of subversion, loyalty, poverty, and religious conflict at this point became theirs to deal with.

Part Five

PROBLEMS OF ESCALATION: AN AMERICAN CRISIS

After the assassination of Ngo Dinh Diem, and despite hopes that a viable government in Saigon would defeat the Communist-led guerrillas, the problem of Vietnam became more of an *American* problem than it had ever been. The American record on the Asian mainland in the two decades after World War II had not been a glorious one, and Vietnam did not improve it any. Donald Zagoria, a knowledgeable writer on Asian affairs and a general supporter of U. S. policies in Vietnam, has suggested the cause of this failure. Zagoria points to the undeniable fact that in Eastern Europe communism did not come to power as a popular movement; it was installed by the Soviets bayonets. But in Asia communism is an indigenous and vital force that has often achieved its successes despite Russian opposition.[1]

Americans persist in viewing Asian communism in the conspiratorial Eastern European pattern—as simply an extension of Soviet or Chinese power. Such views have long been dominant in Washington, too. Men like Dean Acheson considered Communist militancy in Asia synonymous with "Soviet Russian imperialism," [2] and thus committed the U. S. to the use of military power in support of the series of lost causes chronicled in the early sections of this book. Currently, American might is directed against what is officially labeled an outside conspiracy to undermine the sovereignty of a free nation—South Vietnam. This view informs the major U. S. policy statement of the escalating war—the "White Paper" of February 1965. Only slightly abridged here,[3] the "White Paper" has been widely recognized as an inadequate defense of a policy that desperately needs defense. Arthur Schlesinger, Jr., who prepared a similar paper in 1961,[4] was tempted to reflect on the gullibility of Sec-

[1] Donald S. Zagoria, "Communism in Asia," Commentary, XXXIX (Februray 1965), pp. 53–58.
[2] Secretary of State Acheson to President Harry Truman (July 30, 1949), quoted in Oliver E. Clubb, Jr., The United States and the Sino-Soviet Bloc in Southeast Asia (Washington, 1962), p. 52.
[3] See pp. 284–316.
[4] Cuba [U.S. Department of State Publication 7171: Inter-American Series, 66] (Washington, D.C., [April], 1961), apparently prepared in order to justify the invasion of Cuba launched on April 17 of that year.

retaries of State after reading the 1965 document.[5] Journalist I. F. Stone carefully measured the conclusions of the "White Paper" against the evidence adduced, and found them wanting.[6]

In addition to the desperate search for an argument to justify American involvement in the affairs of Vietnam, the U. S. has also been hard put to find a method by which military power can be made effective there. Frank Trager suggests some of the strategic considerations that go into the making of American military policy.[7] Eqbal Ahmad, on the other hand, argues that a military response to guerrilla warfare in Vietnam cannot counter the political advantages of the revolutionary side.[8] These advantages are clearly indicated in the solid reporting of Max Clos on the situation within Vietnam.[9]

The problems of an escalating war have given rise to a wave of protest in the United States. Isaac Deutscher may err when he compares this protest movement to the "thaw" in Russia, or may be too optimistic when he interprets both as a sign of the genuine possibility of coexistence. But whatever the ultimate significance of this wave of dissent, it is unparalleled in recent American history. One center of this protest has been the U. S. Senate, where Wayne Morse, Ernest Gruening, and others have vigorously and frequently questioned the basic premises of American policy in Vietnam.[10] Dissent has also been prominent in academic circles. The teach-in movement, originating at the Ann Arbor campus of the University of Michigan,[11] has generated a nationwide movement [12] that promises to continue until the United States finds an honorable and humane way to end its military involvement in the war-weary nation of Vietnam.

---

[5] The New York Times (May 16, 1965). See also p. 334.
[6] See pp. 317–323. [7] See pp. 337–350.
[8] See pp. 351–362. [9] See pp. 429–438.
[10] See pp. 376–388. On a different plane altogether is the partisan critique prepared by the Republican Conference Committee ("Vietnam: Some Neglected Aspects of the Historical Record") reprinted in the Congressional Record (August 25, 1965), and available as a pamphlet from Rep. Melvin R. Laird.
[11] See Marc Pilisuk in The Correspondent, No. 34 (Summer, 1965).
[12] Also included is a description of a local teach-in, which may remedy the misconception that teach-ins are like primitive "Hate America" rallies.

United States Government
"White Paper" (February 1965)*

INTRODUCTION

South Vietnam is fighting for its life against a brutal campaign of terror and armed attack inspired, directed, supplied, and controlled by the Communist regime in Hanoi. This flagrant aggression has been going on for years, but recently the pace has quickened and the threat has now become active.

The war in Vietnam is a new kind of war, a fact as yet poorly understood in most parts of the world. Much of the confusion that prevails in the thinking of many people, and even many governments, stems from this basic misunderstanding. For in Vietnam a totally new brand of aggression has been loosed against an independent people who want to make their own way in peace and freedom.

Vietnam is *not* another Greece, where indigenous guerrilla forces used friendly neighboring territory as a sanctuary.

Vietnam is *not* another Malaya, where Communist guerrillas were, for the most part, physically distinguishable from the peaceful majority they sought to control.

Vietnam is *not* another Philippines, where Communist guerrillas were physically separated from the source of their moral and physical support.[1]

Above all, the war in Vietnam is *not* a spontaneous and local rebellion against the established government.

There are elements in the Communist program of con-

* Aggression From the North: The Record of North Vietnam's Campaign to Conquer South Vietnam [U.S. Department of State Publication 7839; Far Eastern Series 130] (Washington, D. C., [February] 1965).

[1] Compare with the "White Paper" of 1961: "The basic pattern of Vietcong activity is not new, of course. It operated with minor variations in China, and Mao Tse-tung's theories on the conduct of guerrilla warfare are known to every Vietcong agent and cadre. Most of the same methods were used in Malaya, in Greece, in the Philippines, in Cuba, and in Laos." A Threat to the Peace: North Vietnam's Effort to Conquer South Vietnam [U.S. Department of State Publication 7308; Far Eastern Series 110] (Washington, D. C., [December] 1961) p. 1.—ed.

quest directed against South Vietnam common to each of the previous areas of aggression and subversion. But there is one fundamental difference. In Vietnam a Communist government has set out deliberately to conquer a sovereign people in a neighboring state. And to achieve its end, it has used every resource of its own government to carry out its carefully planned program of concealed aggression. North Vietnam's commitment to seize control of the South is no less total than was the commitment of the regime in North Korea in 1950. But knowing the consequences of the latter's undisguised attack, the planners in Hanoi have tried desperately to conceal their hand. They have failed and their aggression is as real as that of an invading army.

This report is a summary of the massive evidence of North Vietnamese aggression obtained by the Government of South Vietnam. This evidence has been jointly analyzed by South Vietnamese and American experts.

The evidence shows that the hard core of the Communist forces attacking South Vietnam were trained in the North and ordered into the South by Hanoi. It shows that the key leadership of the Vietcong (VC), the officers and much of the cadre, many of the technicians, political organizers, and propagandists have come from the North and operate under Hanoi's direction. It shows that the training of essential military personnel and their infiltration into the South is directed by the Military High Command in Hanoi.

The evidence shows that many of the weapons and much of the ammunition and other supplies used by the Vietcong have been sent into South Vietnam from Hanoi. In recent months new types of weapons have been introduced in the VC army, for which all ammunition must come from outside sources. Communist China and other Communist states have been the prime suppliers of these weapons and ammunition, and they have been channeled primarily through North Vietnam.[2]

The directing force behind the effort to conquer South

[2] *Compare with the "White Paper" of 1961: "By hitting such targets [police stations, army outposts, etc.] suddenly and in superior force, the VC are able to assure themselves a supply of arms and ammunition. This reduces their dependence on the long supply line from the North. The weapons of the VC are largely French- or U.S.-made, or handmade on primitive forges in the jungles."* A Threat to the Peace, p. 9.—ed.

Vietnam is the Communist Party in the North, the Lao Dong (Workers) Party. As in every Communist state, the party is an integral part of the regime itself. North Vietnamese officials have expressed their firm determination to absorb South Vietnam into the Communist world.

Through its Central Committee, which controls the Government of the North, the Lao Dong Party directs the total political and military effort of the Vietcong. The Military High Command in the North trains the military men and sends them into South Vietnam. The Central Research Agency, North Vietnam's central intelligence organization, directs the elaborate espionage and subversion effort. . . .

Under Hanoi's overall direction the Communists have established an extensive machine for carrying on the war within South Vietnam. The focal point is the Central Office for South Vietnam with its political and military subsections and other specialized agencies. A subordinate part of this Central Office is the Liberation Front for South Vietnam. The front was formed at Hanoi's order in 1960. Its principal function is to influence opinion abroad and to create the false impression that the aggression in South Vietnam is an indigenous rebellion against the established Government.

For more than 10 years the people and the Government of South Vietnam, exercising the inherent right of self-defense, have fought back against these efforts to extend Communist power south across the 17th Parallel. The United States has responded to the appeals of the Government of the Republic of Vietnam for help in this defense of the freedom and independence of its land and its people.

In 1961 the Department of State issued a report called *A Threat to the Peace*. It described North Vietnam's program to seize South Vietnam. The evidence in that report had been presented by the Government of the Republic of Vietnam to the International Control Commission (ICC). A special report by the ICC in June 1962 upheld the validity of that evidence. The Commission held that there was "sufficient evidence to show beyond reasonable doubt" that North Vietnam had sent arms and men into South Vietnam to carry out subversion with the aim of overthrowing the legal Government there. The ICC found the authorities in Hanoi in specific violation of four provisions of the Geneva Accords of 1954.[3]

Since then, new and even more impressive evidence of Hanoi's aggression has accumulated. The Government of the United States believes that evidence should be presented to its own citizens and to the world. It is important for free men to know what has been happening in Vietnam, and how, and why. That is the purpose of this report.

I. HANOI SUPPLIES THE KEY PERSONNEL
FOR THE ARMED AGGRESSION AGAINST
SOUTH VIETNAM

The hard core of the Communist forces attacking South Vietnam are men trained in North Vietnam. They are ordered into the South and remain under the military discipline of the Military High Command in Hanoi. Special training camps operated by the North Vietnamese army give political and military training to the infiltrators. Increasingly the forces sent into the South are native North Vietnamese who have never seen South Vietnam. A special infiltration unit, the 70th Transportation Group, is responsible for moving men from North Vietnam into the South via infiltration trails through Laos. Another special unit, the maritime infiltration group, sends weapons and supplies and agents by sea into the South.

The infiltration rate has been increasing. From 1959 to 1960, when Hanoi was establishing its infiltration pipeline, at least 1,800 men, and possibly 2,700 more, moved into South Vietnam from the North. The flow increased to a minimum of 3,700 in 1961 and at least 5,400 in 1962. There was a modest decrease in 1963 to 4,200 confirmed infiltrators, though later evidence is likely to raise this figure.

For 1964 the evidence is still incomplete. However, it already shows that a minimum of 4,400 infiltrators entered the South, and it is estimated more than 3,000 others were sent in.

There is usually a time lag between the entry of infiltrating troops and the discovery of clear evidence they have entered. This fact, plus collateral evidence of increased use of the infiltration routes, suggests strongly that 1964 was probably the year of greatest infiltration so far.

[3] *See pp. 186–189 for the Special Report of 1962, which mentions violations by other parties as well. See also, pp. 165–166.*

Thus, since 1959, nearly 20,000 VC officers, soldiers, and technicians are known to have entered South Vietnam under orders from Hanoi. Additional information indicates that an estimated 17,000 more infiltrators were dispatched to the South by the regime in Hanoi during the past 6 years. It can reasonably be assumed that still other infiltration groups have entered the South for which there is no evidence yet available.

To some the level of infiltration from the North may seem modest in comparison with the total size of the armed forces of the Republic of Vietnam. But one-for-one calculations are totally misleading in the kind of warfare going on in Vietnam. First, a high proportion of infiltrators from the North are well-trained officers, cadres, and specialists. Second, it has long been realized that in guerrilla combat the burdens of defense are vastly heavier than those of attack. In Malaya, the Philippines, and elsewhere a ratio of at least 10-to-1 in favor of the forces of order was required to meet successfully the threat of the guerrillas' hit-and-run tactics.

In the calculus of guerrilla warfare the scale of North Vietnamese infiltration into the South takes on a very different meaning. For the infiltration of 5,000 guerrilla fighters in a given year is the equivalent of marching perhaps 50,000 regular troops across the border, in terms of the burden placed on the defenders.

Above all, the number of proved and probable infiltrators from the North should be seen in relation to the size of the VC forces. It is now estimated that the Vietcong number approximately 35,000 so-called hard-core forces, and another 60,000–80,000 local forces. It is thus apparent that infiltrators from the North—allowing for casualties—make up the majority of the so-called hard-core Vietcong. Personnel from the North, in short, are now and have always been the backbone of the entire VC operation.

It is true that many of the lower level elements of the VC forces are recruited within South Vietnam.[4] However, the

---

[4] Compare with the "White Paper" of 1961: "During the months after the Geneva Agreements went into effect, most of the military units loyal to Ho Chi Minh were transferred to North Vietnam; but some of the best-trained guerrilla units moved to remote and inaccessible regions in the South . . . [that is, they remained]. Individual agents and many members of Communist

thousands of reported cases of VC kidnapings and terrorism make it abundantly clear that threats and other pressures by the Vietcong play a major part in such recruitment.

A. THE INFILTRATION PROCESS

The infiltration routes supply hard-core units with most of their officers and noncommissioned personnel. This source helps fill the gaps left by battle casualties, illness, and defection and insures continued control by Hanoi. Also, as the nature of the conflict has changed, North Vietnam has supplied the Vietcong with technical specialists via the infiltration routes. These have included men trained in armor and ordnance, antiaircraft, and communications as well as medical corpsmen and transport experts.

There is no single infiltration route from the North to South Vietnam. But by far the biggest percentage of infiltrators follow the same general course. The principal training center for North Vietnamese army men assigned to join the Vietcong has been at Xuan Mai near Hanoi. Recently captured Vietcong have also reported an infiltration training camp at Thanh Hoa. After completion of their training course —which involves political and propaganda work as well as military subjects—infiltrating units are moved to Vinh on the east coast. Many have made stopovers at a staging area in Dong Hoi where additional training is conducted. From there they go by truck to the Laos border.

Then, usually after several days' rest, infiltrators move southward through Laos. Generally they move along the Laos-South Vietnam border. Responsibility for infiltration from North Vietnam through Laos belongs to the 70th Transportation Group of the North Vietnamese army. After a time the infiltration groups turn eastward, entering South Vietnam in Quang Nam, Quang Tri, Thua Thien, Kontum, or another of the border provinces.

The Communists have established regular lanes for infiltration with way-stations established about one day's march apart. The way-stations are equipped to quarter and feed the Vietcong passing through. Infiltrators who suffer from ma-

---

cells were told to stay in place, to lead normal lives, and to wait until they received orders to carry out Party assignments." These assignments were mainly to prepare for the nationwide elections that the Geneva Agreements provided for in 1956. A Threat to The Peace, p. 3.—ed.

laria or other illnesses stay at the stations until they recover sufficiently to join another passing group moving South.

[A map] shows the infiltration route from North Vietnam to the South followed by VC Sgt. Huynh Van Tay and a group of North Vietnamese army officers and men in September 1963. Tay was captured during an engagement in Chuong Thien Province in April 1964.[5]

Local guides lead the infiltration groups along the secret trails. Generally they direct the infiltrators from halfway between two stations, through their own base station, and on halfway to the next supply base. Thus the guides are kept in ignorance of all but their own way-stations. Only group leaders are permitted to talk with the guides in order to preserve maximum security. The men are discouraged from asking where they are or where they are going.

The same system of trails and guides used along the Laos infiltration routes is used within South Vietnam itself. Vietcong infiltrators may report directly to a reassignment center in the highlands as soon as they enter South Vietnam. But in the past year or more some groups have moved down trails in South Vietnam to provinces along the Cambodian border and near Saigon before receiving their unit assignment. Within South Vietnam infiltration and supplies are handled by VC units such as the Nam Son Transportation Group.

At the Laos border-crossing point infiltrators are re-equipped. Their North Vietnamese army uniforms must be turned in. They must give up all personal papers, letters, notebooks, and photographs that might be incriminating. Document control over the infiltrators has been tightened considerably over the past two years. A number of Vietnamese infiltrators have told of being fitted out with Lao "neutralist" uniforms for their passage through Laos.

Infiltration groups are usually issued a set of black civilian pajama-like clothes, two unmarked uniforms, rubber sandals, a sweater, a hammock, mosquito netting, and waterproof sheeting. They carry a 3–5 day supply of food. A packet of medicines and bandages is usually provided.

The size of infiltration groups varies widely. Prisoners

[5] *Although* Aggression From The North *supplies many capsule biographies of alleged infiltrators, there is no further data included about Huynh Van Tay. The map is omitted here.*—ed.*

have mentioned units as small as five men and as large as 500. Generally the groups number 40–50. When they arrive in South Vietnam these groups are usually split up and assigned to various VC units as replacements, although some have remained intact.

B. MILITARY PERSONNEL

The following are individual case histories of North Vietnamese soldiers sent by the Hanoi regime into South Vietnam. They are only an illustrative group. They show that the leadership and specialized personnel for the guerrilla war in South Vietnam consists in large part of members of the North Vietnam armed forces, trained in the North and subject to the command and discipline of Hanoi.

1. Tran Quoc Dan

Dan was a VC major, commander of the 60th Battalion (sometimes known as the 34th Group of the Thon-Kim Battalion). Disillusioned with fighting his own countrymen and with Communism and the lies of the Hanoi regime, he surrendered to the authorities in South Vietnam on February 11, 1963.

At the age of fifteen he joined the revolutionary army (Vietminh) and fought against the French forces until 1954 when the Geneva Accords ended the Indochina War. As a regular in the Vietminh forces, he was moved to North Vietnam. He became an officer in the so-called People's Army.

In March 1962 Major Dan received orders to prepare to move to South Vietnam. He had been exposed to massive propaganda in the North which told of the destitution of the peasants in the South and said that the Americans had taken over the French role of colonialists. He said later that an important reason for his decision to surrender was that he discovered these propaganda themes were lies. He found the peasants more prosperous than the people in the North. And he recognized quickly that he was not fighting the Americans but his own people.

With the 600 men of his unit, Major Dan left Hanoi on March 23, 1962. They traveled through the Laos corridor. His group joined up with the Vietcong First Regiment in central Vietnam.

The thirty-five-year-old major took part in forty-five actions and was wounded once in an unsuccessful VC attack on an outpost. As time passed he became increasingly discouraged by his experience as a VC troop commander. Most of all, he said, he was tired of killing other Vietnamese. After several months of soul-searching he decided to surrender to the authorities of the Republic of Vietnam. He has volunteered to do "anything to serve the national cause" of South Vietnam.

2. Vo Thoi

Sergeant Vo Thoi (Communist Party alias Vo Bien) was an assistant squad leader in the VC Tay Son 22d Battalion. On the night of October 7, 1963, his unit attacked An Tuong village in Binh Dinh Province. After overrunning the village, Vo's company was assigned to set up an ambush against Republic of Vietnam troops rushing to defend the village. In the ensuing fight Vo was seriously wounded. He was picked up by local farmers and turned over to the authorities.

Vo's life and experiences were similar to those of thousands of Vietcong. Born in Quang Ngai Province [6] in 1932, he went through five years of school and then worked on his parents' small farm. During the war against the French he joined the Vietminh forces. When the fighting ended, he was transferred to North Vietnam with his unit, the 210th Regiment. He remained in the North Vietnamese army until 1960 when he was sent to work on a state farm in Nghe An Province. Vo said 3,000 men and women worked on the farm, of whom 400 were soldiers. In September 1962 Vo was told he must join the newly activated 22d Battalion. All the members of the battalion came from provinces in South Vietnam, from Quang Tri to Phu Yen. But it was not an ordinary battalion; two-thirds of its members were cadre with ranks up to senior captain.

The group was put through an advanced training course that lasted six months. The training program included combat tactics for units from squad to company and the techniques of guerrilla and counterguerrilla fighting. There were heavy doses of political indoctrination.

On March 5, 1963, the 22d Battalion received orders to move South. They were transported in trucks from Nghe An Province to Dong Hoi in Quang Binh, just north of the 17th Parallel. From there the unit was moved westward to the Laos border. Then the more than 300 men began walking to

[6] *South Vietnam where all the others mentioned in this section also originated.—ed.*

the South following mountain trails in Laos and the Vietnam border area. They marched by day, rested at night. Every fifth day they stopped at a way-station for a full day's rest. One company dropped off at Thua Thien Province. Vo and the remainder of the group marched on to Pleiku Province. Two fully armed companies from a neighboring province were assigned to the battalion. The assignment given to the battalion was to harass strategic hamlets in the Hoai An district of Binh Dinh, to round up cattle and rice, to kill or kidnap cadres of the Government forces, and to recruit local youth for service with the Vietcong.

5. Nguyen Truc

Corp. Nguyen Truc was born in 1933, the son of a farmer in Phu Yen Province in South Vietnam. From 1949 to 1954 he served as a courier and then as a guerrilla fighter with the Vietminh. In early 1955 he boarded a Soviet ship [7] and moved with his unit, the 40th Battalion, to North Vietnam. He remained in the army, but in 1959, bothered by illness, he went to work on a state farm.

In August 1962 Nguyen Truc was notified that he was back in the army and that he was being sent to South Vietnam. He reported to the Xuan Mai training center and underwent six months of military and political reeducation. His unit was the newly activated 22d Battalion. The training course was completed in February 1963, but departure for South Vietnam was delayed until April.

For infiltration purposes the battalion was divided into two groups. On April 27, Nguyen Truc and his group boarded trucks at Xuan Mai. They went first to Vinh, then on to Dong Hoi, and finally to the Laos-North Vietnam border. There they doffed their North Vietnamese army uniforms and put on black peasants' clothing. The march to the South began, sometimes in Lao territory, sometimes in Vietnam. They passed through Thua Thien Province, then Quang Nam, Quang Tin, and Quang Ngai, and finally to their destination, Pleiku. Each day they had a new guide, generally one of the mountain people of the area.

Nguyen said that he and most of the troops who were sent North after the Indochina War wanted to return to their homes and rejoin their families. In August 1963 Nguyen

[7] *Those who moved from North to South at this time were transported in French and American vessels.—ed.*

ruc was sent out on a foraging expedition to find food or his unit. He took the opportunity to defect to Government forces at An Tuc in Binh Dinh Province.

. Nguyen Cam

Cam is the son of a farmer in Quang Tin Province. Born n 1929, he joined the Vietminh youth group in his home village in 1946. In one year he became a guerrilla fighter. n 1954, as the Indochina War was drawing to a close, he was serving with the Vietminh 20th Battalion. In May 1955 he went to North Vietnam with his unit.

Ill health caused his transfer to an agricultural camp in 1958. By 1960 he was back in uniform, serving in the 210th Regiment. In May of that year he was assigned to a small group that was to set up a metallurgical workshop. Early in 1961 he was sent to a metallurgical class in Nghe An Province. They were taught a simple form of cast-iron production, simple blast furnace construction, and similar skills. Their instructor was an engineer from the Hanoi Industrial Department.

Their special course completed, Cam and his group of thirty-five men prepared to go to South Vietnam. They went by truck from their training center at Nghe An to the Laos border. After nineteen days marching through Laos, they arrived in the vicinity of Tchepone. There they waited for three days until food supplies could be airdropped by a North Vietnamese plane. Nineteen days of walking took them to the Laos-South Vietnam border.

Delayed en route by illness, Cam finally reached his destination in November 1961. It was a secret VC iron foundry in Kontum Province. Several iron ore deposits were nearby, and the hill people had long used the iron to make knives and simple tools. Cam's job was building kilns to smelt the ore. The Vietcong hoped to use the iron for mines and grenades.

On August 4, 1963, Sergeant Cam went to a nearby village to buy salt for his group. On his return he found his comrades had gone to one of their cultivated fields to gather corn, and he joined them. The group was interrupted at their work by a Vietnamese Ranger Company. After a brief fight Cam was taken prisoner. . . .

[Five biographies also of South Vietnamese captured in battle are omitted.—ed.]

These are typical Vietcong. There are many other officers like Tran Quoc Dan, technicians like Nguyen Thao, and simple soldiers like Nguyen Truc. They were born in South Vietnam, fought against the French, and then went North and served in the army of North Vietnam. They were ordered by the Communist rulers in Hanoi to reenter South Vietnam. Violating the Geneva Accords of 1954 and 1962, they used the territory of neighboring Laos to infiltrate into the South. They are the means by which Communist North Vietnam is carrying out its program of conquest in South Vietnam.

C. INFILTRATION OF NATIVE NORTH VIETNAMESE

The Communist authorities in Hanoi are now assigning native North Vietnamese in increasing numbers to join the VC forces in South Vietnam. Heretofore, those in charge of the infiltration effort have sought to fill their quotas with soldiers and others born in the South. The 90,000 troops that moved from South Vietnam to the North when the Geneva Accords ended the Indochina War have provided an invaluable reservoir for this purpose. Now, apparently, that source is running dry. The casualty rate has been high, and obviously many of those who were in fighting trim ten years ago are no longer up to the rigors of guerrilla war.

In any case, reports of infiltration by native North Vietnamese in significant numbers have been received in Saigon for several months. It is estimated that as many as seventy-five percent of the more than 4,400 Vietcong who are known to have entered the South in the first eight months of 1964 were natives of North Vietnam.

Vo Thanh Vinh was born in Nghe An Province in North Vietnam in 1936. He was captured by South Vietnamese forces on May 5, 1964. He described himself as a military security officer. He infiltrated into South Vietnam in April 1964 with a group of thirty-four police and security officers from the North.

Another native North Vietnamese captured in the South was VC Private First Class Vo Quyen. His home was in Nam Dinh Province. He was a member of the 2d Battalion of the North Vietnamese army's 9th Regiment. He said the entire battalion had infiltrated into South Vietnam between February and May last year. He was captured in an action in Quang Tri Province on July 4. He told interrogators that the bulk of his unit was composed of young draftees from North Vietnam. . . .

[Three biographies of North Vietnamese are omitted. —ed.]

These reports destroy one more fiction which the authorities in Hanoi have sought so long to promote—that the fighting in the South was a matter for the South Vietnamese. They underline Hanoi's determination to press its campaign of conquest with every available resource.

D. INFILTRATION OF VIETCONG AGENTS

No effort to subvert another nation as elaborate as that being conducted by the Ho Chi Minh regime against South Vietnam can succeed without an intelligence-gathering organization. Recognizing this, the authorities in Hanoi have developed an extensive espionage effort. An essential part of that effort is the regular assignment of secret agents from the North to South Vietnam.

The heart of the VC intelligence organization is the Central Research Agency in Hanoi. Communist agents are regularly dispatched from North Vietnam, sometimes for brief assignments but often for long periods. Many of these agents move into South Vietnam along the infiltration trails through Laos; others are carried by boats along the coasts and landed at prearranged sites. A special maritime infiltration group has been developed in North Vietnam, with its operations centered in Ha Tinh and Quang Binh Provinces just north of the 17th Parallel.

1. Maritime Infiltration

The following case illustrates the methods of maritime infiltration of secret agents used by the Communist regime in North Vietnam:

In July 1962 a North Vietnamese intelligence agent named Nguyen Viet Duong began training to infiltrate South Vietnam. A native Southerner, he had fought against the French and had gone to North Vietnam after the war ended. Selected for intelligence work, he was assigned to the Central Research Agency in 1959.

After a period of intensive instruction in radio transmission, coding and decoding, and other skills of the intelligence trade, he was given false identity papers and other supplies and was transported to the South. His principal task was to set up a cell of agents to collect military information. He flew from Hanoi to Dong Hoi, and from there the maritime infiltration group took him by boat to South Vietnam. That was in August 1962.

In January 1963 Duong reported to Hanoi that he had run into difficulties. His money and papers had been lost, and he had been forced to take refuge with VC contacts in another province. Another agent was selected to go to South Vietnam. One of his assignments was to contact Duong, find out details of what happened to him, and help Duong re-establish himself as a VC agent. The man selected for the task was Senior Captain Tran Van Tan of the Central Research Agency.

Tan had already been picked to go to the South to establish a clandestine VC communications center. Making contact with Duong was one of his secondary assignments. After intensive preparations Tan was ready to move to South Vietnam in March. He was transferred to an embarkation base of the maritime infiltration group just north of the 17th Parallel.

He was joined by three other VC agents and the captain and three crewmen of the boat that would take them South. All were given false identity papers to conform to their false names. They also were provided with fishermen's permits, South Vietnamese voting cards, and draft cards or military discharge papers. The boat captain received a boat registration book, crew lists, and several South Vietnamese permits to conduct business.

The agents and boatmen were given cover stories to tell if captured. Each man had to memorize not only the details of his own story but the names and some details about each of the others. The agents had to become familiar with simple boat procedures so they could pass as legitimate fishermen.

The expedition left the embarkation port on April 4. In addition to the four agents the boat carried six carefully sealed boxes containing a generator, several radios, some weapons, and a large supply of South Vietnamese currency. They also carried some chemicals and materials for making false identification papers. Their destination was a landing site on the coast of Phuoc Tuy Province.

Soon after leaving North Vietnam the VC boat encountered high winds and rough seas. On April 7 the storm became violent. The boat tossed and threatened to capsize. Strong northeasterly winds forced it ever closer to shore. Finally the boat captain, Nguyen Xit, ordered that the six boxes be thrown overboard. This was done, and the boat then was beached. The eight men decided to split up into pairs and try to make contact with VC forces. They buried their false papers and set out. Six of the eight were captured almost immediately by authorities in Thua Thien Province, and the other two were taken several days later.

2. Student Propaganda Agents

The student population of South Vietnam is an important target group for VC propagandists. These agents seek to win adherents for the Communist cause among young workers, students in high schools and universities, and the younger officers and enlisted men in the armed forces of the Republic of Vietnam.

Typical of the agents sent into South Vietnam for this purpose is Nguyen Van Vy, a 19-year-old VC propagandist. He is a native of the Vinh Linh District in North Vietnam, just north of the Demilitarized Zone. He was a member of a Communist Party youth group in his native village. He was recruited for propaganda work in the South in the fall of 1962. He was one of forty young persons enrolled in a special political training course given by the Communist Party in his district.

The first phase of the training consisted of political indoctrination covering such subjects as the advance of Communism, the North Vietnamese plan for winning control of the country, the responsibility of youth in furthering this plan, the war in the South, and the need for propaganda supporting the Liberation Front.

Those who successfully completed the first phase were selected for the second level of training, the so-called technical training phase. In this the trainees were given their mission in the South. Vy was told he should infiltrate into South Vietnam and there surrender to the authorities, describing himself as a defector who was "tired of the miserable life in the North." He was to say he wanted to complete his schooling, which was impossible in the North. He was told to ask to live with relatives in the South so he could go to school. Once his story was accepted and he was enrolled in a school, he was to begin his work of propagandizing other students. He was to wait for three or four months, however, until he was no longer the subject of local suspicion. He was assigned to work under an older agent to whom he had to report regularly.

A third member of the team was a younger man who was to assist Vy. The three were to infiltrate into South Vietnam separately and to meet there at a rendezvous point.

At first Vy was to do no more than to observe his fellow students carefully, collecting biographical data on them and studying their personalities, capabilities, and aspirations. He was then to select those he thought might be most influenced by Communist propaganda and try to make friends with them.

Once he had selected targets, he was to begin to influence them favorably toward the North and to implant Communist propaganda. He was responsible then for bringing into his organization those he had influenced effectively. These individuals were to be given their own propaganda assignments to work on other students.

Students who wanted to evade military service in the Government forces were considered prime targets. Where possible, Vy was to help them get to North Vietnam. He was also told to make contact with any students who had been picked up by the authorities for suspected Communist activities. These, too, were to be helped to escape to North Vietnam. Any useful information concerning developments in the South or military activities were to be reported through his superior, Nguyen Van Phong.

In case he became suspect, he was either to make his own way back to North Vietnam or to go into the jungle and try to contact a VC unit.

Vy entered South Vietnam on January 2, 1963, by swimming across the Ben Hai River. He encountered an elderly farmer who led him to the local authorities in Hai Gu. There he told his story but it was not believed. He then admitted his true mission.

3. Other Agents

The Communist authorities in North Vietnam send their agents into South Vietnam by a wide variety of means. A few like Nguyen Van Vy cross the Demilitarized Zone, more infiltrate by sea, and still more along the infiltration route through Laos. But there are other methods for entering South Vietnam. VC espionage agent Tran Van Bui attempted one such method.

Bui was a graduate of the espionage training school in Haiphong, North Vietnam. He completed a special six-month course in July 1962. The training included political indoctrination, but most of the time was spent on such things as use of weapons, preparing booby traps, and methods of sabotage. He was also given instruction in methods of enlisting help from hoodlums, draft dodgers, and VC sympathizers. Once in South Vietnam, he was to organize a small unit for sabotage and the collection of information. On specific assignment by his superiors he was to be ready to sabotage ships in Saigon harbor and to blow up gasoline and oil storage points and Vietnamese Army installations. He was told to be prepared to assassinate Vietnamese officials and American personnel.

In September 1962 Bui was given his mission assignment. He was to hide aboard a foreign ship. When discovered, he was to claim to be a refugee who wanted to "escape" to South Vietnam. He was given an automatic pistol with silencer, some explosive devices, and a small knife that could inject poison into the body of a victim.

Bui stole aboard a foreign ship in Haiphong harbor. After three days at sea—when he was sure the ship would not turn around—Bui surrendered to the ship's captain. When the ship arrived in Bangkok, Bui was turned over to the Thai authorities. They in turn released him to the South Vietnamese as he had requested. But in Saigon his true mission was disclosed and he made a full confession.

II. HANOI SUPPLIES WEAPONS, AMMUNITION, AND OTHER WAR MATERIAL TO ITS FORCES IN THE SOUTH

When Hanoi launched the VC campaign of terror, violence, and subversion in earnest in 1959, the Communist forces relied mainly on stocks of weapons and ammunition left over from the war against the French. Supplies sent in from North Vietnam came largely from the same source. As the military campaign progressed, the Vietcong depended heavily on weapons captured from the Armed Forces in South Vietnam. This remains an important source of weapons and ammunition for the Vietcong. But as the pace of the war has quickened, requirements for up-to-date arms and special types of weapons have risen to a point where the Vietcong cannot rely on captured stocks. Hanoi has undertaken a program to reequip its forces in the South with Communist-produced weapons.

Large and increasing quantities of military supplies are entering South Vietnam from outside the country. The principal supply point is North Vietnam, which provides a convenient channel for material that originates in Communist China and other Communist countries.

An increasing number of weapons from external Communist sources have been seized in the South. These include such weapons as 57-mm. and 75-mm. recoilless rifles, dual-purpose machine guns, rocket launchers, large mortars, and antitank mines.

A new group of Chinese Communist-manufactured weapons has recently appeared in VC hands. These include the 7.62 semiautomatic carbine, 7.62 light machine gun, and the 7.62 assault rifle. These weapons and ammunition for them, manufactured in Communist China in 1962, were first captured in December 1964 in Chuong Thien Province. Similar weapons have since been seized in each of the four Corps areas of South Vietnam. Also captured have been Chinese Communist antitank grenade launchers and ammunition made in China in 1963.

One captured Vietcong told his captors that his entire company had been supplied recently with modern Chinese weapons. The reequipping of VC units with a type of weapons that require ammunition and parts from outside South Vietnam indicates the growing confidence of the authorities in Hanoi in the effectiveness of their supply lines into the South.

Incontrovertible evidence of Hanoi's elaborate program to supply its forces in the South with weapons, ammunition, and other supplies has accumulated over the years. Dramatic new proof was exposed just as this report was being completed.

On February 16, 1965, an American helicopter pilot flying along the South Vietnamese coast sighted a suspicious vessel. It was a cargo ship of an estimated 100-ton capacity, carefully camouflaged and moored just offshore along the coast of Phu Yen Province. Fighter planes that approached the vessel met machine gun fire from guns on the deck of the ship and from the shore as well. A Vietnamese Air Force strike was launched against the vessel, and Vietnamese Government troops moved into the area. They seized the ship after a bitter fight with the Vietcong.

The ship, which had been sunk in shallow water, had discharged a huge cargo of arms, ammunition, and other supplies. Documents found on the ship and on the bodies of several Vietcong aboard identified the vessel as having come from North Vietnam. A newspaper in the cabin was from Haiphong and was dated January 23, 1965. The supplies delivered by the ship—thousands of weapons and more than a million rounds of ammunition—were almost all of Communist origin, largely from Communist China and Czechoslovakia, as well as North Vietnam. At least 100 tons of military supplies were discovered near the ship.

A preliminary survey of the cache near the sunken vessel from Hanoi listed the following supplies and weapons:

—approximately 1 million rounds of small-arms ammunition;
—more than 1,000 stick grenades;
—500 pounds of TNT in prepared charges;
—2,000 rounds of 82-mm. mortar ammunition;
—500 antitank grenades;
—500 rounds of 57-mm. recoilless rifle ammunition;
—more than 1,000 rounds of 75-mm. recoilless rifle ammunition;
—1 57-mm. recoilless rifle;
—2 heavy machine guns;
—2,000 7.92 Mauser rifles;
—more than 100 7.62 carbines;
—1,000 submachine guns;
—15 light machine guns;
—500 rifles;
—500 pounds of medical supplies (with labels from North Vietnam, Communist China, Czechoslovakia, East Germany, Soviet Union, and other sources).

The ship was fairly new and had been made in Communist China. Documents aboard the ship included three North Vietnamese nautical charts (one of the Haiphong area and one of Honggay, both in North Vietnam, and one of the Tra Vinh area of South Vietnam). The military health records of North Vietnamese soldiers were found. One man had a political history sheet showing he was a member of the 338th Division of the North Vietnamese army.

Also aboard the North Vietnamese ship were: an instruction book for a Chinese Communist navigational device; postcards and letters to addresses in North Vietnam; snapshots, including one of a group of men in North Vietnamese army uniforms under a flag of the Hanoi government.

Members of the ICC and representatives of the free press visited the sunken North Vietnamese ship and viewed its cargo. The incident itself underlined in the most dramatic form that Hanoi is behind the continuing campaign of aggression aimed at conquering South Vietnam. It made unmistakably clear that what is happening in South Vietnam is not an internal affair but part of a large-scale, carefully directed and supported program of armed attack on a sovereign state and a free people. . . .

[*Some further details about shipment of arms and materiel from the North are omitted.—ed.*]

The Communists have shown extreme sensitivity to exposure of the fact that war materiel is going to the Vietcong from North Vietnam, Communist China, and other Communist countries. A secret document captured from a VC agent last year reflected this sensitivity. The document was sent from VC military headquarters in Bienhoa Province to subordinate units. It ordered them to "pay special attention to the removal of all the markings and letters on weapons of all types currently employed by units and agencies and manufactured by friendly East European democratic countries or by China." It said incriminating markings should be chiseled off "so that the enemy cannot use it as a propaganda theme every time he captures these weapons."

III. NORTH VIETNAM: BASE FOR
CONQUEST OF THE SOUTH [8]

The Third Lao Dong Party Congress in Hanoi in September 1960 set forth two tasks for its members: "to carry out the socialist revolution in North Vietnam" and "to liberate South Vietnam."

The resolutions of the congress described the effort to destroy the legal Government in South Vietnam as fol-

[8] *Much of the material in this section is identical to that in the "White Paper" of 1961. See* A Threat to the Peace, *especially, pp. 14–25.—ed.*

lows: "The revolution in the South is a protracted, hard, and complex process of struggle, combining many forms of struggle of great activity and flexibility, ranging from lower to higher, and taking as its basis the building, consolidation, and development of the revolutionary power of the masses."

At the September meeting the Communist leaders in the North called for formation of "a broad national united front." Three months later Hanoi announced creation of the "Front for Liberation of the South." This is the organization that Communist propaganda now credits with guiding the forces of subversion in the South; it is pictured as an organization established and run by the people in the South themselves. At the 1960 Lao Dong Party Congress the tone was different. Then, even before the front existed, the Communist leaders were issuing orders for the group that was being organized behind the scenes in Hanoi. "This front must rally . . ."; "The aims of its struggle are . . ."; "The front must carry out . . ."—this is the way Hanoi and the Communist Party addressed the "Liberation Front" even before its founding.

The Liberation Front is Hanoi's creation; it is neither independent nor Southern, and what it seeks is not liberation but subjugation of the South.

In his address to the Third Lao Dong Party Congress, party and government leader Ho Chi Minh spoke of the necessity "to step up the Socialist revolution in the North and, at the same time, to step up the national democratic people's revolution in the South."

The year before, writing for *Red Flag*, the Communist Party newspaper of Belgium, Ho had said much the same thing:

> We are building socialism in Vietnam, but we are building it in only one part of the country, while in the other part we still have to *direct and bring to a close* the middle-class democratic and anti-imperialist *revolution.*

In the same vein, the commander-in-chief of the North Vietnamese armed forces, Vo Nguyen Giap, spoke at the 1960 Party Congress of the need to *"step up* the national democratic people's *revolution in the South."* Earlier in the year, writing for the Communist Party journal *Hoc Tap* in Hanoi, General Giap described the North as *"The revolution-*

ary base for the whole country."

Le Duan, a member of the Politburo and first secretary of the Lao Dong Party, was even more explicit when he talked at the Party Congress about the struggle in the South and the party's role. After noting the difficulties involved in overthrowing the existing order in South Vietnam, Le Duan said:

> Hence the Southern people's revolutionary struggle will be long, drawn out, and arduous. It is not a simple process but a complicated one, combining many varied forms of struggle—from elementary to advanced, *legal and illegal*—and based on the building, consolidation, and development of the revolutionary force of the masses. In this process, *we must constantly intensify our solidarity and the organization* and education *of the people of the South. . . .*

Another high official of the Hanoi regime, Truong Chinh, writing in the party organ *Hoc Tap* in April 1961, expressed confidence in the success of the struggle to remove the legal Government in South Vietnam because: "North Vietnam is being rapidly consolidated and strengthened, *is providing good support to the South Vietnamese revolution, and is serving as a strong base for the struggle for national reunification."*

He outlined the steps by which the Communists expect to achieve control over all Vietnam as follows: The "Liberation Front" would destroy the present Government in the South; a "Coalition Government" would be established; this Government would agree with the North Vietnamese Government in Hanoi regarding national reunification "under one form or another." It takes little imagination to understand the form that is intended.

"Thus," wrote Truong Chinh, "though *South Vietnam will be liberated by nonpeaceful means,* the party policy of achieving peaceful national reunification is still correct."

The official government radio in Hanoi is used both overtly and covertly to support the Vietcong effort in South Vietnam. Captured agents have testified that the broadcasts are used sometimes to send instructions in veiled code to Vietcong representatives in the South.

Hoc Tap stated frankly in March 1963: "They [the authorities in South Vietnam] are well aware that *North Vietnam is the firm base for the Southern revolution* and the point on which it leans, and that *our party* is the steady and experienced vanguard unit of the working class and people and *is the brain and factor that decides all victories of the revolution."*

In April 1964 the Central Committee of the Lao Dong Party issued a directive to all party echelons. It stated:

> "When the forces of the enemy and the plots of the enemy are considered, it is realized that *the cadres, party members, and people in North Vietnam must . . . increase their sense of responsibility in regard to the South Vietnam revolution by giving positive and practical support to South Vietnam in every field."*

Nguyen Chi Thanh, writing in a Hanoi newspaper in May 1963, underlined the importance of the role of the North Vietnamese army in Hanoi's plans to unify Vietnam under Communist rule:

> "Our party set forth two strategic tasks to be carried out at the same time: to transform and build socialism in the North and to struggle to unify the country. *Our army is an instrument of the class struggle in carrying out these two strategic tasks."*

IV. ORGANIZATION, DIRECTION, COMMAND AND CONTROL OF THE ATTACK ON SOUTH VIETNAM ARE CENTERED IN HANOI

The VC military and political apparatus in South Vietnam is an extension of an elaborate military and political structure in North Vietnam which directs and supplies it with the tools for conquest. The Ho Chi Minh regime has shown that it is ready to allocate every resource that can be spared—whether it be personnel, funds, or equipment—to the cause of overthrowing the legitimate Government in South Vietnam and of bringing all Vietnam under Communist rule.

A. POLITICAL ORGANIZATION

Political direction and control of the Vietcong is supplied by the Lao Dong Party, i.e. the Communist Party, led by Ho Chi Minh. Party agents are responsible for indoctrination, recruitment, political training, propaganda, anti-Government demonstrations, and other activities of a political nature. The considerable intelligence-gathering facilities of the party are also at the disposal of the Vietcong.

Overall direction of the VC movement is the responsibility of the Central Committee of the Lao Dong Party. Within the Central Committee a special Reunification Department has been established. This has replaced the "Committee for Supervision of the South" mentioned in intelligence reports two years ago. It lays down broad strategy for the movement to conquer South Vietnam. . . .

[*Some detail on VC Administrative Structure is omitted.—ed.*]

1. The "Liberation Front"

The National Front for the Liberation of South Vietnam is the screen behind which the Communists carry out their program of conquest. It is the creature of the Communist Government in Hanoi. As noted above, the Communist Party in the North demanded establishment of such a "front" three months before its formation was actually announced in December 1960. It was designed to create the illusion that the Vietcong campaign of subversion was truly indigenous to South Vietnam rather than an externally directed Communist plan.

The front has won support primarily from the Communist world. Its radio faithfully repeats the propaganda themes of Hanoi and Peking. When its representatives travel abroad, they do so with North Vietnamese passports and sponsorship.[9] The front's program copies that of the Lao Dong Party in North Vietnam.

B. MILITARY ORGANIZATION

Military affairs of the Vietcong are the responsibility of High Command of the People's Army of North Vietnam and the Ministry of Defense, under close supervision from the Lao Dong Party. These responsibilities include operational plans, assignments of individuals and regular units, training programs, infiltration of military personnel and supplies, military communications, tactical intelligence, supplies, and the like. The six military regions are the same as those of the VC political organization.

The military structure of the Vietcong is an integral part of the political machinery that controls every facet of VC activity in South Vietnam under Hanoi's overall direction.

---

[9] *Pictures of North Vietnamese passports and other travel documents used by officials of the National Liberation Front are included in appendix F of this "White Paper," not reproduced here. One doubts that NLF members would find it easy to get passports from Saigon authorities.—ed.*

Each political headquarters from the Central Office down to
the village has a military component which controls day-to-
day military operations. Similarly, each military headquarters
has a political element, an individual or a small staff. This
meshing of political and military activity is designed to insure the closest co-operation in support of the total Communist mission. It also gives assurance of political control over the military. . . .

The size of the Vietcong regular forces has grown steadily
in recent years. For example, the Vietcong have five regimental headquarters compared with two in 1961. And the
main VC force is composed of 50 battalions, 50 percent
more than before. There are an estimated 139 VC companies. Hard-core VC strength now is estimated at about
35,000, whereas it was less than 20,000 in 1961 . . .

Supporting the main force units of the Vietcong are an
estimated 60,000–80,000 part-time guerrillas. They are generally organized at the district level where there are likely
to be several companies of fifty or more men each. These
troops receive only half pay, which means they must work at
least part of the time to eke out a living.

Below the irregular guerrilla forces of the district are the
part-time, village-based guerrillas. They are available for assignment by higher headquarters and are used for harassment and sabotage. They are expected to warn nearby VC
units of the approach of any force of the legal government. They provide a pool for recruitment into the VC district forces.

The record shows that many of the village guerrillas are
dragooned into service with the Vietcong. Some are kidnaped; others are threatened; still others join to prevent their
families from being harmed. Once in the Vietcong net, many
are reluctant to leave for fear of punishment by the authorities or reprisal by the Communists. . . .

Officials and wealthy people have been kidnaped for ran-
som. The VC have often stopped buses and taken the money
and valuables of all on board. For the most part, the VC
have concentrated their attention on individuals, isolated or
poorly defended outposts, and small centers of population.
They have mercilessly killed or kidnaped thousands of village
chiefs and other local officials. But over the past year the VC
have moved into larger unit operations. Their ability to oper-

ate on a battalion level or larger has substantially increased.

C. INTELLIGENCE ORGANIZATION

A key element in the Vietcong effort is an elaborate organization in Hanoi called the Central Research Agency (C.R.A.) (Cuc Nghien-Cuu Trung-Uong). Though it handles Hanoi's intelligence effort on a worldwide scale, the main focus of its operation is on South Vietnam. This agency is able to draw on the intelligence capabilities of both the Lao Dong Party and the North Vietnamese armed forces for information, personnel, and facilities. . . .

[*Details of the C.R.A. operation are omitted.—ed.*]

Taken as a whole, the North Vietnamese intelligence operation in support of the Vietcong is one of the most extensive of its kind in the world.

V. A BRIEF HISTORY OF HANOI'S CAMPAIGN OF AGGRESSION AGAINST SOUTH VIETNAM

While negotiating an end to the Indochina War at Geneva in 1954, the Communists were making plans to take over all [10] former French territory in Southeast Asia. When Vietnam was partitioned, thousands of carefully selected party members were ordered to remain in place in the South and keep their secret apparatus intact to help promote Hanoi's cause. Arms and ammunition were stored away for future use. Guerrilla fighters rejoined their families to await the party's call. Others withdrew to remote jungle and mountain hideouts. The majority—an estimated 90,000—were moved to North Vietnam.

Hanoi's original calculation was that all of Vietnam would fall under its control without resort to force.[11] For this purpose, Communist cadres were ordered to penetrate official and nonofficial agencies, to propagandize and sow confusion, and generally to use all means short of open violence to aggravate war-torn conditions and to weaken South

---

[10] *But, as we have seen (p. 134) the Vietminh at Geneva gave up their claims to sponsorship of insurgent groups in Cambodia and Laos. In at least the case of Cambodia the Vietminh scrupulously carried out the bargain it had struck.—ed.*

[11] *At this point in the historical section of the "White Paper" of 1961 there is a discreet reference to the "nationwide elections" which the Vietminh hoped to win. As I. F. Stone points out, there is no such reference in the comparable document of 1965, here reprinted. (see p. 322).—ed.*

Vietnam's Government and social fabric.

South Vietnam's refusal to fall in with Hanoi's scheme for peaceful takeover came as a heavy blow to the Communists. Meantime, the Government had stepped up efforts to blunt Vietcong subversion and to expose Communist agents. Morale in the Communist organization in the South dropped sharply. Defections were numerous.

Among South Vietnamese, hope rose that their nation could have a peaceful and independent future, free of Communist domination. The country went to work. The years after 1955 were a period of steady progress and growing prosperity.

Food production levels of the prewar years were reached and surpassed. While per capita food output was dropping 10 percent in the North from 1956 to 1960, it rose 20 percent in the South. By 1963, it had risen 30 percent—despite the disruption in the countryside caused by intensified Vietcong military attacks and terrorism. The authorities in the North admitted openly to continuing annual failures to achieve food production goals.

Production of textiles increased in the South more than 20 percent in one year (1958). In the same year, South Vietnam's sugar crop increased more than 100 percent. Despite North Vietnam's vastly larger industrial complex, South Vietnam's per capita gross national product in 1960 was estimated at $110 a person while it was only $70 in the North.

More than 900,000 refugees who had fled from Communist rule in the North were successfully settled in South Vietnam. An agrarian reform program was instituted. The elementary school population nearly quadrupled between 1956 and 1960. And so it went—a record of steady improvement in the lives of the people. It was intolerable for the rulers in Hanoi; under peaceful conditions, the South was outstripping the North. They were losing the battle of peaceful competition and decided to use violence and terror to gain their ends.

After 1956 Hanoi rebuilt, reorganized, and expanded its covert political and military machinery in the South. Defectors were replaced by trained personnel from party ranks in the North. Military units and political cells were enlarged and were given new leaders, equipment, and intensified training. Recruitment was pushed. In short, Hanoi and its

forces in the South prepared to take by force and violenc
what they had failed to achieve by other means.

By 1958 the use of terror by the Vietcong increased ap
preciably. It was used both to win prestige and to back u
demands for support from the people, support that politica
and propaganda appeals had failed to produce. It was als
designed to embarrass the Government in Saigon and rais
doubts about its ability to maintain internal order and t
assure the personal security of its people. From 1959 throug
1961, the pace of Vietcong terrorism and armed attacks ac
celerated substantially.

The situation at the end of 1961 was so grave that th
Government of the Republic of Vietnam asked the Unite
States for increased military assistance.[12] That request wa
met. Meantime, the program of strategic hamlets, designed t
improve the peasant's livelihood and give him some protec
tion against Vietcong harassment and pressure, was pushe
energetically.

But the Vietcong did not stand still. To meet the chang
ing situation, they tightened their organization and adopte
new tactics, with increasing emphasis on terrorism, sabotage
and armed attacks by small groups. They also introduce
from the North technicians in fields such as armor and anti
aircraft. Heavier weapons were sent in to the regular guer
rilla forces.

The military and insurgency situation was complicated by
a quite separate internal political struggle in South Vietnam,
which led in November 1963 to the removal of the Diem
government and its replacement with a new one. Effective
power was placed in the hands of a Military Revolutionary Council. There have been a number of changes in the
leadership and composition of the Government in Saigon in
the ensuing period.

These internal developments and distractions gave the
Vietcong an invaluable opportunity, and they took advantage
of it. Vietcong agents did what they could to encourage
disaffection and to exploit demonstrations in Saigon and elsewhere. In the countryside the Communists consolidated
their hold over some areas and enlarged their military and
political apparatus by increased infiltration. Increasingly
they struck at remote outposts and the most vulnerable of

[12] See pp. 206–209.–ed.

he new strategic hamlets and expanded their campaign of ggressive attacks, sabotage, and terror.

Any official, worker, or establishment that represents a ervice to the people by the Government in Saigon is fair ame for the Vietcong. Schools have been among their favor-e targets. Through harassment, the murder of teachers, and abotage of buildings, the Vietcong succeeded in closing undreds of schools and interrupting the education of tens f thousands of youngsters.

Hospitals and medical clinics have often been attacked as art of the anti-Government campaign and also because uch attacks provide the Vietcong with needed medical sup-lies. The Communists have encouraged people in rural areas o oppose the Government's antimalaria teams, and some of he workers have been killed. Village and town offices, police tations, and agricultural research stations are high on the ist of preferred targets for the Vietcong.

In 1964, 436 South Vietnamese hamlet chiefs and other Government officials were killed outright by the Vietcong and 1,131 were kidnaped. More than 1,350 civilians were killed in bombings and other acts of sabotage. And at least 3,400 civilians were kidnaped by the Vietcong.

Today the war in Vietnam has reached new levels of ntensity. The elaborate effort by the Communist regime in North Vietnam to conquer the South has grown, not dimin-shed. Military men, technicians, political organizers, propa-gandists, and secret agents have been infiltrating into the Republic of Vietnam from the North in growing numbers. The flow of Communist-supplied weapons, particularly those of large caliber, has increased. Communications links with Hanoi are extensive. Despite the heavy casualties of three years of fighting, the hard-core VC force is considerably larger now than it was at the end of 1961.

The Government in Saigon has undertaken vigorous action to meet the new threat. The United States and other free countries have increased their assistance to the Vietnamese Government and people. Secretary of State Dean Rusk visited Vietnam in 1964, and he promised the Vietnamese: "We shall remain at your side until the aggression from the North has been defeated, until it has been completely rooted out and this land enjoys the peace which it deserves."

President Johnson has repeatedly stressed that the United

States' goal is to see peace secured in Southeast Asia. But he has noted that "that will come only when aggressors leave their neighbors in peace."

Though it has been apparent for years that the regime in Hanoi was conducting a campaign of conquest against South Vietnam, the Government in Saigon and the Government of the United States both hoped that the danger could be met within South Vietnam itself. The hope that any widening of the conflict might be avoided was stated frequently.

The leaders in Hanoi chose to respond with greater violence. They apparently interpreted restraint as indicating lack of will. Their efforts were pressed with greater vigor and armed attacks and incidents of terror multiplied.

Clearly the restraint of the past was not providing adequately for the defense of South Vietnam against Hanoi's open aggression. It was mutually agreed between the Governments of the Republic of Vietnam and the United States that further means for providing for South Vietnam's defense were required. Therefore, air strikes have been made against some of the military assembly points and supply bases from which North Vietnam is conducting its aggression against the South. These strikes constitute a limited response fitted to the aggression that produced them.

Until the regime in Hanoi decides to halt its intervention in the South, or until effective steps are taken to maintain peace and security in the area, the Governments of South Vietnam and the United States will continue necessary measures of defense against the Communist armed aggression coming from North Vietnam.

VI. CONCLUSION

The evidence presented in this report could be multiplied many times with similar examples of the drive of the Hanoi regime to extend its rule over South Vietnam.

The record is conclusive. It establishes beyond question that North Vietnam is carrying out a carefully conceived plan of aggression against the South. It shows that North Vietnam has intensified its efforts in the years since it was condemned by the International Control Commission. It proves that Hanoi continues to press its systematic program of armed aggression into South Vietnam. This aggression violates the United Nations Charter. It is directly contrary to the Geneva Accords of 1954 and of 1962 to which North

Vietnam is a party. It shatters the peace of Southeast Asia. It is a fundamental threat to the freedom and security of South Vietnam.

The people of South Vietnam have chosen to resist this threat. At their request, the United States has taken its place beside them in their defensive struggle.

The United States seeks no territory, no military bases, no favored position. But we have learned the meaning of aggression elsewhere in the post-war world, and we have met it.

If peace can be restored in South Vietnam, the United States will be ready at once to reduce its military involvement. But it will not abandon friends who want to remain free. It will do what must be done to help them. The choice now between peace and continued and increasingly destructive conflict is one for the authorities in Hanoi to make.

APPENDIX C

Detail on Military Infiltration with Case Studies

The following table shows the scale of infiltration of military personnel from North Vietnam into the South since 1959. The confirmed list is based on information on infiltration groups from at least two independent sources.

Year	Confirmed	Estimated additional	Total
1959-60	1,800	2,700	4,500
1961	3,750	1,650	5,400
1962	5,400	7,000	12,400
1963	4,200	3,200	7,400
1964	4,400	3,000	7,400
Total.	19,550	17,550	37,100

Nine brief biographies of "typical Vietcong who were sent into South Vietnam by The Authorities in Hanoi" are omitted.—ed.

APPENDIX D

List of Communist Weapons Captured in South Vietnam

On January 29, 1964, the Government of Vietnam submitted to the International Control Commission a list of weapons and other military equipment which had been captured from the Vietcong.

I. CHINESE COMMUNIST ORIGIN

Type	Quantity	Date of capture	Place
75-mm. recoilless rifle	1	9/10/63	An Xuyen Province
	1	12/2-6/63	An Xuyen Province
	1	12/22/63	Dinh Tuong
Total	3		
57-mm. recoilless gun	1	11/25/62	Phuoc Chau in Quang Tin (1 gun and 7 gun carriages)
		12/5/62	Phu Bon (1 gun carriage)
	2	8/31/63	Province of Quang Ngai
Total	3 guns (8 gun carriages)		
Shells for 75-mm. gun (shells bear markings in Chinese characters. On some shells, markings were scratched out and replaced by "American" markings.)	8	11/24/63	Province of An Xuyen
	120	12/22/63	Operation Due Thang at Dinh Tuong
Total	128		

I. CHINESE COMMUNIST ORIGIN—Continued

Type	Quantity	Date of capture	Place
Shells for 57-mm. gun	49	11/25/62	Phuoc Chau, Province of Quang Tin
	8	2/20/63	Vietcong attack on the post of Ben Heo (Tah Ninh)
	33	5/24/63	On a Vietcong vessel on the Bassac River
	6	8/31/63	Quang Ngai
	1	10/8/63	Province of Binh Dinh
	58	12/22/63	Dinh Tuong
Total	155		
80-mm. mortar	1	3/25/63	Province of Tay Ninh
60-mm. mortar	1	1/7/63	Phuoc Thanh
	2	12/22/63	Dinh Tuong
Total	3		
Shells for 60-mm. mortar . .	18	9/10/63	Province of An Xuyen
	165	12/22/63	Dinh Tuong
Total	183		
90-mm. bazooka	1	12/22/63	Dinh Tuong
Caliber 27-mm. rocket launcher .	2	6/10/62	Provinces of Quang Ngai and Quang Duc
Total	3		

I. CHINESE COMMUNIST ORIGIN—Continued

Type	Quantity	Date of capture	Place
Caliber 7.92-mm. model 08 Maxim machine gun	2	9/10/63	Province of An Xuyen
	4	12/21/63	Chuong Thien
Total	6		
MP-82 rocket	142	4/24/63	Quang Ngai
TNT explosives	365 charges	6/13/62	Quang Duc
	43	11/25/62	Phuoc Chau (Quang Tin)
	29	5/7/63	Can Tho
	140	12/22/63	Dinh Tuong
Total	577 charges		
Red phosphorus	5 kg.	4/19/63	Province of Kien Phong
Potassium chlorate	17 tons	Sept. '62	On a Vietcong vessel at Phu Quoc
	2 tons	4/19/63	Province of Kien Phong
	150 kg.	7/10-15/63	Phu Quoc
Total	19 tons 155 kg.		
Cartridges for 7.92-mm. machine gun.	100,000	12/22/63	Dinh Tuong
Detonating fuses for 60-mm. mortar shell.	150	. . . . do	Do.

II. SOVIET ORIGIN

Type	Quantity	Date of capture	Place
MP-82 rifle	. . . .	5/10/62	Binh Dinh
Launching cartridges	. . . .	. . . do . . .	Do.
Mossin Nagant carbine (with automatic bayonet).	1	6/13/63	Kien Phong
	2	7/13/63	Long An
	5	7/20/63	Dinh Tuong
	7	9/8/63	Dinh Tuong
Total	**15**		
Rifles	6	10/6/63	Long An
	1	10/19/63	Dinh Tuong
	11	11/6/63	Vinh Binh
	1	11/17/63	Dinh Tuong
	1	11/25/63	Hau Nghia
	1	12/6/63	Dinh Tuong
	8	12/7/63	Phong Dinh
	1	12/12/63	Kien Tuong
	1	12/13/63	An Xuyen
	1	12/16/63	Kien Giang
	1	. . . do . . .	Ba Xuyen
	3	. . . do . . .	An Xuyen
	1	12/17/63	Phong Dinh
	1	12/20/63	Kien Hoa
	6	12/21/63	Chuong Thien
	2	12/22/63	Dinh Tuong
Total	**46**		

II. SOVIET ORIGIN—Continued

Type	Quantity	Date of capture	Place
Automatic pistol	1	10/19/63	Phan Thiet
Grenades	5		Long An
Rifle cartridges	160,000	12/22/63	Dinh Tuong
Submachine gun (machine pistol)	2	9/23/63	Long Xuyen

III. CZECH ORIGIN

Type	Quantity	Date of capture	Place
7.65-mm. automatic pistol . .	1	1/2/63	On person of Vietcong leader arrested at Phu Yen
K-50 submachine gun	2	11/25/62	Quang Tin
	1	11/29/62	Phuoc Long
	7	4/24/63	Quang Ngai
	5	5/9/63	Quang Tin
	2	7/11/63	Operation Ha Giang
	3	8/31/63	Quang Ngai
	1	9/8/63	Dinh Tuong
	1	9/16/63	Long An
	1	10/17/63	Quang Nam
	2	11/13/63	Phu Yen
	1	. . . do . . .	Hué
	9	10/8/63	Binh Dinh
	1		Operation Phuoc Binh Thang
	1	12/20/63	Kien Hoa
	1	12/26/63	Chuong Thien
	1	12/17/63	Long Xuyen
Total	**40**		

III. CZECH ORIGIN—Continued

Type	Quantity	Date of capture	Place
Rifles	9	9/10/63	An Xuyen
	1	10/19/63	Chuong Thien
	1	11/6/63	Ba Xuyen
	2	11/9/63	Chuong Thien
	3	11/13/63	Kien Giang
	1	11/17/63	Ba Xuyen
	2	11/26/63	Hau Nghia
	1	12/2/63	Phong Dinh
	6	12/21/63	Chuong Thien
Total	**26**		
Machine gun cartridges	14,000	12/22/63	Dinh Tuong
Grenade launcher	1	7/14/63	Long An
3.5 antitank bazooka	1	12/22/63	Dinh Tuong

A Reply to the White Paper

BY I. F. STONE*

That North Vietnam supports the guerrillas in South Vietnam is no more a secret than that the United States supports the South Vietnamese government against them. The striking thing about the State Department's new White Paper is how little support it can prove. "Incontrovertible evidence of Hanoi's elaborate program to supply its forces in the South with weapons, ammunition, and other supplies," the White Paper says, "has accumulated over the years." A detailed presentation of this evidence is in Appendix D; unfortunately few will see the appendices since even *The New York Times* did not reprint them, though these are more revealing than the report. Appendix D provides a list of weapons, ammunition, and other supplies of Chinese Communist, Soviet, Czech, and North Vietnamese manufacture, with the dates and place of capture from the Vietcong guerrillas, over the 18-month period from June 1962, to January 29 last year, when it was presented to the International Control Commission. The Commission was set up by the Geneva Agreements of 1954. This list provides a good point at which to begin an analysis of the White Paper.

The Pentagon's Figures

To put the figures in perspective, we called the Pentagon press office and obtained some figures the White Paper does not supply—the number of weapons captured from the guerrillas and the number lost to them in recent years:

	Captured From Guerrillas	Lost to Them
1962	4,800	5,200
1963	5,400	8,500
1964	4,900	13,700
3-Year Total	15,100	27,400

* Publisher and editor of *I. F. Stone's Weekly*, a notable exercise in American journalism, author of *The Haunted Fifties* (New York, 1964) and other books. The selection is from *I. F. Stone's Weekly*, XIII (March 8, 1965), pp. 1-4. By Permission.

In three years, the guerrillas captured from our side 12,300 more weapons than they lost to us.

What interests us at the moment is not this favorable balance but the number of guerrilla weapons our side captured during the past three years. The grand total was 15,100. If Hanoi has indeed engaged in an "elaborate program" to supply the Vietcong, one would expect a substantial number of enemy-produced weapons to turn up. Here is the sum total of enemy-produced weapons and supplies in that 18-month tally to the Control Commission—

72 rifles (46 Soviet, 26 Czech)
64 submachine guns (40 Czech, 24 French but "modified" in North Vietnam)
15 carbines (Soviet)
8 machine guns (6 Chinese, 2 North Vietnamese)
5 pistols (4 Soviet, 1 Czech)
4 mortars (Chinese)
3 recoilless 75-mm. rifles (Chinese)
3 recoilless 57-mm. guns (Chinese)
2 bazookas (1 Chinese, 1 Czech)
2 rocket launchers (Chinese)
1 grenade launcher (Czech)

179 total

This is not a very impressive total. According to the Pentagon figures, we captured on the average 7,500 weapons each 18 months in the past three years. If only 179 Communist-made weapons turned up in 18 months, that is less than 2½ percent of the total. Judging by these White Paper figures, our military are wrong in estimating, as they have in recent months, that 80 percent of the weapons used by guerrillas are captured from us. It looks as if the proportion is considerably higher. The material of North Vietnamese origin included only those 24 French submachine guns "modified" in North Vietnam, 2 machine guns made in North Vietnam, 16 helmets, a uniform, and an undisclosed number of mess kits, belts, sweaters, and socks. Judging by this tally, the main retaliatory blow should be at North Vietnam's clothing factories.

There is another way to judge this tally of captured Communist weapons. A Communist battalion has about 450 men. It needs 500 rifles, four 80-mm. mortars, eight 60-mm. mortars, and at least four recoilless rifles. The weapons of Communist origin captured in 18 months would not adequately outfit one battalion. The figures in the appendix on ammunition captured provide another index. We captured 183 (Chinese) shells for a 60-mm. mortar. This fires about 20 shells a minute, so that was hardly enough ammunition for 10 minutes of firing. There were 100,000 (Chinese) cartridges for 7.26-mm. machine guns. That looks impressive until one discovers on checking with knowledgeable military sources that these machine guns fire 600 rounds a minute. A machine gun platoon normally has four machine guns. This was enough ammunition for about 40 minutes of firing by one platoon. Indeed, if the ratio of Communist-made weapons captured is the same for weapons used, then only 12½ days of those 18 months were fought by the guerrillas on the basis of Communist-made supplies.

If these figures were being presented in a court of law, they would run up against a further difficulty: one would have to prove the arms actually came from the Communist side. There is a world-wide market in second-hand weapons. One can buy Soviet, Czech, and Chinese Communist weapons of all kinds only two miles from the Pentagon through Interarmco, Ltd., 10 Prince Street, Alexandria, Va. Interarmco, one of the world's foremost dealers, can provide more Communist weapons than we picked up in 18 months on Vietnamese battlefields. The supply of East European Communist weapons comes in large part from the huge stocks of Soviet and Czech arms captured by the Israelis in the Suez campaign. Many Chinese Communist weapons were captured by our side in the Korean War. There is also, of course, a wide selection of our own military surplus. This has turned up in strange places.

For example, a book on the Algerian war, *Les Algeriens en guerre,* by Dominique Darbois and Phillippe Vingneau, was published in Milan in 1960 by Feltrinelli. It shows pictures of FLN (National Liberation Front) Algerian rebels wearing U. S. Marine Corps uniforms from which the "USM" and the eagle and globe insignia have not even been removed. It shows Algerians carrying U. S. 80-mm. mortars and U. S. 50-caliber machine guns. Such photos could have been used by France to accuse the U. S. of supplying the Algerian rebels.

The State Department's White Paper says "dramatic new proof was exposed just as this report was being completed" in the discovery of a suspected Vietcong arms cargo ship on Feb. 16. *The New York Times* commented astringently on this in an editorial Feb. 28:

> Apparently, the major new evidence of a need for escalating the war, with all the hazard that this entails, was provided by the sinking in a South Vietnamese cove earlier this month of a 100-ton cargo ship loaded with Communist-made small arms and ammunition. A ship of that size is not much above the Oriental junk class. The standard Liberty or Victory ship of World War II had a capacity of 7,150 to 7,650 tons.

The affair of the cargo ship is curious. Until now there has been little evidence of arms coming in by ship. A huge fleet of small vessels patrols the coast and there have been glowing stories in the past of its efficiency. "About 12,000 vessels," the AP reported from Saigon (*The New York Times,* Feb. 22) "are searched each month by the South Vietnamese coastal junk patrol force but arrests are rare and no significant amounts of incriminating goods or weapons ever have been found." This lone case of a whole shipload of arms is puzzling.

Few Northern Infiltrees Cited

The White Paper's story on the influx of men from the North also deserves a closer analysis than the newspapers have given it. Appendix C provides an elaborate table from 1959-60 to 1964 inclusive, showing the number of "confirmed" military infiltrees per year from the North. The total is given as 19,550. One way to measure this number is against that of the military we have assigned to South Vietnam in the same years. These now total 23,500, or 25 percent more, and 1,000 are to be added in the near future. The number of North Vietnamese infiltrees is "based on information . . . from at least two independent sources." *Nowhere are we told how many men who infiltrated from the North have actually been captured.* There is reason to wonder whether the count of infiltrees may be as bloated as the count of Vietcong dead; in both cases the numbers used are estimates rather than actual bodies.

The White Paper claims "that as many as 75 percent of the more than 7,000 Vietcong who are known to have entered the South in 1964 were natives of North Vietnam." But a careful reading of the text and the appendices turns up the names of only six North Vietnamese infiltrees. In Part I of the White Paper, Section B gives "individual case histories of North Vietnamese soldiers" sent South by Hanoi but all nine of these are of South Vietnamese origin. The next Section, C, is headed "Infiltration of Native North Vietnamese." It names five infiltrees but one of these is also from the South. That leaves four North Vietnamese natives. Then, in Appendix C, we are given the case histories and photographs of nine other Vietcong sent South by Hanoi. The report does not explain which ones were originally from the South but it does give the names of the provinces in which they were born. When these are checked, it turns out that only two of the nine were born in North Vietnam. This gives us a total of six Northern infiltrees. It is strange that after five years of fighting, the White Paper can cite so few.

None of this is discussed frankly in the White Paper. To do so would be to bring the war into focus as a rebellion in the South, which may owe some men and materiel to the North but is largely dependent on popular indigenous support for its manpower, as it is on captured U. S. weapons for its supply. The White Paper withholds all evidence which points to a civil war. It also fails to tell the full story of the July 1962 Special Report by the International Control Commission. Appendix A quotes that portion in which the Commission 2-to-1 (Poland dissenting) declared that the North had in specific instances sent men and material south in violation of the Geneva accords. But nowhere does the State Department mention that the same report also condemned South Vietnam and the U. S., declaring that they had entered into a military alliance in violation of the Geneva Agreements. The U. S. was criticized because it then had about 5,000 military advisers in South Vietnam. The Geneva accords limited the U. S. military mission to the 684 in Vietnam at the time of the 1954 cease-fire. The U. S. and South Vietnam were also criticized by the ICC for hamstringing the Commission's efforts to check on imports of arms in violation of the Geneva Accords.[1]

The reader would never guess from the White Paper that the Geneva Accords promised that elections would be held

[1] *See p. 188.—ed.*

in 1956 to reunify the country. The 1961 Blue Book [2] at least mentioned the elections, though somehow managing to make them seem a plot. "It was the Communists' calculation," the Blue Book put it, "that nationwide elections scheduled in the Accords for 1956 would turn all of South Vietnam over to them. . . . The authorities in South Vietnam refused to fall into this well-laid trap." The White Paper omits mention of the elections altogether and says, "South Vietnam's refusal to fall in with Hanoi's scheme for peaceful takeover came as a heavy blow to the Communists." This is not the most candid and objective presentation. From the Vietminh point of view, the failure to hold the elections promised them when they laid down thei· arms was the second broken promise of the West. The earlier one was in 1946 when they made an agreement to accept limited autonomy within the French union, and welcomed the returning French troops as comrades of the liberation. Most of the French military did not want to recognize even this limited form of independence, and chose instead the road which led after eight years of war to Dienbienphu.[3]

That "Economic Miracle" Again

The most disingenuous part of the White Paper is that in which it discusses the origins of the present war. It pictures the war as an attack from the North, launched in desperation because the "economic miracle" in the South under Diem had destroyed Communist hopes of a peaceful takeover from within. Even the strategic hamlets are described as "designed to improve the peasant's livelihood" and we are asked to believe that for the first time in history a guerrilla war spread not because the people were discontented but because their lot was improving!

The true story is a story of lost opportunities. The Communist countries acquiesced in the failure to hold elections. Diem had a chance to make his part of the country a democratic showcase.

---

[2] *Stone is accurately citing here* A Threat to the Peace [*p. 3*], *which I have called the "White Paper" of 1961. The State Department document of 1961 indeed does appear within blue covers; but what Stone and I both call the "White Paper" of 1965 has light brown covers. "White Papers" in general are major official policy statements.—ed.*

[3] *Jean Sainteny,* Histoire d'une paix manquée (*Paris, 1953*); *Ellen J. Hammer,* The Struggle for Indochina (*Stanford, Calif., 1954*). [See pp. 63-86.—ed.]

The year 1956 was a bad one in the North. There was a peasant uprising and widespread resentment among the intellectuals over the Communist Party's heavy-handed thought control. But Diem on the other side of the 17th Parallel was busy erecting a dictatorship of his own. In 1956 he abolished elections even for village councils. In 1957 his mobs smashed the press of the one legal opposition party, the Democratic Bloc, when it dared criticize the government. That was the beginning of a campaign to wipe out every form of opposition. It was this campaign and the oppressive exactions imposed on the peasantry, the fake land reform and the concentration camps Diem set up for political opponents of all kinds, which stirred ever wider rebellion from 1958 onward in the grass roots *before* North Vietnam gave support.[4] It was this which drove oppositionists of all kinds into alliance with the Communists in the National Liberation Front.

Long before the North was accused of interference, its government was complaining to the Control Commission of "border and air-space violations by the South and infringements of the Geneva Agreements by the introduction of arms and U. S. servicemen." [5] For four years after Geneva, both North Vietnam and China followed the "peaceful co-existence" policy while the U. S. turned South Vietnam into a military base and a military dictatorship. It is in this story the White Paper does not tell, and the popular discontent it does not mention, that the rebellion and the aid from the North had their origins.

A Pattern for Peace in Southeast Asia: the Johns Hopkins Speech

BY LYNDON B. JOHNSON*

. . . Tonight Americans and Asians are dying for a world where each people may choose its own path to change.

---

[4] *Philippe Devillers, "The Struggle for the Unification of Vietnam,"* China Quarterly [See pp. 210-235.—ed.].

[5] *Survey of International Affairs 1956-58, by Geoffrey Barraclough, a publication of Britain's Royal Institute of International Affairs. p. 420.*

* President of the United States, former U. S. Senator from Texas. The selection is from *Department of State Bulletin*, LII (April 26, 1965), pp. 606-610.

This is the principle for which our ancestors fought in the valleys of Pennsylvania. It is the principle for which our sons fight in the jungles of Vietnam.

Vietnam is far from this quiet campus. We have no territory there, nor do we seek any. The war is dirty and brutal and difficult. And some 400 young men, born into an America bursting with opportunity and promise, have ended their lives on Vietnam's steaming soil.

Why must we take this painful road?

Why must this nation hazard its ease, its interest, and its power for the sake of a people so far away?

We fight because we must fight if we are to live in a world where every country can shape its own destiny. And only in such a world will our own freedom be finally secure.

This kind of a world will never be built by bombs or bullets. Yet the infirmities of man are such that force must often precede reason, and the waste of war, the works of peace.

We wish this were not so. But we must deal with the world as it is, if it is ever to be as we wish.

The world as it is in Asia is not a serene or peaceful place. The first reality is that North Vietnam has attacked the independent nation of South Vietnam. Its object is total conquest.

Of course, some of the people of South Vietnam are participating in this attack on their own government. But trained men and supplies, orders and arms, flow in a constant stream from North to South.

This support is the heartbeat of the war.

And it is a war of unparalleled brutality. Simple farmers are the targets of assassination and kidnapping. Women and children are strangled in the night because their men are loyal to their Government. Small and helpless villages are ravaged by sneak attacks. Large-scale raids are conducted on towns, and terror strikes in the heart of cities.

The confused nature of this conflict cannot mask the fact that it is the new face of an old enemy. It is an attack by one country upon another. And the object of that attack is a friend to which we are pledged.

Over this war, and all Asia, is another reality: the deepening shadow of Communist China. The rulers in Hanoi are urged on by Peking. This is a regime which has destroyed freedom in Tibet, attacked India, and been condemned by the United Nations for aggression in Korea. It is a nation which is helping the forces of violence in almost every continent. The contest in Vietnam is part of a wider pattern of aggressive purpose.

Why are these realities our concern? Why are we in South Vietnam? We are there because we have a promise to keep. Since 1954 every American President has offered support to the people of South Vietnam.[1] We have helped to build, and we have helped to defend. Thus, over many years, we have made a national pledge to help South Vietnam defend its independence. And I intend to keep our promise.

To dishonor that pledge, to abandon this small and brave nation to its enemy, and to the terror that must follow, would be an unforgivable wrong.

We are also there to strengthen world order. Around the globe, from Berlin to Thailand, are people whose well-being rests, in part, on the belief that they can count on us if they are attacked. To leave Vietnam to its fate would shake the confidence of all these people in the value of American commitment, the value of America's word. The result would be increased unrest and instability, and even wider war.

We are also there because there are great stakes in the balance. Let no one think for a moment that retreat from Vietnam would bring an end to conflict. The battle would be renewed in one country and then another. The central lesson of our time is that the appetite of aggression is never satisfied. To withdraw from one battlefield means only to prepare for the next. We must say in Southeast Asia, as we did in Europe, in the words of the Bible: "Hitherto shalt thou come, but no further."

There are those who say that all our effort there will be futile, that China's power is such it is bound to dominate all Southeast Asia. But there is no end to that argument until all the nations of Asia are swallowed up.

There are those who wonder why we have a responsibility there. We have it for the same reason we have a responsibility for the defense of freedom in Europe. World War II was fought in both Europe and Asia, and when it ended

[1] *See President Eisenhower's letter of October 23, 1945, pp. 204–206 and President Kennedy's of December 14, 1961, p. 209—ed.*

we found ourselves with continued responsibility for the defense of freedom.

Our objective is the independence of South Vietnam, and its freedom from attack. We want nothing for ourselves, only that the people of South Vietnam be allowed to guide their own country in their own way.

We will do everything necessary to reach that objective. And we will do only what is absolutely necessary.

In recent months, attacks on South Vietnam were stepped up. Thus it became necessary to increase our response and to make attacks by air. This is not a change of purpose. It is a change in what we believe that purpose requires.

We do this in order to slow down aggression.

We do this to increase the confidence of the brave people of South Vietnam who have bravely borne this brutal battle for so many years and with so many casualties.

And we do this to convince the leaders of North Vietnam, and all who seek to share their conquest, of a very simple fact:

We will not be defeated.

We will not grow tired.

We will not withdraw, either openly or under the cloak of a meaningless agreement.

We know that air attacks alone will not accomplish all these purposes. But it is our best and prayerful judgment that they are a necessary part of the surest road to peace.

We hope that peace will come swiftly. But that is in the hands of others beside ourselves. And we must be prepared for a long, continued conflict. It will require patience as well as bravery, the will to endure as well as the will to resist.

I wish it were possible to convince others with words of what we now find it necessary to say with guns and planes: Armed hostility is futile. Our resources are equal to any challenge because we fight for values and we fight for principles, rather than territory or colonies. Our patience and determination are unending.

Once this is clear, then it should also be clear that the only path for reasonable men is the path of peaceful settlement.

Such peace demands an independent South Vietnam securely guaranteed and able to shape its own relationships to all others, free from outside interference, tied to no alliance, a military base for no other country.

These are the essentials of any final settlement.

We will never be second in the search for such a peaceful settlement in Vietnam.

There may be many ways to this kind of peace: in discussion or negotiation with the governments concerned; in large groups or in small ones; in the reaffirmation of old agreements or their strengthening with new ones.

We have stated this position over and over again fifty times and more, to friend and foe alike. And we remain ready, with this purpose, for unconditional discussions.

And until that bright and necessary day of peace we will try to keep conflict from spreading. We have no desire to see thousands die in battle, Asians or Americans. We have no desire to devastate that which the people of North Vietnam have built with toil and sacrifice. We will use our power with restraint and with all the wisdom we can command. But we will use it.

This war, like most wars, is filled with terrible irony. For what do the people of North Vietnam want? They want what their neighbors also desire: food for their hunger, health for their bodies and a chance to learn, progress for their country, and an end to the bondage of material misery. And they would find all these things far more readily in peaceful association with others than in the endless course of battle.

These countries of Southeast Asia are homes for millions of impoverished people. Each day these people rise at dawn and struggle until the night to wrest existence from the soil. They are often wracked by disease, plagued by hunger, and death comes at the early age of 40.

Stability and peace do not come easily in such a land. Neither independence nor human dignity will ever be won by arms alone. It also requires the works of peace.

The American people have helped generously in times past in these works.

Now there must be a much more massive effort to improve the life of man in the conflict-torn corner of our world.

The first step is for the countries of Southeast Asia to associate themselves in a greatly expanded cooperative effort for development. We would hope that North Vietnam will take its place in the common effort just as soon as peaceful cooperation is possible.

The United Nations is already actively engaged in development in this area, and as far back as 1961 I conferred with our authorities in Vietnam in connection with their work there.

I would hope that the Secretary-General of the United Nations could use the prestige of his great office, and his deep knowledge of Asia, to initiate, as soon as possible, with the countries of the area, a plan for cooperation in increased development.

For our part I will ask the Congress to join in a billion-dollar American investment in this effort as soon as it is underway.

And I hope all other industrialized countries, including the Soviet Union, will join in this effort to replace despair with hope, and terror with progress.

The task is nothing less than to enrich the hopes and existence of more than a hundred million people. And there is much to be done.

The vast Mekong River can provide food and water and power on a scale to dwarf even our own TVA.

The wonders of modern medicine can be spread through villages where thousands die every year from lack of care. Schools can be established to train people in the skills that are needed to manage the process of development.

And these objectives, and more, are within the reach of a cooperative and determined effort.

I also intend to expand and speed up a program to make available our farm surplus to assist in feeding and clothing the needy in Asia. We should not allow people to go hungry and wear rags while our own warehouses overflow with an abundance of wheat and corn, rice and cotton.

I will very shortly name a special team of patriotic and distinguished Americans to inaugurate our participation in these programs. This team will be headed by Mr. Eugene Black, the very able former president of the World Bank.

In areas still ripped by conflict, of course, development will not be easy. Peace will be necessary for final success. But we cannot wait for peace to begin the job.

This will be a disorderly planet for a long time. In Asia, as elsewhere, the forces of the modern world are shaking old ways and uprooting ancient civilizations. There will be turbulence and struggle and even violence. Great social change, as we see in our own country, does not always come without conflict.

We must also expect that nations will on occasion be in dispute with us. It may be because we are rich, or powerful, or because we have made mistakes, or because they honestly fear our intentions. However, no nation need ever fear that we desire their land, or to impose our will, or to dictate their institutions.

But we will always oppose the effort of one nation to conquer another nation.

We will do this because our own security is at stake.

But there is more to it than that. For our generation has a dream. It is a very old dream. But we have the power and now we have the opportunity to make it come true.

For centuries, nations have struggled among each other. But we dream of a world where disputes are settled by law and reason. And we will try to make it so.

For most of history men have hated and killed one another in battle. But we dream of an end to war. And we will try to make it so.

For all existence most men have lived in poverty, threatened by hunger. But we dream of a world where all are fed and charged with hope. And we will help to make it so.

The ordinary men and women of North Vietnam and South Vietnam—of China and India—of Russia and America—are brave people. They are filled with the same proportions of hate and fear, of love and hope. Most of them want the same things for themselves and their families. Most of them do not want their sons ever to die in battle, or see the homes of others destroyed. . . .

Every night before I turn out the lights to sleep, I ask myself this question: Have I done everything that I can do to unite this country? Have I done everything I can to help unite the world, to try to bring peace and hope to all the peoples of the world? Have I done enough?

Ask yourselves that question in your homes and in this hall tonight. Have we done all we could? Have we done enough?

We may well be living in the time foretold many years ago when it was said: "I call heaven and earth to record this day against you, that I have set before you life and death, blessing and cursing: therefore choose life, that both thou and thy seed may live."

This generation of the world must choose: destroy or build, kill or aid, hate or understand.

We can do all these things on a scale never dreamed of before.

We will choose life. And so doing we will prevail over the enemies within man, and over the natural enemies of all mankind.

American Foreign Policy and International Law

BY DEAN RUSK*

. . . American foreign policy is at once principled and pragmatic. Its central objective is our national safety and well-being—to "secure the Blessings of Liberty to ourselves and our Posterity." But we know we can no longer find security and well-being in defenses and policies that are confined to North America, or the Western Hemisphere, or the North Atlantic community.

This has become a very small planet. We have to be concerned with all of it—with all of its land, waters, atmosphere, and with surrounding space. We have a deep national interest in peace, the prevention of aggression, the faithful performance of agreements, the growth of international law. Our foreign policy is rooted in the profoundly practical realization that the purposes and principles of the United Nations Charter must animate the behavior of states if mankind is to prosper or is even to survive. Or at least they must animate enough states with enough will and enough resources to see to it that others do not violate those rules with impunity. . . .

Unhappily, a minority of governments is committed to different ideas of the conduct and organization of human affairs. They are dedicated to the promotion of the Communist world revolution. And their doctrine justifies any

---

* United States Secretary of State, former President of the Rockefeller Foundation. The selection is from an address to the American Society of International Law (April 23, 1965), in *Department of State Bulletin*, LII (May 10, 1965), pp. 694-700.

technique, any ruse, any deceit, which contributes to that end. They may differ as to tactics from time to time. And the two principal Communist powers are competitors for the leadership of the world Communist movement. But both are committed to the eventual communization of the entire world.

The overriding issue of our time is which concepts are to prevail: those set forth in the United Nations Charter or those proclaimed in the name of a world revolution.

Charter Prohibitions on Use of Force

The paramount commitment of the charter is article 2, paragraph 4, which reads:

> All Members shall refrain in their international relations from the threat or use of force against the territorial integrity or political independence of any state, or in any other manner inconsistent with the Purposes of the United Nations.

This comprehensive limitation went beyond the Covenant of the League of Nations. This more sweeping commitment sought to apply a bitter lesson of the interwar period—that the threat or use of force, whether or not called "war," feeds on success. The indelible lesson of those years is that the time to stop aggression is at its very beginning.

The exceptions to the prohibitions on the use or threat of force were expressly set forth in the charter. The use of force is legal:

—as a collective measure by the United Nations, or

—as action by regional agencies in accordance with chapter VIII of the charter, or

—in individual or collective self-defense. . . .

What Is a "War of National Liberation"?

What is a "war of national liberation"? It is, in essence, any war that furthers the Communist world revolution—what, in broader terms, the Communists have long referred to as a "just" war. The term "war of national liberation" is used not only to denote armed insurrection by people still under colonial rule—there are not many of those left outside the Communist world. It is used to denote any effort led by Communists to overthrow by force any non-Communist government.

Thus the war in South Vietnam is called a "war of national liberation." And those who would overthrow various other non-Communist governments in Asia, Africa, and Latin America are called the "forces of national liberation."

Nobody in his right mind would deny that Venezuela is not only a truly independent nation but that it has a government chosen in a free election. But the leaders of the Communist insurgency in Venezuela are described as leaders of a fight for "national liberation"—not only by themselves and by Castro and the Chinese Communists but by the Soviet Communists.

A recent editorial in *Pravda* spoke of the "peoples of Latin America . . . marching firmly along the path of struggle for their national independence" and said, ". . . the upsurge of the national liberation movement in Latin American countries has been to a great extent a result of the activities of Communist parties." It added:

> The Soviet people have regarded and still regard it as their sacred duty to give support to the peoples fighting for their independence. True to their international duty the Soviet people have been and will remain on the side of the Latin American patriots.

In Communist doctrine and practice, a non-Communist government may be labeled and denounced as "colonialist," "reactionary," or a "puppet," and any state so labeled by the Communists automatically becomes fair game—while Communist intervention by force in non-Communist states is justified as "self-defense" or part of the "struggle against colonial domination." "Self-determination" seems to mean that any Communist nation can determine by itself that any non-Communist state is a victim of colonialist domination and therefore a justifiable target for a "war of liberation."

As the risks of overt aggression, whether nuclear or with conventional forces, have become increasingly evident, the Communists have put increasing stress on the "war of national liberation." The Chinese Communists have been more militant in language and behavior than the Soviet Communists. But the Soviet Communist leadership also has consistently proclaimed its commitment in principle to support wars of national liberation. This commitment was reaffirmed as recently as Monday of this week by Mr. Kosygin [Aleksai N. Kosygin, Chairman of the U.S.S.R. Council of Ministers].

International law does not restrict internal revolution

within a state or revolution against colonial authority. But international law does restrict what third powers may lawfully do in support of insurrection. It is these restrictions that are challenged by the doctrine, and violated by the practice, of "wars of liberation."

It is plain that acceptance of the doctrine of "wars of liberation" would amount to scuttling the modern international law of peace which the charter prescribes. And acceptance of the practice of "wars of liberation," as defined by the Communists, would mean the breakdown of peace itself.

South Vietnam's Right of Self-Defense

Vietnam presents a clear current case of the lawful versus the unlawful use of force. I would agree with General Giap [Vo Nguyen Giap, North Vietnamese Commander-in-Chief] and other Communists that it is a test case for "wars of national liberation." We intend to meet that test.

Were the insurgency in South Vietnam truly indigenous and self-sustained, international law would not be involved. But the fact is that it receives vital external support—in organization and direction, in training, in men, in weapons and other supplies. That external support is unlawful for a double reason. First, it contravenes general international law, which the United Nations Charter here expresses. Second, it contravenes particular international law: the 1954 Geneva accords on Vietnam and the 1962 Geneva agreements on Laos.

In resisting the aggression against it, the Republic of Vietnam is exercising its right of self-defense. It called upon us and other states for assistance. And in the exercise of the right of collective self-defense under the United Nations Charter, we and other nations are providing such assistance.

The American policy of assisting South Vietnam to maintain its freedom was inaugurated under President Eisenhower and continued under Presidents Kennedy and Johnson. Our assistance has been increased because the aggression from the North has been augmented. Our assistance now encompasses the bombing of North Vietnam. The bombing is designed to interdict, as far as possible, and to inhibit, as far as may be necessary, continued aggression against the Republic of Vietnam.

When that aggression ceases, collective measures in defense against it will cease. As President Johnson has declared:

> . . . if that aggression is stopped, the people and Government of South Vietnam will be free to settle their own future, and the need for supporting American military action there will end. . . .[1]

Nature of Struggle in Vietnam

I continue to hear and see nonsense about the nature of the struggle there. I sometimes wonder at the gullibility of educated men and the stubborn disregard of plain facts by men who are supposed to be helping our young to learn—especially to learn how to think.[2]

[1] *White House Statement (March 25, 1965) in* Department of State Bulletin, *LII (April 12, 1965), p. 527.—ed.*

[2] A group of faculty members from Harvard, MIT, and other institutions in the Boston area took notice of this speech in *The New York Times* (May 9, 1965). They observed that Secretary Rusk's . . . *abusive language suggests that the Administration wants to silence its critics.*

This suggestion is confirmed by insinuations from other Administration spokesmen about the loyalty of such critics. Precisely in this time of crisis, however, the academic community has both a right and an obligation to point out hazards and inconsistencies in our military and diplomatic policy.

It is easy to see why the Secretary of State is angry. The reasons have nothing to do with "gullibility" in the academic community. He is angry because the facts and wider considerations brought up by these critics have contradicted so many official pronouncements. It is not the scholars but the leaders of the Administration who have shown a "stubborn disregard of plain facts." For example, on March 25, 1965, President Johnson said, "We seek no more than a return to the essentials of the agreements of 1954—a reliable agreement to guarantee the independence and security of all in Southeast Asia." But the "plain fact" is that the Geneva agreement did not provide for a division of Vietnam into two nations. On the contrary, the agreement spoke of the two parts of Vietnam as "regrouping zones" and said that "the military demarcation line is provisional and should not in any way be interpreted as constituting a political or territorial boundary." It provided that " . . . general elections shall be held in July 1956, under the supervision of an international commission . . ." No such unifying elections have been held. The Saigon regime, with United States approval, refused. Ever since, the United States has insisted that Vietnam remain divided.

On April 7, 1965, the President gave another description of the Administration's goals. He said, "Tonight Americans and Asians are dying for a world where each people may choose its own

Hanoi has never made a secret of its designs. It publicly proclaimed in 1960 a renewal of the assault on South Vietnam. Quite obviously its hopes of taking over South Vietnam from within had withered to close to zero—and the remarkable economic and social progress of South Vietnam contrasted, most disagreeably for the North Vietnamese Communists, with their own miserable economic performance.

The facts about the external involvement have been documented in white papers [3] and other publications of the Department of State. The International Control Commission has held that there is evidence "beyond reasonable doubt" of North Vietnamese intervention.[4]

There is no evidence that the Vietcong has any significant popular following in South Vietnam. It relies heavily on terror. Most of its reinforcements in recent months have been North Vietnamese from the North Vietnamese Army.

Let us be clear about what is involved today in Southeast Asia. We are not involved with empty phrases or conceptions that ride upon the clouds. We are talking about the vital national interests of the United States in the peace of the Pacific. We are talking about the appetite for aggression—an appetite that grows upon feeding and that is proclaimed to be insatiable. We are talking about the safety of nations with whom we are allied—and in the integrity of the American commitment to join in meeting attack.

It is true that we also believe that every small state has a

[3] *See pp. 284–316—ed.*
[4] *See pp. 187–188—ed.*

---

path to change," and further on: "Our objective is the independence of South Vietnam, and its freedom from attack. We want nothing for ourselves—only that the people of South Vietnam be allowed to guide their own country in their own way." The "plain fact" is that the scale of American intervention is incompatible with the goal of self-determination. North Vietnam has, to be sure, intervened by helping the Vietcong. But at every stage of the war the scale of American intervention has been far greater. The manner of combat shows that we have saturated South Vietnam with every kind of military equipment the terrain allows. We air-lift troops and supplies continually. We drop napalm on civilian populations intermingled with guerrillas. We burn and defoliate crops and forests. We have resorted to incapacitating gas. An intervention as massive as this does not furnish a choice to the people. It deprives them of one. . . .—ed.

right to be unmolested by its neighbors even though it is within reach of a great power. It is true that we are committed to general principles of law and procedure that reject the idea that men and arms can be sent freely across frontiers to absorb a neighbor. But underlying the general principles is the harsh reality that our own security is threatened by those who would embark upon a course of aggression whose announced ultimate purpose is our own destruction.

Once again we hear expressed the views that cost the men of my generation a terrible price in World War II. We are told that Southeast Asia is far away—but so were Manchuria and Ethiopia. We are told that, if we insist that someone stop shooting, that is asking them for unconditional surrender. We are told that perhaps the aggressor will be content with just one more bite. We are told that, if we prove faithless on one commitment, perhaps others would believe us about other commitments in other places. We are told that, if we stop resisting, perhaps the other side will have a change of heart. We are asked to stop hitting bridges and radar sites and ammunition depots without requiring that the other side stop its slaughter of thousands of civilians and its bombings of schools and hotels and hospitals and railways and buses.

Surely we have learned over the past three decades that the acceptance of aggression leads only to a sure catastrophe. Surely we have learned that the aggressor must face the consequences of his action and be saved from the frightful miscalculation that brings all to ruin. It is the purpose of law to guide men away from such events, to establish rules of conduct which are deeply rooted in the reality of experience. . . .

> An incisive analysis on this subject is now available: American Policy Vis-A-Vis Vietnam In Light of Our Constitution, the United Nations Charter, the 1954 Geneva Accords, and the Southeast Asia Collective Defense Treaty, Memorandum of Law prepared by Lawyers Committee on American Policy Towards Vietnam (38 Park Row, New York City, 10038). It is regretted that the Memorandum is too lengthy to reprint here, but it is available on request from the Lawyers Committee, and it has been inserted by Senator Wayne Morse in The Congressional Record (September 23, 1965) pp. 24010ff.—ed.

Military Requirements for U. S. Victory In Vietnam

BY FRANK N. TRAGER*

THE THREE MILITARY REQUIREMENTS

The Vietcong in South Vietnam are organized into three main groups. The regulars comprise the hard-core, highly trained units of paid soldiers organized into platoons, companies, battalions, and regimental headquarters. In 1962 it was estimated that there were between eight and ten thousand of these professionals operating in the provinces of Vietnam. By September 1964 this number had grown to some 28,000 to 32,000 men—mostly by infiltration from the north and some recruitment from the more highly trained members of the second group, the territorial forces. The latter are usually organized in the provincial districts in groups of fifty. They work on a part-time basis, receive some pay, and are eligible for promotion to the regular forces. The third group of local guerrillas, farmers-by-day and fighters-by-night, are organized on a squad basis of four or five to as many as sixteen per village. They are not paid and are usually poorly armed, but they are the suppliers, the drawers of water, and hewers of wood, for the Vietcong regulars and territorials. The number of territorials and local guerrillas reportedly had declined during 1963-64 in proportion to the success of the central Government. Their numbers had been estimated at more than 100,000, but they may have lost as many as one-fifth of their forces. Backing the Vietcong in North Vietnam are at least 300,000 well-trained, disciplined, and modestly equipped armed forces, with a common experience dating back to the early 1940's. These regular forces are reinforced by a local militia.

The regular forces of the Saigon Government, mainly

* Professor of International Affairs at the Graduate School of Public Administration, New York University, author of *Building a Welfare State in Burma* (New York, 1958) and other works. The selection is from "Vietnam: The Military Requirements for Victory," *Orbis*, VII (Fall 1964), pp. 563-583, slightly condensed. By permission.

army, number in excess of 200,000 and are supported by paramilitary bodies such as the Civil Guard, Self-Defense Corps, and Citizens Irregular Defense Groups, which may total another 200,000. Thus, in mid-1964, the forces of the RV [Republic of (South) Vietnam] outnumbered those of the communists in South Vietnam roughly four to one. Prior military experience with communist insurgency under more favorable conditions in Malaya and elsewhere in Southeast Asia indicated that a successful campaign required ten to fifteen patriotic troops to one communist guerrilla.

The forty-two provinces of Vietnam have been grouped by the RV into four military corps areas and the capital area, all closely related to the military-civilian provincial chiefs. But the communist "war of liberation" ignores such provincial arrangements. Communist military operations are based on strategy and tactics applied in "areas of concentration" and "areas of opportunity." To carry out their plans in the first of these, they have concentrated on establishing a "four corner" or quadrilateral stranglehold on the capital city—on the well-founded assumption that, if Saigon falls, the country or most of it would be theirs. Thus they have invested heavily in the provinces surrounding Saigon. Tay Ninh, Kien Tuong, and Kien Phong—from the northwest to the southwest of Saigon—border on Cambodia and thus provide the Vietcong an easy sanctuary. Cambodian "neutrality" in this area (which includes the so-called Duck's Bill, pointing at Saigon, and the Plain of Reeds, to the west of Saigon) is a fiction carefully nurtured by Prince Sihanouk and his Chinese and French friends—and unnecessarily tolerated by the U. S. Department of State. To the north and northeast of Saigon the communists control considerable sectors of the three provinces of Long Khanh, Phuoc Thanh, and Phuoc Long. Along the coast, especially in the dense so-called mangrove swamps of Phuoc Tuy, Go Cong, and Kien Hoa, they have strong forces and have been able to conceal camps and small arsenals. The Vietcong have also moved in force along the southern line of the quadrilateral from Kien Tuong to Long An, Dinh Tuong, Kien Hoa, and Go Cong. If they were to win permanent control over this line they would not only split South Vietnam but would also dispose over the fertile, food-rich section of the Mekong Delta.

This roughly quadrilateral zone is here designated as Military Requirement II. Considered as part of the same military problem are the Camau Peninsula at the southern end of South Vietnam and a small section of the northern coastal zone in the provinces of Quang Tin and Quang Ngai. Thus the zones of Military Requirement II include significant portions of the coast, the Central Lowlands, and the Mekong Delta, including the Camau Peninsula.

Military Requirement III is created by communist operations in "areas of opportunity." These include the Central Highlands stretching north from the province of Tuyen Duc —the provincial seat of which is the well-known hill station, Dalat—in a random pattern to the province of Quang Nam. In this sparsely inhabited area are a number of towns which occasionally appear in the news, such as Ban Me Thuot, Pleiku, An Tuc, Kontum, and Ban Het, all close to the Laotian border and the Ho Chi Minh Trail. They are accessible to the Lao town of Tchepone, its airstrip and motorable road. The Central Highlands is the home of the Montagnards and other minorities; it is also perfectly situated for communist hit-and-run raids and for large-scale infiltration via Laos and, to a lesser extent, by sea.

Thus three Military Requirements, in the border areas, the areas of communist concentration, and the areas of communist opportunity, require three different sets of war plans and forces because they represent three different types of warfare.

The War of the Border Areas

Military Requirement I, the war of the border areas, is initially a garrison and patrol war designed to seal off the boundaries and simultaneously to serve as a defense against an invasion from Communist North Vietnam. This is a very difficult and costly undertaking, but it is a traditional military task clearly set forth in classic treatises on warfare. Vietnamese and allied naval forces have already given considerable though incomplete protection to Vietnam's long irregular coastline. If the current effort is sustained, very little more will be required to secure the sea flank—as the recent encounters in the Gulf of Tonkin demonstrated. Similarly, regular Vietnamese armed forces trained and supplied by U. S. military assistance teams provide security along the fifty miles of the northern border of Quang Tri province close to the 17th Parallel—except where at its northwest corner the RV abuts on Laos. It is the 800-mile Vietnamese border with Laos and Cambodia that represents the major problem in Military Requirement I. The task here is assigned to the Vietnamese Special Forces—counter-guerrilla forces capable of military and civic action—supported and advised by U. S. Special Armed Forces trained for this type of warfare. They are the "advance" troops of the four RV military corps areas mentioned above.

Communist regular forces in South Vietnam can be resupplied with trained manpower from the North across these borders. It has been estimated that from 3,500 to 6,000 communists have entered annually in this way. The soldier, whether a recruit from the South trained in the North, or a Northerner, requires about five pounds of supplies a day, half in food, half in ammunition. Though he lives partially off the land and captures weapons and ammunition, his supply of "quality" matériel must come by bearers over the trails or by sea. Hence it is necessary to seal the western borders of Vietnam and close the sea lanes. However "classical" in military tradition, the task is enormous because of the terrain. All the lessons of the Chindits, Marauders, Rangers, and other World War II Special Forces active in the China-Burma-India theater should be reapplied here; additional doctrine can be derived from related experiences in Malaya and the Philippines. There are no "secrets" about this type of warfare; it is the oldest form known in history.

The RV needs specially trained, equipped, and well-led air and ground forces and labor battalions to clear, hold and patrol these 800 miles of border terrain. To do this, the RV should create a border defile or *cordon sanitaire* by relocating the inhabitants on the Vietnamese side of the boundary. This will interrupt the traditional trans-border village trading pattern, but it is a small price to pay for security. The sparse Vietnamese-Montagnard population near the border can be easily moved to new villages which will have the protection and the civic action services of the Special Forces. *All* persons then found in or seeking entrance to the border defile—except at prescribed checkpoints— would be regarded as enemies and so treated.

The creation and defense of this border is regarded in some quarters as an operation so large as to force the United States to withdraw some of our forces from NATO. This is nonsense. The build-up of the U. S. armed forces under the Kennedy-Johnson Administration, to a large extent influenced by General Taylor . . . has prepared the United States to cope with this type of unconventional warfare. This was confirmed by Secretary of Defense Robert S. McNamara in his speech at the Forrestal Memorial Awards Dinner in Washington on March 26, 1964.[1] The task is difficult but feasible. It requires a large-scale effort at bulldozing and defoliating the jungle—carving out a zone of visibility—and building a long north-south military road and intercommuncations base system. On a comparative basis, the similar jobs in World War II of building the Ledo Road between India and Burma and the Burma Road from Lashio to Kunming were infinitely more difficult and expensive. Allied forces had to conquer higher mountains and more dense malaria jungles than their Vietnamese counterparts. They contributed, however, to the victory of the Allies in the China-Burma-India theater.

If Vietnamese Special Forces are assigned to garrison and incessant day and night patrol duties, and engage in the necessary road building, transportation, communication, and related logistic and civic operations, the regular armed and auxiliary forces of Vietnam will have to be enlarged. For these purposes there is *no* shortage of available manpower,

---

[1] *"I have pointed out on other occasions the enormous strategic nuclear power which the United States has developed to cope with the first of Mr. Khrushchev's types of war [world war]. . . . With respect to our general purpose forces designed especially for local wars [Khrushchev's second type], within the past three years we have increased the number of our combat-ready army divisions by about 45 per cent, tactical air squadrons by 30 per cent, airlift capabilities by 75 per cent, with a 100 per cent increase in ship construction and conversion. . . . President Kennedy and President Johnson have recognized, however, that our forces for the first two types of war might not be applicable or effective against what the communists call 'wars of liberation,' or what is properly called covert aggression or insurgency. We have therefore undertaken and continue to press a variety of programs to develop skilled specialists, equipment and techniques to enable us to help our allies counter the threat of insurgency." Pp. 5-6 of the mimeographed text of Secretary McNamara's address, released by the Office of Assistant Secretary of Defense for Public Affairs, Doc. No. 249-64, March 26, 1964.*

The military requirements for Vietnam demand the kind of U. S. forces Secretary McNamara describes as available in the latter two categories, i.e., "local wars" and "wars of liberation."

although there is a shortage of training facilities. U. S. Engineer, Signal Corps, Transportation, and related elements of our active and reserve military forces will be needed to accomplish this task. In addition, the sea patrol for close coastal defense must be stepped up. Above all, the U. S. Special Armed Forces in South Vietnam must be augmented. They now represent a very small fraction, perhaps no more than 10 per cent, of U. S. forces in Vietnam.

This classical approach to border defense is easier to describe than to achieve. It is not quickly accomplished, and could lead to interim war-weariness, loss of American patience, and deflation of Vietnamese morale. Thus, in order to fulfill Military Requirement I, it might behoove us to heed Von Clausewitz's advice and proceed to the "swift transition to the attack [as] the most brilliant point of the defensive."

This calls for a major decision, beyond the defensive action in the Gulf of Tonkin, to reject the notion that the war must be fought solely on RV soil. The way to defend Saigon is by threatening, penetrating, undermining and attacking North Vietnam.[2] If this "swift transition" is confined to a limited objective—namely, the defense of South Vietnam—the risk of escalation is small. Interdiction of communist resupply of men and matériel, not the conquest of North Vietnam, is the goal. In February 1964 Senator Thomas J. Dodd (D., Conn.) called for "unleashing" the Vietnamese against the North by covert and overt means. The Vietnamese cannot be unleashed effectively for this type of action unless the United States shares in the operation by means of a unified command. Such a unified command need not mean U. S. domination of Vietnam; it could take the form of a Joint War Council with a majority of senior Vietnamese officers. The Council would make decisions based upon the planning of a Vietnamese-American operations staff. In mid-August 1964 a similar scheme was being examined in Saigon, but at this writing there is no indication that a decision has been reached. It is strongly urged here that a unified command for offensive and defensive action be established in South Vietnam.

[2] See Frank N. Trager, "The Far East," in David Abshire and Richard V. Allen, editors, National Security, Political, Military and Economic Strategies in the Decade Ahead (New York, 1963).

The accomplishment of this strategic mission—sealing of the borders against infiltration and invasion by offensive and defensive tactics—would eventually lighten the Vietnamese burden in countering communist insurgency, for the Vietcong would henceforth be deprived of external land and sea resupply of trained manpower and matériel.[3] It would advance the timetable for victory.

War in the Areas of Communist Concentration

Victory against insurgency in areas of communist concentration designated as Military Requirement II, calls for another type of warfare. In its present stage this form of conflict is on the threshold of becoming a species of conventional land warfare in the Central Lowlands and Mekong Delta regions. The enemy holds certain salients in the quadrilateral outside the capital and in the Camau Peninsula. He has been there so long that he can now levy taxes, control food and shelter, and infect sectors of the population with his propaganda. In these areas the Vietcong has demonstrated a capability of mounting battalion-strength attacks on the RV, and, when these attacks are successful, of acquiring U. S. weapons. Here he holds what the clandestine radio of the National Liberation Front of South Vietnam calls his "liberated areas." These are such Vietcong bases as Duong Minh Chau in Tay Ninh province, and elsewhere in Phuoc Thanh and Phuoc Long provinces north of Saigon; various clusters in the Dong Thap Muoi, the swampy Plain of Reeds in the Mekong Delta, southwest of Saigon, and U Minh at the end of the Camau Peninsula.

This type of warfare can best be illustrated by describing the present situation in the five provinces composing the southwest to southeast line of the quadrilateral bounding Saigon. Of these, Kien Tuong, the largest and least dense in population (about 56,000), is located at the Cambodian border in the Plain of Reeds. Any Vietcong forces here have easy access into the sanctuary of Cambodia, particularly in the "Duck's Bill" salient. During the monsoon the "roads" of

[3] *It should be noted that the day of the "home-made" Vietcong weapon is past. The Vietcong have acquired a wide variety of captured American weapons from the RV and from Korea, and others from the Sino-Soviet bloc. Their heavy and successful mortar attack on the Bienhoa American air installation (New York Times, November 1, 1964) gives evidence of their modern equipment.*

his province are waterways. The two center provinces, Long
An and Dinh Tuong (with populations, respectively, of
882,000 and 528,000), are rich agriculturally and have main
north and south as well as some lateral roads, all of which
are frequently mined by the Vietcong. Dinh Tuong is the
regional headquarters for the rapidly expanding RV Seventh
Army Infantry Division. The U. S. advisory team in that
province is headed by an army colonel. The two coastal
provinces, Go Cong (population 171,000) and Kien Hoa
(population 587,000), are equally rich in resources. It was
only in the summer of 1964 that the provincial capital of Go
Cong and nearby areas were made secure by an RV Marine
Battalion. More progress has been made in Kien Hoa, a
province divided into three main "fingers," or peninsulas.
Here, as in Go Cong, the Vietcong is capable of establishing
production centers and military bases in the "mangrove"
swamps on the edge of the waterways entering the sea. The
swamps, dense with foliage of many kinds including scrub
oak and palm, effectively conceal human activity.

The Vietcong rarely disturb the farmers in these provinces.
They grant them safe conduct to the provincial capitals and
even to Saigon. But they tax them in both cash and crops,
and terrorize them whenever necessary by making an example of a collaborator, i.e., one who rejects Vietcong control. In these five provinces the Vietcong military and civilian
cadres control at least one-third of the population; the RV
controls at best one-third; and the rest have no permanent
political overlord. In order to cope with this situation, the
Diem regime began to build "strategic hamlets"—a good
idea badly executed—throughout the countryside on an irregular pattern. Unfortunately, RV officials, seeking to please
U. S. officials, carefully exaggerated the progress of this
program, engaging in what became known as "the statistical
hamlet numbers game." U. S. officials (State, CIA, and
DOD) were frequently "taken in" by this. They ignored or
rejected the advice of U. S. advisers in the field who repeatedly pointed out that the hamlets were neither strategically located for security nor adequately supplied and prepared for self-
defense. The decision, taken after the fall of Diem, to change
the name to "New Rural Life Hamlet" and to inaugurate the
"pacification" program (described below) was designed to help
the farmers to forget past mistakes.

These five provinces are treated as a single region by the Vietcong command. It has at least one highly trained, mobile (over land and water) inter-provincial battalion composed of several companies and subdivided into two sections totaling more than 600 men. These are the best equipped and best trained communist soldiers. From squad leader on up, they received their training in North Vietnam. Their mobility and equipment permit each section, even if physically separated by a day's journey, to strike simultaneously. In these strikes they may join with the regular provincial battalions and district companies. Each province has a Vietcong battalion and one or more district companies of about 120 men with cadre-trained leadership down to the platoon leader. Because of the tri-peninsular character of Kien Hoa province, the Vietcong maintain there three separate battalions and related district companies.

Other areas of the Vietcong quadrilateral around Saigon are similarly staffed and provisioned, for the Mekong Delta is the critical food area of South Vietnam and the lifeline of Saigon. Without its products the South Vietnamese Government would lose whatever authority it still possesses in the countryside. Hence the primary task of the RV is to clear the Mekong Delta area step by step and then hold it. This is the purpose of the "pacification" program, which seeks to identify the Vietcong and their supporters in control of the villages, draw up an inventory of the human and other resources of the area, ferret out and destroy the Vietcong, and replace their infrastructure with a loyal civilian regime capable of winning the villagers' support. The task of identification in any village or district is carried out by repetitive private interrogation about every fifteen days by different squads. This is followed by recruitment among the villagers for local services and regular RV forces, while government forces provide defense and social services to the area.

An experienced RV colonel in Kien Hoa province summed up for this writer the task to be done:
1. separate the people from the Vietcong,
2. destroy the Vietcong infrastructure and units,
3. encourage the Vietcong to return to legitimacy,
4. strengthen security and government for the people, and
5. reconstruct and redevelop the life of the people.
He hoped to achieve these objectives through securing firm

"intelligence," carrying on psychological and military warfare, creating self-defense militia and paramilitary local forces, and establishing a number of model villages and districts with tight security and socio-economic improvement programs.

With U. S. aid the RV has continued to mount its conventional and anti-guerrilla attacks in the general area of communist strongholds in the Mekong Delta; it also has attempted to woo the villagers, to build or rebuild new, secure hamlets, and to deny the enemy food and shelter. It has initiated an amnesty program designed to encourage defections among the Vietcong forces and to assure villagers who may have been forced to assist the communists that if they come into the protected hamlets they will not be punished for past activities.

Yet even a successful program of this sort would not be enough. After pursuing these anti-guerrilla tactics, psychological warfare, and economic deprivation campaigns, the RV, with U. S. assistance, will have to mount large-scale conventional warfare operations against Vietcong bases such as Duong Minh Chau in Tay Ninh province, and especially U Minh in the Camau Peninsula. These and other areas must be treated as enemy sectors. Some innocent people will inevitably be killed in this war. But large-scale, continuing attacks on the enemy will cost him casualties which he will be increasingly unable to replace quickly and deprive him of further logistic support. It may be argued that a campaign of this magnitude will merely "scatter" the enemy and permit him to regroup elsewhere or encourage him to go underground for the duration only to reappear later. This possibility cannot be dismissed. But the break-up and destruction of Vietcong "Yenans," or "liberated areas," is so necessary for the attainment of victory that we must accept the risks attendant on a communist decision to "scatter" and go into temporary hiding.

Even this is not enough. No government in Saigon has yet been able to assure the ordinary peasant that loyalty to it will obtain for him *security* and require him to pay only *one* set of taxes. Nor has any government provided the villagers with sustained police protection to establish and maintain ordinary law and order which they have a right to expect. During Diem's rule and under succeeding regimes, strategic

hamlets have been overrun by the Vietcong. In late July 1964
for instance, the Vietcong attacked and executed some forty
village women and children whose menfolk were out on duty
for the RV; to point up the lesson, the "neutral" villager
were left unharmed. If the present pacification program is to
succeed, it must move only on a "clear and hold" basis with
sufficient "hold" to guarantee to the villager at least two or
three crop years under single taxation—the government's
No Vietnamese government has yet mobilized sufficient resources, human and material, on such a sustained, 24-hours-
a-day, 365-days-a-year basis. Until this is carried out concurrently with a major effort to wipe out the Vietcong and its
supporters, there will be no victory in Vietnam. In the quadrilateral area this does *not* require U. S. army divisions. But it
does require some form of joint RV-U. S. command and some
additional U. S. combat teams at battalion or regimental
strength. These should buttress enlarged regular RV armed
forces deployed on an around-the-clock patrol.

The RV and U. S. military in Vietnam are fighting against
a foe supplied with sophisticated conventional weapons
which include recently manufactured Chinese 75-mm recoilless rifles and heavy machine guns, 90-mm. rocket launchers,
60-mm. mortars, carbines, and rounds of appropriate kinds of
ammunition and explosives. They are also fighting against an
enemy who has put some 30,000 trained troops into a relatively small area, troops who can rely upon another 80,000
secondary forces. The 10-to-1 or 15-to-1 proportion which has
thus far obtained in other successful campaigns against communist insurgents in Southeast Asia cannot be achieved by
the RV. At best it musters a 4-to-1 advantage. It would be
unwise to attempt to reach the proportion which the British
were able to use in Malaya, for such an effort would "bleed"
Saigon. Alternatively, therefore, in addition to a modest increase in RV-U. S. force levels, North Vietnam must be inter-
dicted and hurt if the Vietcong are to be defeated.

In the areas of communist concentration, Military Requirement II, the RV and the United States must create a military
organization and command and control system capable of
dealing with this form of conventional land warfare and the
more mobile counter-insurgency warfare. Provincial chiefs
appointed by Saigon to rule within their province must be
subordinate to a unified military command responsible for

arrying out pacification missions which may overlap several
rovinces. The quadrilateral area and the Camau Peninsula
nust come under government control by day and by night
o prevent the "choking" of Saigon. The political significance
f this undertaking far outweighs that of any other military
lans in South Vietnam. Until the Saigon area, its environs,
he Delta, and the Camau Peninsula are firmly under government rule, the fight against the Vietcong cannot be won.

War in the Areas of Communist Opportunity

The areas of "communist opportunity," especially those in
he Central Highlands, the area of mixed Vietnamese and
Montagnards, constitute Military Requirement III. It is here,
n contrast to the "border areas," that RV and U.S. forces
must employ the doctrine and practice of "counterinsurg-
ency"—a term in popular usage since the spring of 1962
when President Kennedy ordered the Departments of Defense
and State to study this type of warfare and train special forces
for it. This concept embraces the application of political,
economic, psychological, military, and paramilitary techniques to maintain government control where it exists, to restore it where it has been lost, and to acquire it in the "back
country" where it had not previously been established.
In these areas, too, the RV is competing with the communists for "the hearts and minds" of men, especially for those
of minority groups. In this form of contest, Vietnamese of
all political persuasions have, in the past, been notoriously
inept. Until recently the RV did not have the opportunity
or ability or inclination to establish a presence in the Central Highlands which would win for it the loyalty of the
inhabitants. The conflict that erupted at Hué in May
1963—and which still continues—between the majority Buddhists and the minority Roman Catholic leadership, who controlled the power structure in part of this area and in Saigon,
is the best known example of this difficulty. Trust and harmony in a society containing minority groups can exist only
where there is toleration and mutual respect. These qualities
have been lacking in the attitude of the Vietnamese toward
all other groups in the society. Like "lowlanders" elsewhere
in mainland Southeast Asia, they must make an effort to
establish friendlier relationships with the "hill peoples" whom
they have commonly disregarded and even despised.

There is no dearth of material on the ingredients of a counter-insurgency campaign. The phases of intelligence gathering and analysis, military operations, securing each area before advancing to the next, and instituting civic action programs to gain and retain the loyalty of the population are too well known to require further comment here. Nearly everyone engaged in the war in Vietnam knows "the book" on this subject. The task is to carry it out as effectively as possible, without corruption or favoritism. But this task is rendered more difficult because the undermanned RV and U. S. armed forces must not only execute their military duties but also serve as doctor, teacher, policeman, judge, rural sociologist, tax-collector, recruiter, trainer and general factotum. Military administration along a "front line" is relatively simple, for there military command and control are clear-cut and enforceable. Military administration is a far more complex and difficult task where there is no front line and where it must create a new, secure civil administration responsive to local needs and desires. The military must gradually and with sensitivity merge with and then give way to the civilian authority which it has created and whose loyalty and support it must win. In addition, these basic RV detachments consisting of nine to eleven men,[4] supported by larger detachments in corps regions and by a general headquarters in Nhatrang, and supplied by air-drop, boat, and foot, must be on constant day and night patrol to flush out and capture or kill Vietcong units.

Military Requirement III rates as the hardest task for the RV Special Forces, for the government, and for the assisting U. S. Special Forces. For it is essentially the task of nation-building under the constant threat of communist insurrectionary activity. It would be difficult under any circumstances; in the present Vietnamese case in the Central Highlands and the relevant portions of the Central Lowlands, it is a herculean task.

CONCLUSION

The successful implementation of Military Requirement I would for the most part choke off Hanoi's supply lines to the Vietcong. It is unlikely that the North Vietnamese communists would risk an open attack south of the border, for they

---

[4] *These detachments normally consist of a leader, two medics, and two experts each in communications, explosives and psychological warfare.*

would invite a swift counterattack. The implementation of Requirement II would reduce, if it did not destroy, the Vietcong's strike-force (company to battalion strength) capability. This in itself would not eliminate the Vietcong, for they have demonstrated their ability to execute the classical guerrilla tactics of surprise, mobility, concentration for attack, and rapid withdrawal and dispersal. In these the enemy has had the advantage of the terrain, the climate, and the as yet shaky reach of the RV Government into the countryside. In addition, the Vietcong has had the advantage of forced and voluntary intelligence, superior thus far to the Government's, on which guerrilla action so heavily depends. Finally, the RV must give high priority to Requirement III, providing security and socio-political programs designed to weld all the peoples of the countryside, Vietnamese and ethnic and religious minorities, into a loyal nation. In this arena the strategy and tactics of "clear and hold" military operations followed by effective civic action programs in the provinces, districts, and villages—whether these be "strategic" or "new life" hamlets or anything else—must be executed by sympathetic, ably led, mobile Vietnamese army and paramilitary forces.

These requirements must be viewed as related parts of one concerted set of war plans under a unified military command. RV forces may be capable of successfully executing these war plans while U. S. forces remain, as at present, "advisers," but this entails considerable risk for the future of South Vietnam. The longer we wait for eventual success in South Vietnam, the greater the risks. On the other hand, if U. S. forces were modestly augmented and permitted to become active partners of the Vietnamese, the length of time required for victory could be reduced and the risks diminished.

The United States is pledged to sustain the Republic of Vietnam which has not enjoyed one full day of peace since its emergence as a sovereign state in 1954. That pledge can be honored if Americans and Vietnamese are able to meet the military and socio-political demands of these three types of warfare in Vietnam. Ultimate success against Vietcong subversion, insurgency, and regular warfare can be achieved only by a clear-cut military victory over the Vietcong and by winning the political loyalty of the population. . . .

Revolutionary Warfare

BY EQBAL AHMAD*

Vice President Humphrey expressed the national concern over guerrilla warfare recently when he spoke of this "bold new form of aggression which could rank with the discovery of gunpowder" as constituting the "major challenge to our security." It is viewed as the latest weapon in the Communist arsenal with Vietnam as its testing ground. "If guerrilla techniques succeed in Vietnam," wrote James Reston in *The New York Times,* "nobody in Washington dare assume that the same techniques will not be applied in all Communist rimlands from Korea to Iran." This view is based on two assumptions and at least one serious misconception. It assumes that the Vietnamese situation is typical, historically and politically, of other underdeveloped countries, and that American policy toward other nations would be comparable to the one pursued in Vietnam. The misconception concerns the nature of revolutionary warfare.

America's interest in revolutionary warfare began from a defensive posture as a result of reverses in China, Korea, Cuba, and Laos, and of protracted involvement in Vietnam. It was natural for its officials to be attracted more to the myths and methods of those who have had to defend themselves against guerrillas than to an understanding of the causes and characteristics of such a war. Americans are therefore unable to avoid the psychological and political pitfalls of colonial powers and feudal regimes like France and Nationalist China. A symptom of his negative posture is that while recognizing "a bold new form" of warfare, government publications, including the course books of Fort Bragg, reject the term "revolutionary war" in favor of old terms which do not suggest the vital distinction between revolutionary and other types of guerrilla conflict.

* Pakistani citizen, Assistant Professor at the School of Labor and Industrial Relations, Cornell University, currently at work on a political biography of Habib Bourguiba. The selection is from "Revolutionary Warfare: How to Tell When the Rebels Have Won," *The Nation,* CCI (August 30, 1965), pp. 95-100. By permission.

The official American interpretation of revolutionary war can be summarized as follows: (1) It is essentially a technical problem i.e., a problem of plotting and subversion on the one hand and of intelligence and suppression on the other. As the chief conspiratorial group, the Communists are believed to be the most likely initiators and beneficiaries of revolution. It was this attitude which led to the recent attempt to nip in the bud what was construed as the Dominican Communist conspiracy. A logical extension of this theory is the belief that any revolutionary movement is inspired, directed, and controlled from abroad. (2) The active sanctuary —from which guerrillas can smuggle supplies and train their troops—is considered the primary factor in their success. (3) The guerrilla movement is believed to enjoy considerable advantage because, in the words of W. W. Rostow, "its task is merely to destroy while the government must build and protect what it is building." (4) The civilian population is considered important for providing information and protection to the guerrillas; it is believed that civilian-guerrilla cooperation is enforced by terror. (Dean Rusk, while complaining of the "gullibility of educated men and their stubborn disregard of plain facts," asserted that the Vietcong "has no significant popular following . . . it relies heavily on terror." [1]) Serious inquiry into other bases of guerrilla support and mass mobilization is therefore deemed of no great importance.

Judging from the failure of Washington's prophecies in Vietnam and from the policies followed to date, it would seem that these assumptions represent the actual official view and cannot be dismissed as myths consciously constructed for public consumption. Wrong premises do not usually produce right policies, and these assumptions are, at best, half truths—credible and misleading. (Oliver Wendell Holmes once remarked that a half truth is like half a brick; it can be thrown a considerable distance.) Studies in the field of revolutionary wars and my personal observation of the Algerian struggle lead to very different conclusions, which may be summarized as follows: (1) Revolutionaries consider mass support the primary condition for their success; winning and maintaining popular support remains their central objective throughout the struggle. (2) The requirements of guerrilla war, as well as the history of its failures and successes,

[1] See pp. 334, 335.—ed.

confirm the primacy of political factors in such a conflict. (3) Popular support for the guerrillas is predicated upon the moral alienation of the masses from the existing government. The revolutionaries' chief aim is to activate and perpetuate the moral isolation of the enemy regime until such isolation has become total and irreversible. (4) The conditions leading to revolutionary wars are not created by conspiracy. They are partly inherent in a situation of rapid social change, but the outbreak normally results mainly from the failure of a ruling elite to respond to the challenge of modernization. (5) A revolutionary guerrilla movement concentrates on "out-administering," not on "out-fighting" the enemy. This is a constructive and not simply a destructive undertaking. (6) The use of terror by guerrillas is highly selective; it does not constitute the main reason for the favorable reaction of the masses to their cause. (7) The external sanctuary has greater psychological and diplomatic than military or political value to the guerrillas. A discussion of these points follows.

Organizers of guerrilla warfare give prime attention, in practice no less than in theory, to the human factor. T. E. Lawrence (of Arabia) spoke of guerrilla war in terms of "the algebraic element of things, the biological element of life, and the psychological element of ideas." In other words, although Lawrence's goals were essentially military, military considerations constituted for him, only one-third of the problem of organizing and sustaining guerrilla troops. When Tito was told of the exceptionally unfavorable terrain in the region of Srem ("the area is level as the palm of your hand . . . and with little forests") he remarked, "What a first-class example it is of the relative unimportance of geographical factors in the development of a rising. The basic factor is studious political work, the attitude of the mass of people, and the fighting leadership—if these are present the population would fight to the last man." Mao Tse-tung states, "Because guerrilla warfare basically derives from the masses and is supported by them, it can neither exist nor flourish if it separates itself from their sympathies and cooperation." This belief in the need to command popular support governs the movement through all stages of its development.

History confirms the sovereignty of the human factor in revolutionary warfare. While shying away from the wars that were "lost," American military analysts are prone to

cite cases of successful anti-guerrilla operations. A heavy
favorite—the British "counter-insurgency" in Malaya—i
faithfully imitated in Vietnam. (Sometimes too faithfully, a
in the case of the strategic hamlets program launched in
April 1962.) But comparisons with Malaya are fallacious, be
cause there the guerrillas were at a severe disadvantage. Their
support was limited to a minority of 423,000 Chinese squat
ters, who were ethnically distinct from and distrusted b
the majority of Malays, and popular grievances were no
acute enough to make the guerrillas look like liberators to
the Malay peasants. Furthermore, the British acted quickly to
remove the grievances on which the rebellion was based
Even then it took thirteen years and a total of 260,000 sol
diers and police (80,000 British, 180,000 Malays) to down
8,000 guerrillas (a ratio of 30 to 1). Another success story, the
joint U.S.-Philippine victory over the Huks, is less fre
quently cited because of its embarrassing aspects. The Huk
movement collapsed dramatically when Magsaysay convinced
the peasants of his will and capacity to introduce reforms
However, the promises made to them were not kept and the
Garcia administration witnessed a resurgence of guerrillas
In April 1962 Macapagal swallowed his embarrassment and
ordered a mop-up operation in Central Luzon. According to
the latest reports, guerrilla strength in the Philippines is in
creasing.

The Algerian revolution, the least studied in this countr
though it comes closest to the Vietnamese situation, ha
actually been crushed militarily but had won politically when
de Gaulle negotiated independence. By 1961 the guerrilla
had been reduced to some 5,000 and their ability to en
gage the French at will had markedly declined. But Franc
faced a sullen Algerian population that it had conquered but
could not rule. The FLN was defeated in the field, but
continued to outadminister and "illegitimize" the French.

Why did the Algerian peasants risk, for seven remorsele
years, their lives, the honor of their women, and the securi
of their paltry belongings? Nationalism alone could not e
plain their violent and resolute rejection of French rul
In no other colony, except Indochina, did the moveme
for independence take so violent a turn. And why did n
the peasants respond earlier to the militants' calls to arm
The answer comes from one of the historic chiefs of th

Algerian revolution. The time was not "ripe," he said. "These events occur where foreign rule is resented, where acute grievances exist, and institutional channels for ventilating and satisfying them are ineffective."

Peasant rebellions had occurred in past years of famine and high taxation, but these spontaneous and periodic disturbances, as expressions of frustration over social and economic conditions, are not a sufficient condition for guerilla revolution. "Revolutionary warfare does not require simply discontent among the masses but a sense of desperation and a grim determination to end injustice and humiliation. It demands patience with prolonged suffering, and a determined conspiracy of silence, and militancy."

A people can summon up that resolution only if they feel morally alienated from their rulers. "The success of a revolutionary war is predicated upon the continual and increasing moral isolation of the enemy. When it becomes total the war has been won, for the population will then fight to the last man." Later, other Algerian leaders told me they had spent more effort fighting the French promises of eventual independence and reforms than fighting the military. The Algerians became increasingly alienated from the French as the latter increased their military effort, which in revolutionary warfare means large-scale killing of civilians (if for no other reason than because the guerrilla is indistinguishable from other peasants), and the FLN became more confident of winning not the military battles but the revolutionary war.

The conditions leading to revolutionary warfare are not created by conspiracy. They are inherent in the dislocations and demands produced by rapid social change, and are predicated on the failure of ruling elites to respond to the challenge of modernization. The pressures for change in the political, economic, and social relationships of the past inevitably lead to a confrontation with those whose interests are in the maintenance of the status quo. In countries and colonies whose rulers are willing to abdicate their monopoly of power and privileges, where genuine reforms are introduced, and new institutions begin to provide for a sharing of power and responsibility, the change is effected in an orderly (if not entirely peaceful) and democratic manner. But when a ruling class resists reforms (which invariably

mean reduction in its power and privileges), its confronta
tion with the new political forces becomes increasingly vio
lent. A regime unwilling to satisfy popular aspirations begins
to lose legitimacy; revolutionary forces deliberately accel
erate this process by weakening the efficacy and cohesion o
the ruling elite and by giving form to the amorphous revolu
tionary conflagration. In the competition for leadership tha
often takes place in this volatile situation, non-Communis
revolutionary groups are handicapped by several factor
the most important of which are the attitudes and policies o
Western powers. By supporting the defenders of the ol
order, a great nation like the United States weakens th
fighting power of the democratic forces, drives the col
war neutralists to seek the help of the Communists, and give
the latter new heroes and martyrs.

Once a revolutionary movement enters the guerrilla pha
its central objective is to confirm, perpetuate, and institu
tionalize the moral isolation of the enemy by providing a
alternative to the discredited regime through the creation o
"parallel hierarchies." The major task of the movement
not to outfight but to outadminister the government. Th
main target in this bid is the village, where the majorit
of the population lives, and where the government's pre
ence is often exploitative (collection of taxes). Here the chi
and his council are the main link between the people an
the government. Breaking this link demands careful plannin
organization, and hard work. The government is systematica
ly eliminated from the countryside by the conversion o
killing of village officials, who are then controlled or r
placed by the political arm of the movement. The rebe
must then build an administrative structure to collect tax
to provide some education and social welfare, and to maintai
a modicum of economic activity. A revolutionary guerril
movement that does not have these administrative con
cerns and structures to fulfill its obligations to the popula
would degenerate into banditry. The official American vie
that the guerrillas' tasks are easier because they only destro
contradicts the findings of those who have studied and o
served these movements. During this phase military co
frontation is normally avoided, and the government als
treats assassinations as a police problem, and ascribes no
payment of taxes to administrative lags, bad harvests, et

The Vietcong is known to have gained control over 70 percent of rural Vietnam during 1957-60—a period when Americans were presenting Uncle Diem as a rival of Uncle Ho and were going around saying: "Look, no Vietnamese army units are attacked. Therefore, there is no guerrilla threat."

Most compelling, but also most self-defeating, is the myth that terror is the basis of civilian support for the guerrillas. Guerrilla warfare requires a highly committed but covert civilian support which cannot be obtained at gun point. Only degenerate and defeated guerrillas are known to have risked the loss of mass support by terrorizing civilians (some Huk and Malayan diehards were reduced to it). An outstanding feature of guerrilla training is the stress on scrupulously "correct and just" behavior toward civilians. Political work, believes General Giap, is "the soul of the army," and a Chinese guerrilla expert explains that "army indoctrination is primarily aimed at training the troops to act in such a way that they will gain this total support [of the people]." Guerrilla use of terror, therefore, is sociologically and psychologically selective. It strikes those who are popularly identified as the "enemy of the people"—officials, landlords, and the like.

Killing a village chief, however, is often a more complicated affair. Since most chiefs are local farmers who command legitimacy and loyalty through tradition and kinship, the militants ideally want to persuade them into the movement. When that fails, it takes painstaking political work to engineer their assassination and to prepare the villagers to accept it. In the early years of the Algerian revolution it took the FLN from two months to a year to kill a village chief without incurring the liability of public hostility, and that was an anticolonial war. I was, therefore, amazed to learn that in Vietnam about 13,000 local officials were killed between 1957 and 1961. Professor Bernard Fall gives a simple explanation: These chiefs, as appointees of Diem, had little legitimacy compared with the Vietminh cadres who had liberated the country from France. Furthermore, the local officials became involved, along with the American-equipped and trained army, in the sordid business of restoring the landlords who had fled the country during the war. (A *de facto* land reform was achieved under the Vietminh.) These absentee aristocrats even demanded eight years' worth of back rent, covering the period from 1945 to 1954. Before the war, the rent had been 50 percent of the yield; the peasant was thus required to pay 400 percent of his produce and to surrender his rights to the land. The Viet cong had no problem preparing them to accept the killing of officials engaged in such work.

Terror is also used to insure survival of the militants and of the movement. Robert Kleiman of *The New York Times* (May 3, 1965) informs us that in Vietnam's "contested areas with 40 percent of the population, Saigon usually gets co operation by day and the Vietcong by night—because that is when their troops and officials are present. It is an old Asian custom." I was amused by the last sentence, for I know it is not our custom, but a universal practice of guer rilla warfare. The population must seem at least neutral if it hopes to escape full enemy treatment from government troops. Rebel troops and officials do not arrive at night from "somewhere in the mountains"; they are present during the day, too, and often lead the show of obedience to the government. At night the loyal peasant turns into a guerrilla and all know him as such. To insure that the popular con spiracy of silence develops no seams, exemplary punishments are given to those suspected of having informed.

Second-degree terror, which normally does not result in killing, is used to sabotage the government's belated effort to gain popular support. Government schoolteachers and health workers are favorite targets of kidnapping and in doctrination. In June 1962 a South Vietnamese UN observer informed UNESCO that the Vietcong had kidnapped more than 1,200 teachers; the government's malaria-eradication campaign collapsed after twenty-two health officers had been killed and sixty kidnapped. Guerrilla sabotage normally guards against causing too much hardship on the population and long-range damages to the economy. Industry and even foreign-owned plantations are spared if they pay their "taxes" to the liberation front. And they normally do so when the government is unable to protect them. (In Vietnam the large European rubber plantations, Michelin, SIPH, Terres Rouges, resisted for a while, but started paying taxes to the Vietcong after their French supervisors were kidnapped.)

It is difficult to say at what point the moral isolation of a government becomes total and irreversible, so that no amount

promises and reforms would restore the lost confidence
nd reduce the peoples' resistance. In Algeria, at least, the
oint seems to have been reached when the French were re-
uced to touring and killing civilians and to "regrouping" the
opulation. Many Algerian leaders believe that their revolu-
on became irreversible at the moment of France's greatest
ilitary victory—General Massu's conquest of the Casbah
he Muslim section of Algiers was reduced to rubble during
957-58). France could no longer expect the confidence,
uch less the loyalty, of a people it was destroying in-
iscriminately, albeit unwillingly and despite itself.

The desertion of the intellectuals and moderates often
gnals, not so much the irreversibility of a revolutionary
ar, but its take-off. Intellectuals, especially the Asian variety,
re a democratic liberal group, who view organized violence
ith distaste. Somewhat alienated from their culture, West-
rnized and city-centered, they distrust the peasants but
esire an improvement of their condition. When an armed
volution breaks out, they are likely to play in the middle,
oping to get some reforms under way by using the armed
reat as a counter for bargaining. They begin to go into
xile or to defect to the rebels after the failure of the re-
ime and the success of the revolution become imminent.

The defending army's pressure for conventional attack or
n external sanctuary is yet another sign that a revolutionary
ar has been lost on home grounds. In revolutionary warfare,
rmies trained for conventional combat follow a vicious logic
f escalation, which derives from acute frustration over an
usive war that puts in question not only their effectiveness
ut the very validity of their training and organization. More-
ver, the morale of professional soldiers cannot be main-
ained if they know they are fighting a popular rebellion.
ence the compulsion to believe that behind the popular be-
avior lies the terror of an army trained, equipped, and di-
ected by a foreign power and the wish to draw the enemy
to open battles. Since reprisals against the population fail
produce the desired result, carrying the war to a sovereign
ation becomes the only road to a conventional showdown.
Algeria this demand led to French participation in the
vasion of Suez, then to the bombing of the Tunisian border
wn of Sakiet Sidi Youssef, and produced a succession of
my revolts, the last of which destroyed the Fourth Re-

public. Had the French Government succumbed to these pre
sures, France would have been the first power to violate t
international practice of respecting the right of sanctuary—
a principle that was observed in Korea, Greece, Cypru
and Malaya.

The importance of an active sanctuary should not be unde
estimated, although it is not essential to guerrilla success.
Cuba, Yugoslavia, and China the revolutionaries did not ha
active sanctuaries. In Burma and to a lesser extent in Gree
sanctuaries proved of limited value. Politically and mi
tarily, revolutionary guerrillas are, by and large, a self-su
taining group who can go on fighting indefinitely even
infiltration from across the border stops. External help, hov
ever, has great psychological and diplomatic value. In a w
of attrition, there can be no decisive victory over a stro
foreign enemy. At best, one hopes to inflict on it hea
losses, tire it out, and, through international pressure, force
to negotiate withdrawal. External help is important in inte
nationalizing guerrilla demands, and keeps alive the ho
of liberation. When a revolutionary army loses an ally,
loses not so much military support; it loses hope. Wh
the world is not watching, when the fear of diploma
sanctions and the threat of a widened war are absent,
foreign power trapped in counter-guerrilla operations is lik
ly to make the final and the only move that may "win"
it starts to commit genocide.

Finally, the assumption that a guerrilla outfit, like a co
ventional army, can be controlled and commanded by
foreign or externally based government, ignores the o
ganizational, psychological, and political facts of revo
tionary warfare. The distrust of the "home-based" guerrill
even for their own government in exile, cannot be ov
stated. The resourceful and tough "interior" leaders a
cadres who face the enemy daily, collect taxes, administ
make promises, and give hopes to the population are n
easily controlled from abroad and make suspicious, exa
ing, and hard-to-please allies. Therefore, zone command
and political commissars are, for the most part, monar
of what they survey. As a group, they are joined together
shared experiences, by a common mood which is defiant a
insular, by a shared suspicion of "politicians and diplom
over there" selling them out, and by a collective will to d

a settlement that is not of their making.

In Vietnam, the signs are clear. The South Vietnames
regime has no legitimacy, and no government backed by
Western power can hope for popular support in a coun
try where the Communists have capitalized on the na
tionalist appeal of restoring independence and unity, an
where the pro-Western leaders have been Bao Dai, Diem, an
the musical-chair generals. The massacre of civilians bega
as early as 1960 (not counting the earlier repressive meas
ures of the Diem regime), as attested by reputable scholar
and even a former Chief U. S. Military Adviser (Lt. Ger
Samuel T. Williams; see *U.S. News & World Report,* Nov. !
1964). It has since escalated. The intellectuals and moderate
have deserted or defected. And North Vietnam is subjecte
to daily bombings. America and its South Vietnamese allie
have lost the revolutionary war because they could not wi
the support of the Vietnamese people, and now their mora
isolation is total.

As an Asian, I am aware of the appeals and threat of con
munism, and I would support policies likely to prevent i
expansion. But I do not believe that communism is the wav
of the future, and therefore I am neither panicked no
paralyzed. I believe that Vietnam is a unique case—cultura
ly, historically, and politically. I hope that the United State
will not repeat its Vietnam blunders elsewhere. I do nc
subscribe to the domino theory and I am anguished by Amer
cans who call Vietnam a test case. Vietnam is the only cour
try in the world where the nationalist movement for ii
dependence was led by the Communists during its mo:
crucial and heroic decades. In new countries where institu
tional loyalties are still weak, the legitimacy and popularit
of a regime derives from its nationalist heroes and martyr:
Unfortunately for the free world the George Washington
Vietnam, its Gandhi, was a Communist nationalist. H
Chi Minh and his associates (including General Giap
Dienbienphu fame) are understandably considered th
founding fathers of modern Vietnam. It was morbid opt
mism to expect an absentee aristocrat to supplant a leade
who had devoted a lifetime to the liberation of his countr
and to defeat a leadership and cadres whose organic tie
with the peasants were cemented by the bitter struggle fc
independence. It is not fair to blame Diem for driving th

Vietnamese to desperation. He had no choice. Given his circumstances his only possible weapons were a power apparatus to regiment the population, all-out support of minorities, and widespread terror. These were not aberrations of a program but the program itself.

Vietnam is also the only country in which the United States gave substantial support to a colonial power in a war of independence. This could not have endeared America to the Vietnamese people. Then in the "Southern zone" America replaced France, and supported the ex-French puppet Bao Dai; next it put up Diem as "the democratic alternative to Vietnam," and also failed to honor its pledge to hold elections for the unification of the country. To most Vietnamese the present war, therefore, is a continuation of the struggle for independence. I know how Asians feel about America's action. They call it neo-colonialism; some think it is imperialism. I know that is very wrong because Americans are naturally sympathetic to peoples' struggles for freedom and justice, and they would like to help if they could. I prefer the term "maternalism" for American policy in countries like Vietnam, because it reminds me of the story of an elephant who, as she strolled benignly in the jungle, stepped on a mother partridge and killed her. When she noticed the orphaned siblings, tears filled the kind elephant's eyes. "Ah, I too have maternal instincts," she said, turning to the orphans, and sat on them.

Fight on In Vietnam

BY HANSON W. BALDWIN*

What should we do—"bug out" or fight? Should we be "Hawks" or "Doves"? Or is there a third choice—negotiations now?

Recent events in Vietnam indicate that "the war that is not a war" has reached a crossroads. Washington's policy of the

* Military editor of The New York Times, author of Great Mistakes of the [Second World] War (New York, 1950), and other works. The selection is from "We Must Choose—(1) 'Bug Out' (2) Negotiate (3) Fight," The New York Times Magazine (February 21, 1965). By permission.

past four years, based on the polite fiction that we were not fighting a war but merely helping the Vietnamese to defeat the Vietcong insurgents within their own territory, has reached a point of no return.

Compromise and consensus—perhaps applicable to some of the nation's great domestic problems—cannot be guideposts to foreign policy. There must be a clearcut and courageous decision. And though in Vietnam we face the hard problem of risking much to gain little, the risk must be taken: we must fight a war to prevent an irreparable defeat. We must use what it takes to win.

Our policy should not be "unconditional surrender" or unlimited victory. Our goal of victory should be the defeat of Communist attempts to conquer South Vietnam and extend their control deep into Southeast Asia.

The reasons we must fight for Vietnam have little to do with making Saigon safe for "democracy" or "freedom." There has been far too much cant on this point, far too much effort devoted to trying to establish a politically legitimate South Vietnamese Government after our own image. Nor does it do much good to argue the past, debating whether or not we should have become involved in Vietnam in the first place. The facts are that Communist expansionism in Asia has been consistent, related, and progressive, that the end of the Korean war, without a simultaneous settlement in Vietnam, gave Peking and North Vietnam's Ho Chi Minh the opportunity in Southeast Asia they have so well exploited.

The psychological and political consequences of a United States defeat in Vietnam, a United States withdrawal, or a negotiated peace likely to lead to a Communist take-over, would be disastrous in much of Asia. It would undermine Thailand (already openly threatened by Peking), Laos (even now half-conquered by Communism), Malaya, the Philippines (with its growing anti-Americanism), Burma, India, Japan, and even Taiwan, Okinawa, and Australia.

Despite the admitted importance of South Vietnam to the United States global position, the current breed of neo-isolationists and the "Doves" who believe we must cut our losses and get out, advance many arguments against deeper involvement and in favor of withdrawal.

Most of the arguments represent the voices of defeat and despair, caution and fear.

Any negotiations opened now would lead from weakness, not strength. If we want to negotiate—and not to surrender —we shall have to raise our ante considerably. And "meaningful" negotiations are "meaningful" to the Communists only if they are faced with superior power and a position of strength.

"Continued fighting or expanded U.S. involvement will mean higher U.S. casualties and greater risks of broadening the war."

Of course. You cannot win a war without spilling blood. We must pay the price of power. Risks are unavoidable in any foreign policy worthy of its name. The question is not whether there will be risks, but the degree of risk. For against the perils of action must be weighed the perils of inaction. Political and military history clearly reveal that compromise, hesitancy, or appeasement merely lead to ultimate disaster. In Vietnam, the longer we wait, the greater the price we shall have to pay for even partial victory (as we are now discovering), and the more restricted our choice of options.

"We have no moral right to be in Vietnam, or to attack North Vietnam."

Neither do the Vietcong. Nor does North Vietnam have the right to support the civil war in the South. Our involvement was a response to the Communist aggression. Since the beginning, Hanoi has organized, supplied, and directed the Vietcong insurgency. We were invited by the South Vietnamese Government to come to its aid. A high moral purpose is an essential element of our foreign policy, but we can be left with no purpose—moral or otherwise—if we are conquered by the doctrine that the ends justify the means. If we are inhibited from action by Hamlet-like indecision over legalistic concepts of international law, we shall lose the world.

What should we do? First and foremost, we must recognize as a Government and as a people that we are fighting a war in Vietnam, and not merely "advising" how to fight one. Such a recognition would awaken a greater sense of national and military determination, inspire a Presidential and Congressional enunciation of purpose, and create a more streamlined military operation in Vietnam.

Continuous and heavy air and sea attacks against staging

areas, supply routes, training fields, camps, and recupera-
tion centers of the Vietcong in North and South Vietnam an
Laos will be necessary for any appreciable diminution in th
flow of men and supplies to the Communists. The one-sho
retaliatory raids have only temporary and minimum military importance; viewed as political and psychological war
ings, they are likely to provoke the Vietcong and North Vie
nam to a redoubled war effort.

How many United States soldiers would be needed is ur
certain—probably a minimum of three to six division
(utilized chiefly in battalion- or brigade-size units), possibl
as many as ten or twelve divisions. Including Air Force, Navy
and supporting units, perhaps 200,000 to 1,000,000 Ameri
cans would be fighting in Vietnam.

Obviously, this would mean a Korean-type conflict,
major war, no matter what euphemisms would be used. No
could we wage it in the present "business-as-usual" economy
We would require partial mobilization, vastly beefed-up mili
tary production. Many weaknesses in our military structur
would need strengthening. Even so, we could not an
ticipate quick success.

No one could relish such a prospect as this; the starl
statistics of war explain the President's reluctance to em
bark upon a path that has no turning.

Vietnam is a nasty place to fight. But there are no nea
and tidy battlefields in the struggle for freedom; there i
no "good" place to die. And it is far better to fight in Viet
nam—on China's doorstep—than fight some years hence i
Hawaii, on our own frontiers.

Vietnam and the National Interest

BY HANS J. MORGENTHAU*

The address which President Johnson delivered on April 7

* Albert A. Michelson Distinguished Service Professor of Po
litical Science and Modern History, University of Chicago, autho
of *Politics Among Nations* (3d ed., New York, 1961), *In De
fense of the National Interest* (New York, 1951), *The Purpose
of American Politics* (New York, 1960), and many other works
The selection is from "We Are Deluding Ourselves in Vietnam,"
The New York Times Magazine (April 18, 1965). By permission

at Johns Hopkins University [1] is important for two reasons. On the one hand, the President has shown for the first time a way out of the impasse in which we find ourselves in Vietnam. By agreeing to negotiations without preconditions he has opened the door to negotiations which those preconditions had made impossible from the outset.

By proposing a project for the economic development of Southeast Asia—with North Vietnam a beneficiary and the Soviet Union a supporter—he has implicitly recognized the variety of national interests in the Communist world and the need for varied American responses tailored to those interests. By asking "that the people of South Vietnam be allowed to guide their own country in their own way," he has left all possibilities open for the future evolution of relations between North and South Vietnam.

On the other hand, the President reiterated the intellectual assumptions and policy proposals which brought us to an impasse and which make it impossible to extricate ourselves. The President has linked our involvement in Vietnam with our war of independence and has proclaimed the freedom of all nations as the goal of our foreign policy. He has started from the assumption that there are two Vietnamese nations, one of which has attacked the other, and he sees that attack as an integral part of unlimited Chinese aggression. Consistent with this assumption, the President is willing to negotiate with China and North Vietnam but not with the Vietcong.

Yet we cannot have it both ways. We cannot at the same time embrace these false assumptions and pursue new sound policies. Thus we are faced with a real dilemma. This dilemma is by no means of the President's making.

We are militarily engaged in Vietnam by virtue of a basic principle of our foreign policy that was implicit in the Truman Doctrine of 1947 and was put into practice by John Foster Dulles from 1954 onward. This principle is the military containment of Communism. Containment had its origins in Europe; Dulles applied it to the Middle East and Asia through a series of bilateral and multilateral alliances. Yet what was an outstanding success in Europe turned out to be a dismal failure elsewhere. The reasons for that failure are twofold.

[1] See pp. 323–330.—ed.

First, the threat that faced the nations of Western Europe in the aftermath of the Second World War was primarily military. It was the threat of the Red Army marching westward. Behind the line of military demarcation of 1945 which the policy of containment declared to be the westernmost limit of the Soviet empire, there was an ancient civilization, only temporarily weak, and able to maintain itself against the threat of Communist subversion.

The situation is different in the Middle East and Asia. The threat there is not primarily military but political in nature. Weak governments and societies provide opportunities for Communist subversion. Military containment is irrelevant to that threat and may even be counter-productive. Thus the Baghdad Pact did not protect Egypt from Soviet influence and SEATO has had no bearing on Chinese influence in Indonesia and Pakistan.

Second, and more important, even if China were threatening her neighbors primarily by military means, it would be impossible to contain her by erecting a military wall at the periphery of her empire. For China is, even in her present underdeveloped state, the dominant power in Asia. She is this by virtue of the quality and quantity of her population, her geographic position, her civilization, her past power remembered, and her future power anticipated. Anybody who has traveled in Asia with his eyes and ears open must have been impressed by the enormous impact which the resurgence of China has made upon all manner of men, regardless of class and political conviction, from Japan to Pakistan.

The issue China poses is political and cultural predominance. The United States can no more contain Chinese influence in Asia by arming South Vietnam and Thailand than China could contain American influence in the Western Hemisphere by arming, say, Nicaragua and Costa Rica.

If we are convinced that we cannot live with a China predominant on the mainland of Asia, then we must strike at the heart of Chinese power—that is, rather than try to contain the power of China, we must try to destroy that power itself. Thus there is logic on the side of that small group of Americans who are convinced that war between the United States and China is inevitable and that the earlier that war comes, the better will be the chances for the United States to win it.

Yet, while logic is on their side, practical judgment is against them. For while China is obviously no match for the United States in overall power, China is largely immune to the specific types of power in which the superiority of the United States consists—that is, nuclear, air, and naval power. Certainly, the United States has the power to destroy the nuclear installations and the major industrial and population centers of China, but this destruction would not defeat China; it would only set her development back. To be defeated, China has to be conquered.

Physical conquest would require the deployment of millions of American soldiers on the mainland of Asia. No American military leader has ever advocated a course of action so fraught with incalculable risks, so uncertain of outcome, requiring sacrifices so out of proportion to the interests at stake and the benefits to be expected. President Eisenhower declared on Feb. 10, 1954, that he "could conceive of no greater tragedy than for the United States to become involved in an all-out war in Indochina." General MacArthur, in the Congressional hearings concerning his dismissal and in personal conversation with President Kennedy, emphatically warned against sending American foot soldiers to the Asian mainland to fight China.

If we do not want to set ourselves goals which cannot be attained with the means we are willing to employ, we must learn to accommodate ourselves to the predominance of China on the Asian mainland. It is instructive to note that those Asian nations which have done so—such as Burma and Cambodia—live peacefully in the shadow of the Chinese giant.

This *modus vivendi*, composed of legal independence and various degrees of actual dependence, has indeed been for more than a millennium the persistent pattern of Chinese predominance on the mainland of Asia. The military conquest of Tibet is the sole exception to that pattern. The military operations at the Indian border do not diverge from it, since their purpose was the establishment of a frontier disputed by both sides.

On the other hand, those Asian nations which have allowed themselves to be transformed into outposts of American military power—such as Laos a few years ago, South Vietnam, and Thailand—have become the actual or prospective victims of Communist aggression and subversion. Thus it appears that peripheral military containment is counter-productive. Challenged at its periphery by American military power at its weakest—that is, by the proxy of client-states—China or its proxies respond with locally superior military and political power.

In specific terms, accommodation means four things: (1) recognition of the political and cultural predominance of China on the mainland of Asia as a fact of life; (2) liquidation of the peripheral military containment of China; (3) strengthening of the uncommitted nations of Asia by nonmilitary means; (4) assessment of Communist governments in Asia in terms not of Communist doctrine but of their relation to the interests and power of the United States.

In the light of these principles, the alternative to our present policies in Vietnam would be this: a face-saving agreement which would allow us to disengage ourselves militarily in stages spaced in time; restoration of the status quo of the Geneva Agreements of 1954, with special emphasis upon all-Vietnamese elections; cooperation with the Soviet Union in support of a Titoist all-Vietnamese Government, which would be likely to emerge from such elections.

This last point is crucial, for our present policies not only drive Hanoi into the waiting arms of Peking, but also make it very difficult for Moscow to pursue an independent policy. Our interests in Southeast Asia are identical with those of the Soviet Union: to prevent the expansion of the *military* power of China. But while our present policies invite that expansion, so do they make it impossible for the Soviet Union to join us in preventing it. If we were to reconcile ourselves to the establishment of a Titoist government in all of Vietnam, the Soviet Union could successfully compete with China in claiming credit for it and surreptitiously cooperate with us in maintaining it.

Testing the President's proposals by these standards, one realizes how far they go in meeting them. These proposals do not preclude a return to the Geneva Agreements and even assume the existence of a Titoist government in North Vietnam. Nor do they preclude the establishment of a Titoist government for all of Vietnam, provided the people of South Vietnam have freely agreed to it. They also envision the active participation of the Soviet Union in establishing and maintaining a new balance of power in Southeast Asia. On the other hand, the President has flatly rejected a withdrawal "under the cloak of a meaningless agreement." The controlling word is obviously "meaningless," and only the future can tell whether we shall consider any face-saving agreement as "meaningless" regardless of its political context.

However, we are under a psychological compulsion to continue our military presence in South Vietnam as part of the peripheral military containment of China. We have been emboldened in this course of action by the identification of the enemy as "Communist," seeing in every Communist party and regime an extension of hostile Russian or Chinese power. This identification was justified 20 or 15 years ago when Communism still had a monolithic character. Here, as elsewhere, our modes of thought and action have been rendered obsolete by new developments.

It is ironic that this simple juxtaposition of "Communism" and "free world" was erected by John Foster Dulles's crusading moralism into the guiding principle of American foreign policy at a time when the national Communism of Yugoslavia, the neutralism of the third world, and the incipient split between the Soviet Union and China were rendering that juxtaposition invalid.

Today, it is belaboring the obvious to say that we are faced not with one monolithic Communism whose uniform hostility must be countered with equally uniform hostility, but with a number of different Communisms whose hostilities, determined by different national interests, vary. In fact, the United States encounters today less hostility from Tito, who is a Communist, than from de Gaulle, who is not.

We can today distinguish four different types of Communism in view of the kind and degree of hostility to the United States they represent: a Communism identified with the Soviet Union—e.g., Poland; a Communism identified with China—e.g. Albania; a Communism that straddles the fence between the Soviet Union and China—e.g., Rumania; and independent Communism—e.g., Yugoslavia. Each of these Communisms must be dealt with in terms of the bearing its foreign policy has upon the interests of the United States in a concrete instance.

It would, of course, be absurd to suggest that the officials responsible for the conduct of American foreign policy are unaware of these distinctions and of the demands they make for discriminating subtlety. Yet it is an obvious fact of experience that these officials are incapable of living up to these demands when they deal with Vietnam.

Thus they maneuver themselves into a position which is antirevolutionary per se and which requires military opposition to revolution wherever it is found in Asia, regardless of how it affects the interests—and how susceptible it is to the power—of the United States. There is a historic precedent for this kind of policy: Metternich's military opposition to liberalism after the Napoleonic Wars, which collapsed in 1848. For better or for worse, we live again in an age of revolution. It is the task of statesmanship not to oppose what cannot be opposed with a chance of success, but to bend it to one's own interests. This is what the President is trying to do with his proposal for the economic development of Southeast Asia.

Why do we support the Saigon Government in the civil war against the Vietcong? Because the Saigon Government is "free" and the Vietcong are "Communist." By containing Vietnamese Communism, we assume that we are really containing the Communism of China.

Yet this assumption is at odds with the historic experience of a millennium and is unsupported by contemporary evidence. China is the hereditary enemy of Vietnam, and Ho Chi Minh will become the leader of a Chinese satellite only if the United States forces him to become one.

Furthermore, Ho Chi Minh, like Tito and unlike the Communist governments of the other states of Eastern Europe, came to power not by courtesy of another Communist nation's victorious army but at the head of a victorious army of his own. He is, then, a natural candidate to become an Asian Tito, and the question we must answer is: How adversely would a Titoist Ho Chi Minh, governing all of Vietnam, affect the interests of the United States? The answer can only be: not at all. One can even maintain the proposition that, far from affecting adversely the interests of the United States, it would be in the interest of the United States if the western periphery of China were ringed by a chain of independent states, though they would, of course, in their policies take due account of the predominance of their powerful neighbor.

The roots of the Vietnamese civil war go back to the very beginning of South Vietnam as an independent state. When President Ngo Dinh Diem took office in 1954, he presided not over a state but over one-half of a country arbitrarily and, in the intentions of all concerned, temporarily severed from the other half. He was generally regarded as a care-taker who would establish the rudiments of an administration until the country was united by nationwide elections to be held in 1956 in accordance with the Geneva accords.

Diem was confronted at home with a number of private armies which were politically, religiously, or criminally oriented. To the general surprise, he subdued one after another and created what looked like a viable government. Yet in the process of creating it, he also laid the foundations for the present civil war. He ruthlessly suppressed all opposition, established concentration camps, organized a brutal secret police, closed newspapers, and rigged elections. These policies inevitably led to a polarization of the politics of South Vietnam—on one side, Diem's family, surrounded by a Praetorian guard; on the other, the Vietnamese people, backed by the Communists, declaring themselves liberators from foreign domination and internal oppression.

Thus, the possibility of civil war was inherent in the very nature of the Diem regime. It became inevitable after Diem refused to agree to all-Vietnamese elections and, in the face of mounting popular alienation, accentuated the tyrannical aspects of his regime. The South Vietnamese who cherished freedom could not help but oppose him. Threatened by the secret police, they went either abroad or underground where the Communists were waiting for them.

Until the end of last February, the Government of the United States started from the assumption that the war in South Vietnam was a civil war, aided and abetted—but not created—from abroad, and spokesmen for the Government have made time and again the point that the key to winning the war was political and not military and was to be found in South Vietnam itself. It was supposed to lie in transforming the indifference or hostility of the great mass of the South Vietnamese people into positive loyalty to the Government.

To that end, a new theory of warfare called "counter-insurgency" was put into practice. Strategic hamlets were established, massive propaganda campaigns were embarked upon, social and economic measures were at least sporadically taken. But all was to no avail. The mass of the population remained indifferent, if not hostile, and large units of the army ran away or went over to the enemy.

The reasons for this failure are of general significance, for they stem from a deeply ingrained habit of the American mind. We like to think of social problems as technically self-sufficient and susceptible of simple, clear-cut solutions. We tend to think of foreign aid as a kind of self-sufficient, technical, economic enterprise subject to the laws of economics and divorced from politics, and of war as a similarly self-sufficient, technical enterprise, to be won as quickly, as cheaply, as thoroughly as possible and divorced from the foreign policy that preceded and is to follow it. Thus our military theoreticians and practitioners conceive of counter-insurgency as though it were just another branch of warfare like artillery or chemical warfare, to be taught in special schools and applied with technical proficiency wherever the occasion arises.

This view derives of course from a complete misconception of the nature of civil war. People fight and die in civil wars because they have a faith which appears to them worth fighting and dying for, and they can be opposed with a chance of success only by people who have at least as strong a faith.

Magsaysay could subdue the Huk rebellion in the Philippines because his charisma, proven in action, aroused a faith superior to that of his opponents. In South Vietnam there is nothing to oppose the faith of the Vietcong and, in consequence, the Saigon Government and we are losing the civil war.

A guerrilla war cannot be won without the active support of the indigenous population, short of the physical extermination of that population. Germany was at least consistent when, during the Second World War, faced with unmanageable guerrilla warfare throughout occupied Europe, she tried to master the situation through a deliberate policy of extermination. The French tried "counter-insurgency" in

Algeria and failed; 400,000 French troops fought the guerrillas in Indochina for nine years and failed.

The United States has recognized that it is failing in South Vietnam. But it has drawn from this recognition of failure a most astounding conclusion.

The United States has decided to change the character of the war by unilateral declaration from a South Vietnamese civil war to a war of "foreign aggression." "Aggression from the North: The Record of North Vietnam's Campaign to Conquer South Vietnam" is the title of a White Paper published by the Department of State on the last day of February, 1965. [2] While normally foreign and military policy is based upon intelligence—that is, the objective assessment of facts—the process is here reversed: a new policy has been decided upon, and intelligence must provide the facts to justify it.

The United States, stymied in South Vietnam and on the verge of defeat, decided to carry the war to North Vietnam not so much in order to retrieve the fortunes of war as to lay the groundwork for "negotiations from strength." In order to justify that new policy, it was necessary to prove that North Vietnam is the real enemy. It is the White Paper's purpose to present that proof.

Let it be said right away that the White Paper is a dismal failure. The discrepancy between its assertions and the factual evidence adduced to support them borders on the grotesque. It does nothing to disprove, and tends even to confirm, what until the end of February had been official American doctrine: that the main body of the Vietcong is composed of South Vietnamese and that 80 to 90 percent of their weapons are of American origin.

This document is most disturbing in that it provides a particularly glaring instance of the tendency to conduct foreign and military policy not on their own merits, but as exercises in public relations. The Government fashions an imaginary world that pleases it, and then comes to believe in the reality of that world and acts as though it were real.

It is for this reason that public officials are so resentful of the reporters assigned to Vietnam and have tried to shut them off from the sources of news and even to silence

[2] See pp. 284–316.—ed.

them. [3] They resent the confrontation of their policies with the facts. Yet the facts are what they are, and they take terrible vengeance on those who disregard them.

However, the White Paper is but the latest instance of a delusionary tendency which has led American policy in Vietnam astray in other respects. We call the American troops in Vietnam "advisers" and have assigned them by and large to advisory functions, and we have limited the activities of the Marines who have now landed in Vietnam to guarding American installations. We have done this for reasons of public relations, in order to spare ourselves the odium of open belligerency.

There is an ominous similarity between this technique and that applied to the expedition in the Bay of Pigs. We wanted to overthrow Castro, but for reasons of public relations we did not want to do it ourselves. So it was not done at all, and our prestige was damaged far beyond what it would have suffered had we worked openly and single-mindedly for the goal we had set ourselves.

Our very presence in Vietnam is in a sense dictated by considerations of public relations; we are afraid lest our prestige would suffer were we to retreat from an untenable position.

One may ask whether we have gained prestige by being involved in a civil war on the mainland of Asia and by being unable to win it. Would we gain more by being unable to extricate ourselves from it, and by expanding it unilaterally into an international war? Is French prestige lower today than it was 11 years ago when France was fighting in Indochina, or five years ago when she was fighting in Algeria? Does not a great power gain prestige by mustering the wisdom and courage necessary to liquidate a losing enterprise? In other words, is it not the mark of greatness, in circumstances such as these, to be able to afford to be indifferent to one's prestige?

The peripheral military containment of China, the indiscriminate crusade against Communism, counter-insurgency as a technically self-sufficient new branch of warfare, the conception of foreign and military policy as a branch of public relations—they are all misconceptions that conjure up terrible dangers for those who base their policies on them.

[3] *See p. 194.—ed.*

One can only hope and pray that the vaunted pragmatism and common sense of the American mind—of which the President's new proposals may well be a manifestation—will act as a corrective upon those misconceptions before they lead us from the blind alley in which we find ourselves today to the rim of the abyss. Beyond the present crisis, however, one must hope that the confrontation between these misconceptions and reality will teach us a long-overdue lesson—to rid ourselves of these misconceptions altogether.

Dissent In the Senate (1963-1965)*
September 6, 1963:

Mr. [Wayne] Morse [D., Oregon]. The policy of our Government to continue to support military dictatorship is costing us heavily in prestige around the world, because the policy proves us to be hypocritical. . . . So long as Diem is the head of the Government of South Vietnam, we continue to support a tyrant, we continue to support a police-state dictator. . . . Everyone in this administration knows that if we withdrew our support from Diem, the anti-Communist forces in South Vietnam would throw him out within ninety days, and that hundreds of the exiles in Paris who are anti-Diem and anti-Communist would return to South Vietnam. Then there would be some chance of establishing in South Vietnam a moderate regime, anti-Communist in nature, but also democratic in purpose.

So I would have the United States get out of South Vietnam and save the American people the hundreds upon hundreds of millions of dollars that our Government is pouring down that rat hole—and I use the descriptive phrase "rat hole" advisedly.

Also, it would save many precious American lives. There are places in this city that do not like to hear that said. They did not like to hear it when the senior Senator from Oregon spoke it the first time. But I shall continue to speak it. On the basis of the present policies that prevail there South Vietnam is not worth the life of a single American

* Selections from the *Congressional Record*. [These selections have appeared in the Marzani and Munsell pamphlet, *The Conscience of the Senate* (New York, 1965), which must be used with great care because some speeches are quoted there out of context to give the appearance of greater dissent than actually exists. In each case I have checked the context of the speech.—ed

boy. The senior Senator from Oregon will not vote to c
tinue to sacrifice the lives of American boys in So
Vietnam.

February 19, 1964:

Mr. [Mike] Mansfield [D., Montana]. Mr. Preside
I refer to this morning's news reports which indicate t
Secretary of Defense McNamara has made it clear that
United States still hopes to bring about a major withdra
of U.S. forces from Vietnam by the end of 1965. . .

That was the hope which originally underlay our supp
of the government of President Ngo Dinh Diem, a h
which had become very slim by last summer. . . . It rem
to be seen whether the latest coup will really lead in t
direction.

That is a key question because the conflict in Vietn
remains a Vietnamese conflict, and in the end it must
resolved by the Vietnamese themselves. We have given
traordinary support to two successive governments in V
nam. We can do no more and should try to do no more
a third. We have teetered for too long on the brink of tu
ing the war in Vietnam which is still a Vietnamese war i
an American war to be paid for primarily with American li

And may I say, too, that it seems to me that Presid
de Gaulle has done well to speak out on Southeast Asia.
has again demonstrated a sense of history and statesmans
in seeking new ways for dealing with the continuing
stability and insecurity which prevails in Vietnam and m
of Southeast Asia.

The possibilities of such a neutralization may be extrem
difficult to realize, but they ought not to be dismissed. .

Mr. [E.L.] Bartlett [D., Alaska]. We are attempt
to find a military solution in Vietnam and if we are de
mined to win, the cost of this solution will have just beg
France tried a military solution in Indochina in the ea
fifties. At the time of the fall of Dienbienphu and the colla
of French resistance in 1954, France had over 200,000
her own troops, 200,000 Vietnamese troops, and suppor
forces numbering 150,000 men in the country.

It would seem evident, Mr. President, that any possibi
of obtaining a diplomatic solution should not be scorn
it is just this possibility that France now intends to expl

As a first step in this exploration our ally, France,
recognized Red China.

[1] *In Senate debates it is customary to address one's remarks to
President* pro tempore.—*ed.*

Our policies need reevaluation, and central to this re-aluation is the defusing of Red China as a domestic policy ue. We must be able to discuss Red China as we discuss er nations, Communist or free.

March 10, 1964:

Mr. [Ernest] Gruening [D., Alaska]. Mr. President, e mess in Vietnam was inherited by President Johnson.

Over ten years ago, after a careful study of the situation in Iochina a report was made to the Senate outlining the lowing conditions for success in that troubled area of the rld:

> The basic problem which confronts all three governments and particularly that of Vietnam is to put down firm roots in their respective populations. They will be able to do so only if they evolve in accord with popular sentiment and they deal competently with such basic problems as illiteracy, public health, excessive population in the deltas, inequities in labor and land tenure, and village and agricultural improvements. . . .

The date of that report was October 27, 1953, over ten ars ago.

The person making the report was our very able and dis-aguished majority leader, the Senator from Montana [Mr. ANSFIELD], whose knowledge of that area of the world is ost extensive. With respect to South Vietnam, the recom-endations of the Senator from Montana, were prophetic . . .

The war in South Vietnam is not and never has been a .S. war. It is and must remain a fight to be fought and won · the people of South Vietnam themselves. . . .

When President Eisenhower took office in January 1953, e war in Indochina was not going well. It was a French war, ught with French troops. . . .

. . . an article in *Look* on February 8, 1955 gave a forceful ccount of maneuverings in high places in Washington and ondon in those fateful, early days of 1954 when the United ates stood on the brink of an all-out invasion of Viet-m.[2]

According to Mr. Knebel, Adm. Arthur W. Radford, then hairman of the Joint Chiefs of Staff, advocated an imme-ate airstrike from carriers: Gen. Matthew B. Ridgway, rmy Chief of Staff, was opposed since he believed that ch a strike could lead to all-out intervention.

President Eisenhower, according to Knebel, agreed with dmiral Radford on two conditions: that the United States be

See p. 90.–ed.

joined in the action by other allies, namely, Great Brita
and that congressional approval be obtained for the actic
Since neither condition could be met, the United Sta
moved back safely from the brink. . . .

Within two months, on September 8, 1954, the Gover
ments of Australia, France, New Zealand, Pakistan, the Phili
pines, Thailand, the United Kingdom, and the Unit
States signed a collective security pact at Manila, known
the Southeast Asia Collective Defense Treaty. . . .[3]

In his address to the nation on September 15, 1954, e
plaining the action taken at Manila, Secretary Dulles fi
reiterated his concept of the domino theory. . . . Dulles al
expounded his massive retaliation theories of how to conta
Communism anywhere in the world, anytime. . . . By Ja
uary 1, 1955, U.S. aid began to flow directly to Sou
Vietnam and on February 12, 1955, a U.S. military assistan
advisory group took over the training of the South Vi
namese army. Previously, U.S. aid had been given throu
France.

In October 1955, the Eisenhower administration pick
Ngo Dinh Diem to rule South Vietnam. . . . In a nationwi
broadcast on March 8, 1955, Secretary Dulles said: "I w
much impressed by Prime Minister Diem. He is a tr
patriot, dedicated to independence and to the enjoyment
his people of political and religious freedoms. He now has
program for agricultural reform."

Ngo Dinh Diem ruled South Vietnam from October 2
1955 until the coup of November 2, 1963 deposed him.
the guerrilla fighting intensified through the years, so did t
mismanagement and corruption of the Diem governmer
It became increasingly oppressive, trampling the rights
individuals and ignoring the necessity for economic reforn
to benefit the people.

There is no room for disagreement concerning the fact th
the United States condoned or ignored actions by Diem ar
his ruling relatives calculated to antagonize the peop
on whose support any stable South Vietnamese Governme
must rest—or fall.

. . . The recent spate of optimistic announcements from th
Pentagon on how well the war in South Vietnam is going
despite contrary reports from trained observers on the scen
—only carries on a tradition. . . .

Thus, in July 1956, in the face of continued Vietcong sab

[3] *See pp. 96–105.—ed.*

ge and virulent propaganda, Vice-President Nixon, ad-
ressing the first Constituent Assembly of South Vietnam
ated that "the militant march of Communism has been
alted." But by the middle of the next year, Vietcong guer-
lla bands stepped up their attacks, bombing U.S., MAAG,
nd USIS installations and attacking settlements near Saigon.

Mr. Nixon's overoptimistic statement in July 1956 is on
par with his statement in October 1960, when he stated:
As far as Indochina was concerned . . . as a result of our
aking the strong stand that we did, the civil war there was
nded, and today we do have a strong free bastion there."

Vietcong guerrilla activities, reinforced by arms and men
rom North Vietnam, increased greatly during Diem's regime.
So did corruption and the oppression of the people. . . .

In the light of Diem's long years of corrupt and repressive
ule, the two coups in Vietnam last year should have come
s no surprise to anyone. The surprise lies in the fact that
ney did not occur sooner. . . .

The theory has been advanced that the United States has
o alternative but to remain in South Vietnam regardless
f the course of action followed by the people and the
overnment of South Vietnam. This theory follows the line
hat if we pulled our support out of South Vietnam now,
t would quickly be taken over by the Vietcong who in turn
vould be controlled by North Vietnam which in turn would
e controlled by Red China. The theory then continues that
f this happens then Cambodia and Laos would also fall
"like a row of dominoes" to Red China. This is a con-
inuance ten years later of Secretary Dulles' domino theory.

Recent actions on the part of Cambodia in seeking its
wn neutralization cast considerable doubt on this theory.
Cambodia, the middle domino, fell out of its own accord.
The $300 million we have spent there was totally wasted. . . .

A few days ago, the senior Senator from Montana [Mr.
MANSFIELD] took an enlightened stand with respect to the at-
empt by the President of France to put forth a solution
or the deteriorating situation in South Vietnam . . . .

I commend the majority leader for his statesmanlike approach. . . .

I also wish to commend the able senior Senator from Oregon [Mr. MORSE] for his splendid speech last week. . . .

To a question from Senator [Allen] ELLENDER [D.,
Louisiana] what Senator MORSE would advise we should do
in South Vietnam, Senator MORSE answered with his usual
forthrightness:

"We should never have gone in. We should never ha
stayed in. We should get out."

And Senator ELLENDER seconded that clear—and in m
judgment thoroughly correct and realistic counsel—by sayin
"I have been advocating such a course of action. After m
last visit there, I again stated that we should never have go
in there and that we should get out. My advice was nev
heeded. That is my advice today."

I consider the life of one American worth more than th
putrid mess. . . . I would feel very definitely that he ha
not died for our country, but had been mistakenly sac
ficed in behalf of an inherited folly. . . .

President Johnson, let me repeat, inherited this mess.
was not of his making. As he approaches the difficult task
making the necessarily hard decisions with respect to t
problems in South Vietnam, problems created long before
was President, he should feel no compunction to act in su
a way as to justify past actions, past decisions, and past m
takes. He should feel entirely free to act in such a mann
and to make such decisions as are calculated best to ser
the interests of the United States and the free world—a wor
changed greatly from the time President Eisenhower a
Secretary Dulles initiated our Southeast Asia policies. . . .

May 27, 1964:

Mr. Morse. Mr. President, I shall speak again in oppo
tion to McNamara's war in South Vietnam. . . .

. . . Mr. President, we are on the brink of a full-scale w
in Asia. I cannot emphasize too much the gravity of th
situation. . . . A nuclear war is in the offing, unless th
war in Asia is stopped. If this war in Asia is escalated in
a war in North Vietnam and beyond, put it down as a ce
tainty, Mr. President, that nuclear power will be used. .

Mr. President, what has happened to us? What has ov
come us? What has happened to the American people? Ha
we forgotten so soon? Have we forgotten the inhumanity
the last war? Have we forgotten the cost of the last war, n
only in material things, not only in human blood, but also
human values?

The Constitution still requires a declaration of war or
treaty obligation before American soldiers can be sent in
battle, and as the Secretary of Defense knows, Americ
soldiers are now fighting in South Vietnam not under a de
laration of war nor in pursuance of a treaty, but on t
orders of Mr. McNamara.

That makes our war illegal under the Constitution of the United States. . . .

August 5, 1964:

The Presiding Officer. The message from the President of the United States will be read.

Last night I announced to the American people that the North Vietnamese regime had conducted further deliberate attacks against U.S. naval vessels operating in international waters, and that I had therefore directed air action against gunboats and supporting facilities used in these hostile operations.

I recommend a resolution expressing the support of the Congress for all necessary action to protect our armed forces and to assist nations covered by the SEATO Treaty. . . .

The joint resolution (S.J. Res. 189) was read, as follows:

Resolved by the Senate and House of Representatives of the United States of America in Congress assembled, That the Congress approves and supports the determination of the President, as Commander-in-Chief, to take all necessary measures to repel any armed attack against the forces of the United States. . . .

Mr. Morse. Mr. President, I rise to speak in opposition the joint resolution. I do so with a very sad heart. But consider the resolution . . . to be naught but a resolution which embodies a predated declaration of war. . . .

I am convinced that a continuation of the U.S. unilateral military action in Southeast Asia, which has now taken on the aspects of open aggressive fighting, endangers the peace of the world. . . .

What about the 21,000 American troops in South Vietnam advising the Government?

What about the American air attack, on North Vietnam naval bases?

What about the shelling of the islands in Tonkin Bay by South Vietnamese vessels? These were all clear acts of war. . . .

I shall not support any substitute which takes the form of military action to expand the war or that encourages our puppets in Saigon to expand the war. . . .

I shall not support any substitute which takes the form of predated declaration of war. In my judgment, that is what the pending joint resolution is. . . .

August 6, 1964:

Mr. [George] McGovern. [D., South Dakota] All of us have been puzzled, if not baffled, as to why a little state such as

North Vietnam should seek a deliberate naval conflict with United States.

. . . There have been references in the press to the eff that General Khanh was in political trouble and that c way he thought he could get out of it was to divert attenti from failure in the conduct of the war in the South to so kind of strike in the North, . . . the press quoting Gene Khanh, the South Vietnamese leader, as saying that the w had to be won by carrying it to North Vietnam. . . .

Does the Senator think there is any danger in this re lution that we may be surrendering to General Khanh's p sition . . . ?

Mr. [J. William] Fulbright. [Arkansas] I do not think t policy that the war be confined to South Vietnam h changed. I think it is still the policy. I think it is the corre one.

Mr. [Daniel] Brewster. [D., Maryland]. . . . [Is there] ar thing in the resolution which would authorize or recomme or approve the landing of large American armies in Vietna or in China.

Mr. Fulbright. There is nothing in the resolution, as I re it. . . .

I do not know how to answer the Senator's question ar give him an absolute assurance that large numbers of troo would not be put ashore. I would deplore it. . . . But would be most concerned if the Congress should say that v intend by the joint resolution to authorize a complete chan; in the mission which we have had in South Vietnam for tl past ten years, and which we have repeatedly stated w not a commitment to engage in a direct land confront tion with our army. . . .

. . . Does the Senator know how close to the North Vie nam coast or the Red China coast our ships were patrollin;

Mr. Fulbright. It was testified that they went in at lea eleven miles in order to show that we do not recognize twelve-mile limit, which I believe North Vietnam had a serted.

Mr. [Gaylord] Nelson. [D., Wisc.] The patrolling was fc the purpose of demonstrating to the North Vietnamese th we did not recognize a twelve-mile limit?

Mr. Fulbright. That was one reason given for going i to a point eleven miles from the coast. . . .

Mr. Nelson. . . . it would be mighty risky, if Cuban P boats were firing on Florida, for Russian armed ships (

stroyers to be patrolling between us and Cuba, eleven
iles out. . . . So the question was whether the patrolling
at close was really necessary to the accomplishment of
ir mission. We are, after all, dealing with the possibility of
cinerating the whole world. . . .

Mr. Fulbright. I do not deny that it is risky. The whole
peration is risky. Mr. President, it is always difficult not
 accede to a request from the President of the United
ates. . . .

Mr. Gruening. But the United States has not pursued
eace as it has pursued and carried out armed intervention
 an ever-increasing scale.

The latest episode—the attack by North Vietnam vessels
 U.S. naval vessels, I consider an inevitable development
 the U.S. steady escalation of our own military activi-
es. . . .

Mr. Morse. My point is, if we are to talk about provoca-
on, that the United States was a provocateur by having
ny ships anywhere within striking distance or bombing
stance; and the South Vietnamese boats did bomb those
lands. We should have been completely out of the scene.

If Senators want my opinion, a "snow-job" is being done
 us by the Pentagon and the State Department in regard
 that bombardment. Not only had we full knowledge of it,
ut it was being done with our tacit approval. If we did
ot want to escalate the war into North Vietnam, that was
e time for the United States to stop escalating. . . .

Mr. [Frank] Lausche. [D., Ohio] I should like to state my
adgment as to what the evidence shows. Our Government
ad no knowledge of any nature about the attacks which
ere made upon the two islands by the North Vietnamese.
he *Maddox* was miles——

Mr. Morse. Do not talk about the *Maddox*; talk about
ur American officialdom in Saigon, and our American of-
cialdom in the Pentagon and the State Department. I state
ategorically that they knew the bombardment was going to
ke place before the ships ever moved.

Mr. Lausche. There is no testimony to that effect whatever. That is an inference made by the Senator from Ore-
on as to the——

Mr. Morse. Get permission of the State Department or
e Pentagon to publicly release the whole of the transcript
ithout a single word deleted, and let the country know
hat they said. . . . I am taking the criticism that, in my

judgment, American armed vessels should not have been as close to the islands as they were on Friday, July 31. In my judgment, that gave cause for the North Vietnamese to assume that there was a cause-and-effect relationship between the bombardment by the South Vietnamese vessels and the presence of the American naval patrol boats in Tonkin Bay at the location where they then were. . . .

So I say we are a provocateur. My colleagues become excited and seem to think I am guilty of some heinous accusation without any substantiation in fact. We would have been in a stronger position before the eyes of the world tonight if, after we had responded as we had a right to respond Tuesday night to the attack on our ships, we had on Wednesday laid that issue before the United Nations and asked the United Nations to proceed to take actions encompassed under the jurisdiction of the United Nations. Oh, no. We had to proceed to bomb the mainland. . . .

August 21, 1964

Mr. Morse. I . . . want to call to the attention of the Senate some of the circumstances surrounding the incident in the Gulf of Tonkin which were not discussed during the recent debate on the Asian resolution.

At the time of the debate on the joint resolution, it may be remembered that the Senator from Oregon, as tactfully as he could, within the rules of the Senate, without violation of any rule of secrecy, charged that the United States was a provocateur in the Gulf of Tonkin. I repeat tonight that the United States was a provocateur in the Gulf of Tonkin episode. The United States was a part and parcel of the escalating of the war. . . .

. . . There is no question that we knew of the escalating of the war. As I said the other day, and repeat tonight, that has been the objective of Secretary McNamara for months and months, to escalate the war. . . .

We had American naval vessels in the vicinity. The Pentagon disputes how far away they were. If they were seventy-five miles away, they were a provoking element. There is no question that one of them was within the twelve-mile limit of North Vietnam at the beginning of the bombardment. . . .

These are not among the facts that Americans were given in the President's television message, nor were they pointed out in the general news coverage of the *Maddox* incident.

But they are the kind of facts that have been withheld

so long that the American people do not know how we ever got started in the Vietnam war.

I repeat what I said before: what do we think would have been the attitude of the United States if Castro had sent two Russian-supplied, armed PT boats off Key West to bombard Key West, and a Russian destroyer or Russian submarines had been 30, 40, 50, or even 75 or 100 miles from Key West at the time?

Mr. President, we cannot have it both ways. We can be provocateurs too—and we were, in Tonkin Bay. . . .

We are making ourselves look absurd when we say through our Government, "The conference table can come later. The conference table can come after we dominate the battlefield."

Mr. President, that is not a country standing for peace. That is a country standing first for war. . . .

February 9, 1965:

Mr. Gruening. Mr. President, in commenting yesterday on the tragic events in South Vietnam last weekend, I stated: "Much of the news thus far released from South Vietnam, the Pentagon, and the White House raises many more questions than it answers. . . ."

Calling the war in Vietnam the "war that cannot be won on the ground where it is being fought," Mr. Walter Lippmann, in his column in the *Washington Post* this morning, pointed out:

> We have had a very clear demonstration of the strategic reality in Southeast Asia. The American Army at Pleiku was unable to protect itself against a comparatively small guerrilla attack, against a force estimated officially at about two squads and one platoon. The American forces got no warning of the attack from the Vietnamese people in the nearby hamlets where the raid was prepared. It got no protection from the Vietnamese security guards. . . .

February 11, 1965

Mr. [Frank] Church [D., Idaho]. Mr. President. . . .

. . . Our troops are now stationed in no less than thirty countries, we are pledged to defend forty-two and we are extending aid, in one form or another, to nearly 100 nations. As a result of this proliferation, Walter Lippmann writes: "We have become grossly overextended in regions where we have no primary vital interest. We have scattered our assistance to such a degree that we help everybody a little and nobody enough."

We have come to treat "Communism," regardless of what form it may take in any given country, as the enemy. We fancy ourselves as guardian of the "free" world, though most of it is not free, and never has been. We seek to immunize this world against further Communist infection through massive injections of American aid, and, wherever necessary, through direct American intervention. Such a vast undertaking has at least two defects: first, it exceeds our national capability; second, among the newly-emerging nations, where the specter of Western imperialism is dreaded more than Communism, such a policy can be self-defeating. As a seasoned, friendly foreign diplomat recently put it: "The United States is getting involved in situations where no one—not even a nation of saints—would be welcome. . . ."

To avoid this, we must understand that, for most Africans and Asians, our concept of self-government and individual freedom is totally unreal, having never been experienced. In many, if not most, of these emergent lands, it is capitalism, not Communism, which is the ugly word. . . .

Due to the degree of our involvement in the internal affairs of Southeast Asia, an area where China has been feared and resisted for centuries, the Peking government is now able to pose as champion of Asia for the Asians, defying the United States in the name of opposing the revival of Western imperialism.

It would be to our national advantage, then, to seek an international agreement for the neutralization of the whole great region that used to be French Indochina.

As the beat of the war drums intensifies, and passions rise on both sides, I recognize that negotiation becomes more difficult. Already cries of "appeasement" are being directed at anyone who speaks up for a negotiated settlement of this escalating war. So soon the country seems to have forgotten the wise words of John F. Kennedy, that we should never negotiate out of fear, but never fear to negotiate. . . .

It is not appeasement to recognize that the problem of Southeast Asia does not lend itself to a military solution. It is not appeasement for the mightiest military power in the history of the world to recognize the limits of that power and to commit it reasonably and wisely. Positive steps toward peace will do more than retaliatory air strikes to replenish the reservoir of good will which is America's greatest source of strength in Asia and throughout the world. . . .

February 24, 1965:

Mr. Gruening, Mr. President, Mr. [Hanson] Baldwin open'y admits [4] that escalation of the war could result in our having up to a million men fighting in South Vietnam in a Korea-type military operation. This does not include the number of military troops we would have to send to Korea if Red China—as is most likely—decided to reopen that front.

Such an escalation of the war would stop our steps towards economy in Government, our war against poverty, and our attempts to establish the Great Society . . . I hope the President will not attach too much significance to the urging he has received that he adopt the position of the "hawks" from such outstanding Republican leaders as the former Vice-President, Richard Nixon, the former GOP presidential candidate, Barry Goldwater, and the able and distinguished minority leader [Mr. (Everett) DIRKSEN (R., Illinois)]. As has been pointed out, if we become involved in a Korea-type, bogged-down foot war in South Vietnam, all three of these distinguished gentlemen will, when the casualty lists from an escalated war start coming in, be among the first to dub the war "Johnson's war" . . . My mail already shows, in a ratio of over 100 to 1, that our Vietnamese policy is not approved by the American people . . . Some of the letters which I receive come from his State.

Mr. [Gale] McGee. [D., Wyoming] I also have received a good bit of mail on this question. . . . I may get some which is even more vituperative, because some of us have been labeled as "war hawks." . . . I believe that our position is much bigger than reflecting public opinion. We should contribute to the molding of public opinion. We are not going to do it if we read letters first and then act. . . .

Mr. [Claiborne] Pell. [D., Rhode Island] I have one question to ask the Senator from Wyoming in connection with the number of people coming South from North Vietnam. I think the number of guerrillas born in North Vietnam and coming from North Vietnam, as opposed to South Vietnamese who have come home to engage in a revolution, is less than the number of American soldiers in South Vietnam. Is that correct?

Mr. Gruening. I should say advisedly that far more aggression has been committed by the United States of America in South Vietnam than has been committed by any of the North Vietnamese. . . . We have been told . . . that the

[4] See Baldwin's article, pp. 362–365.—ed.

16,000, 18,000, or 23,000 men we had in South Vietnam were advisers. We learned painfully that they were not advisers, but that they were in combat. The American people have not been given the full truth about this situation.

Mr. McGee. I agree with the Senator from Alaska that we have been less than candid about our activities, and that is unfortunate. . . .

*National Teach-in, Washington, D. C. (May 15, 1965)**

MORNING SPEECHES: Arthur Schlesinger Jr., on the Government position; Hans J. Morgenthau, a critique of the Administration; Isaac Deutscher on the policy and the cold war; Eric Wolf, moderator, on the history of the teach-in.

AFTERNOON POLICY CONFRONTATION: SPEAKERS: George McT. Kahin, professor of government and director of the Southeast Asia Program, Cornell University. INTERROGATORS:

On behalf of United States policy; Zbygniew Brzezinski, professor of public law and government and director, Research Institute for Communist Affairs, Columbia University; Wesley R. Fishel, professor of political science, Michigan State University; Robert A. Scalapino, professor of political science, University of California, Berkeley.

Again United States policy: Hans J. Morgenthau, professor of political science and director, Center for Study of American Foreign Policy, University of Chicago; Stanley Millet, professor of government, Briarcliff College; Mary Wright, professor of history, Yale University.

MODERATOR (Ernest Nagel, professor of philosophy at Columbia University): I have a very important announcement to read. I've been requested to read to you a text of a statement by Mr. McGeorge Bundy: "I greatly regret that it is impossible for me to take part in the discussion this afternoon of our policy in Vietnam.

* *New York Times* (May 17, 1965). [Further information about the Teach-in movement is available from Alternate Perspectives on Vietnam, P.O. Box 1385, Ann Arbor, Michigan 48106, or through the "communication network" established through the *BiWeekly Information Action Report,* P.O. Box 1995, Ann Arbor, Michigan 48106. The complete proceedings of the Washington Teach-in are to be published soon by Basic Books. —ed.]

"I have looked forward to this meeting and I hate to miss it. When I accepted your invitation, I did so with a warning that I might be unable to attend because of other duties. It gives me no pleasure that this warning has come true.

"I regret my absence the more because I wholly disagree with those who have argued that it is inappropriate for a government official to take part in a discussion of this kind.

"It may be true, although I have no first-hand knowledge, that some of your meetings on Vietnam have failed to meet the standards appropriate to university and college discussions. It may also be true, and I have thought so once or twice myself, that a few of those who feel strongly about the situation in Vietnam have been more interested in pressure upon the Administration than in fair discussion with its representatives.

"But the preliminary arrangements for this particular meeting, so far as I have knowledge of them, have been fair to a fault. I'm confident the discussion this afternoon will be a model of its kind.

"Members of the academic community and members of the Administration share a deep interest in the encouragement of such fair and open discussion. It has been argued that debate of this kind should be avoided because it can give encouragement to the adversaries of our country. There is some ground for this argument, since it is true that Communists have little understanding of the meaning of debate in a free society. The Chinese will continue to pretend, and perhaps in part to believe, that American policy is weaker because 700 faculty members have made a protest against our policy in Vietnam.

"The American people, whatever their opinions, know better. They know that those who are protesting are only a minority, indeed a small minority, of American teachers and students. They know also that even within that minority the great majority accept and respect the rights and duty of the American Administration to meet its constitutional responsibilities for the conduct of our foreign affairs.

"The American people know that the real day of danger will come when we are afraid of any unpopular minority or unwilling to reply to its voices. They understand what Communists cannot understand at all: That open discussion between our citizens and their government is the central nervous system of our free society. We cannot let the propaganda of totalitarians divert us from our necessary arguments with one another any more than we should let them be misled by such debates if we can help it.

"I will not take your time in this brief message for a rehearsal of the policy of this Administration on Vietnam. Let me take only a word to speak of our purpose there. That purpose is peace for the people of Vietnam, the people of Southeast Asia and the people of the United States.

"We evidently differ on the choice of ways and means to peace, in what we all must recognize to be a complex, ugly, and demanding situation. Those differences may go deep to the nature of the politics of Asia, to the legitimacy of force in the face of armed attack, and to the true prospects and purposes of the people of Vietnam themselves.

"But my own assessment is that what divides us is less than what unites us. None of us wants the war to be enlarged. All of us want a decent settlement. None of us wants other men to be forced under a totalitarian political authority. All of us seek a solution in which American troops can be honorably withdrawn. None of us, I hope, believes that these are easy goals. All of us, I trust, are prepared to be steadfast in the pursuit of our purposes.

"I recognize the entire sincerity of the great majority of those who now disagree with our policy in Vietnam. I think many of these critics have been wrong in earlier moments of stress and danger and I think many of them misunderstand the hard realities of this dangerous world. But their good faith and good intent are not in question, and on other issues at other times their efforts have been of great service to the country.

"Having said this much, perhaps I can ask you in return that these critics should recognize that the Administration which now bears responsibility for the conduct of our foreign affairs, does not admire force for its own sake, or brinkmanship of any sort. The purpose of its foreign policy in Vietnam as elsewhere is that diplomacy and power and progress and hope shall be held together in the service of the freedom of us all.

"So I trust that the discussion this afternoon will not turn upon charge and countercharge against the motives of those with whom we disagree.

"Let it turn, instead, upon analysis of the situation as it is, and of choices for the future which can serve the purposes we share.

"I repeat my apologies for my forced absence; and I take comfort in the thought that I shall miss the meeting more than you will miss me."

PROF. NAGEL: This meeting has come into being because of widespread doubt in many academic communities as well as elsewhere concerning the wisdom of current United States policy in Vietnam. It needs to be emphasized, however, that the meeting has been sponsored by university teachers throughout the country and organized by the Inter-University Committee for a Public Hearing on Vietnam on the basis of two assumptions:

The first is that whether or not those doubts are well-founded, there has been insufficient responsible debate in public of the great issues raised by our actions in Southeast Asia.

The second assumption is that since a thorough airing of these issues by competent students is a condition for an enlightened public opinion on them, in a liberal democracy such as ours in which governmental policies require the assent of its citizens, students who possess knowledge pertinent to those issues have a special duty to discuss them openly and critically. . . .

PROF. KAHIN: Mr. Nagel, ladies and gentlemen, I am indeed very sorry to learn that Mr. Bundy finds it impossible to be with us this afternoon. I see no reason therefore for altering in any significant way the remarks I'd planned to make. I will perhaps have a few additional things to say in closing concerning his absence.

Since the end of the last war, American officials have made such grave errors in policy toward Southeast Asia that we have every right to be skeptical about their ability to respond intelligently to the present situation in Vietnam. Their most consistent failure has been an inability both to appreciate the importance of Asian nationalism and to work with rather than against this powerful force. This is a major reason why Burma, Cambodia, Indonesia have become so distrustful of the United States, and why they have either broken or come close to breaking their relations with us. Moreover, the obsession of American policymakers with what they still see as monolithic Communism has blinded them to the fact that Communism in Asia has adapted itself to nationalism. And they have confused the broad but nationally differentiated force and potential of Communism with the threat of specifically Chinese power.

Despite the immense information gathering facilities of the Government, serious policy mistakes have been made because decisions have been taken on the basis of inappropriate criteria, wrong analyses, and a disregard for the relevant facts. At the same time essential information has been withheld from the American public and crucial policy decisions concerning Southeast Asia have been made before the public has even been aware that a problem exists. And once taken, these decisions have set in motion events which severely circumscribed any moderating influence which an informed public opinion might bring to bear.

Moreover in recent months the tendency has increased to dismiss even thoughtful criticism of Government policy as irresponsible meddling.

In Vietnam, American policy has been wrong from the outset. In the decade following World War II, because of our illusory hope that we could induce France to become the keystone in an American-designed European military organization, we temporized with our commitment to national self-determination and backed France in her efforts to reestablish control over Vietnam.

By supporting her attempt to establish a Vietnamese regime which lacked nationalist support, we helped insure that Vietnamese patriots would have no real alternative but to rally to the banner of Ho Chi Minh. France's humiliating defeat at Dienbienphu in 1954 was a military defeat, but it was made inevitable by the political failure that preceded it.

Then came the Geneva Agreements clearly specifying that Vietnam was one country. They stipulated that the 17th Parallel was a temporary demarcation line, not in any way to be interpreted—and here I'm using the text of the agreement—not in any way to be interpreted as constituting a political or territorial boundary.

The United States in its own unilateral declaration at Geneva spoke only of one Vietnam, not of a South, and not of a North, and with respect to the conference's provision for national elections, the United States also stated—

again in its own unilateral declaration—that it would continue to seek to achieve unity through free elections supervised by the United Nations.

Nevertheless the United States soon thereafter set out to build up a separate state in the South. And again we made the mistake of thinking we could establish a viable government on an inadequate nationalist base. The United States supported Ngo Dinh Diem giving him, as you know, massive amounts of—economic initially and later—military assistance.

But American aid was no substitute for nationalist support, something Diem's regime never really acquired, despite what our officials told Congress and the American people.

Diem himself had said in 1953—repeatedly, I might add—that Ho Chi Minh—and I'm quoting him—"gained in popularity as a leader of the resistance, not as a Communist," and that the vast majority of his followers were nationalist and in no way pro-Communist.

What the United States failed to recognize was that in these conditions Ho Chi Minh, who for at least nine years had been the acknowledged head of the Vietnamese nationalist movement, could not be replaced as the leader of the Vietnamese people by a man supported from the outside, a man little known and who had spent the critical years—nearly all of them—of the independence struggle abroad.

America's failure, of course, to build up an effective government under Diem is now well known. . . . [Also] . . . with American encouragement Diem refused to permit the elections in 1956 and France washed her hands of the responsibilities which she had assumed at Geneva.

Regardless of what sophistry has been employed to demonstrate otherwise, by encouraging Diem to defy this central provision of the Geneva agreements, the United States reneged on the position it had taken there in its own unilateral declaration.

Civil war in Vietnam became inevitable, for when a military struggle for power ends on the agreed condition that the competition will be transferred to the political level, can the side which violates the agreed conditions legitimately expect that the military struggle will not be resumed?

Faced with [the] decline in political cohesion, and the evident inability of the South Vietnamese military to stave off the Vietcong, the present Administration has enlarged the war in Vietnam by bombing the north and increasing American military activity in the south.

It has endeavored to compensate for the continuing erosion of Saigon's political and military base by introducing more American troops, more American air power.

It has justified this in terms of our pledge to support Vietnam, a commitment which, as you know, the Administration regards as a test case.

And here I think it might be appropriate to recall the caveat of Secretary Acheson in 1950 when he stated that America could not by itself create politically stable states in Asia.

President Kennedy also recognized these limitations when, in September 1963, he said of the South Vietnamese, "In the final analysis it's their war—they're the ones who have to win it or lose it. We can help them, give them equipment. We can send our men out there as advisers, but they have to win it."

In the context of these cautions, does an unconditional American military pledge to a weak and factious regime which lacks popular backing—does that make common sense? Is our pledge of support completely unqualified? Does it not demand a minimum degree of performance and cooperation from Saigon—political as well as military? Is our pledge automatically to any military or civilian group which happens to control Saigon? What happens if our current policy of brinkmanship induces Hanoi to send its 300,000-man army into South Vietnam?

Because this it may very well do if the damage inflicted by the United States becomes so great that the north has little to lose by undertaking a retaliatory attack and little to save through compromise and negotiation. . . .

If we are going to salvage anything in Vietnam, we will achieve more through a cease-fire and a negotiated political settlement than through the futile infusion of more and more American military power.

The United States must recognize that the historic Vietnam fear of—fear of and antagonism toward—China continues—continues despite the common adherence to Communist ideology. And inasmuch as the character of Vietnamese Communism is inseparable from Vietnamese nationalism,

Vietnamese power will not necessarily be exerted in concert with Chinese power.

This is likely to depend upon whether such actions conform with Vietnamese national interests as the Vietnamese people define that interest.

Those who still are impressed by the simplistic domino theory must realize that non-Communist governments of Southeast Asia will not automatically collapse if the Communists should come to control all of Vietnam. So long as Southeast Asian governments are in harmony with their nations' nationalism, so long as they are wise enough to meet the most pressing economic and social demands of their people, they are not likely to succumb to Communism.

Nationalism and the demand for social and economic progress are the dominant forces in Southeast Asia today. If we can work with these forces we will make a major contribution to maintaining the territorial integrity of the states of Southeast Asia and provide them with a better opportunity to develop along non-Communist lines.

The first step in that direction must be to negotiate a settlement in Vietnam.

What has our position been thus far? I think you know it well. The Administration tells us that it is prepared to negotiate unconditionally but in effect on condition that the Vietcong cease all operations immediately and on condition that the state of South Vietnam—and this is the most important condition, I would say—continue its separate existence in permanent violation of the Geneva Agreements.

Furthermore, we have made clear that the Vietcong and its political arm, the National Liberation Front, cannot be party to such negotiations. Not only is that one more condition, but it flies squarely in the face of political reality.

It is, I think, widely acknowledged that at least half of the South is today under the control of the Vietcong. Is it not utopian to assume that Hanoi is in a position to insist upon the Vietcong's yielding up the position it has won there?

In 1954, the Vietminh could induce its numerous supporters in the South to accept Vietnam's partition and to abandon their gains south of the 17th Parallel, because partition was regarded as a temporary measure to last only until elections.

But we cannot assume that once again the insurgent in the South will give up what they have won through lon and difficult campaigns.

Over the last five years, the doctrine of uncompromisin struggle and a real expectation of victory have been assid uously nurtured among the Vietcong. While there i undoubtedly a considerable congruence of interest betwee Hanoi and the Vietcong, under these circumstances w cannot assume that Hanoi can abruptly call off the South erners' resistance.

And whatever influence Hanoi can exert over the Viet cong, we cannot expect it to exert this so long as we con tinue bombing the North.

The morale of the North Vietnamese is, of course, n more likely to be broken by bombs than was that of th British or the Russians in the last war. Indeed their will i likely to be stiffened. President Johnson said after our em bassy in Saigon had been bombed that outrages like thi will only reinforce the determination of the American peopl and Government. What is true for Americans is true fo the Vietnamese. . . .

And finally, for those many Americans who still regard full public discussion of vitally important national issues as essential to our brand of democracy, there is a partic ularly disquieting domestic aspect of this situation:

Realizing as they do that an informed public discussion requires access to the relevant facts, these Americans can only be deeply disturbed when a spokesman for the news paper editors of this country feels compelled to state as he did last month that the American press in Vietnam faces stronger restrictions than it ever has in wartime and that we are getting contradictions, double-talk, and half-truths from the Government concerning the situation in Vietnam.

And surely Americans have grounds for concern when *The New York Times* can editorialize, as it did shortly after this, less than three weeks ago, that high-ranking rep resentatives of government in Washington and in Saigon have so obscured, confused, or distorted news from Vietnam or have made such fatuously erroneous evaluations about the course of the war that the credibility of the United States Government has been sacrificed.

I had indeed hoped that Mr. Bundy's appearance would

e an indication of a change in the Administration's attitude s to the value of informed public discussion. I can only ope that his indispensability in meeting some major crisis f policymaking is really of greater importance than the ontribution he might have made this afternoon toward our etter understanding of the Administration's aims and to hat kind of enlightened public discussion which is so ssential to the wisest conduct of foreign policy.

MR. NAGEL: The second principal speaker is Professor calapino.

PROF. SCALAPINO: Mr. Moderator, ladies and gentlemen f the panel, ladies and gentlemen of the audience, both here nd unseen:

First, it should be perfectly clear that I am not here as a pokesman for the Government. I do not know what Mr. Bundy would have said. As the moderator has made clear, we knew about this on both sides of this panel only about 2:30 and consequently my remarks will be strictly those of myself as prepared rather hastily after that time.

Now it seems to me that in beginning I would not start my remarks with an historical background as did Professor Kahin. I would rather prefer to work those into some of the critical questions to which I would like to address myself.

The first of these questions, which is, I think, critical, is as follows:

Is the Vietcong a truly indigenous force in South Vietnam and has it achieved its strength for its support such as it is through promoting socio-economic reform?

To me, the answer to this question, while complicated, is, on balance, no.

Let me cite, to begin, an editorial from *The Peking Daily Worker* of April 15 of this year and reproduced in *The Peking Review* on April 23. "The Vietnamese people's anti-U. S. struggle for national salvation is a just revolutionary struggle against aggression. It is certain to win, because there is the wise leadership of the Marxist-Leninist Workers Party of Vietnam, because there is the unity of the 30 million Vietnamese people, and because there is sympathy and support from people the world over."

I call to your attention the first phrase in that statement: Because there is the wise leadership of the Marxist-Leninist

Workers Party of Vietnam. I think that there is little ques
tion that the Vietcong is a carbon copy of the Vietminh
which preceded it. This is certainly not to say that it doe
not have indigenous support and leadership in nominal term
at least. Clearly most of the leaders of the National Liberation Front originated from the South as that front is
now structured. And whatever the bewildering difference
in figures, I am prepared to say that a significant segmen
of the National Liberation Front is still Southern in origin

But what are the truly critical factors? These factors, i
seems to me, are as follows:

First, who does know the leadership of the National
Liberation Front? Individuals like Nguyen Wuc Ngo. How
many either in or out of Vietnam really subscribe to their
leadership? The real leaders of the Vietcong are, and have
always been, those in small hard-core elements that are also
members of the Communist Party—and that party has
Hanoi as its headquarters now as in the past.

The South Vietnamese Revolutionary Party numbers no
more than 500 or so. It could not possibly be expected to
dominate the 500,000-man party of the North. Not only is
the leadership of this movement shadowy indeed, but take
a look at its basic principles. I urge you to read them
carefully, because I suggest that though there may have
been differences in tactics between the South National Liberation Front and the North Workers Party, or Lao Dong group,
there have been no differences up to date on the question of
basic policies or of fundamental programs. . . .

Let me raise another question: Does the Vietcong really
command the support and allegiance of the people of South
Vietnam?

I think again, though the answer is complicated, the answer, on balance, must be no.

What is a true phenomenon is that though the Diem
Government made many mistakes, and I am not here in any
sense to defend it, although the Diem Government made
many mistakes, one of the interesting things is that very
few, if any, significant anti-Diem leaders in the South
joined the Vietcong. One of the significant things is that
today still, the great popular elements of South Vietnam
are not a part of the Vietcong, nor have they ever
been. . . .

I think it is also significant, quite frankly, to point out that the successes of the Vietcong are neither attributable alone to the appeals which they have been able to make on social, economic, or nationalist grounds.

I would not depreciate those appeals, or their success in some quarters. But what I would emphasize and re-emphasize is the fact that Communist strength in South Vietnam, as in many other areas, is also heavily attributable to organizational skill.

If one takes hold of a movement politically and can organize it, mobilize it, and utilize all of the organizational technique, then one has, indeed, a powerful weapon—particularly when one works in a truly diverse, heterogeneous, nonorganized society.

It does not necessarily mean, however, that because one has organizational control, one has public support. I think anyone familiar with American big city politics must know that.

The fact is that organization is critical to Communist success in Asia and elsewhere and very frequently coercion as much as persuasion is involved. How many village officials, good, bad, and indifferent, have been killed by the Vietcong in recent years?

Some estimates are 6,000. I have no doubt that some of them were bad, many of them indifferent, some of them good, but the only question that was really asked was, do they support the Government or don't they?

And if they do, then they're finished. For to root out the willful bases of power is critical in the development of a movement like this, and it has little to do quite frankly with the appeal of issues, socio-economic or others.

Now I make these points because I think that if the true allegiance of the people of South Vietnam could really be tested, it is very doubtful that they would vote for the Vietcong. And this question of elections, in Geneva or after the Geneva Agreements or elsewhere, troubles me greatly.

For I do not know, frankly, of any state that has been controlled by the Communists which could afford to allow free elections. And quite frankly in recent announcements coming out of Hanoi, I have seen nothing to indicate that Hanoi is interested in elections in the north.

I have seen nothing to indicate that they would really relinquish the mass media communications system for purposes of a true dialogue, that they would allow the establishment of class enemy parties.

I have seen nothing to indicate that the formula of free elections which is meaningful in the democratic context can be meaningful in a Communist context. And if that is true, then was the Geneva Agreement always a fraudulent one? Then was it clearly fraudulent from the beginning to assume that you could have free elections in a society dominated by men who regard class enemies as susceptible to control through whatever means possible?

Now, I think that when it comes to the basic issues that confront us today . . . , we are confronted, at least theoretically, with three broad alternatives: Withdrawal. Negotiation. Or escalation.

It seems to me clear that the arguments against withdrawal are so powerful and so strong that at least as yet they have not been answered.

It is not merely that withdrawal would reduce American credibility with her allies and neutrals round the world, but it is also that it would be a green light to the new national liberation movements which are even now getting under way. I do not need to remind you that Peking has broadcast repeatedly its intent to support the Thai national liberation movement and has already launched the first propaganda with this matter in hand.

If socio-economic interests are the critical question, we would have some curious new kinds of analyses to make. We cannot ignore the ingredient of power. And central to this, it seems to me, is the fact that for more than five years Peking and Moscow have been arguing vigorously about the way in which to handle American imperialism. That argument, which has gone down to this present month, is roughly speaking as follows, and I think you know it well:

American imperialism, argues Peking, is a paper tiger. Push and attack—it will retreat. It is not to be taken as a nuclear blackmail threat. The problem with the Russians, argues Peking, is that they have been too sensitive to American power, too willing to compromise, too unwilling to push the revolutionary movement forward.

It seems to me that, above all, withdrawal—withdrawal would prove that Peking was right and make it virtually impossible for moderation to prevail inside the world Communist movement. For if the strategy of pushing American power and forcing it into a unilateral retreat works—if it works in Vietnam, it will work elsewhere and be tried everywhere. . . .

Let me then move to this question of negotiation: I suspect the overwhelming majority of people in this room, and listening to us, favor negotiation. And I suspect that the critical issue, therefore, to come is: who is willing to negotiate and on what terms.

Up to date, and we can certainly hope that this will change, the Chinese have indicated very little willingness to negotiate. . . . And we are still hoping that at least Hanoi will come forward and break its tie, now more than two years old, with Peking and move into a new orbit of independence.[1]

The whole history of Vietnam indicates that while there has always been a stout resistance to China on the one hand there has always been a strong element willing to cooperate and collaborate with China on the other. And this brings to me—I think—the focus of this problem: namely, the question of the containment of China. . . . I suggest that the pressures which Communist China is putting upon the small neutralist countries today—unless they are counteracted by some balance of power in this region—will be antinationalist and increasingly satellite in character.

These are small states, the survival of which depends upon some balance of power—a balance of power, I say, that must be a combination of both Western and Asian power, that must represent a fusion, for today it is critical that we come into line with such major societies in Asia as Japan and India, and I would hope some day, Indonesia. For these are societies with whom we can work in forwarding the social, economic and nationalist revolutions. . . .

[Professor Scalapino, after announcing he would do so, neglected to discuss "escalation."—ed.]

I say that this policy can run along these lines:

---

[1] *Later in the Teach-in Professor Scalapino clarified his view on the question of Hanoi's allegiances. Having followed DRV publications in translation for three years, Scalapino concluded that the North Vietnamese leaders have gone over to the Chinese camp.—ed.*

First, our broad objective should be a neutral, nonaligned Asia that is truly neutral and nonaligned, not the Communist version of the Vietcong.

Secondly we should, of course, negotiate. But we should make it clear that we are not negotiating just with labels, that we are negotiating with men representing forces. We should negotiate with the Communists in South Vietnam as Communists, and we should negotiate with the other elements in terms of whatever representation they truly represent. It must be remembered that the Buddhists are the largest functional group in South Vietnam and they certainly dwarf the Vietcong in numbers and supporters.

And lastly I would say this, that I think that as long as we maintain two open channels not only for the neutrals but for the Communists, one in which we urge social, economic, cultural exchange, one in which we urge peaceful coexistence, one in which we desire the exchange of scholars, journalists and economic development—yes, with China, as with others. And the other channel in which we say we will not surrender unconditionally, we will not be driven out by a philosophy that regards compromise as evil as long as it takes that stand, as long as we keep these channels open and operative in an imaginative sense, I do not see how we can fail in the long run to reach a solution to our problems.

PROF. MORGENTHAU: Let me suppose that Professor Scalapino's analysis of the facts in Southeast Asia is correct in every particular—a mere hypothetical assumption on my part.

What would the consequences for American policy be?

Professor Scalapino speaks very softly about the establishment of a balance of power. I speak very crudely about war against China.

For I see here one of the basic inner contradictions of our official policy which makes, as speakers have reminded us this morning and this afternoon, those problems so terribly complicated.

It is because we set ourselves goals in Asia and we have done so, I should say in parting, for half a century, which cannot be achieved with the means we are willing to employ.

And as it is in philosophy and in pure logic, if you pose a wrong question you find it extremely complex to give a simple and correct answer.

And the uneasiness in the country of which this assembly is an impressive manifestation, I think stems from this instinctive recognition that there's something basically wrong in the modes of thought and action of our Government, that there is an essential contradiction or a number of contradictions between what we profess to want and the policies we want to employ and the risks which we want to take.

And I submit again, as I have done this morning, and have done before in lectures many times, that if you really want to achieve in Asia what the spokesmen for our Government say they want to achieve, you must be ready to go to war with China, with all that that implies.

I would also say a word . . . about negotiations. Much has been made of our willingness to negotiate. There is, of course, no doubt, and Mr. McGeorge Bundy didn't need to emphasize it, that our Government wants a peaceful solution. No decent government which isn't out of its mind would want anything else.

But this is not the point. The point is not what you intend, but the point is what you do regardless of your intentions. The history of the world is full of instances where well-meaning, high-principled people have brought unspeakable misery upon their own nation in spite of their good intentions, because it used the wrong policies.

Let me turn to the problem of negotiations. Of course we want a negotiated settlement, and I'm sure there are people in our Government who pray for a negotiated settlement. If only the other side would make a move.

But those people cannot see that the implicit conditions which we have made—the unspoken conditions—make a negotiated settlement at the moment impossible.

For, first of all, we refuse to negotiate with the Vietcong.

Secondly, we make it an implicit condition that we remain —at least for the time being—in South Vietnam—that is to say, as long as no stable government is established there, which will take a very long time.

Now the other side is fully aware of the blind alley in which we find ourselves in South Vietnam. We don't have the courage to retreat and we don't dare to advance too far.

And so obviously from the point of view of Peking, which hasn't lost a single man in that conflict and has only lost, as far as we can tell, one gun, which Mr. McNamara showed the other day in a press conference.

Of course from the point of view of Peking, nothing better could happen than the United States waging a war in Vietnam which it is not able to win and which it cannot afford to lose.

Why should Peking under such circumstances recommend negotiations?

Negotiations are possible only under the conditions such as when one recognizes the inevitable facts of life in Asia which, as I have said before, can only be changed by war.

PROF. SCALAPINO: If I may risk a simplification of Professor Morgenthau's thesis: It seems to me that he is coming pretty close to saying that either war or withdrawal from Asia is inevitable for the United States—that we must either get out or we must go to war with China.

I may be misinterpreting him, but that's the way I read his remarks and he'll have a chance to rebut this if I'm wrong.

Now, I would just like to reiterate what's been said by other people here. I don't believe in historical inevitability. But if I did, I would put this in precisely the opposite framework. I would say that withdrawal at this point will mean war. Because I think it will inevitably settle, at least for the time being, the issue of how to meet American imperialism, as the Communists put it.

I think it will inevitably cause the launching not of a thousand ships, but a thousand revolts not just in Asia, but wherever this movement can get under way. And I think that that means war. Under what conditions, I cannot predict, nor can you.

Now it seems to me that that's the critical issue.

We are engaged in the hard, difficult, complex task of trying again to build a containment policy, if you will, but one that is more broadly gauged than the past. And I would simply end my answer to Mr. Morgenthau's comment by suggesting that if you take the last ten years, I think that the United States, itself a late-developing society in terms of world leadership, has learned a great deal; has moved a great distance.

Ten years ago we were still saying—some of us, not I, but some—that neutralism was immoral. Today, we are prepared

—and I think this is true of both of our major parties—to work with and underwrite when we can, neutral and non-aligned states.

We have people—and this point ought to be underlined and re-emphasized—who are not reactionary; who are not committed to the past, and who have found that between us and the Communists they'd rather take their chances on socio-economic reform and development with us.

And I maintain that in some of the areas where the American commitment has been heaviest in Asia, the standard of living is going up most rapidly.

This is important, not because I want to whitewash American policy, I think we've made many mistakes in the past, we're still making some—I've been a frequent critic of American policy myself—but I think the time has come, both to face up to alternatives and at the same time to point out again and again that, if we can't do something to preserve a certain openness in these societies, then, it seems to me, the balance of power will be abruptly changed and global war will shortly ensue.

PROF. MARY WRIGHT: My differences with Professor Scalapino and his analysis of the situation are very deep and very profound and we are talking about a very serious matter here. It's a good deal more serious than I expected it to be when we came onto this platform today.

I agree with him, with his very curious and earnest statement, that I, too, will fight for American soil. But when he makes that plea for Asia—we will not be moved out of Asia. We will not give up unilaterally—I am absolutely dumfounded, because he links it to a policy of getting into alignment with nations like India and Japan.

He surely is as well aware as I am and all of you are of what our policy and the kind of policy he poses, the kind of tensions that this has placed on our sound relation with Japan and India.

Professor Scalapino would like Asia a certain way. I agree with Professor Morgenthau that to have the Asia that he has outlined is not only impossible within the means which we are willing to use, it is impossible within the means at our command.

Because we sit here with an Asia projected of how we would want it. We are trying to disavow the Communist revolution in China. We pretend it doesn't exist there. We talk against the advice of our best friends of Europe, against our best allies as far as Asia goes. We upset the nonaligned countries. We bring in far more military aid than the opposition is bringing in as far as that goes.

We've got some lessons of history here to learn and Mr. Brzezinski's parallels are those very dangerous intellectual exercises—faulty parallels—to the position of Hitler's Germany or Imperial Japan.[2] Because this is not the first time that a great power has used military force to try to save Asia from Communism.

I find myself in very profound opposition to my friends and colleagues on the panel and on the other side.

It appears to me that the Communist revolution has been won in China; as Mr. Brzezinski says, a great deal has happened in the last 20 years. The one place it's not happened is in Chinese-American relations. . . .

*Decentralization of Dissent: Local Teach-In, Brooklyn, New York (May 13, 1965)**

The Universities Committee on the Problems of War and Peace of Greater New York in co-operation with the Pratt Institute chapter of The National Student Association are honored by your attendance and the participation of all students and faculty members of the Polytechnic Institute of Brooklyn, Long Island University, Brooklyn College, and Pratt Institute in the Joint Brooklyn Colleges Teach-in on Vietnam and the Dominican Crisis

TENTATIVE PROGRAM OF THE TEACH-IN

4:00 P.M. Opening Remarks by Dr. Josef E. Garai, Assistant Professor of Psychology, Pratt Institute.

---

[2] *Brzezinski had said earlier: "There are those who say that it can never be, for China is the predominant power in the region. Let us assume for a second that it is. So was Japan in 1940. Does that mean we should not have taken the course we did? So was Germany in Europe in 1940. So was the Soviet Union in Europe in 1945-46. Yet this did not justify the conclusion that one should therefore disengage and in a self-fulfilling prophecy make right the assertion—make right the assertion that China is the predominant power and prove it by disengaging."—ed.*

* From the program of the teach-in, distributed at Pratt Institute.

4:30 P.M. "Political Developments in Vietnam since 1954," by David Mermelstein, Assistant Professor of Economics, Polytechnic Institute of Brooklyn.

5:20 P.M. "Memories from Germany Revived by the Present International Tension," by Sibyl Moholy-Nagy, Chairman, Department of History of Architecture, Pratt Institute.

6:10 P.M. "Social Structure of Vietnam," by John McDermott, Assistant Professor of Philosophy, Long Island University.

7:00 P.M. "The Only Solution Is Ultimate Victory," by Henry Litchfield, Director, Foreign Affairs Committee, Conservative Party.

7:50 P.M. "The Background of the Crisis in the Dominican Republic," by Professor Louis Menashe, Assistant Professor of History, Polytechnic Institute of Brooklyn.

8:40 P.M. "Impressions from the Universities Committee's Lobby for Peace (Washington, April 8)," by Marvin E. Gettleman, Assistant Professor of History, Polytechnic Institute of Brooklyn.[1]

8:40 P.M. "Impressions from the Universities Committee's Lobby for Peace Today," by Robert Slutzky, Instructor in Architecture, Pratt Institute.[2]

9:10 P.M. "In Defense of President Johnson's Foreign Policy in Vietnam," by Chris Emmet, American Friends of Vietnam.[3]

10:00 P.M. "The 'Rationality' of President Johnson's Foreign Policy," by Shane Mage, Assistant Professor of Economics, Polytechnic Institute of Brooklyn.

[1] *The Universities Committee on Problems of War and Peace, which organized the Washington Lobby of April 8–9, is an academic peace group. Information about it may be obtained from P.O. Box 7228, Detroit 2, Michigan. A description of the Washington lobbying project is available from Professor Everett W. Bovard, Department of Anatomy, Albert Einstein College of Medicine, Bronx, New York. (I might add at this point that while the original impetus behind this book was my participation in the peace movement, its content is dictated by canons of scholarly objectivity. On the distinction between inspiration and objectivity, see Max Weber, "Science as a Vocation," in H. H. Gerth and C. Wright Mills [eds. and translators], From Max Weber: Essays in Sociology [New York, 1958], pp. 136ff.). —ed.*

[2] *Mr. Slutzky arrived from Washington just a few moments before he was scheduled to speak; he and I shared the platform.—ed.*

[3] *For the activities of this organization, see pp. 250–251.—ed.*

10:45 P.M.[4] Closing Remarks by Dr. Josef E. Garai, Assistant Professor of Psychology, Pratt Institute.

In case Erich Fromm will be able to address the meeting, one of the speakers with a viewpoint sympathetic to his will make room for him.[5]

Each speaker is allowed a maximum time of thirty minutes to provide twenty minutes for a question-and-answer period from the audience. Chairmen will rigorously enforce time requirements to permit each speaker to state his point of view.

Chairmen of the teach-in are:

—6:10 Josef Garai, Department of Social Studies, Pratt
—9:10 Jacob Landau, Chairman of the Department of Graphic Art, Pratt Institute
0–11:00 Helmut Gruber, Associate Professor of History, Polytechnic Institute of Brooklyn.

The participants in the teach-in are requested to observe the usual decorum of academic learning and to listen to all speakers regardless of their disagreements with any views enunciated. The teach-in is designed to assist students and faculty in obtaining more profound understanding of the issues and the dangers inherent in the present political situation.

Militancy of the National Liberation Front (March 1965) *

For more than ten years now, the U.S. imperialists have continuously interfered in, and committed aggression against, South Vietnam. Of late, they have brought into South Vietnam many more units of U.S. combat troops composed of missle units, marines, B-57 strategic bombers, together with mercenary troops from South Korea, Taiwan, the Philippines, Australia, Malaya, etc. They even frenziedly ordered the air

[4] *The early closing time makes this teach-in atypical; usually they last all night long, or even longer. See Mitchel Levitas, "Vietnam Comes to Oregon U." New York Times Magazine (May 9, 1965).—ed.*

[5] *Fromm, after having indicated that he might come to the teach-in, was finally not able to make it.—ed.*

* Statement of the Central Committee of the South Vietnam National Liberation Front (March 22, 1965), in *Vietnam Courier: Information and Documents* [Hanoi], no. 23 (April 3, 1965).

forces of the U. S. A. and its henchmen to conduct repeated air raids on North Vietnam and Laos. At present, not only are they stubbornly stepping up their criminal aggressive war in South Vietnam but are also attempting to fan up the flames of war throughout Indochina and Southeast Asia.

The puppet administration, hangers-on of the U. S. A., in South Vietnam is daily committing more heinous crimes against the country. The impudent traitors are kowtowing before the aggressors and are bringing in snakes to kill chickens of the home coop, inviting troops of the United States and many of its satellite countries to come to South Vietnam to massacre our people, occupy and trample the territory of our sacred fatherland, and oppress and exploit our people most harshly.

The Vietnamese people and the people throughout Indochina and Southeast Asia and peace- and justice-loving people all over the world are highly indignant at, and strongly protest against, the criminal warmongering and aggressive acts of the U.S. imperialists.

Faced with the present situation of utmost gravity, the South Vietnam National Front for Liberation deems it necessary to reaffirm once again in a formal way its unswerving will to carry out the war of resistance against the U.S. imperialists.

1—The U.S. imperialists are the saboteurs of the Geneva Agreements, the most brazen warmongers and aggressors and the sworn enemy of the Vietnamese people.

As is known to everyone, in their extremely glorious war of resistance the Vietnamese people defeated the aggression of the French colonialists and the intervention and assistance of the U.S. imperialists. In fact, during the past war of resistance of the Vietnamese people the U.S. imperialists supplied to the French colonialists 2,600 million dollars, hundreds of thousands of tons of weapons, and 200 military advisers to frustrate the aspiration for independence and freedom of the Vietnamese people. However, with their undauntedness and their determination to die rather than be enslaved, their courage and their staunch resolve to fight, and due to the wholehearted support of the people throughout the world, the heroic Vietnamese people won great victories, liberated half of their beloved country from the clutches of the enemy, which led to the conclusion of an international agreement in Geneva in 1954 formally recognizing the sovereignty, independence, and territorial integrity of Vietnam, Laos, and Cambodia, restoring peace in this area, and laying the basis for the reunification of Vietnam by peaceful means.[1]

The Vietnamese people are deeply aware of the value of these Agreements. Now as in the past they have been correctly implementing these Agreements and are resolved to have these Agreements implemented in their spirit and letters as all international agreements with full legal validity should be. On the contrary, the U.S. imperialists and their henchmen in South Vietnam have step by step and daily more brazenly trampled on the Geneva Agreements and have in fact scrapped them. They have brazenly conducted an atrocious war of aggression in South Vietnam during the past eleven years in an attempt to enslave and oppress the South Vietnamese people, turn South Vietnam into one of their colonies and military bases, and perpetuate the division of Vietnam.

Hardly had the ink dried on the Geneva Agreements when the U.S. imperialists hastily dragged their henchmen satellites into setting up the SEATO military bloc and brazenly placed South Vietnam in the "protection" area of this bloc, which amounted in reality to putting South Vietnam under the command of the United States. Ever since, the U. S. A. has undertaken deeper and more and more cynical intervention in South Vietnam.

From the end of 1954 to 1959 the U.S. imperialists and the puppet Ngo Dinh Diem Administration carried out repeated barbarous terrorist raids and operations. . . . In order to step up their large-scale and barbarous raids, the U.S. imperialists and their henchmen enacted the fascist law 10/59,[2] outlawing the South Vietnamese people and all other political groupings and individuals who opposed them and whom they termed "Communists". At the same time, they dragged the guillotine all over South Vietnam. In this period, according to incomplete figures, the U.S. hangmen and their henchmen massacred or detained hundreds of thousands of patriots in

[1] *See pp. 137–154 for the text of these Agreements.—ed.*
[2] *See pp. 256–262 for the text of this law.—ed.*

South Vietnam for the only reason that they struggled for peace and demanded the execution of the Geneva Agreements, demanded the consultative conference on general elections to reunify the country, or simply because they refused to submit to them.

The criminal acts of the U.S. imperialists and their henchmen naturally stirred up the flames of hatred throughout Vietnam and roused a seething indignation throughout the world. Public opinion in Vietnam and Asia and the honest public opinion all over the five continents severely condemned the tyrannical acts of the U.S. imperialists and their henchmen and raised its voice to demand that they stop their warlike and aggressive activities against the South Vietnamese people and correctly implement the 1954 Geneva Agreements.

During the past eleven years, by carrying out a policy of aggressive colonialism in South Vietnam, the U.S. government has poured 4,000 million dollars disguised under the signboard of "aid", more than 80 percent of which has been direct military expenditures.

The aggressive war in South Vietnam has enjoyed the special concern of the U.S. ruling circles. The late U.S. President Kennedy and the present U.S. President Johnson, the U.S. National Security Council, the Defense Department, State Department, and the Central Intelligence Agency have daily been following all developments in South Vietnam. Honolulu has become the site for regular monthly meetings of the ringleaders of the White House, Pentagon, and the U.S. generals in the Pacific area to discuss plans of invading South Vietnam. . . .

To cover up their piratical nature, the U.S. imperialists have resorted to deceitful signboards which nevertheless cannot fool the world's peoples. It is necessary to recall that the so-called "White Paper" [3] recently issued by Washington carries no conviction at all. This clumsy thief-crying-stop-thief trick has thrown more light on their intention to intensify and expand their aggressive war. At present, the fact in South Vietnam is that the U.S. imperialists are waging a criminal aggressive war, that the U.S. imperialists are the most impudent saboteurs of the Geneva Agreements, the

³ See pp. 284–316—ed.

most dangerous war provocateurs and aggressors, and the sworn enemy [sic] of the peoples of Vietnam, Indochina, and of the other peoples of the world.

> 2—*The heroic South Vietnamese people are resolved to drive out the U.S. imperialists in order to liberate South Vietnam, achieve an independent, democratic, peaceful, and neutral South Vietnam and eventual national reunification.*

The South Vietnamese people have always cherished peace, but are determined not to sit with folded arms and let the U.S. aggressors and their henchmen do what they like and let them trample upon their homeland and ride on them. They had rather die than be enslaved. The fourteen million valiant South Vietnamese people have stood up as one man in a gallant struggle to defeat the U.S. aggressors and their traitors so as to liberate South Vietnam, achieve independence, democracy, peace, and neutrality in South Vietnam, in contribution to the maintenance of peace in Indochina and Southeast Asia.

The patriotic war of the South Vietnamese people is fully consistent with the most elementary and basic principles of international law concerning the people's rights to self-determination and to wage a patriotic and self-defense war against foreign aggression.

In their sacred liberation war, the South Vietnamese people have used all kinds of weapons to fight against the enemy. The chief and biggest arms supplier for the South Vietnamese people's armed forces is nobody else than the U.S. imperialists themselves who have sustained heavy and repeated setbacks over the past years.

From scratch the South Vietnamese people have built a great fortune and recorded extremely glorious military exploits. They are firmly convinced that thanks to their own strength and the wholehearted support of the peoples throughout the world, they will certainly win complete victory. The U.S. imperialists and their lackeys are at the end of their tether. They are being swept off by the powerful storm of the South Vietnamese people's revolution and they still are only writhing in the throes of death. To retrieve that serious situation, the U.S. imperialists are blindly taking the risk of embarking headlong on extremely dangerous military adventures.

The fact that the U.S. imperialists have dispatched to South Vietnam more weapons and combat troops . . . is no indication of their strength, but only of the frenzied behavior of a truculent enemy who has gone out of his senses. It can intimidate nobody. . . .

The South Vietnamese people want to tell the U.S. imperialists and their agents this:

At present, the only way for you, U.S. imperialists, is to pull out of South Vietnam. If you stubbornly continue plunging headlong into the war you will sustain the biggest and most shameful failures. On behalf of the fourteen million valiant South Vietnamese people, the South Vietnam National Front for Liberation solemnly declares: The South Vietnamese people and their armed forces are resolved never to lose hold of their arms so long as they have not reached these goals of theirs: independence, democracy, peace, and neutrality. The South Vietnamese people are determined to go on dealing thunder blows at the U.S. aggressors and their lackeys, and they will surely win final victory. All negotiations with the U.S. imperialists at this moment are entirely useless if they still refuse to withdraw from South Vietnam all their troops and all kinds of war materials and means and those of their satellites, if they still do not dismantle all their military bases in South Vietnam, if the traitors still surrender the South Vietnamese people's sacred rights to independence and democracy to the U.S. imperialists, and if the South Vietnam National Front for Liberation—the only genuine representative of the fourteen million South Vietnamese people—does not have its decisive say.

> 3—*The valiant South Vietnamese people and the South Vietnam liberation army are resolved to fully accomplish their sacred duty to drive out the U.S. imperialists so as to liberate South Vietnam and defend North Vietnam.*

Vietnam is one, the Vietnamese people are one. North and South Vietnam are of the same family. This sentiment is higher than mountains and deeper than the sea. This truth is like the sun rising in the East and cannot be shaken by any force whatsoever. In the present state of blood and fire, in a life-and-death struggle against the U.S. imperialists and their lackeys, the heart cannot but feel a pain when the hand is cut. That the people in North Vietnam are resolved to fulfil their duty toward their kith and kin in South Vietnam is just sense and reason.

On behalf of the fourteen million South Vietnamese people, the South Vietnam National Front for Liberation conveys to their seventeen million relatives in the North their steel-like confidence and unchanging pledge: "The heroic South Vietnamese people and the South Vietnam liberation army are determined to fully accomplish their sacred duty to drive out the U.S. imperialists, liberate South Vietnam, and defend the North, with a view to the reunification of their fatherland."

Recently, to escape from their critical situation and their inevitable collapse in South Vietnam, the U. S. imperialists and their flunkeys recklessly sent aircraft and warships to bomb, strafe, and shell North Vietnam, but they have received due punishment. Over fifty American jet planes have been shot down. The South Vietnam army and people greatly rejoice at, and warmly hail, those brilliant feats of arms of the North Vietnam army and people.

The heart feels a pain when the hand is cut! To defend the beloved North, the army and people of the South have given vent to their anger at the U. S. aggressors and their agents. If the U.S. imperialists lay hands upon the North of our fatherland once, the army and people of the South are resolved to strike twice or thrice as hard at them.

In February, while the aggressors and traitors attacked the North, in the South the liberation army launched stormy attacks on important enemy military bases and main forces, putting out of action 20,706 enemy troops (among them nearly 600 U.S. aggressors killed, wounded, and captured), seizing 4,144 guns of various kinds, and shooting down, damaging, or destroying 111 aircraft of various types.

The South Vietnam National Front for Liberation warns the U. S. imperialists and the Vietnamese traitors: As you have not been able to vanquish the fourteen million people of South Vietnam, give up all hope of defeating the more than thirty million people of Vietnam. Your military adventure and war expansion definitely cannot help you out of your quagmire, and instead will lead you quickly to a sort of suicide. . . .

The South Vietnam National Front for Liberation and the South Vietnamese people warn the U. S. imperialists and their lackeys: Should you dare expand the aggressive war to the whole of Vietnam and fan up the flames of war in the whole of Indochina, the invincible strength of the more than thirty million people of Vietnam and the strength to move mountains and drain up seas of the hundreds of millions of people in Indo-china and Asia will wipe you out and bury you.

> 4—*The South Vietnamese people express their profound gratitude to the wholehearted support of the peace-and justice-loving people all over the world and declare their readiness to receive all assistance, including weapons and all other war materials from their friends in the five continents.*

The just and patriotic struggle of the South Vietnamese people has enjoyed the sympathy, support, and encouragement of the peace-and-justice-loving people throughout the world. Not only have the world peoples supported the South Vietnamese people morally, but have also assisted and are assisting them materially. Of course the South Vietnamese people and their representative—the South Vietnam National Front for Liberation—are fully entitled to accept, and greatly appreciate, such valuable assistance.

The South Vietnam National Front for Liberation has always relied mainly on its own strength and capacity, but it is ready to accept all assistance both moral and material, including weapons and all other war materials from all the Socialist countries, the Nationalist countries, as well as all the international organizations, and peace-loving people the world over. Besides, the Front reserves for itself the right to buy weapons and war materials from other countries to strengthen the potential of its self-defense war. . . .

The South Vietnam National Front for Liberation will [also] call on the peoples of various countries to send young men and army men to South Vietnam to fight shoulder-to-shoulder with the South Vietnamese people and together annihilate the common enemy.

While the U. S. imperialists are constantly sowing suffering and death in South Vietnam, the South Vietnam National Front for Liberation, if need be, cannot but call back the sons and daughters of South Vietnam who regrouped to the North in observance of the cease-fire agreement and who have had to live far from South Vietnam during ten long years, to take arms to annihilate the enemy to save their country and homes.

A Vietnamese proverb says: "To peel the thick skin of a mandarin there must be a sharp fingernail." The invincible fingernail of the Vietnamese people and the peace-loving people all over the world decidedly will not leave the U. S. imperialists and their lackeys unpunished. They will have to bear all the extremely serious consequences arising from their aggressive and warlike actions.

Once again, on behalf of the fourteen million people of South Vietnam, the Central Committee of the South Vietnam National Front for Liberation expresses deep gratitude to the peoples of the Socialist countries, the Nationalist countries, the international organizations, and the peace-and-justice-loving people throughout the world who have wholeheartedly supported the just, patriotic war of resistance of the South Vietnamese people. More than ever we consider it our glorious internationalist duty to devote all our energy and make every sacrifice to contribute a worthy share to the very great common cause of struggle of all nations to defend independence, democracy, peace, and social progress in Indochina, Southeast Asia, and all over the world and to defeat the international gendarme—the warlike and aggressive U. S. imperialists.

> 5—*The whole people to unite, the whole people to take up arms, to continue to march forward heroically, and to resolve to fight and to defeat the U.S. aggressors and Vietnamese traitors.*

The armed struggle waged by the South Vietnamese people against the U. S. aggressors and their henchmen has won very great victories. The U. S. imperialists and their lackeys are formidable in appearance but are inwardly very weak and very confused and more isolated than ever. The South Vietnamese people, bearing in mind their vow "rather to die than to be enslaved," will definitely smash the barbarous and predatory enemy.

The South Vietnam National Front for Liberation and the South Vietnamese people not only have justice on their side but have also developed and are developing rapidly their material and organizational strength. They have been and are the glorious victors. The more they fight the stronger they become and the more numerous and greater their victories.

We are worthy successors to, and have upheld to a high degree, the Dienbienphu tradition and the heroic tradition of the Vietnamese nation credited with 4,000 years of history against the invaders. Moreover, the South Vietnam National Front for Liberation and the South Vietnamese people are fighting heroically in the extremely favorable conditions of the present era, that of the revolutionary rising tide of the oppressed nations in Asia, Africa, and Latin America. The Socialist countries and the forces of democracy and peace all over the world are an important factor stimulating the advance of mankind, overwhelming and annihilating imperialism and colonialism of all brands. If the U. S. imperialists and their henchmen are rash enough to spread the flames of war all over Indochina, the people of this area and Southeast Asia are resolved to stand up as one man and sweep them out into the ocean.

The South Vietnamese people and their only genuine representative—the South Vietnam National Front for Liberation —will undoubtedly win final victory. . . .

Even if we are to carry out the struggle for ten, twenty years or longer and have to suffer greater difficulties and hardships, we are prepared and resolved to fight and fight to the end until not a single U. S. soldier can be seen in our country.

The Vietnamese people's history is thousands of years old. That is the heroic history of a heroic nation. During the past ten years of fighting against the U. S. imperialist aggressors and their quislings, the people and liberation armed forces of South Vietnam have written a golden page in the glorious history of their people. We have won and we are winning; the U. S. imperialists and their agents have lost and are losing. This proves that our strength is invincible, that the U. S. aggressors and their agents are weak. If we have triumphed over the U. S. during the past ten years, we are now provided with far more favorable conditions to defeat them. If the U. S. aggressors and their lackeys have been defeated during the past ten years, they are now all the weaker and will suffer heavier defeats. Especially if the U. S. imperialists extend the war to the North, they will certainly incur more shameful defeats.

We are absolutely confident that victory belongs to us.

We are determined to fight, hit vigorously and accurately at the U. S. aggressors and their quislings to liberate the South, defend the North, and reunify our fatherland.

"Johnson's Swindle Will Certainly Fail"

BY HOANG QUOC VIET*

. . . U.S. President Lyndon Johnson [has] spread the smokescreen of independence, freedom, peace, and negotiations in an attempt to whitewash the towering crimes and aggressive and war-seeking policy of the U.S. imperialists in Vietnam.

Johnson said that the United States is in South Vietnam to oppose aggression by foreign countries. The truth is that, throughout the past twenty years, the U.S. imperialists have never ceased to carry out their scheme to invade Vietnam. In December 1945 President Roosevelt declared that it was necessary to entrust to the United Nations the right to administer the Indochinese countries, and schemed to use the United Nations to invade Vietnam, Cambodia, and Laos. Afterward, the U.S. imperialists intervened in the Indochina War, helped the French colonialists with money, weapons, and even military advisers and war plans to prolong that dirty aggressive war.

After the French colonialists were defeated and ousted from Vietnam, for the past ten or more years the sole foreign country present in South Vietnam has been that of the interventionist and aggressive U.S. imperialists. Opposing that intervention and aggression are the heroic fourteen million South Vietnamese people united under the patriotic banner of the NFLSV. To slander North Vietnam with carrying out aggression against South Vietnam is a trick of "thief crying stop thief" that cannot deceive anybody!

Johnson said that the United States is in South Vietnam because it must keep its pledge to defend the independence of South Vietnam.

But the essence of the 1954 Geneva Agreements is the

* Chairman of the Standing Committee of the International Conference for Solidarity with the Vietnamese People, Against U.S. Imperialist Aggression, and for the Defense of Peace. The selection is from the Hanoi daily paper *Nhan Dan* (April 21, 1965), as broadcast the same day by Radio Hanoi.

recognition of the independence, sovereignty, unity, and territorial integrity of Vietnam. These agreements clearly stipulate that the 17th Parallel is only a temporary military demarcation line and should not in any way be interpreted as constituting a political or territorial boundary, and that by 1956 Vietnam should be reunified through nationwide free general elections.

It is starkly clear that the Geneva Agreements recognize that Vietnam is a single territory from Langson to Point Cameau, as it has always been. Yet, the U.S. imperialists intervened in South Vietnam, set up there a stooge administration, rigged up the so-called Republic of Vietnam in an attempt to divide united Vietnam into two different states. To sabotage the unity of Vietnam, the U.S. imperialists have completely violated the Geneva Agreements.

They have deliberately forgotten their pledge to refrain from infringing upon those agreements, and instead made a pledge with the traitors to the people and the nation who oppose the entire Vietnamese people.

If Johnson wants to return to the 1954 Geneva Agreements as he declared, then the United States should immediately withdraw its troops and weapons from South Vietnam and respect the independence, sovereignty, unity, and territorial integrity of Vietnam. That is the basic condition to restore peace in Indochina.

Johnson said the United States is in South Vietnam to defend freedom in Asia and to strengthen world order. Clearly the U.S. Government has bluntly declared its vicious design to bring the world under its sway and has installed itself as an international gendarme. With that vicious design, wherever they go, the U.S. imperialists sabotage independence and freedom and plunder the people and provoke war instead of defending freedom and order for anybody!

The peoples of Asia and of the world have all along shouted in their face, "U.S. imperialists, go home!"

Peace, Negotiations, and the Bait of Aid

Johnson said that the United States desires peace and seeks no wider war, but the truth is that every day U.S. troops, U.S. planes, U.S. guns, U.S. napalm bombs, and U.S. poison gases are killing South Vietnamese people! The truth is that almost daily U.S. aircraft and warships have attacked North Vietnam! The truth is that right after Johnson harped about peace, the U.S. continued to introduce large numbers of aircraft and two more U.S. marine battalions into South Vietnam. Many U.S. generals and other senior officers have gone to Honolulu to discuss the intensification of the aggressive war in South Vietnam and fan up the flames of war to the whole of Vietnam. Condemned by public opinion, Johnson tried to plead that if the United States continued bombing the DRV it was because the United States had been attacked. But the Vietnamese people, who live tens of thousands of kilometers away from the United States, have never done anything that harms the security of the United States. Instead, it is precisely the United States which has come from tens of thousands of kilometers away from Vietnam to attack Vietnam, has conducted an aggressive war against South Vietnam, and has provoked war against North Vietnam!

Johnson further lied that the U.S. attacks on the DRV were aimed at military targets, and not to massacre the people, that they were carefully limited. But everybody knows that the so-called military targets attacked by the United States in North Vietnam are populated areas, villages, provincial capitals, townships, schools, markets, and even churches and hospitals!

Everybody knows that the United States is carrying out a so-called escalation, leap-frogging plan, gradually increasing the tempo of attacks, climbing from one parallel to another, expanding the war to North Vietnam, and even provoking the CPR [*Chinese Peoples' Republic*]!

Johnson said the United States was ready for unconditional discussion next week, tomorrow, or tonight. But what does that so-called readiness for unconditional discussions mean? It means that the United States completely ignores, does not recognize the NFLSV, the sole legitimate representative of the South Vietnamese people, which has the right to participate in the settlement of the South Vietnam problem.

It also means that in Johnson's opinion the South Vietnamese, although they are winning, should unconditionally lay down their arms and stop opposing U.S. aggression! That they station troops and set up military bases in South Vietnam, and maintain there a puppet regime and prolong the partition of Vietnam!

It means that the United States should be allowed to bolster up the forces of the United States and their stooges, which are weakening and disintegrating, so that the United States will be able to continue sabotaging the independence, sovereignty, unity, and territorial integrity of Vietnam, continue sabotaging peace in Indochina and Southeast Asia!

If the Vietnamese people do not accept these conditions, then, in Johnson's views, the United States would not withdraw, instead would use force and talk with guns and planes, regarding it as a necessary part of the surest road to peace.

Johnson repeatedly said the United States will remain in South Vietnam as long as necessary, whatever the risk and whatever the cost.

Really, these are arguments of corsairs, fallacious yet stupid! The U.S. imperialists think they can cow the Vietnamese people and deceive the world's people! But the Vietnamese people are a heroic people; they have never retreated before any aggressor, however truculent he might be. Profoundly indignant at the U.S. imperialists, the South Vietnamese people are dealing staggering blows at the U.S. aggressors and have driven them into a state of defeat, of being bogged down and of stalemate in South Vietnam.

The North Vietnamese people have resolutely hit back at the U.S. aggressors and have brought down over 200 U.S. aircraft during their raids on North Vietnam.

The world's people are still more angry at seeing clearly that the U.S. imperialists are trying by all means to hold on to South Vietnam in an attempt to turn it into a new-type colony and military base of the United States. . . .

More ridiculous still, Johnson tried to dangle his dollars before the eyes of the Vietnamese and other peoples of Southeast Asia! He said: The United States will earmark one billion dollars as an effort toward cooperation for the development of the Southeast Asian region, and hopes that North Vietnam would join in that effort!

He thought that the Vietnamese people and the other peoples of Southeast Asia have the same mood as the U.S. monopoly capitalists, that their eyes are dimmed by the sight of dollars, and that they are ready to sell off their independence and freedom and their fatherland!

Really, he cannot understand how the revolutionary people prize justice and slight money! . . .

Johnson's Swindle Laid Bare

Johnson's recent speeches reflect the cunning U.S. double dealing policy of brandishing a sword while paying at the same time, and expose the ugly, aggressive, and bellicose features of the U.S. imperialists. They also reflect the inevitable bog and failure of the United States in Vietnam, its isolation and embarrassment before world public opinion, and its dismay in face of the antiwar movement which is surging ever more powerfully among the American people.

Johnson may repeat such things many times again but he cannot deceive the people of the world. Clear-sighted opinion in all countries is laying bare Johnson's swindle. In the United States itself, to protest against the aggressive and bellicose policy of the U.S. Government, 8,000 representatives of the American people of all strata on April 10 demonstrated in front of the U. N. Headquarters. Seven days later, over 20,000 American youths, students, and other people held a protest demonstration in front of the White House. These were slaps in Johnson's hypocritical face! [1]

. . . Through their own experiences, the Vietnamese people have long seen clearly the aggressive and bellicose nature of the U.S. imperialists, regarding them as the chieftain of the most reckless warmongering imperialists, the most dangerous neocolonialists, international gendarmes, and war criminals, the number one enemy of peace and freedom, and the common enemy of the peoples all over the world.

The allegations spread by Johnson . . . have thrown more light on the U.S. stubborn policy of continuing its aggression in South Vietnam and conducting acts of war against the DRV. In the face of this arrogant attitude, the Vietnamese people are still more determined to oppose the U.S. imperialists. So long as the U.S. imperialists refuse to get out of South Vietnam and continue attacking socialist North Vietnam and encroaching upon the independence and freedom of the Vietnamese people, the Vietnamese people will fight against them, unite millions as one man, and are resolved to defeat the U.S. aggressors, as President Ho Chi Minh has said.

[1] *Much is made by Radio Hanoi of expressions of dissent such as these. But even Barry Goldwater's statements about the war are cited as proof that dissatisfaction with the war exists in the U.S. See Radio Hanoi (October 2, 1964).—ed.*

Only One Solution to the Vietnam Problem

In his speech on April 10 at the National Assembly, President Ho Chi Minh once again reiterated the unswerving stand of the Government of the DRV and the Vietnamese people, that is, to resolutely defend Vietnam's independence, sovereignty, unity, and territorial integrity. Vietnam is one, the Vietnamese people are one, nobody is allowed to infringe upon this sacred right of our people. The U.S. imperialists must respect the Geneva Agreements and withdraw from South Vietnam! That is the only measure to solve the problem of war in Vietnam, to carry out the 1954 Geneva Agreements to defend the peace of Indochinese and Southeast Asian countries. There is no other solution. That is the answer of our people and government to the U.S. imperialists.

The stand is a fully just one because it fully conforms to the 1954 Geneva Agreements, to international law, to the interests of peace and national independence, and to the interests and honor of the American people. It is also in keeping with the resolutions on Vietnam adopted by the international conference held in November last year in Hanoi.

If the U.S. imperialists, blinded by their selfish interests, stubbornly follow the path of intensifying and expanding their aggressive war in Vietnam, they not only cannot get out of their present stalemate, but they will also invite upon themselves even heavier defeats.

Seeing clearly through Johnson's deceitful maneuvers and criminal acts, and approving the correct stand of the Government of the DRV and the Vietnamese people, the delegates who took part in the international conference in November 1964 in Hanoi as well as the peace- and justice-loving governments, organizations, and individuals in the world, including the American people, will certainly give stronger and stronger support to the just struggle of the Vietnamese people against U.S. imperialist aggression and step up further the mass movements of struggle to demand that the U.S. imperialists withdraw from South Vietnam, stop their acts of war against the DRV, and observe and scrupulously implement the 1954 Geneva Agreements on Vietnam.

With the solidarity and support of the socialist countries, of the people of Indochina and Southeast Asia, and the world's people as a whole, including the American people, more than thirty million Vietnamese people, united as one and determined to fight to the end, will surely defeat the U.S. aggressors, liberate the South, defend the North with a view to the reunification of the country, defend an outpost of the socialist camp, win a big victory for the national liberation movement in Asia, Africa, and Latin America, and contribute to the safeguarding of peace in Southeast Asia and the world.

" 'Escalation' Means Getting Closer and Closer to the Grave": Mainland China's Warning (April 1965)*

Each time the Johnson Administration chants from its "peace" script, it pours oil on its war of aggression in Vietnam. This has become a rule.

On April 19, two days after Johnson in his new statement declared that "the window to peace is still open," U. S. military chieftains called an emergency meeting in Honolulu to plot further expansion of the war.

The U. S. officials tried their utmost to describe the conference as "routine," declaring that the chief subject under discussion was nothing more than the expansion of their puppet troops in South Vietnam. But who will believe this? If this were true, why did the U. S. Defense Secretary and the Chairman of the U. S. Joint Chiefs of Staff take the trouble to attend the meeting? Why did the chiefs of the U. S. Navy, Army, and Air Force in the Pacific region find it necessary to take part? In fact, as the Western press reported, there was "an examination of the whole spectrum of Vietnamese war" at the meeting, and "the conference aims to put into effect various decisions designed to 'escalate' military operations in Vietnam." According to initial disclosures, the United States will continue to send more ground forces to South Vietnam, extend air raids against North Vietnam, dispatch more aircraft carriers to the Pacific, and increase air reconnaissance flights over China. McNamara even openly announced after the conference that the United States will

---

* Editorial in *Renmin Ribao* (April 24, 1965) in *Peking Review*, VIII (April 30, 1965), pp. 13-14.

step up its blockade of Vietnam's coastline.

There are many indications that the Honolulu conference was called by the United States to plan an even bigger military adventure after its war, blackmail, and peace hoax had failed, and that the conference represented the desperate struggle of the U. S. aggressors at a time when they face a more and more unfavorable situation.

The U. S. imperialist war machine is operating at an increased tempo. It can be predicted that the Johnson Administration will continue to lay down its peace smokescreen. War expansion, peace fraud, and then war expansion again —these two tactics will be employed alternatively in a pattern of cyclical repetition. This is the customary practice of the Johnson Administration on the Vietnam question.

Let us take a look at the Johnson Administration's record over more than the past two months.

On February 7, big U. S. air raids against North Vietnam started when the White House was trying strenuously to show that the United States "seeks no wider war." At about the same time, a U. S. battalion of Hawk missiles was introduced into South Vietnam.

On February 18, the U. S. State Department declared that the United States was exploring "all avenues of peaceful settlement." Immediately, Washington ordered the direct participation of the U. S. air force in the assault against the South Vietnamese people's armed forces and decided to increase the number of puppet troops by another 100,000 and send several hundred more U. S. military "advisers." Shortly afterward, the United States announced the dispatching of two battalions of marines, the first contingent of marines to be sent to South Vietnam. What the United States was exploring turned out to be an avenue to war expansion.

On March 7, Rusk spread the speculation that for the United States the "political channels" to the solution of the Vietnam question "remain open." Four days later, U. S. planes began to extend their bombing deeper into the interior of North Vietnam. Then, six days afterward, 2,000 South Korean mercenaries arrived in South Vietnam. In fact, the United States was widening the channel to war further.

On March 25, Johnson issued a statement boasting that the United States "will never be second in seeking a settlement." Right after these high-sounding words were mouthed,

U. S. air strikes against North Vietnam went farther than the 20th Parallel.

On April 7, Johnson, in his Baltimore address, expressed his willingness to conduct "unconditional discussions" on the Vietnam question in order to achieve a "peaceful settlement." But only three days later, the United States sent its second contingent of two battalions of marines and a squadron of naval jet planes to South Vietnam. U. S. planes even carried out provocation against China by intruding into the airspace over Hainan Island.

In face of this series of iron-clad facts, even the most slow-witted person will not believe that the Johnson Administration is really concerned about peace rather than expanding step by step its war of aggression in Vietnam. By its own increasingly truculent military actions, U. S. imperialism has torn off its "peaceful settlement" mask and slapped those who have made Herculean efforts to describe the U. S. Government as "restrained" and "prudent" in the face.

Therefore, when Johnson in his April 17 statement talked glibly about "window to peace" and "come to the meeting room—we will be there," we knew what U. S. imperialism was up to. Sure enough, into the "war room" of the U. S. Pacific military command two days later walked McNamara, the U. S. Defense Secretary, followed by a group of top-ranking military officers. The subject discussed was an even more adventurous step to expand the war.

For more than two months, the Johnson Administration has professed repeatedly that its military action of aggression against Vietnam is "appropriate," "measured," and "carefully limited." But the actual facts are that the United States, from sending "advisers" to South Vietnam, has gone on to taking a direct part in the war; from aggression in the South to attacks on the North; from bombing raids south of the 18th Parallel to bombing raids north of the 20th Parallel; from day raids to round-the-clock raids; and from bombing of military targets to bombing of civilians. All this shows that what the Johnson Administration called "appropriate," "measured," and "carefully limited" military action is a planned gradual expansion of the war.

A so-called theory of "escalation" on the unleashing of an aggressive war is now prevalent among U. S. ruling groups.

They divide a war into a number of thresholds, each consisting of a number of rungs. They have advocated strengthening and expanding the use and threat of force according to these methods. The tactics used by the Johnson Administration are very similar to Hitler's gradual expansion of aggression before World War II. The aim is nothing less than to slacken the vigilance of the world's people, so that they will be faced with a *fait accompli* by the U. S. aggressor before they know it. While taking "escalation" steps, the Johnson Administration continuously waves its olive branch in a vain attempt to demoralize its victims, hoodwink public opinion, and conceal its crimes of deliberately expanding the war. This is precisely what it is doing in Vietnam.

This theory of "escalation" demonstrates that the Johnson Administration is more adventurous than its predecessors. Johnson is so obstinately placing blind faith in force and so feverishly using it that he puts Eisenhower, Kennedy, and their kind to shame. This theory also reflects the weakness of the Johnson Administration. Not daring to rashly launch a big war of aggression, Washington waits to see the response of its victim and world opinion as it measures every step it takes. The Johnson Administration's image is a mixture of gangster and swindler.

This theory of "escalation" owes its existence to the bankruptcy of the U. S. imperialist strategies of "massive retaliation" and "flexible response." Dulles dreamt of forbidding all the oppressed nations and people to rise in revolution by intimidating them with the use of nuclear weapons for "massive retaliation." But faced with the national liberation movement and the people's revolutionary struggle, which have shaken the five continents, U. S. imperialism is at its wit's end. Learning a lesson from the failure of Dulles, Kennedy formulated the strategy of "flexible response." He resorted to "special warfare" in a futile attempt to suppress the national liberation movement and the people's revolutionary struggle. He chose South Vietnam as his testing ground. The result of almost four years' trial of strength is the complete defeat of this "warfare." Foundering in this impasse, U. S. imperialism has cooked up the theory of "escalation" in order to push forward with policies of war and aggression.

Embarking on the military adventure of "escalation," the

Johnson Administration is attempting to save itself from defeat in South Vietnam. But confronted by the people of the world, who are daring to struggle and to win, any use or threat of force by U. S. imperialism is futile, no matter what force, what threat of force is used, or on what rung it takes place. This theory has been tested in Vietnam for months. The result is that U. S. imperialism is faring worse, not better, there. Even the noted U. S. bourgeois commentator Lippmann has admitted that U. S. imperialist bombing of North Vietnam, far from "doing what it is supposed to do," has greatly strengthened the Vietnamese people's "will to fight on." The U. S. imperialist road of "escalation" is one gradually leading to the grave. Lying ahead is not an arch of triumph, but a dark hell of death.

"The window to peace" opened by Johnson in his April 17 statement has been shrouded in the dark clouds of war rising from Honolulu. Facing U. S. imperialism, teacher by negative example, the world's people know that when the Johnson Administration goes out of its way to preach "peace," this only demonstrates intensified efforts to press ahead with steps to expand the war. They know even more clearly that it is completely reasonable for the Vietnamese people to insist on their four-point proposition. If U. S. imperialism refuses to withdraw all its armed forces from Vietnam, there will be no peace in Vietnam and Indochina, no matter how many times Johnson may repeat his words of "peace." The most important task of the people of Asia and the rest of the world today is to give resolute support to the Vietnamese people's just struggle against U. S. aggression and for national salvation, to shatter Johnson's peace-talk schemes completely, curb his plans for escalating the war, and drive the U. S. aggressors out of Vietnam.

The Situation in Vietnam

BY MAX CLOS*

The bar on the fifth floor of the Hotel Majestic in Saigon overlooks the harbor. At night from time to time muffled explosions can be heard from the other side of the river.

* French journalist, correspondent for the Associated Press (1950–1963), *Le Monde* (1953–1955), *Figaro* (1965–), has reported from Cuba, the Congo, and North Africa, as well as from Indochina. The selection is from *Le Figaro Litteraire*

From time to time a brilliant flare shoots up and glitters for some minutes. What we have again is a probe by a Vietcong patrol.

Some young American officers with crewcuts and with the red patch of their Vietnamese parachute battalion tilted over the ear are drinking whiskey amid peals of laughter. They are charming and just like the French officers who ten years ago were sitting in the same place recounting their exploits in the rice paddies and in the jungles.

Don't they know that this war is lost, that their deaths will accomplish nothing, that their hardships are useless and their sacrifice without point, that we have seen the start of the usual comedy of threatening statements which are the prelude to settlement talks? Probably not. It is no doubt part of the charm of young officers that to the very end they do not realize that their death in Vietnam will be futile.

The Can Tho area seventy-five miles southwest of Saigon is one of the most far gone of the delta. A night operation is in progress. For three days the Vietnamese battalion has slogged through the mud without finding anything. Some villages were burnt, some hundreds of scared peasants were terrorized, and to vary the menu a certain number of chickens and black pigs which squeal unbelievably shrilly have been commandeered. And then just when everyone thinks that it is all over the leading company is ambushed. In a flash: eight dead and thirty wounded. Night has fallen. Nearby the day's dead, already turned gray, are piled up under canvas. I was seated at the side of an old friend, a colonel in the Vietnamese army. Let us call him X.

"The Americans," he said, "are jaunty fellows, but they are inexperienced. Like a young dog they wish to dig out everything. The sad thing is that here the war does not obey the rules of the textbooks and of the manuals. My corporal knew perfectly well that if we went in a certain direction we would find a 'bone.' My people were not eager to go, but the Americans insisted." X used his fingers to show the number of dead, saying, "This was the result."

"The truth is," he said, sipping a cup of coffee, "that the game is up. We are fed up with this war now, and no one

(March 3, 1965), translated by Molly Kealy and inserted in the *Congressional Record* [April 21, 1965], pp. 7860-7862) by Sen. Wayne Morse.

wants to prolong the killing. Take me. I've been in the army for twenty years. If I were given a choice between stars and a discharge, I'd take the discharge without a moment's delay. You know wars are not won with men who think of only one thing: to become civilians again."

The relations between Vietnamese and American officers are cool, not to use a worse term. The Vietnamese are critical of the Americans for understanding little or nothing about this war. The Americans often have a poor opinion of the Vietnamese generals, find their officers mediocre and their soldiers without stomach for combat.

But it is certainly not a matter of the Vietnamese lacking physical courage. At the end of the first Indochinese War, practically all of the French units were half "yellow," and most of the officers would agree that combat operations were first-rate. The Vietcong, who attack well-defended positions, are exposed to heavy artillery fire and to the Government's air power, undergo at times frightful ordeals, and always display real courage, if not fanaticism. Their opponents admire them for their courage. And these men, with the exception of a small majority who have come down from the North, are peasants of Indochina who have got their training at places only miles from the American training centers in South Vietnam.

What then is the explanation of the combat inefficiency of the government forces? In a few years, when this war will be over, it will be seen that the American defeat in Vietnam was caused by two things. First, the guerrillas depend not merely on military training and professional skill, but also on the creation of warm personal ties among their men. Second, they make a detailed and exact analysis of the political and social setting and climate in which the war is carried on. In these two areas the second Indochinese War is ending in an American defeat.

In Vietnam the American "advisers" do a job, or, if you prefer, they perform their duty conscientiously. They serve with devotion and competence. But all this is not enough. They are merely guerrilla warfare professionals. The French when they were here made of the Indochinese War a sentimental and romantic adventure. French officers and men fell in love with the country, infected with what Larteguy aptly calls "the yellow sickness." They played their part in a stirring adventure, which, it is true, ended badly, but which gave them a sense of glory. It was because of this that they were able to make contact with the Vietnamese, to form emotional ties with them, and to draw them into that cruel adventure. Contrary to appearances, there exist few peoples more passionate, more sentimental, and more sensitive than the Vietnamese. They have a need to be loved. The stiff ways of the American military, its love for formality, its taste for following military regulations to the letter greatly upset the Vietnamese. The Vietnamese can't understand how a military order can be treated as anything else but a topic for debate and discussion. In this they found that the French often shared their point of view. This divergence in military philosophy creates problems, and in the case of Vietnam it is evident that it has taken its toll.

Intimate contact has never been established between the Vietnamese and the Americans. The French, spellbound with the exotic, took up the Vietnamese way of life. They were delighted with Chinese soups flavored with exotic ingredients, they smoked opium, they organized riproaring parties with their yellow friends, and topped off the night in their company with the girls. This of course was not particularly decent, but what connection is there anyway between decency and war?

The Americans, on the other hand, have tried to introduce puritan morality and the American way of life in Vietnam. At the doors of the hotels restricted to Americans there are signs reading: "Women are forbidden to enter." Their food comes directly from the United States in sealed packages. A recent article written by one of the better American war correspondents describes the Vietnamese war. It is all a matter of bad odors, of food contaminated by the natives, and of the resulting stomachaches. In short, it is a hell from which each American is eager to escape. In Saigon, marine sergeants in mufti sport silk jackets on which you can read embroidered in yellow letters: "When I die I shall go straight to heaven. I have put in my purgatory here."

The 25,000 American advisers live in Vietnam like in the States." At Can Tho, for example, the headquarters for one of the four military districts it is like this: at staff headquarters every Vietnamese office is duplicated by an American opposite number. At 5 P.M. it's closing time, and the Americans return immediately to their compound at the edge of the city. It is a big camp ringed with barbed wire and protected by Vietnamese guards. The lowest private is entitled to quarters of his own furnished with a refrigerator and air conditioning. He has a shower with hot water. A PX supplies him with all that he can desire, from shaving cream to record players, with whiskey in between—all at ridiculously low prices. The bar offers thirty brands to choose from. Every night at eight there is a new movie shown on a wide screen in color at a theater furnished with lounge chairs.

Vietnamese officers are rarely at American messes. It is not that they must eat separately, but Americans and Vietnamese do not enjoy one another's company. I went to the compound at Can Tho with Colonel X, whom I mentioned before. On leaving, he said to me: "I have a feeling these Americans have come from another planet."

Then he told me: "When I came out of school in 1948, I was assigned to a French port unit. The first night at table I was a little shy. I didn't know how to use a fork very well. The CO was a naval lieutenant. He said to me: 'Tell me, X, do you eat with a fork or a pitch-fork?' Afterwards, we made the rounds of the girls together. With the Americans there is no danger that anyone will talk about anything of this kind. No one goes to the girls anymore."

Now there is no objection to movies, hot water, and refrigerators. Except this: If you want to persuade people to join your side, it's not a good idea to set up what in the eyes of the Vietnamese soldiers appears to be excessive luxury.

More or less confused, Nguyen, a Vietnamese GI Joe of the second class, tells himself that it's not normal to see people engaged in the same war treated in such an unequal fashion. He not only says this to himself, but the Vietcong tell it to him. Communication is easy. There are women who act as messengers. They are the ones who spread the good word. They have only simple things to explain. This, for example:

"The Americans whom you see down there in their well-lit compounds are the masters. As for you, you are poorly fed and poorly paid. You are going to die for them—and for nothing."

Nguyen gets 1,750 piastres a month, about eighteen dollars. His lieutenant receives a salary of eighty dollars. Eighteen dollars is not a small sum in Vietnam, but Nguyen thinks he would be more useful in his own village. But it's not only a question of this. Theoretically he is drafted for three years, but this is already the fifth year he's been in uniform. The war continually gets harder. The Vietcong continually are better armed. Life for him is very tough. The Vietcong propaganda says: "Why do you fight us? The war will eventually end. The Americans will leave. Go over the hill now, or do not fight when you are attacked. Keep still, and nothing will happen to you."

Nguyen, to say the least, is upset. He knows his village is controlled by the Vietcong. He knows also that if he is wounded, he will be poorly cared for because there is a scarcity of doctors and medicine. Moreover, the military hospitals are crowded with wounded. They are stacked four and five high under the tarpaulins which extend to the roofs of the hospitals. The wounded painfully line up to go to the latrines, which are always jammed, and to get a drink of water at the scarce fountains. Nguyen knows also that if he loses an arm or a leg, he will be left without any chance to make a living—and he is not more than twenty. So, sometimes, when he is on guard around the compound of the big-shot Americans with their laughter ringing in his ears, he asks himself what he will do if the Vietcong attack.

The Americans are bitter. They have been disillusioned by Vietnam. They say: "These people are incomprehensible. We come here to save them from Communist slavery, and they couldn't care less."

The Americans carry with them their almost insane horror of Communism. They apply here all the fatuous ideas they have on the subject in the States. For them the problem is simple: the Vietnamese are divided neatly into two groups, the Vietcong and the anti-Vietcong, that is, the pro- and the anti-Communists. These two groups, by the iron law of logic and history, cannot but hate each other, and fight each other to the death.

This is unfortunately a mental picture which in Vietnam has little basis in reality.

In the first place the pro- and anti-Vietcong are not isolated from each other. There hardly exists in Vietnam a single family which is not divided between the two factions. It is rare that a Government minister or general does not have one or more relatives more or less close to him on the other side. Between the two sides of the family the ties are not cut. News is exchanged, and sometimes, visits. It is necessary also to take into account the problem of nationalism, which complicates things even more. On this score ambiguity existed all during the first Vietnamese war. Large numbers of anti-Communist Vietnamese fought with the Vietminh, nevertheless, in order to get independence for their country. Today there is a bit of the same problem. The continuous line of Vietcong propaganda is that the Americans have stepped into the shoes of the French, that national independence is again in jeopardy, that the Vietcong fight chiefly to end the interference of the foreigner. You have to be pretty ignorant of the Vietnamese to imagine that this line of argument does not carry weight.

Officially, the American intervention has for its objective "the fight against Communism." This is a notion which to the Vietnamese peasants means absolutely nothing. The Vietcong never mention the subject of Communism. They don't present themselves as the exponents of an ideology. The whole thing is infinitely more simple than that. Their political staff doesn't hold meetings of the peasants to conduct seminars in political theory. What they do is propose concrete solutions to concrete problems. These problems are not difficult to state. They are, in the order of their importance, the return of peace, the re-establishment of law and order, and better management of public affairs.

What the Vietcong leaders say to the peasants, and what all the officials down the line repeat, is this:

"You have nothing to pay to the landlords who have taken refuge in Saigon. The land belongs to the man who farms it. Don't worry, if someone tries to persecute you, we will protect you."

When the Government tries to draft, the Vietcong tells the parents: "Don't let your children go. The Saigon government wants them to be killed to advance the objectives of the Americans. Hide them. In an emergency, send them to the areas we hold. We will make use of them."

The families with boys in service are told: "Have them desert, and no harm will come to them. If they don't we will be forced to kill them."

In a revolutionary period, propaganda is worthless if it does not put out a concrete action program. The Vietcong tells the population: "You are oppressed by corrupt men representing a government which has sold out to a foreign country."

On hearing this the peasants look around. The chief of the province appointed by the Saigon Government lives in a big house, drives a Mercedes, and loads his wife with jewelry. The Governor is a man of importance who is approached with deference, protected by police, soldiers, and assistants. His Vietcong opposite number can be seen every day. He is out among the people. He is dressed like a peasant, in black calico and with sandals cut from an old tire. He makes his rounds in his district on foot, walking along the public roads. You can be sure of one thing: he is not getting rich on the back of the people.

When the Vietcong began their revolution in 1959 and 1960, it was opened with a wave of terrorism. In isolated places, in hamlets, then in villages and cities, officials and private persons loyal to Saigon were assassinated. Government propaganda strove mightily to exploit these facts to arouse popular indignation. This backfired. It was understood too late that in most cases the peasants had fearlessly helped in the brutal liquidation of the men on whose death the Saigon Government was basing its case. Instead of murders, the terrorists were considered dispensers of justice.

All this was not exactly an unplanned reaction. The Vietcong do not leave anything to chance. The heart of their system is always to explain the reasons for the course of action they adopt. Before killing a man they explain at length, repeating tirelessly the same arguments, giving the reasons for which the victim must be punished. And they don't stop there. The population too must repeat the arguments, learn them by heart, and tell everyone about them. The Vietcong want the people themselves to demand the punishment of the guilty. And no one is satisfied with mere lip service.

The difference between the two Vietnams, official Vietnam, that of the Saigon Government and the real Vietnam, that of the Vietcong, is undoubtedly here. The Vietcong is a great, perfectly oiled machine which organizes the people after winning their inner conviction, after becoming master of their heart and head. The Saigon government also has tried to win over the people. This was under Diem, but it was all a matter of externals. I was well acquainted with Ngo Dinh Nhu, the brother of the dead President. He was the regime's man of theory. He was obsessed with the idea of having at his command, as the Vietcong does, an army of fanatical partisans who would go from village to village, from man to man, doing the kind of work the Vietcong has done. He never could develop a corps of this kind, however, because there are no competent people of this kind who side with the Saigon Government, and he didn't have time to create them.

With the fall of Diem the Vietcong machine preempted this field of activity. One Saigon government after another fell. There was a confusing succession of heads of state and commanders-in-chief. There was a continual turnover of important civil and military officials who were killed, jailed, silenced, fired, and recalled.

The people have this picture to look at. On one side there is a real government, law and order, and responsible people. On the other side, chaos, anarchy, and disorder. The people chose those who had won the contest. Against this, bombs and strafing mean nothing.

If the National Liberation Front imposed itself by clever propaganda and by professional leadership, it also offered a political program designed to win adherence.

The Vietnamese are by nature distrustful and sensitive to possible trickery. They don't swallow naively the arguments of the Vietcong leaders. They know perfectly well what they have to fear from the installation in South Vietnam of a government comparable to the one imposed by the Vietminh on North Vietnam. They don't want a government of that kind at any price. They passionately want two things: First, not to be subjected to the North Vietnamese Government which they detest, and second, not to see installed in the south a political and economic system less humane than that of Hanoi.

The National Liberation Front, with the approval of Hanoi, gives pleasing assurances on all of these different points. First, it stresses that it is a question of a front, and not of a single party. It's not the Marxist Party alone, but the Popular Revolutionary Party—a party made up of twenty other groups. It is therefore necessary to make out that the Popular Revolutionary Party plays an essential role in the conduct of the struggle, but it is known that neither the president nor the secretary of the front are members of the Popular Revolutionary Party, and that only one of the front's five vice presidents is affiliated with the Popular Revolutionary Party.

The program of the front [1] is one that could not be more reassuring. To read it, it is for a sort of liberal Socialist government. It is precise in providing for the retention of the right to private property, that private industry and commerce will be encouraged, that the property of French citizens will be protected. In foreign affairs, diplomatic relations will be established with all countries "without distinction as to political system." Economic, cultural, and technical aid will be sought from countries "having different political systems." It is the same as saying that Vietnam will be a friend of the United States. Lastly, the separate existence of South Vietnam is promised. On reunification of the two Vietnams the program says: "The question will be determined by the two parts * * * subject to the proviso that one part will not swallow up the other."

All observers are in agreement on the point: The program and the conduct of the National Liberation Front have won it the adherence, enthusiastic or resigned, of a very large part of the Vietnamese population. This is a fact which becomes particularly clear when one interviews middle class and intellectual people in Saigon. One of them summarizes the problem in this way: "We have a choice between two solutions: to wage an endless war while every day placing ourselves more at the mercy of the Americans, and without any guarantee that this will end in a clearcut victory, or categorically to demand the end of the war and trust to the good faith of the National Liberation Front's leaders and to their willingness to carry out a program which to us appears acceptable."

Before that vast majority who above all want peace and the fulfillment of their hopes, there is one minor obstacle: some generals who command troops ready to die like the troops of all ages. There is also a major obstacle presented by the open intervention of the United States in the Indochinese War. One thing at least is sure: the fiction that American military power has been introduced upon demand of a people fighting Communism no longer holds today.

[1] See pp. 253–256.—ed.

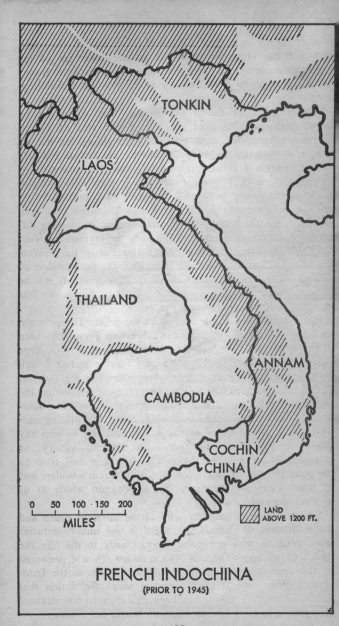

TONKIN

LAOS

THAILAND

ANNAM

CAMBODIA

COCHIN
CHINA

0   50 100 150 200
MILES

LAND
ABOVE 1200 FT.

FRENCH INDOCHINA
(PRIOR TO 1945)

CHINA

N. VIETNAM

RED R.

YUNGNING

(SONG KOI)

DIENBIENPHU

HANOI

HAIPHONG

LAOS

HOÀ BINH

PLAINE DES JARRES

LUANG PRABANG

GULF OF
TONKIN

VINH

VIENTIANE

HAINAN

UDON

THAILAND

HUÉ

DA NANG

SARAVANE

PAKSE

BANGKOK

CAMBODIA

PLEIKU

QUI NHON

NHA TRANG

PHNOM
PENH

MEKONG RIVER

S.
VIETNAM

GULF OF
SIAM

CHAU DOC

BIEN HOA

SAIGON

MY THO

LONG XUYEN

CAN THO

SOUTH CHINA
SEA

0   50 100 150 200

MILES

MEKONG
RIVER
DELTA

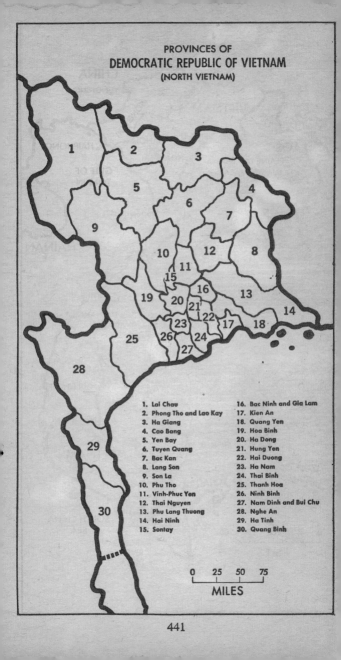

PROVINCES OF
DEMOCRATIC REPUBLIC OF VIETNAM
(NORTH VIETNAM)

1. Lai Chau
2. Phong Tho and Lao Kay
3. Ha Giang
4. Cao Bang
5. Yen Bay
6. Tuyen Quang
7. Bac Kan
8. Lang Son
9. Son La
10. Phu Tho
11. Vinh-Phuc Yen
12. Thai Nguyen
13. Phu Lang Thuong
14. Hai Ninh
15. Sontay
16. Bac Ninh and Gia Lam
17. Kien An
18. Quang Yen
19. Hoa Binh
20. Ha Dong
21. Hung Yen
22. Hai Duong
23. Ha Nam
24. Thai Binh
25. Thanh Hoa
26. Ninh Binh
27. Nam Dinh and Bui Chu
28. Nghe An
29. Ha Tinh
30. Quang Binh

0   25   50   75
MILES

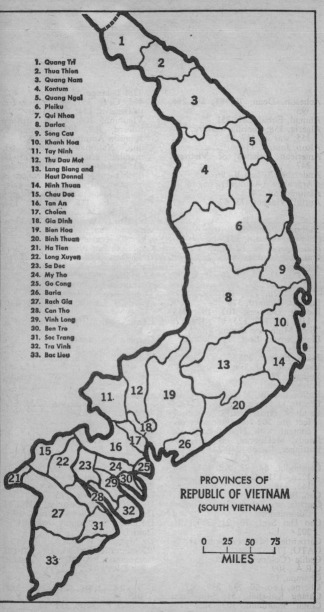

1. Quang Tri
2. Thua Thien
3. Quang Nam
4. Kontum
5. Quang Ngai
6. Pleiku
7. Qui Nhon
8. Darlac
9. Song Cau
10. Khanh Hoa
11. Tay Ninh
12. Thu Dau Mot
13. Lang Biang and
    Haut Donnai
14. Ninh Thuan
15. Chau Doc
16. Tan An
17. Cholon
18. Gia Dinh
19. Bien Hoa
20. Binh Thuan
21. Ha Tien
22. Long Xuyen
23. Sa Dec
24. My Tho
25. Go Cong
26. Baria
27. Rach Gia
28. Can Tho
29. Vinh Long
30. Ben Tre
31. Soc Trang
32. Tra Vinh
33. Bac Lieu

PROVINCES OF
REPUBLIC OF VIETNAM
(SOUTH VIETNAM)

0   25   50   75
MILES

INDEX

A

Acheson, Dean, 79, 81, 88, 296, 395
Ahmad, Eqbal, 283, 351
Algeria, 358; guerilla warfare, 354-355; war in, 357
Alsop, Joseph, 114
American Friends of Vietnam, 247
Anderson, Robert B., 96
d'Argenlieu (Admiral), 66, 69
Assimilation, 24
Auriul, Vincent, 73, 82

B

Baghdad, Pact, 367
Baldwin, Hanson, 362
Ball, George W., 62-63
Bandung Conference, principals of, 226
Bao Dai, 41, 58, 59, 60, 61, 69, 70, 71, 72, 73, 74, 79, 82, 83, 108, 115, 122n, 125, 161, 199, 217
Bartlett, Richard, 376
Bidault, Georges, 102, 103, 118, 119, 120, 122, 125, 127, 128. 129
"Big" Minh. see Duong Van Minh
Binh Xuyen Sect, 71, 200, 201, 250
Black, Eugene, 328
Blum, Léon, 68, 90n
Bollaert, 79
Bonnet, Henri, 107
Boston faculty, 334n
Brzezinski, Zbygniew, 407, 407n
Budd'ist crisis, 262; Catholic affect on, 262-269, 348; over discontent with Ngo family, 268
Bundy, McGeorge, 389, 397, 404
Buttinger, Joseph, 240-241

C

Cambodia, 64, 82, 85, 101, 116, 122n, 131, 134, 135, 151, 161, 163, 338
Can, Bishop, 237
Canada. see International Control Commission
Cao Dai Sect, 70, 71, 200, 201, 202
Carpentier, Marcel (General), 80
CATO, 173
Cedile (Colonel), 44, 45
C.R.A., 309
Champa, 15
Cherne, Leo, 60, 238, 239, 243
Chiang Kai-shek, 51, 53n, 260n
China: mainland, 303, 325, 377-
378; balance of power in, 402, 403; CPR, 151, 421; delegation to Geneva, 134; "Sanctuary" for Vietminh, 108; U. S. attitude toward, 369, 393; warning to Johnson Administration, 425
China, Nationalist: Army, 67; mandate after World War II, 43; temporary occupation of Indochina, 51 passim; troops in Vietnam, 61; see also Kuomintang, Chiang Kai-shek, cumshau
Chou En-lai, 115, 120, 125, 131, 132, 134, 154
Christianity, hostility to, 28, 30
Chu Van Tan, 59
Church, Senator Frank, 386
Churchill, Sir Winston, 101, 102
Civil guard, 249
Clements, Earle C., 97
Clos, Max, 283, 430, 430n
Cochinchinese, 65-66, 84
Cogny, René, 106
Collins, J. Lawton (General), 239, 240
Communist Party of Indochina, 33, 35
Communists: containment of, 326, 366; in Asia, 282; in France, 78; in NLF, 231; in North, 286; in Vietminh, 77; in world, 370; resistance in South, 225; strength, 234; subversion in South, 226
Confucianism, 205
Cong Hoa (Republican), 276
CPR, 421
Cu Huy Can, 59
Cuba, 282n, 375
Cumshaw, 51, 53
Cuong De, 82

D

Dao Trong Kim, 59
De Behaine, Pignean, 16
De Gaulle, Charles, 75
De la Croix de Castries, 106, 111
De la Grandière (Admiral), 19
De Lattre de Tassigny, Jean, 84
Deltiel, Henri, 135, 150
De Margerie, R., 126
"Democratic Freedoms," 180-181
Democratic Republic of Vietnam, see DRV
Desai, 165
Deutscher, Isaac, 283, 298, 389, 405
Devillers, Philippe, 211

Dienbienphu, 62, 102, 105-114, 118, 119, 120, 122, 123, 124, 127, 127n, 128, 325, 393
Do Cao Tri, 271
Dodd, Senator Thomas J., 342
Dooley, Tom, 242-243
Douglas, William O., 237
Doumer, Paul, 22
DRV, 37, 122, 152, 213, 214, 216-218, 219, 220, 226-228, 231, 232, 261n, 424
Due Nghiep, 266, 269
Dulles, Allen, 241
Dulles, John Foster, 89, 92, 96, 98, 99, 100, 101, 102, 103, 115, 118, 120, 121, 122, 126, 132, 133, Duong Duc Hien, 59
Duong Van Minh, 270, 271, 275, 280

E

East Germany, 215
EDC, 119, 120, 129, 130, 133, 136, 137n
Eden, Anthony, 101, 102, 103, 104, 118, 119, 122, 125, 126, 127, 128, 131, 136, 154
Eisenhower, Dwight D., 89, 96, 119, 121, 164, 206-207, 214, 237, 251
Ely, Paul, 99, 100
Elysee Agreements, 81, 83, 85
Enmet, Chris, 409
Escalating War, 194, 492, 425-429. see also "White Paper"
European imperialism, 15

F

Fall, Bernard B., 105-114, 242, 357
Fishel, Wesley R., 193, 197, 237, 239, 248, 253, 253n, 254
FLN (Algeria), 354, 355, 357
French 13; in Algeria, 113; Army, 74, 322; Communist Party, 76; defeat at Dienbienphu, 114, 118, 119; at Geneva Conference, 151; Impact of, 20-25, 34; Imperialism, 57; Indochinese policy, 128; revolutionary tradition, 38; sentiment against, 37; Socialist Party, 82; troops in Cambodia, 151; Foreign Legion, 107, 237; Union, 65, 72, 76, 84, 138, 139, 142, 143

G

Garai, Josef E., 409, 410
General Confederation of Labor, 260
Geneva Agreements of 1954, 160-167, 209, 210, 334; Burial of, 220; consolative conference at,

296; observance of, 165; violation of, 164, 165; see also International Control Commission; Interim Reports; Conference, 103-105, 107-108, 114-137, 198; close of (1954), 154-159; final declaration of, 151-154
Ghana, 198
Gracey, General Douglas, 45
Great Britain, 15, 42-47, 78, 80, 119, 151
Greece, 284
Gruber, Helmut, 409
Gruening, Senator Ernest, 280, 377-386
Gulf of Tonkin, 339, 342

H

Halberstam, David, 262, 270
Hanoi, 140, 218, 219, 233, 286, 287, 307; Central Research Agency, 296
Heath, Donald, 206
Ho Chi Minh (alias Nguyen Ai Quoc), 27, 30, 31, 32, 33, 35, 52, 55, 56, 59, 61, 70, 71, 73, 75, 76, 78, 87, 98, 116, 211, 212, 220, 230, 236, 296, 304, 316, 371, 393, 323; Trail, 339
Hoa Hao Sect, 70, 71, 200, 201, 202
Hoang Hoa Tham, 56
Hoang Quoc Viet, 419
Hoc Tap, 305
Hué, 264, 269
Humphrey, Hubert, 351
Hungarian Revolution, 223
Huynh Van Cao, 269, 272, 279, 280

I

India. see International Control Commission
Individualism, 203
Indochinese Communist Party (ICP), 26, 27, 28, 261; Union, 65-66; Federation of 65, 66, 84; War, 62, 64, 66
Infiltration process, 289-291
Interarm Co., Ltd., 219
Interim Reports, see International Control Commission
International Commission for Supervision and Control in Vietnam. see International Control Commission
International Conference for Solidarity with Vietnamese people, 419
International Control Commission, 129, 146, 147, 167, 168, 248, 286; interim reports of, 163, 164, 168; majority vote of, 149;

tasks of, 148; *see also*, Geneva Agreements, Geneva Conference
Isaacs, Harold, 36, 37, 86*n*
"Isabelle," 106, 107

J

Jacquet, Marc, 122
Japanese: Army, 86; coup against French 40; Fascists, 35, 57; occupation of Vietnam, 39; surrender, 41; troops, 46; war against Indochina, 114
Jessup, Philip, 79
"Johns Hopkins Speech," 323-330, 366
Johnson, Lyndon B., 97, 98, 116, 160, 312, 325-330; attacks on, 419-420, 425-429
Joint Commission; Attitude toward: certain internees, 144; consultations, 172; costs of truce supervision, 145; nationwide elections, 172; prisoners of war, 144; punishment, 145; reunification, 172
Juin, Alphonse (general), 83

K

Kahin, George, 389, 392
Kennedy, John F., 196, 208-210, 238, 276, 348, 395
Khmer: empire, 15; government, 123, 124
Knowland, William K., 97
Korea: South, 236; war, 81, 108
Kosygin, Aleksai N., 332
Kuomintang government, 51
Kyes, Roger, 96

L

Ladejinsky, Wolf, 238, 252
Lam Van Phat, 279
Landau, Jacob, 409
Lansdale, Edward, 240, 241, 234
Lao Dong Party, 217, 219, 229, 230, 286, 306, 307; Third Congress of, 313, 314
Lao Issara, 124
Laos; election in, 151, 163; Kingdom of, 64, 82, 85
Law, 10/59, 226, 256-260
Le Duan, 230, 305
Le Loi, 12
Le Quang Tung, 275, 277, 278, 280
Le Van Hien, 60
Le Van Hoach, 68
Le Van Kim, 270
League of Nations, 34
Lenin, V. I., 31, 229
Letourneau, Jean, 83, 84
Li Fu-ch'un, 229

Liberation Front, 286, 298, 304
Lien Viet, 77, 211, 260
Litchfield, Henry, 408
Lodge, Henry Cabot, 273, 281
Long, Gia, 16-17, 18
Lu Han, 53
Luong Ngoc Quyen, 56

Mc

MacArthur, Douglas (general), 46
MacDonald, Malcolm, 79
McCarthy, Joseph, 99
McCormack, John W., 97, 99
McDermott, John, 408
McNamara, Robert, 114, 116, 341, 405

M

Mage, Shane, 408
Malaya, 284
Mandarinate, 13-14, 236
Mansfield, Mike, 95, 238, 263, 376
Mao Tse-tung, 284
Marchand, Father, 171
Marshall, George C., 75*n*
Marshall Plan, 78
Martin, Joseph, 97
Massigli, René, 119
Mekong, 108, 109, 280, 328, 345
Menashe, Louis, 408
Mendès-France, Pierre, 123, 130, 131, 131*n*, 132, 133, 134, 136, 137*n*, 154, 155, 198, 212
Mermelstein, David, 408
Minh Mang, 17-18, 28
Moholy-Nagy, Sibyl, 408
Molotov, Vyacheslav, 120, 125, 126, 127, 129, 130, 135, 136, 154, 158
Monopolies, 23
Montagnards, 339, 340, 348
Morgenthau, Hans J., 365, 389, 403
Morse, Wayne, 283, 336*n*, 376
Morton, Thruston B., 96
M.S.U. Project, 247-251
My Thu, 276

N

Nagel, Ernest, 389, 405
Nam Il, 120
Nam Phan, 260
Nam-bô Veterans of the Resistance Association, 227
"National Liberation Front," 230-233, 307, 319, 323, 399, 437; communism in, 231, 232, 233; militancy of, 411-418
National Security Council, 100
Nationalism: Growth of, 26; non-Communist, 235
Navarre, Henri-Eugene, 102, 109, 111

Nehru, Pandit, **79**
Netherlands, 15
Nghe An, 223
Ngo Dinh Can, 223
Ngo Dinh Diem, 81, **161**, 193-279
  passim., 372
Ngo Dinh Nhu (Mrs.), 262, 263,
  264, 265, 266, 268, 275
Ngo Dinh Nhu, 262, 263, 264,
  266, 268, 269, 270, 271-273, 274,
  275, 276, 278, 279, 281, 282
Ngo Dinh Thuc, 263, 264, 270
Nguyen Ai Quoc, (Nguyen the
  Patriot), *see* Ho Chi Minh
Nguyen Anh, 16
Nguyen Cam, 294
Nguyen Chi Thanh, 306
Nguyen Dynasty, 12
Nguyen Hun Co, 275, 278, 279
Nguyen Hun Tri, 81
Nguyen Kanh, 271
Nguyen Manh Ha, 60
Nguyen Ngoc Khoi, 277
Nguyen Ngoc Tho, 266
Nguyen Quoc Dinh, 122, 125
Nguyen Phan Long, 81
Nguyen Tat Thanh; *see* Ho Chi
  Minh
Nguyen Truc, 293
Nguyen Van Hinh, 200
Nguyen Van Thieu, 278
Nguyen Van Thinh, 68
Nguyen Van To, 60
Nguyen Van Vy, 298, 299
Nguyen, Van Xuan, 60
Nguyen Viet Duong, 296
Nixon, Richard, 91, 100
North Vietnam: aggression by,
  282-321; attacked by U.S.A.,
  342; changes in government,
  311; influence over NLF, 396-
  397; intelligence operation, 309;
  "peaceful co-existence policy,"
  323; policy, 216; raids on, 422

O

Operation Bravo, 276

P

"Pacification" program, 345
Pathet Lao, 124, 127, 134, 195,
  223
Pau Conference, 82
P.A.V. (People's Army of Viet-
  nam), *see* Vietminh
P.C. (penal colony): *see* Poulo
  Condore
Pham Ngoh Thach, 44, 60
Pham Van Bach, 256
Pham Van Dong, 60, 122, 123,
  124, 132, 134, 155, 161, 218
Phan Dinh Phung, 56
Phan Quang Dan, 163n, 228

Philippines, 284
Phoui Sananikong, 154
Phu Loi (concentration camp),
  225
Pignon, Léon, 73
Piroth (Colonel), 111
Pondicherry, 16
Popular Front, 28, **77**
Portugal, 15
Potsdam, 42, 51
Poulo Condore, 38, 42
Priest, J. Percy, 97

R

Racism, 38
Radford, Arthur (Admiral), **96**,
  97, 98, 99, 102
Red Flag, 304
Richardson, John, 275
Richter, Gustave, *see* Buttinger,
  Joseph
Roberts, Chalmers M., 96
Robertson, Walter S., 162
Rusk, Dean, 36, 116, 234, 312,
  330-336, 351, 426
Russell, Senator Richard B., **97**

S

"Saigon Government," *see* South
  Vietnam, government of
Sainteny, Jean, 322; mission, 218
Sary, Sam, 124
Scalapino, Robert, 398, 402-403,
  405
Scheer, Robert, 215n., 235, 253n
Schlesinger, Arthur, Jr., 282, 389
SEATO, 101-102, 115, 214, 367
Slutsky, Robert, 408
Smith, Walter Bedell, 121, **132**,
  133, 135, 158
Socialist world strategy, 226
Southeast Asia Collective Defense
  Treaty, 95
Soviet Union, 33, 34, 51, 78, 151,
  229; conciliation, 126; delega-
  tion to Geneva Conference, 133;
  Foreign Minister, *see* Molotov.
Spellman, Francis Cardinal, 201,
  237, 239
Stalingrad, 102
Stone, I. F., 282, 317
South Vietnam: army, 337-338,
  341-342; attitude toward U.S.
  imperialism, 411-418; concentration camps, 223; coup in,
  269-281; government of, 15,
  207, 226, 234, 272, 282; insurrection in, 231; intervention in,
  224; legitimacy in, 345; Liberation Front, 235, 236n; policy
  toward former resistance members, 260; refugees to, 200, 201,
  215; repression of (*see* Law 10/

59), 223; Republic of (RV), 338, 340; U.S. influence in, 223; Vietcong support in, 399; weapons captured in, 314-316

Sudrat, André (Major), 110

Sukarno, Achmed, 202; "guided democracy," 198

T

Ta Quang Buu, 129, 135, 150

Tay Son Rebellion, 12, 15

Teach-In Movement, 280; National (Washington, D. C., 5/15/65), 389; Local (Brooklyn, N. Y., 5/13/65), 408-409

Tehran, 42

Tep Phan, 135, 154

Terauchi (General), 46

Thailand, 77, 80, 101

Thich Quang Duc, 265-266

Thich Tri Quang, 264, 280

Thieu Tri, 18

Third International, 31, 32

A Threat to Peace, 284n, 286

Tito, Josip, 353; Titoism, 369-370, 371-372

Ton That Dinh, 271ff.

Tong Bo, 77

Trager, Frank, 283, 337

Tran Huy Lieu, 60

Tran Quoc Dan, 291

Tran Van Bui, 300

Tran Van Do, 133, 134, 134n, 136, 159

Tran Van Don, 271, 279

Tran Van Giau, 78

Tran Van Huu, 82, 83

Treaty of Manila, 92-96, 214

Trotskyites, 29, 236

Truman, Harry, 81, 282; Doctrine, 366

Truong Chinh, 305

Tu Duc, 18-19

U

UNESCO, 358

United Nations, 126, 201, 330

Universities Committee on Problems of War and Peace, 408n; *see also* Teach-In Movement

University of Michigan, *see* Teach-In.

U.S.A.: assistance to France, 81, 88; attacks North Vietnam, 342; attitude toward China, 393; CIA, 272, 274; delegation to Geneva Conference, 127, 132; distrust of, 119; fear of French defeat, 91; foreign policy: [criticism by academicians, 389-407, by senators, 376-388; goals, 366; progress, 405]; influence in

South, 223; intervention in South, 222; "Johns Hopkins" speech, 323-330; military: command, 542; mission, 82; requirements for victory, 337-350; strategy, 373-374; negotiations, 404-405; objective in Vietnam, 326, 334; opposition to spread of Communism, 89; policy, 275; prestige of, 375; protests against, 282-283, 376, 429-432; protests in, 423; relations with other Asian states, 406-407; role at Geneva Conference, 121, 151; support for Ngo Dinh Diem, 208-210, 236-255; sympathy for Bao Dai, 77-80; "White Paper" (Feb. 1965), 284

V

Vanguard Youth Organization, 260

Venezuela, 332

"Vietcong," 260-262 and see National Liberation Front

Vietminh, 39, 40, 55, 62, 67-68, 77, 85, 108, 114, 124, 128, 137, 138, 160, 163, 166, 211, 212, 234, 242, 307; definition of, 211, League, 260; organization of, 337

Vietnam Doc Lap Dong Minh Hoi, *see* Vietminh

Vietnam Quoc Dan Dang (VNQDD), 26, 27, 28

Vietnam: Agrarian conditions in, 23; American Friends of, 247; borders, 340; Buddhist crisis in, 262-269; "Bureau of Investigation," 249; Catholics in, 262; Chinese influence on, 11, 14; Democratic Republic of, 74, 75, 76, 77; Elections in, 140, 151, 195, 216, 319, 400-401; [U.S. attitude toward, 393-394]; historical background of, 10; independence of, 160, 161; Kingdom of, 64; nationalism in, 394; Nationalist, 212; partition of, 129, 132; prohibition of military bases in, 144; reunification of, 211-236; State of, 151; U.S. military requirements for victory in, 337-350

Vietnamese Nationalist Party, 26

Vo Nguyen Giap, 60, 68, 77, 78, 110, 170, 304, 338

Vo Quyen, 295

Vo Thanh Vinh, 295

Vo Thoi, 292

Vu Din Hoc, 59

Vu Trong Khanh, 59

W

Weapons, Communist, seized in Vietnam, 317-318, 331-332
World War II, 325, 336, 340, 341; end of, 37-42
"War of National Liberation," 331
"Welfare State," 204
White Paper: (1961), 284, 373; (1965), 282-321; reply to, 317

Women's Solidarity Movement, 264
Woodward, C. Vann, 9, 9n
World trade unions, 260
Wright, Mary, 406-407

XYZ

Zagoria, Donald, 282

————

ABOUT THE AUTHOR

Marvin E. Gettleman, who is assistant professor of United States history at the Polytechnic Institute of Brooklyn, has been a student of philosophy and history at The City College of New York and Johns Hopkins University, and has taught at The City College and the University of Baltimore. In addition to numerous articles and reviews for scholarly publications, Professor Gettleman has been a consultant to the Association of the Bar of the City of New York for its project on the impact of technological progress on privacy in the United States. Professor Gettleman lives with his wife and two young children in Manhattan.